ASIAN ECONOMIC AND POLITICAL ISSUES. VOLUME 14

ASIAN ECONOMIC AND POLITICAL ISSUES

Additional books in this series can be found on Nova's website under the Series tab.

Additional E-books in this series can be found on Nova's website under the E-books tab.

ASIAN ECONOMIC AND POLITICAL ISSUES

ASIAN ECONOMIC AND POLITICAL ISSUES. VOLUME 14

DAVID A. MAREK
EDITOR

Nova Science Publishers, Inc.
New York

For permission to use material from this book please contact us:
Telephone 631-231-7269; Fax 631-231-8175
Web Site: http://www.novapublishers.com

LIBRARY OF CONGRESS CATALOGING-IN-PUBLICATION DATA
Available upon request

ISBN: 978-1-61728-019-1

Published by Nova Science Publishers, Inc. ✦ New York

Contents

Preface		**vii**
Chapter 1	China and the Global Financial Crisis: Implications for the United States *Wayne M. Morrison*	**1**
Chapter 2	Japan-U.S. Relations: Issues for Congress *Emma Chanlett-Avery, William H. Cooper and Mark E. Manyin*	**11**
Chapter 3	North Korea: Economic Leverage and Policy Analysis *Dick K. Nanto and Emma Chanlett-Avery*	**35**
Chapter 4	Sri Lanka: Background and U.S. Relations *K. Alan Kronstadt and Bruce Vaughn*	**93**
Chapter 5	Taiwan's Political Status: Historical Background and Ongoing Implications *Kerry Dumbaugh*	**123**
Chapter 6	Afghanistan: Government Formation and Performance *Kenneth Katzman*	**133**
Chapter 7	Pakistan's Nuclear Weapons: Proliferation and Security Issues *Paul K. Kerr and Mary Beth Nikitin*	**151**
Chapter 8	Human Rights in China: Trends and Policy Implications *Thomas Lum and Hannah Fischer*	**167**
Chapter 9	North Korean Counterfeiting of U.S. Currency *Dick K. Nanto*	**205**
Chapter 10	Indonesia: Domestic Politics, Strategic Dynamics, and American Interests *Bruce Vaughn*	**221**
Index		**255**

PREFACE

Asia has entered the 21st century as an economic superpower and is inevitably also becoming a political superpower. This evolution is the subject of Politics and Economics of Asia. This new book includes in its scope the entire spectrum of contemporary politics and economics of Asia. The coverage is intended to deal with Asia, its political dynamics, economic policies, institutions, and its future. This book reviews information on the politics and economics of Asia including China and the Global Financial Crisis; Japan-U.S. Relations; the economic leverage and policy analysis of North Korea; background and U.S. relations with Sri Lanka; Taiwan's political status; human rights in China and Pakistan's nuclear weapons.

Chapter 1 - Over the past several years, China has enjoyed one of the world's fastest growing economies and has been a major contributor to world economic growth. However, the current global financial crisis threatens to significantly slow China's economy. Several Chinese industries, particularly the export sector, have been hit hard by crisis, and millions of workers have reportedly been laid off. This situation is of great concern to the Chinese government, which views rapid economic growth as critical to maintaining social stability. China is a major economic power and holds huge amounts of foreign exchange reserves, and thus its policies could have a major impact on the global economy. For example, the Chinese government in November 2008 announced plans to implement a $586 billion package to help stimulate the domestic economy. If successful, this plan could also boost Chinese demand for imports. In addition, in an effort to help stabilize the U.S. economy, China might boost its holdings of U.S. Treasury securities, which would help fund the Federal Government's borrowing needs to purchase troubled U.S. assets and to finance economic stimulus packages. However, some U.S. policymakers have expressed concerns over the potential political and economic implications of China's large and growing holdings of U.S. Government debt securities.

Chapter 2 - The post-World War II U.S.-Japan alliance has long been an anchor of the U.S. security role in East Asia. The alliance, with its access to bases in Japan, where about 53,000 U.S. troops are stationed, facilitates the forward deployment of U.S. military forces in the Asia-Pacific, thereby undergirding U.S. national security strategy. For Japan, the alliance and the U.S. nuclear umbrella provide maneuvering room in dealing with its neighbors, particularly China and North Korea.

During the Bush Administration, the alliance initially made significant strides in broadening U.S.-Japan strategic cooperation and encouraging Japan to assume a more active international role. Following the September 11, 2001 terrorist attacks, Japan made its first-ever military deployments in non-combat support of U.S. and allied forces in Afghanistan. In 2004 Tokyo sent non-combat troops to Iraq, despite considerable domestic opposition. In 2005 the United States and Japan announced a sweeping new agreement to strengthen military cooperation. The plan calls for U.S. forces to be realigned and Japan to take on a more active (non-combat) role in maintaining regional and global security.

Political turmoil in Tokyo has slowed or stalled some of this progress in security relations. The ruling party's historic defeat in Upper House elections in July 2007 and the abrupt resignations of both Shinzo Abe and Yasuo Fukuda from the Prime Minister post has shaken the traditional power structure in Japan. Premier Taro Aso has clung to power while watching his approval ratings dip increasingly lower. When parliamentary elections are eventually held, an emboldened opposition party may take control of the government. As a result of this uncertainty, some of the earlier defense relations platform may be placed on hold. If political jockeying weakens Tokyo's focus on U.S.-Japan relations as an aging Japanese population demands more attention to domestic economic issues, the U.S.-Japan relationship may struggle to regain the momentum enjoyed in the early part of the decade.

Chapter 3 - In 2009, the Democratic Peoples Republic of Korea (DPRK or North Korea) embarked on a course that includes a series of extremely provocative military actions, a shift in power toward the military, emphasis on ideological purity, rising criticism of the United States, and going forward with its nuclear and missile program in spite of sanctions and objections from much of the rest of the world. Two factors that seem to be operating to compel this more "aggressive" behavior by Pyongyang. The first is the apparent stroke by North Korea's leader, Kim Jong-il, in August 2008. The country appears to be preparing for succession, and in jockeying for position, the military seems to be gaining in policy precedence over the civilian side of government, and the military- first doctrine is prevailing over economic reform. The second factor has been the preparations for the 100th anniversary of the birth of Kim Il Sung, the founder of the DPRK, in 2012. By then the country wants to join the club of nuclear and space powers and to be an Asian tiger economy.

North Korea's dire economic straits provide one of the few levers to move the country to cooperate in attempts by the United States, China, South Korea, Japan, and Russia to halt and dismantle its nuclear program. These five countries plus North Korea comprise the "six parties" who are engaged in talks to resolve issues raised by the DPRK's development of a nuclear weapon. The Six-Party Talks are now stalled. Western leverage over the DPRK remains limited, but China, and to some extent Russia, are in a position to exert pressure on Pyongyang.

The economy of North Korea is of interest to Congress because it provides the financial and industrial resources for the Kim Jong-il regime to develop its military and to remain in power, constitutes an important "push factor" for potential refugees seeking to flee the country, creates pressures for the country to trade in arms or engage in illicit economic activity, is a rationale for humanitarian assistance, and creates instability that affects South Korea and China in particular. The dismal economic conditions also foster forces of discontent that potentially could turn against the Kim regime—especially if knowledge of the luxurious lifestyle of communist party leaders becomes better known or as poor economic performance hurts even the elite.

North Korea has extensive trading relationships with China and Russia and, until recently, with South Korea. U.S. and Japanese trade with North Korea since 2006 has been virtually nil except for U.S. aid deliveries. The DPRK has been running an estimated $1.5 billion deficit per year in its international trade accounts that it funds primarily through receipts of foreign assistance and foreign investment as well as through various questionable activities.

Following the DPRK's second nuclear test and subsequent actions, the focus in mid-2009 has been on negative incentives and increasing sanctions. The larger question, however, is how to move beyond tit-for-tat actions to a three-fold transformation of the DPRK: a transformation in its international relations, in the Stalinist methods by which Communist regime maintains its support, and in its moribund economy that cannot feed its own population.

Chapter 4 - Sri Lanka, an island nation in the Indian Ocean, is a constitutional democracy with a relatively high level of development. Political, social, and economic development has, however, been seriously constrained by ethnic conflict between the majority Sinhalese and minority Tamil ethnic groups. Since 1983, a separatist war costing at least 70,000 lives has been waged against government forces by the Liberation Tigers of Tamil Eelam (LTTE), a rebel group that sought to establish a separate state or internal self-rule in the Tamil-dominated areas of the North and East. The United States designated the LTTE as a Foreign Terrorist Organization in 1997. Open fighting in this conflict came to a close with the defeat of LTTE field forces and the combat death of their leader Velupillai Prabhakaran in May 2009. The government now faces the challenge of consolidating peace with the Tamil community now that LTTE forces have been defeated. Sri Lanka also suffered a huge natural disaster in December 2004. A massive tidal wave killed up to 35,000 citizens in Sri Lanka's worst-ever natural disaster.

The current state of affairs in Sri Lanka presents the United States and the international community with several key challenges. Chief among these is how to help the government of Sri Lanka to win the peace now that it has won the war against LTTE forces in the field. Many observers feel that the manner in which the post conflict period is addressed will have a great impact on the degree to which the grievances of the Tamil minority can be put to rest. A policy that would address these grievances is perceived by many to be more likely to avert a resurgence of conflict than one that ignores or exacerbates them. Another key challenge is how to recast foreign aid to assist those in need and those displaced by the civil war.

Chapter 5 - In 1979, official U.S. relations with Taiwan (the Republic of China) became a casualty of the American decision to recognize the government of the People's Republic of China (PRC) as China's sole legitimate government. Since then, U.S. unofficial relations with Taiwan have been built on the framework of the Taiwan Relations Act (P.L. 96-8) and shaped by three U.S.-China communiqués. Under these agreements, the United States maintains its official relations with the PRC while selling Taiwan military weapons and having extensive economic, political, and security interests there. But developments in both the PRC and Taiwan political systems mean U.S. officials continually are facing new policy choices. These developments include ongoing transformations in both Taiwan's and the PRC's political systems, economic and trade cycles and, in 2008, a renewal of the long-stalled contacts, talks, and agreements between the two sides. This chapter, intended as a background overview, briefly summarizes U.S. political history with Taiwan and discusses the complications it has for current U.S. policy and for congressional actions. For analysis of current developments in Taiwan and their implications for U.S. policy, see CRS Report R40493, *Taiwan-U.S. Relations: Developments and Policy Implications*, by Kerry Dumbaugh.

Chapter 6 - The central government's limited writ and widespread official corruption are helping sustain a Taliban insurgency, and have fed pessimism about the Afghanistan stabilization effort. However, ethnic disputes remain confined largely to political debate and competition, enabling President Hamid Karzai to focus on trying to build Afghan institutions, and on his bid for re-election in presidential elections slated for August 20, 2009. Karzai has faced substantial loss of public confidence, in large part due to widespread official corruption, but his opponents—divided by ethnicity and personal ambition—were unable to form a strong electoral coalition as the presidential election registration process closed on May 8, 2009.

At the same time, U.S. officials have been shifting away from reliance on building the central government and toward promoting local governing bodies and security initiatives. That trend is to accelerate, according to the Obama Administration's review of U.S. strategy, the results of which were announced on March 27, 2009. The core of the new strategy is a so-called "civilian surge" that will virtually double, to about 900, the number of U.S. civilian personnel to deploy to Afghanistan to help build its governing and security institution, and to increase economic development efforts. The Administration also says it will develop "metrics" by which to judge the performance and legitimacy of the Afghan government, including its efforts to curb official corruption, although the Administration and many in Congress appear reluctant to tie any U.S. funds or other activities to Afghanistan's performance on such metrics. The review did not emphasize building democracy in Afghanistan, although that goal appears implicit within its recommendations.

Chapter 7 - Pakistan's nuclear arsenal consists of approximately 60 nuclear warheads. Pakistan continues fissile material production for weapons, and is adding to its weapons production facilities and delivery vehicles. Pakistan reportedly stores its warheads unassembled with the fissile core separate from non-nuclear explosives, and these are stored separately from their delivery vehicles. Pakistan does not have a stated nuclear policy, but its "minimum credible deterrent" is thought to be primarily a deterrent to Indian military action. Command and control structures have been dramatically overhauled since September 11, 2001 and export controls and personnel security programs have been put in place since the 2004 revelations about Pakistan's top nuclear scientists, A.Q. Khan's international proliferation network.

Pakistani and some U.S. officials argue that Islamabad has taken a number of steps to prevent further proliferation of nuclear-related technologies and materials and improve its nuclear security. A number of important initiatives such as strengthened export control laws, improved personnel security, and international nuclear security cooperation programs have improved the security situation in recent years.

Instability in Pakistan has called the extent and durability of these reforms into question. Some observers fear radical takeover of a government that possesses a nuclear bomb, or proliferation by radical sympathizers within Pakistan's nuclear complex in case of a breakdown of controls. While U.S. and Pakistani officials express confidence in controls over Pakistan's nuclear weapons, continued instability in the country could impact these safeguards. For a broader discussion, see CRS Report RL33498, *Pakistan-U.S. Relations*, by K. Alan Kronstadt.

Chapter 8 - Human rights has been a principal area of U.S. concern in its relations with the People's Republic of China (PRC), particularly since the violent government crackdown on the Tiananmen democracy movement in 1989. Some policy makers contend that the U.S.

policy of engagement with China, particularly since granting the PRC permanent normal trade relations status in 2000, has failed to produce meaningful political reform. Others argue that U.S. engagement has helped to accelerate economic and social change and build social and legal foundations for democracy and human rights in the PRC. This chapter analyzes China's mixed record on human rights – major human rights problems, new human rights legislation, and the development of civil society, legal awareness, and social and political activism. This chapter discusses major areas of interest but does not provide an exhaustive account of all human rights abuses or related incidents.

Fear of social unrest, particularly during times of economic uncertainty, appears to motivate the PRC government's resistance toward major political reform. The PRC government has attempted to respond to public grievances and popular calls for redress while subduing activists who attempt to organize mass protests and dissidents who openly call for fundamental change. This approach has both produced incremental improvements in human rights conditions and allowed for continued, serious abuses. Major, ongoing problems include excessive use of violence by security forces, unlawful detention, torture, arbitrary use of state security laws against political dissidents, coercive family planning policies, state control of information, and religious and ethnic persecution. Tibetans, ethnic Uighur Muslims, and Falun Gong adherents have been singled out for especially harsh treatment.

China's leadership has addressed rising public expectations through a combination of economic growth policies and carrot-and-stick political tactics. In so doing, it has planted seeds of potential change. China's developing legal system, while plagued by corruption and political interference, has provided activists with new ways of defending rights. Although generally supportive of the status quo, the urban middle class has begun to engage in narrowly targeted protests against local government policies, following over a decade of social unrest among wage laborers and farmers. Despite a massive censorship effort, the Internet and other communications technologies have made it impossible for the government to clamp down on information as fully as before.

In December 2008, over 300 PRC citizens signed and posted online a document entitled "Charter '08" calling for fundamental changes in China's political system. An additional 8,000 people signed the manifesto before the PRC government shut down the Charter's website. One of its drafters, democratic activist Liu Xiaobo, remained in detention at the time of this writing.

The U.S. government's multifaceted efforts to promote human rights in China have included open or formal criticisms and assessments of the PRC government's human rights policies, official bilateral dialogue, sanctions, and congressionally sponsored legislation, hearings, and investigations. Some Members of the 111th Congress have called for the release of political prisoners and introduced resolutions supporting human rights in China. In March 2009, the House passed H.Res. 226, a resolution recognizing the plight of the Tibetan people. In June 2009, the House and Senate passed H.Res. 489 and S.Res. 171, respectively, commemorating those who demonstrated for democracy or died in the military crackdown in 1989 in Beijing and expressing continued support for human rights and democracy activists in China. The U.S. government also provides funding for rule of law, civil society development, participatory government, labor rights, Tibetan culture, Internet access, and other programs in the PRC.

Chapter 9 - The United States has accused the Democratic People's Republic of Korea (DPRK or North Korea) of counterfeiting U.S. $100 Federal Reserve notes (Supernotes) and passing them off in various countries, although there is some doubt by observers and other governments that the DPRK is capable of creating Supernotes of the quality found. What has been confirmed is that the DPRK has passed off such bills in various countries and that the counterfeit bills circulate both within North Korea and around its border with China. Defectors from North Korea also have provided information on Pyongyang's counterfeiting operation, although those statements have not been corroborated. Whether the DPRK is responsible for the actual production or not, trafficking in counterfeit has been one of several illicit activities by North Korea apparently done to generate foreign exchange that is used to purchase imports or finance government activities abroad.

Chapter 10 - Indonesia is the world's fourth most populous country and the most populous Muslim nation. It is also a moderate Muslim state that is strategically positioned astride key sea lanes that link East Asia with the energy resources of the Middle East. Indonesia is seen by many as a valuable partner in the struggle against radical Islamist militants in Southeast Asia. Indonesia is continuing to democratize and develop its civil society and rule of law under the leadership of President Susilo Bambang Yudhoyono (SBY), who many view as reform-minded. However, a legacy of abuse of human rights by the military that stems from the three-decade reign of former President Suharto, who stepped down in 1998, remains unresolved.

The parliamentary elections of 2009 further consolidated Indonesian democracy and marked a continued preference by Indonesian voters for secular-nationalist parties rather than Islamic or Islamist political parties. President Yudhoyono's Democrat party made significant gains due to the voters' approval of the president. Observers predict that President Yudhoyono will win the presidential election scheduled for July 2009.

U.S. foreign policy concerns have focused on building relations with Indonesia to more effectively counter the rise of militant Islamist extremists, as well as to develop relations with a geopolitically important state. The United States has sought to promote democracy, the rule of law, and human rights in Indonesia in addition to American trade and investment interests there.

The election of President Barack Obama, who spent part of his childhood in Indonesia, and his subsequent outreach to the Muslim world has done much to spur expectations in Indonesia and the United States that the bilateral relationship will be enhanced during his administration. Expectations for development of the bilateral relationship were also lifted by the November 2008 proposal by President Yudhoyono to develop a strategic partnership between Indonesia and the United States. This initiative was followed by Secretary of State Hillary Clinton's decision to travel to Indonesia during her first trip abroad as Secretary of State in February 2009.

This chapter surveys key aspects of Indonesia's domestic politics and strategic dynamics in addition to provide general background information on Indonesia. It also provides an overview of the bilateral relationship between the United States and Indonesia. The report examines issues of ongoing congressional interest, including Indonesia's role in the struggle against violent Islamist extremists, security assistance, human rights, religious freedom, promotion of democracy and good governance, trade, foreign assistance, and regional geopolitical and strategic interests. The report seeks to provide a broader context for understanding the complex interrelated nature of many of these issues.

In: Asian Economic and Political Issues, Volume 14
Editor: David A. Marek
ISBN: 978-1-61728-019-1

Chapter 1

CHINA AND THE GLOBAL FINANCIAL CRISIS: IMPLICATIONS FOR THE UNITED STATES*

Wayne M. Morrison

SUMMARY

Over the past several years, China has enjoyed one of the world's fastest growing economies and has been a major contributor to world economic growth. However, the current global financial crisis threatens to significantly slow China's economy. Several Chinese industries, particularly the export sector, have been hit hard by crisis, and millions of workers have reportedly been laid off. This situation is of great concern to the Chinese government, which views rapid economic growth as critical to maintaining social stability. China is a major economic power and holds huge amounts of foreign exchange reserves, and thus its policies could have a major impact on the global economy. For example, the Chinese government in November 2008 announced plans to implement a $586 billion package to help stimulate the domestic economy. If successful, this plan could also boost Chinese demand for imports. In addition, in an effort to help stabilize the U.S. economy, China might boost its holdings of U.S. Treasury securities, which would help fund the Federal Government's borrowing needs to purchase troubled U.S. assets and to finance economic stimulus packages. However, some U.S. policymakers have expressed concerns over the potential political and economic implications of China's large and growing holdings of U.S. Government debt securities.

* This is an edited, reformatted and augmented version of a CRS Report for Congress publication, Report#RS22984, dated June 3, 2009.

China's Stake in the Current Crisis

China's economy is heavily dependent on global trade and investment flows. In 2007, China overtook the United States to become the world's second largest merchandise exporter after the European Union (EU). China's net exports (exports minus imports) contributed to one-third of its GDP growth in 2007. China's exports of goods and services as a share of GDP rose from 9.1% in 1985 to 37.8% in 2008 (see Figure 1). The Chinese government estimates that the foreign trade sector employs more than 80 million people, of which 28 million work in foreign-invested enterprises.[1] Foreign direct investment (FDI) flows to China have been a major factor behind its productivity gains and rapid economic growth. FDI flows to China in 2007 totaled $75 billion, making it the largest FDI recipient among developing countries and the third largest overall, after the EU and the United States. The current global economic slowdown (especially among its major export markets—the United States, the EU, and Japan) is having a significant negative impact on China's export sector and industries that depend on FDI flows.

The Chinese economy has slowed sharply in recent months. China's 4th real GDP growth (year-on-year basis) was 6.8%, and its 1st quarter 2009 growth (year-on-year basis) was 6.1% (reportedly, the slowest quarterly growth in 10 years). Some analysts contend annual economic growth of less than 8% could lead to social unrest in China, given that an estimated 20 million people seek jobs every year (including migrant workers that move to urban centers and high school and college graduates).[2] According to the International Monetary Fund (IMF), China was the single most important contributor to world economic growth in 2007.[3] Thus, a Chinese economic slowdown (or recovery) could also have significant global implications.

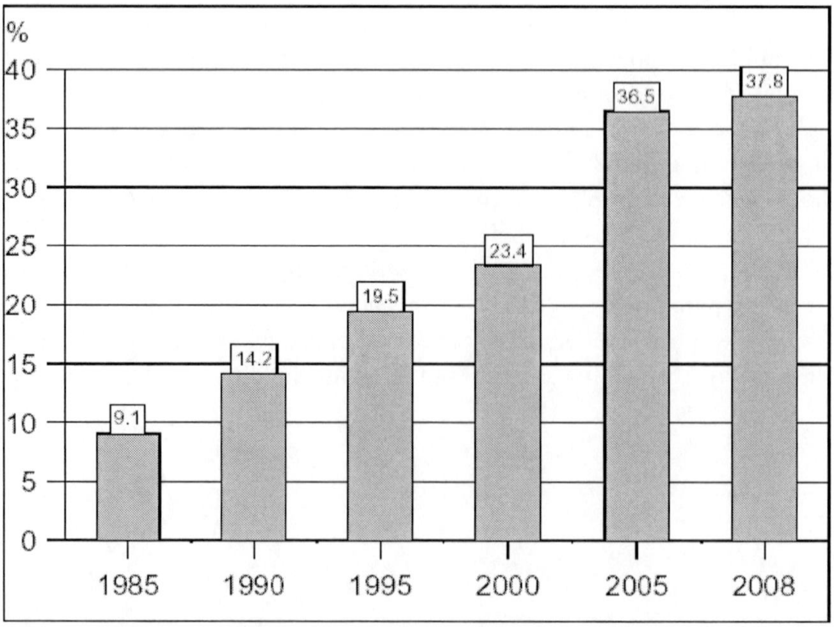

Source: Economist Intelligence Unit.

Figure 1. Chinese Exports of Goods and Services as a Percent of GDP: 1985-2008

CHINA'S EXPOSURE TO THE GLOBAL FINANCIAL CRISIS

The extent of China's exposure to the current global financial crisis, in particular from the fallout of the U.S. sub-prime mortgage problem, is unclear.[4] On the one hand, China places numerous restrictions on capital flows, particularly outflows, in part so that it can maintain its managed float currency policy.[5] These restrictions limit the ability of Chinese citizens and many firms to invest their savings overseas, compelling them to invest those savings domestically, (such as in banks, the stock markets, real estate, and business ventures), although some Chinese attempt to shift funds overseas illegally. Thus, the exposure of Chinese private sector firms and individual Chinese investors to sub-prime U.S. mortgages is likely to be small.

Moreover, Chinese government entities, such as the State Administration of Foreign Exchange, the China Investment Corporation (a $200 billion sovereign wealth fund created in 2007),[6] state banks, and state-owned enterprises, may have been more exposed to troubled U.S. mortgage securities. Chinese government entities account for the lion's share of China's (legal) capital outflows, much of which derives from China's large and growing foreign exchange reserves. These reserves rose from $403 billion in 2003 (year end) to $1.95 trillion as of December 2008.[7] In order to earn interest on these holdings, the Chinese government invests in overseas assets. A large portion of China's reserves are believed to be invested in U.S. securities, such as long-term (LT) Treasury debt (used to finance the federal deficit), LT U.S. agency debt (such as Freddie Mac and Fannie Mae mortgage-backed securities), LT U.S. corporate debt, LT U.S. equities, and short-term (ST) debt.[8] The Treasury Department estimates that, as of June 2008, China's holdings of U.S. securities totaled $1,205 billion (up from $922 billion in June 2007), making it the 2nd largest foreign holder of such securities (after Japan).[9] Of this total, $527 billion were in LT U.S. agency securities,[10] $522 billion were in LT Treasury securities, $100 billion in LT equities, $26 billion in LT corporate securities, and $30 billion in ST debt.

If China held troubled sub-prime mortgage backed securities, they would likely be included in the corporate securities category and certain U.S. equities (which include investment company share funds, such as open-end funds, closed-end funds, money market mutual funds, and hedge funds) which may have been invested in real estate. However, these were a relatively small share of China's total U.S. securities holdings.[11] China's holdings of Fannie Mae and Freddie Mac securities (though not their stock) were likely to have been more substantial, but less risky (compared to other mortgage-backed securities), especially after these two institutions were placed in conservatorship by the Federal Government in September 2008 and thus have government backing.

The Chinese government generally does not release detailed information on the holdings of its financial entities, although some of its banks have reported on their level of exposure to sub-prime U.S. mortgages.[12] Such entities have generally reported that their exposure to troubled sub-prime U.S. mortgages has been minor relative to their total investments, that they have liquidated such assets and/or have written off losses, and that they (the banks) continue to earn high profit margins.[13] For example, the Bank of China (one of China's largest state-owned commercial banks) reported in March 2008 that its investment in asset-backed securities supported by U.S. sub-prime mortgages totaled $10.6 billion in 2006 (accounting for 3.5% of its investment securities portfolio). In October 2008, it reported that it had reduced holdings of such securities to $3.3 billion (1.4% of its total securities investments) by the end of September 2008, while its holdings of debt securities issued or backed by Freddie Mac and Fannie Mae were at $10 billion. *Fitch Ratings* service reported that the Bank of China's exposure to U.S. sub-prime-related investments was the largest among Asian financial institutions, and that further losses from these investments were likely, but went on to state that the Bank of China would be able to absorb any related losses "without undue strain."[14]

However, China's economy has not been immune to effects of the global financial crisis, given its heavy reliance on trade and foreign direct investment (FDI) for its economic growth. Numerous sectors have been hard hit.[15] To illustrate:

- The real estate market in several Chinese cities has exhibited signs of a bubble that is bursting, including a slowdown in construction, falling prices and growing levels of unoccupied buildings. This has increased pressure on the banks to lower interest rates further to stabilize the market.
- The value of China's main stock market index, the Shanghai Stock Exchange Composite Index, lost nearly two-thirds of its value from December 31, 2007, to December 31, 2008.
- China's trade and FDI have plummeted over the past six months or so (see Figure 2). For example, China's exports and imports in February 2009 were down 25.7% and 24.1%, respectively on a year-on-year basis; the decline in exports was the biggest monthly decline ever recorded. The level of FDI flows to China has declined in each of the past seven months (November 2008-April 2009) on a year-on-year basis. FDI flows to China in April 2009 were down 22.5%, compared to April 2008 when FDI surged by 70.2%
- The Chinese government in January 2009 estimated that 20 million migrant workers alone had lost their jobs in 2008 because of the global economic slowdown.
- For the first four months of 2009, industrial output rose by 5.5% year-on-year, well below 12.9% growth rate in 2008.
- *Global Insight*, an international forecasting firm, estimates that China's real GDP growth will slow to 6.6% in 2009 (compared to growth rates of 13% in 2007 and 9% in 2008).[16] Some analysts contend annual economic growth of less than 8% could lead to social unrest, given that every year there are 20 million new job seekers in China.[17]

CHINA'S RESPONSE TO THE CRISIS

China has taken a number of steps to respond to the global financial crisis. On September 27, 2008, Chinese Premier Wen Jiabao reportedly stated that "what we can do now is to maintain the steady and fast growth of the national economy, and ensure that no major fluctuations will happen. That will be our greatest contribution to the world economy under the current circumstances."[18] In addition to cutting interest rates and boosting bank lending, China has implemented a number of policies to stimulate and rebalance the economy increase consumer spending, restructure and subsidize certain industries, and boost incomes for farmers and rural poor.

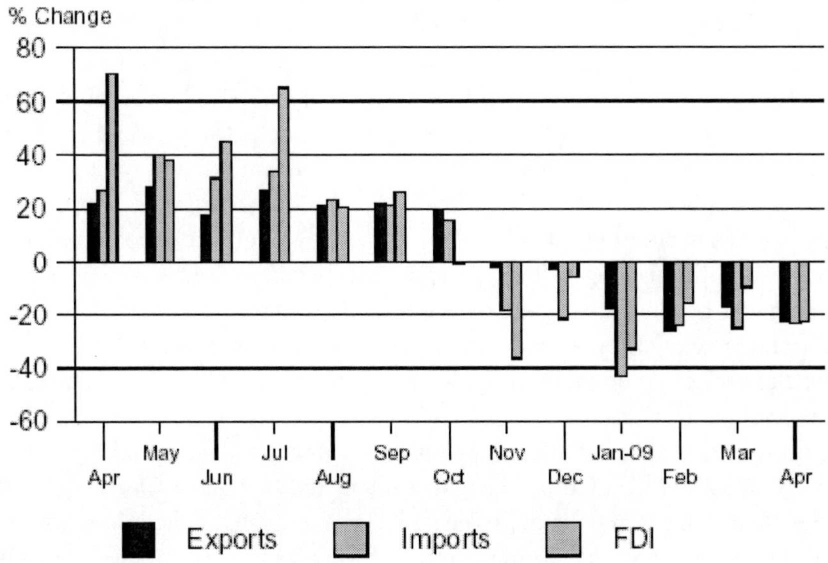

Source: Global Insight and China's Customs Administration.

Figure 2. Changes in China's Monthly Trade and FDI Inflows: April 2008-April 2009 year-on-year basis

Table 1. China's November 2008 Domestic Stimulus Package

	In Chinese Yuan (billions)	In U.S. Dollars (billions)	As a Percent of Total Stimulus Package	As a Percent of China's 2008 GDP
Transport infrastructure investment	1,500	220	37.5	5.0
Post-earthquake reconstruction	1,000	146	25.0	3.3
Public housing	400	59	10.0	1.3
Rural infrastructure	370	54	9.3	1.2
Research and development and structural change	370	54	9.3	1.2
Environmental development	210	31	5.3	0.7
Healthcare and education	150	22	3.8	0.5
Totals	4,000	586	100.0	13.3

Source: Global Insight

Notes: Ranked according to planned spending levels.

China's Stimulus Program

On November 9, 2008, the Chinese government announced it would implement a two-year 4 trillion yuan ($586 billion) stimulus package (equivalent to 13.3% of China's 2008 GDP), largely dedicated to infrastructure projects.[19] The package would finance public transport infrastructure (including railways, highways, airports, and ports) affordable housing, rural infrastructure (including irrigation, drinking water, electricity, and transport), environmental projects, technological innovation, health and education, and rebuilding areas hit by disasters (such as areas that were hit by the May 12, 2008 earthquake, primarily in Sichuan province).[20] China's stimulus, if fully implemented, would likely constitute one of the largest economic stimulus packages (both in spending levels and as a percent of GDP) that have been announced by the world's major economies to date, although it is unclear to what extent the stimulus package represents new spending versus projects that were already in the works before the economic downturn hit China.[21] Table 1 provides a breakdown of the stimulus program spending priorities.

The Chinese stimulus program includes steps the government intends to take to assist 10 pillar industries (i.e., industries deemed by the government to be vital to China's economic growth) to promote their long-term competitiveness. These industries include autos, steel, shipbuilding, textiles, machinery, electronics and information, light industry (such as consumer products), petrochemicals, non-ferrous metals, and logistics. Government support policies for the 10 industries are expected to include tax cuts and incentives (including export tax rebates), industry subsidies and subsidies to consumers to purchase certain products (such as consumer goods and autos), fiscal support, directives to banks to provide financing, direct funds to support technology upgrades and the development of domestic brands, government procurement policies, the extension of export credits, and funding to help firms invest overseas.[22]

On April 7, 2009, the Chinese government announced plans to spend $124 billion over the next three years to create a universal health care system.[23] The plan would attempt to extend basic coverage to most of the population by 2011, and would invest in public hospitals and training for village and community doctors. A number of efforts have been made to boost rural incomes and spending levels and to narrow the gap in living standards between rural and urban citizens (as well as between coastal and western regions of the country). For example, since February 2009, an estimated 900 million Chinese rural residents have been eligible to receive a 13% rebate for purchase of home appliances. Public housing projects, education, and infrastructure projects are largely targeted to rural areas. The government has also announced plans to boost agricultural subsidies to farmers. China has taken a number of steps to respond to the global financial crisis.

Has China's Economy Bottomed Out?

Chinese officials contend that their economic policy efforts are beginning to produce results. For example, in 2009 (through June 3 15, 2009) the Shanghai Stock Exchange Composite Index has risen by 45%. Industrial output rose by 7.3% in April 2009 on a year-on-year basis (it was up 8.3% in March 2009). In addition, retail sales in April 2009 were up

14.8% while investment in real estate was up 6.4% (year-on-year). However, China's trade and FDI flows continue to show sharp declines. Many analysts contend that China's large-scale bank lending and infrastructure spending projects have helped boost the domestic economy, but warn that these can not be maintained indefinitely. Many Chinese analysts have raised concerns that the large level of borrowing by local governments and state-owned enterprises will lead to a rise in non-performing loans on the balance sheets of China's major banks and could undermine efforts to reform the banking system. Others are concerned over the long term effects of expanded local government debt.[24] China's long-term economic growth prospects will likely depend on the ability of the government to rebalance the economy by promoting greater domestic consumption.

China's Potential Role and Implications for the United States

Analysts debate what role China might play in responding to the global financial crisis, given its huge foreign exchange reserves but its relative reluctance to become a major player in global economic affairs and its tendency to be cautious with its reserves. Some have speculated that China may, in order to help stabilize its most important trading partner (the United States), boost purchases of U.S. securities (especially Treasury securities) in order to help fund the hundreds of billions of dollars that are expected to be spent by the U.S. government to purchase troubled assets and stimulate the economy.[25] Additionally, China might try to shore up the U.S. economy by buying U.S. stocks. On September 21, 2008, the White House indicated that President Bush had called President Hu about the financial crisis and steps the Administration was planning to take. An unnamed Chinese trade official was reported as stating that "the purpose of that call was to ask for China's help to deal with this financial crisis by urging China to hold even more U.S. Treasury bonds and U.S. assets." The official was further quoted as saying that China recognized that it "has a stake" in the health of the U.S. economy, both as a major market for Chinese exports and in terms of preserving the value of U.S.-based assets held by China" and that a stabilized U.S. economy was in China's own interest.[26] During her first visit to China in February 2009, Secretary of State Clinton urged China to continue to buy U.S. Treasury securities. Some contend that taking an active role to help the United States (and other troubled economies) would boost China's image as a positive contributor to world economic stability, similar to what occurred during the 1997-1998 Asian financial crisis when it offered financial aid to Thailand and pledged not to devalue its currency.

On the other hand, there are a number of reasons why China might be reluctant to significantly increase its investments of U.S. assets. One concern could be whether increased Chinese investments in the U.S. economy would produce long-term economic benefits for China. Some Chinese investments in U.S. financial companies have fared poorly, and Chinese officials could be reluctant to put additional money into investments that were deemed to be too risky.[27] Secondly, a sharp economic downturn of the Chinese economy would likely increase pressure to invest money at home, rather than overseas. Many analysts (including some in China) have questioned the wisdom of China's policy of investing a large volume of foreign exchange reserves in U.S. government securities (which offer a relatively low rate of return) when China has such huge development needs at home.[28] China's holdings of U.S. securities at the end of 2008 are estimated to be roughly equivalent to over $1,000 per person in China, a significant figure for a country with a per capita GDP of about $3,190 (2008).[29] On March 13, 2009, Wen Jiabao at a news conference stated that he was "a little bit worried" about the safety of Chinese assets in the United States[30] On March 24, 2009, the governor of the People's Bank of China, Zhou Xiaochuan, published a paper calling for the replacing the U.S. dollar as the international reserve currency with a new global system controlled by the International Monetary Fund.[31] Many analysts (including some in China) have questioned the wisdom of China's policy of investing a large level of foreign exchange reserves in U.S. government securities, which offer a relatively low rate of return when China has such huge development needs at home.

While additional large-scale Chinese purchases of U.S. securities might provide short-term benefits to the U.S. economy and may be welcomed by some policymakers, they could also raise a number of issues and concerns. Some U.S. policymakers have expressed concern that China might try to use its large holdings of U.S. securities as leverage against U.S. policies it opposes. For example, various Chinese government officials reportedly suggested on a number of occasions in the past that China could dump (or threaten to dump) a large share of its holdings in order to counter U.S. pressure (such as threats of trade sanctions) on various trade issues (such as China's currency policy). In exchange for new purchases of U.S. debt, China would likely want U.S. policymakers to lower expectations that China will move more rapidly to reform its financial sector and/or allow its currency to appreciate more substantially against the dollar.[32] Some analysts have suggested that China could choose to utilize its reserves to buy stakes in various distressed U.S. industries. However, this could also raise concerns in the United States that China was being allowed to buy equity or ownership in U.S. firms at rock bottom prices, that technology and intellectual property from acquired firms could be transferred to Chinese business entities (boosting their competitiveness vis-a-vis U.S. firms), and that becoming a large stakeholder in major U.S. companies would give the Chinese government enormous new political influence in the United States.[33] U.S. policymakers in the past have sometimes opposed attempts by Chinese firms to acquire shares or ownership of U.S. firms.[34]

While attending the G-20 summit in London on the global financial crisis on April 1, 2009, President Obama President Hu met separately to discuss a number issues. The two sides agreed "to work together to resolutely support global trade and investment flows" and to "resist protectionism."[35]

End Notes

[1] *Invest in China*, September 10, 2007.

[2] According to *Xinhua Net* (March 9, 2008), China's Labor and Social Security Minister Tian Chengping warned that the employment situation in China in 2008 was expected to be "very severe."

[3] *IMF Survey Magazine: What the Numbers Show*, October 17, 2007.

[4] Some analysts contend that China's policy of keeping the value of its currency low against the dollar and large purchases of U.S. debt may have been a contributing cause to the current global financial crisis.

[5] China's central bank manages its currency (the renminbi or yuan) against a basket of major currencies (largely the U.S. dollar) by heavily intervening in international currency markets to maintain targeted exchange rates. See CRS Report CRS Report RL32165, *China's Currency: Economic Issues and Options for U.S. Trade Policy*, by Wayne M. Morrison and Marc Labonte.

[6] For an overview of the China Investment Corporation, see CRS Report RL34337, *China's Sovereign Wealth Fund*, by Michael F. Martin.

[7] China's large and growing reserves are largely the result of China's currency policy (which requires the government to intervene in currency markets to prevent the renminbi from appreciating), large levels of FDI, and large trade surpluses.

[8] ST debt includes Treasury, agency, corporate, and equity debt with less than one year maturity.

[9] Although the Chinese government does not make public the dollar composition of its foreign exchange holdings, many analysts estimate this level to be around 70%. Based on this estimate, China's holdings of such securities may have risen to about $1.4 trillion through the end of 2008, and it is likely that China surpassed Japan by the end of 2008 as the largest foreign holder of U.S. securities.

[10] China was the largest foreign holder of U.S. agency debt, accounting for 36% of total as of June 2008.

[11] According to the Treasury Department, China was not among the top 10 global investors of U.S. corporate mortgage-backed securities.

[12] *Financial Times*, September 11, 2008.

[13] According to Caijing.com, Chinese banks held $670 million worth of bonds issued by U.S. investment bank Lehman Brothers when it went bankrupt in September 2008.

[14] *Fitch Ratings*, Press Release, January 24, 2008.

[15] China's economy was already slowing down before the global financial crisis hit. This was in large part the result of government efforts to slow the rate of inflation. China's real GDP growth fell from 13% in 2007 to 9% in 2008. The global financial crisis has sharply diminished economic growth. Thus, the Chinese government has abandoned its anti-inflation policies and instead has sought to stimulate the economy.

[16] Global Insight, *China*, May 29, 2009.

[17] According to *Xinhua Net* (March 9, 2008), China's Labor and Social Security Minister Tian Chengping warned that the employment situation in China in 2008 was expected to be "very severe," noting that towns and cities would be able to provide only 12 million new jobs.

[18] *Chinaview*, September 27, 2008.

[19] China's currency is officially called the renmibi (RMB) and is denominated in units of yuan. Both terms are used to describe China's currency.

[20] Shortly after the central government announced its stimulus package, numerous local government officials announced their own stimulus package. Thus, the total level of China's economic stimulus could be much higher than the official 4 trillion yuan ($586 billion) figure.

[21] In dollar terms, China's stimulus would be larger than the combined stimulus packages of Japan and the European Union, but smaller than levels announced by the United States. See CRS Report RL34742, *The Global Financial Crisis: Analysis and Policy Implications*, coordinated by Dick K. Nanto.

[22] On May 18, 2009, China's State Council, announced plans to create 3 million new jobs in light industry over the next three years by providing financial support to small and medium-sized light industry firms with "good development potential."

[23] It is not yet clear whether this is part of the November 2008 stimulus package or constitutes new spending commitments,

[24] The central government has indicated that it will fund 1.2 million yuan out of the 4 million yuan stimulus package; local governments are expected to fund the rest.

[25] According to the Treasury Department, China overtook Japan in September 2008 as the largest foreign holder of U.S. Treasury securities. As of January 2009, China's holdings totaled $740 billion, accounting for 24.1% of total foreign holdings of U.S. Treasury securities. China accounted for more than one-third of total new purchases of these securities by foreign investors from January 2008 to January 2009.

[26] *Inside U.S. Trade, China Trade Extra*, September 24, 2008.

[27] For example, in June 2007, China's sovereign wealth fund bought $3 billion worth of shares from Blackstone LP (a U.S. private equity firm) at $31 each, but the value of those shares fell to $7.3 as of Aprill 1, 2009.

[28] China could use some of these reserves to purchase foreign imports, such as food, equipment, raw materials, consumer goods, etc. However, a significant sell-off of U.S. assets could destabilize the value of China's remaining U.S. assets and could weaken its ability to maintain its exchange rate goals. A similar result would occur if the government sold off its dollar holdings in China to obtain renminbi to be used to stimulate the domestic economy—it would cause the value of the renminbi to depreciate against the dollar, which could decrease exports.

[29] As long as the Chinese government continues to intervene in currency markets to keep the value of the renminbi low against the dollar, and continues to experience large trade surpluses, it will have relatively few options for dealing with additional foreign exchange reserves, other than to keep buying U.S. assets.

[30] Xinhua News Agency, March 13, 2009.

[31] *Financial Times*, "China calls for new reserve currency," March 24, 2009.

[32] China's currency has appreciated by about 19% to the dollar since reforms were made in July 2005, but many U.S. policymakers contend that it remains significantly undervalued.

[33] Most Chinese firms that have been allowed to invest overseas are state-owned enterprises.

[34] For example, efforts by a Chinese state owned oil company (CNOOC) in 2005 to purchase a U.S. energy company (Unocal) was widely opposed in Congress and eventually led the Chinese company to drop its bid. In 2007 a Chinese firm (Huawei) attempted to buy a stake in a U.S. technology company (3Com), but dropped its bid after a number of national security concerns were raised in a review by the U.S. Committee on Foreign Investment in the United States.

[35] White House Pres Release, April 1, 2009.

In: Asian Economic and Political Issues, Volume 14
Editor: David A. Marek
ISBN: 978-1-61728-019-1

Chapter 2

JAPAN-U.S. RELATIONS: ISSUES FOR CONGRESS*

Emma Chanlett-Avery, William H. Cooper and Mark E. Manyin

SUMMARY

The post-World War II U.S.-Japan alliance has long been an anchor of the U.S. security role in East Asia. The alliance, with its access to bases in Japan, where about 53,000 U.S. troops are stationed, facilitates the forward deployment of U.S. military forces in the Asia-Pacific, thereby undergirding U.S. national security strategy. For Japan, the alliance and the U.S. nuclear umbrella provide maneuvering room in dealing with its neighbors, particularly China and North Korea.

During the Bush Administration, the alliance initially made significant strides in broadening U.S.-Japan strategic cooperation and encouraging Japan to assume a more active international role. Following the September 11, 2001 terrorist attacks, Japan made its first-ever military deployments in non-combat support of U.S. and allied forces in Afghanistan. In 2004 Tokyo sent non-combat troops to Iraq, despite considerable domestic opposition. In 2005 the United States and Japan announced a sweeping new agreement to strengthen military cooperation. The plan calls for U.S. forces to be realigned and Japan to take on a more active (non-combat) role in maintaining regional and global security.

Political turmoil in Tokyo has slowed or stalled some of this progress in security relations. The ruling party's historic defeat in Upper House elections in July 2007 and the abrupt resignations of both Shinzo Abe and Yasuo Fukuda from the Prime Minister post has shaken the traditional power structure in Japan. Premier Taro Aso has clung to power while watching his approval ratings dip increasingly lower. When parliamentary elections are eventually held, an emboldened opposition party may take control of the government. As a result of this uncertainty, some of the earlier defense relations platform may be placed on hold. If political jockeying weakens Tokyo's focus on U.S.-Japan relations as an aging

* This is an edited, reformatted and augmented version of a CRS Report for Congress publication, Report #RL33436, dated June 3, 2009.

Japanese population demands more attention to domestic economic issues, the U.S.-Japan relationship may struggle to regain the momentum enjoyed in the early part of the decade.

Japan is one of the United States's most important economic partners. Outside of North America, it is the United States' second largest export market and second-largest source of imports. Japanese firms are the United States' second-largest source of foreign direct investment, and Japanese investors are the second largest foreign holders of U.S. treasuries, helping to finance the U.S. deficit and reduce upward pressure on U.S. interest rates. Bilateral trade friction has decreased in recent years, partly because U.S. concern about the trade deficit with Japan has been replaced by concern about a much larger deficit with China. The exception was U.S. criticism over Japan's decision in 2003 to ban imports of U.S. beef, which have since resumed.

However, the economic problems in Japan and United States associated with the credit crisis and the related economic recession and how the two countries deal with those problems will likely dominate the their bilateral economic agenda for the foreseeable future. In 2008, Japan's economy contracted 0.7%, having declined 3.8% alone in the final quarter of 2008. The contraction has accelerated in 2009, as Japan's gross domestic product (GDP) declined 4.0% in the first quarter. Japan is experiencing its steepest recession since the end of World War II. Japan is also experiencing its highest unemployment rate in three years. This trend will likely curtail Japanese demand for imports. In addition, the value of the yen has hit 13-year highs in terms of the U.S. dollar, which has adversely affected Japanese exports to the United States and other countries, contributing to the downturn in Japanese economic growth. The United States is the midst of a recession that will also likely affect trade flows in both directions.

RECENT DEVELOPMENTS

North Korean Nuclear Test and Missile Launches

North Korea's nuclear test in May and long-range missile launch in April re-ignited Japanese security fears about the capabilities and intentions of the regime in Pyongyang. In the wake of the tests, Japan has been actively engaged in working with the United Nations Security Council (UNSC) to craft a robust response to the provocation. Tokyo also has threatened to add to its already stringent suite of sanctions, potentially imposing a full embargo. Regardless of how the UNSC ultimately responds, the launch is likely to reinforce a trend of beefing up national defense, particularly the joint U.S.-Japan missile defense system. In another indication of how North Korean actions are affecting Japan's security consciousness, a parliamentary subcommittee composed of ruling party officials has proposed that Japan consider developing an attack capability. In addition, the United States, South Korea, and Japan held their first-ever trilateral defense ministerial on the sidelines of a regional security conference in Singapore to coordinate responses to the series of provocations.

The Global Financial Crisis and Economic Downturn

The U.S. and Japan economic agendas are likely to be dominated by the efforts of the two countries to resolve the financial crisis and the sharpest recessions each has seen since the end of World War II. Both countries have taken steps to ease credit conditions in their respective economies and to boost domestic demand through stimulus packages. The United States and Japan each pushed the other members of the G-20 to increase government spending at the April 2009 G-20 summit in London. A bilateral issue will be how each country can stimulate employment and other domestic economic activity while maintaining their obligations not to erect new barriers to trade and investment.

Political Paralysis in Tokyo Continues

For months, Japanese policymaking has been complicated—and in some cases, stalled—by three inter-related factors: divided government, a succession of weak LDP prime ministers, and a scandal involving the leader of the largest opposition party, the Democratic Party of Japan (DPJ). Hanging over all these developments are upcoming national elections for the Lower House, the more powerful of Japan's two Parliamentary chambers. Polls indicate the vote, which must be held by October, is likely to be closer than any previous one taken in decades. While many forecasters predict a muddled result in which no party has a clear victory, it is possible that the opposition Democratic Party of Japan (DPJ) could win, thereby assuming power. A DPJ victory would amount to a political earthquake in Japan, which except for a ten-month period in the 1990s has been ruled by the Liberal Democratic Party (LDP) since 1955. While most members of the DPJ are broadly supportive of the U.S.-Japan alliance and the general thrust of Japanese foreign policy, many features of the relationship could come under greater questioning if the DPJ won the Lower House.

In the most recent major political development, the DPJ in mid-May selected Yukio Hatoyama to be its party president. Hatoyama succeeded Ichiro Ozawa, the veteran politician who had masterminded the DPJ's victory in 2007 elections for the (less powerful) Upper House of Japan's legislature. Ozawa resigned after prosecutors arrested his chief aide on charges of violating campaign contributions laws. Throughout the early spring of 2009, the scandal over Ozawa's political finances, combined with Aso's unveiling of a series of large economic stimulus packages, sapped the DPJ's momentum. While Ozawa's resignation appears to have restored the DPJ's slight lead in many polls, its popularity remains below the levels it had enjoyed before the Ozawa scandal broke.

THE ROLE OF CONGRESS IN U.S.-JAPAN RELATIONS

Congressional powers, actions, and oversight form a backdrop against which both the Administration and the Japanese government must formulate their policies. In the 111th Congress, it is unlikely that Members' attention to Japan will increase significantly, although some Members showed interest in the 109th and 110th Congresses. In the 109th, Congress held four hearings on Japan in 2005-2006, after holding only two Japan-specific public hearings from 2001 through 2004. Members of Congress were particularly critical of Japan's two-year ban on imports of U.S. beef and of the Bush Administration's handling of the beef dispute. On security issues, members expressed concern that steps taken by the Japanese government are harming U.S. interests in East Asia by worsening Sino-Japanese and South Korean-Japanese relations. Former Chairman of the House International Relations Committee Henry Hyde suggested in an April 2006 letter to Speaker Dennis Hastert that Prime Minister Koizumi should not address a joint session of Congress unless he pledged to stop visiting Yasukuni Shrine, which enshrines the names of several Class A war criminals from World War II, and convened a hearing on Japan's "history problem" in September 2006.

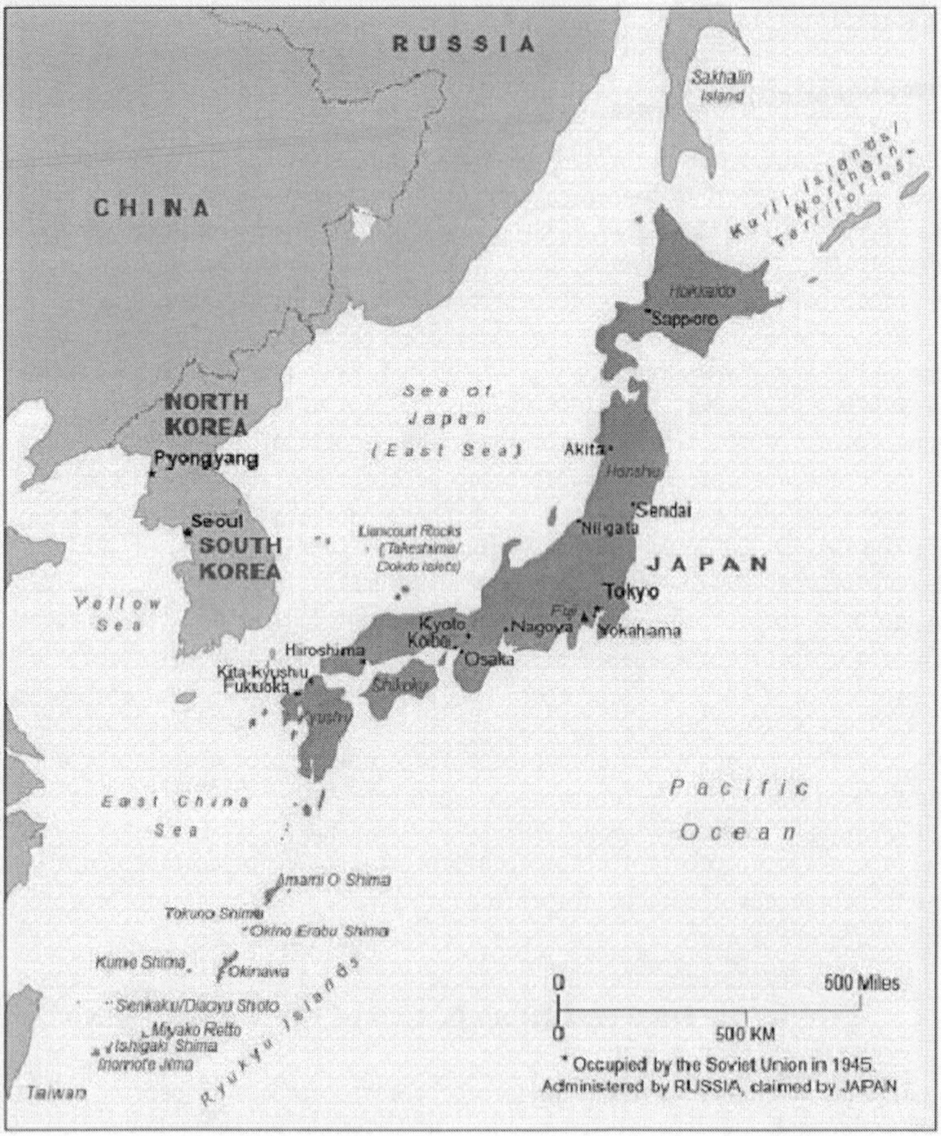

Source: Map Resources. Adapted by CRS.

Figure 1. Map of Japan

The "comfort women" controversy in the 110th Congress reignited congressional concern about revisionist views of history in Japan. In September 2007, the House passed H.Res. 121, calling on the government of Japan to "formally acknowledge, apologize, and accept historical responsibility in a clear and unequivocal manner" for its treatment of women forced to serve as prostitutes for the Japanese military during its colonization and occupation of Asia in the 1930s and 1940s. The resolution passed by voice vote and attracted 167 co-sponsors, reportedly driven in part by a June 2007 *Washington Post* advertisement signed by several Japanese legislators and academics rejecting the historical basis of the resolution. A few days later, the House also passed H.Res. 508, which praised the U.S.-Japan alliance and Japan's contributions to the effort against international terrorism. The bill was seen as an attempt to blunt the negative diplomatic impact of the former resolution. The question of historical truth and memory has emerged as a prominent theme in congressional relations with Japan. (See the "Selected Legislation" section.)

MAJOR DIPLOMATIC AND SECURITY ISSUES[1]

Two high-level bilateral meetings between senior officials in Tokyo and Washington in February 2009, early in the Obama Administration, provided a symbolic yet reassuring boost to the relationship amid concerns about some drift in the alliance. Secretary of State Hillary Clinton chose to make Japan her first official foreign visit, followed by embattled Prime Minister Taro Aso's reception as President Obama's first foreign guest in the White House. Both Clinton and Obama reaffirmed the axiom that the U.S.-Japan alliance is "the cornerstone of U.S. Asia-Pacific strategy."

JAPAN COUNTRY DATA

Population: 127.4 million (July 2006 est.)
% of Population over 64: 21% (U.S. = 12.4%) (2007)
Area: 377,835 sq km (slightly smaller than California)
Life Expectancy: 82 years (2007 est.)
Per Capita GDP: $33,800 (2007 est.) purchasing power parity
Primary Export Partners: US 22.8%, China 14.3%, South Korea 7.8%, Taiwan 6.8% (2006)
Primary Import Partners: China 20.5%, U.S. 12%, Saudi Arabia 6.4%, UAE 5.5%, Australia 4.8%, South Korea 4.7% (2006)
Yen:Dollar Exchange Rate: 117.99 (2007), 116.18 (2006), 110.2 (2005), 108.2 (2004), 115.9 (2003), 125.4 (2002)
Foreign Exchange Reserves: $881 billion (2006 est.)

Source: CIA *World Factbook*, February 2008

Global Issues

Support for U.S. Policy toward Iraq and Afghanistan

Following the terrorist attacks of September 11, 2001, the government of former Prime Minister Junichiro Koizumi initiated a series of unprecedented measures to protect American facilities in Japan and provide nonlethal, "rear area" logistical support to U.S. military operations against Al Qaeda and the Taliban in Afghanistan. The latter mainly took the form of at-sea replenishment of fuel oil and water to U.S., British, French, and other allied warships operating in the Indian Ocean. The dispatch of Japan's Maritime Self-Defense Forces (MSDF) was the first such deployment since World War II.

While strongly preferring a clear United Nations role in resolving the U.S./British confrontation with Iraq, Japan nonetheless gave almost unqualified support to the Bush Administration's position. During an open debate in the U.N. Security Council, Japan was one of only two out of 27 participating countries (the other being Australia) to support the U.S. contention that even if the U.N. inspections were strengthened and expanded, they were unlikely to lead to the elimination of Iraq's weapons of mass destruction. Since 2003, Japan has provided $1.5 billion in grant assistance to Iraq, has pledged to provide $3.5 billion in yen loans, and has agreed to a phased cancellation of 80% of the approximately $7.5 billion in debt Iraq owed Japan. In addition, in January 2004, the Koizumi government deployed about 600 military personnel—mainly ground troops—to carry out humanitarian aid and reconstruction activities in Iraq. The ground troops were withdrawn from the southern area of Samawah in June-July 2006, but the air division of the Self Defense Forces (the official name of Japan's military) remained. The Lower House of the Diet approved a two-year extension of the air force transport mission in May 2007, but subsequently Japan ended its participation in Iraq in late 2008 as U.N. authorization for multinational forces in Iraq expired.

In Afghanistan, Japan has dispatched refueling vessels that provide about 30% of the fuel used by U.S. and allied warships. After a suspension due to political opposition in 2007, the refueling mission has been renewed and will continue through at least January 2010. Japan has also sent a civilian assistance team to assist in reconstruction efforts. Although the dispatch of troops has been considered, Japan faces resistance from its public to send its military overseas as well as considerable restrictions in its rules of engagement due to its pacifist constitution. Japan has pledged a total $2 billion of assistance for Afghanistan to contribute to security efforts, the promotion of the political process and reconciliation, and economic and human resource development.

North Korea and the Six-Party Talks

As the Obama Administration's North Korea policy forms, Japan has watched closely for signs of any shift. President Obama and Secretary Clinton strongly condemned the 2009 nuclear device and missile tests by North Korea and called for coordinated UNSC action, similar to Japan's reaction. However, Japan continues to hold the hardest position in the negotiations and is wary that their concerns will not be given enough weight in the overall talks.

As the Bush Administration moved aggressively to reach a deal on denuclearization with North Korea in the Six-Party Talks, distance emerged between Washington and Tokyo. Former Prime Minister Abe rose to prominence based on his hardline position on

Pyongyang's responsibility to disclose the fate and/or whereabouts of several Japanese citizens abducted by North Korean agents in the 1970s and 1980s.[2] Japan pledged that it would not provide economic aid to North Korea without resolution of the abductees' issue. The abductee issue remains an emotional topic in Japan, and the opposition party has not taken a substantially different position from the LDP. Although some Japanese officials and media figures privately acknowledge that Japan may need to compromise in order to remain relevant in the ongoing talks, the political potency and widespread anger surrounding the abductees make it difficult for leaders to adopt a softer position.

Before the United States announced it planned to remove North Korea from the list of state sponsors of terrorism in June 2008 in exchange for North Korean concessions on its nuclear program, Japanese officials had expressed alarm about the anticipated removal. In the past, U.S. leaders linked North Korea's inclusion on the list to the abduction issue, although State Department officials reportedly claimed that the issue was not a legal obstacle for removal. In December 2007, the Committee on Abduction of Japanese Citizens by North Korea of the Lower House adopted a resolution urging the United States to refrain from "de-listing" North Korea. Although conservative groups in Japan have protested the move, the overall reaction has been somewhat muted. Tokyo officials maintain that U.S. and Japanese goals remain the same.

Until the shift toward negotiation in Washington, Japan's policy toward North Korea aligned closely with the U.S. position in the Six-Party Talks. Japan has insisted on North Korea abandoning its nuclear weapons, has taken steps to squeeze North Korea economically, and participates in the U.S.-led Proliferation Security Initiative (PSI). After North Korea test-fired several missiles in July 2006 and tested a nuclear device in October 2006, Japan strongly supported punitive United Nations Security Council resolutions that condemned the actions and called for trade restrictions. In addition, Japan imposed unilateral sanctions more stringent than the UNSC resolutions, including a ban on all North Korean ships in Japanese ports, restrictions on imports and on most North Koreans entering Japan, and a freeze on bank remittances to North Korea from the ethnic Korean community in Japan.

United Nations Security Council Reform

In 2004, Japan accelerated its longstanding efforts to become a permanent member of the United Nations Security Council by forming a coalition with Germany, India, and Brazil (the so-called "G-4") to achieve non-veto membership for all four countries. Though the Bush Administration backed Japan's bid, it did not support the G-4 proposal and opposed taking a vote on expanding the Security Council until a "broader consensus" on reforming the entire organization can be reached. To become a member, Japan must obtain support from two-thirds (128 countries) of all U.N. member countries. Japan is the second-largest contributor to the U.N. regular budget, paying 22% of the total, more than twice the percentage paid by the third-largest contributor. Efforts to gain membership appear to have stalled in the past few years, but Japanese officials have voiced optimism that the Obama Administration will take a positive stance on advancing U.N. reform, including potentially expanding the membership of the Security Council.

Kyoto Protocol and Climate Change Negotiations

Tokyo has sought to highlight Japan's leadership on environmental issues, which has long been recognized as a global leader in increasing energy efficiency and development of green energy technology, including hybrid cars. At the 2008 G-8 summit in Hokkaido hosted by Japan, the forum agreed to work towards halving the amount of greenhouse gas emissions by 2050, marking the first time that the United States has signed on to such a goal. Japan is the fourth-leading producer of greenhouse gases after the United States, the Russian Federation, and China. Under the Kyoto Protocol, which Tokyo ratified in 2002, Japan is obligated to reduce its emissions to 6% below its 1990 levels by 2012, although it is unlikely to meet this goal. Japanese industry shares many of the concerns of U.S. industry about the cost and feasibility of the plan. A U.N. climate negotiations summit slated to be held in December 2009 in Copenhagen, Denmark, aims to find a replacement for the Kyoto Protocol, which will expire in 2012. Japan is considered to be a close ally of the Obama Administration in international climate negotiations.

Regional and Historical Issues

Historical issues have long dominated Japan's relationships with its neighbors, with many Asians, and particularly those in China and South Korea, still resentful of Japan's occupation policies and aggression in the World War II period. Despite underlying distrust, Tokyo's relationships with Beijing and, until recently, Seoul appear to be on a solid upward trajectory. Part of this was due to former Prime Minister Fukuda's emphasis on developing friendly relations with Japan's neighbors; his pledge not to visit the controversial Yasukuni Shrine was perhaps the most significant in terms of improving the diplomatic atmosphere. (The Shinto shrine honors Japanese soldiers who died in war, including 14 war criminals who were convicted by the International Military Tribunal for the Far East following Japan's defeat in World War II.) Despite his reputation as a nationalist conservative, Aso appears to be following the same course. This is in marked contrast to the period under former Prime Minister Koizumi (2001-2006), when relations with China and South Korea suffered, largely because of Koizumi's annual visits to the site.

Despite some progress, however, reminders of Japan's imperial past continue to emerge. In October 2008, it was revealed that Toshio Tamogami, the head of Japan's Air Self Defense Forces, won an essay contest with a piece that glorified Japan's conquests of Asia and denied any wrongdoing on the part of Japan's military. Aso moved quickly to terminate his position, but the episode reinforced the perception that such revisionist views remain within Japan's security establishment. Aso also faced criticism for denying that his family's mining company employed Allied prisoners during World War II, a charge that was later confirmed by the release of government documents.

China

In concert with the leadership in Beijing, which has been keen to shore up its foreign relations before the 2008 Summer Olympics, both Abe and Fukuda substantially warmed Sino-Japanese ties, and Aso appears to be following their lead. Although analysts emphasize that geopolitical rivalry between China and Japan is likely to endure, the short-term outlook is positive. The past year has seen several notable accomplishments, including successful reciprocal visits by heads of state and a breakthrough agreement to jointly develop gas fields in the East China Sea, the site of long-standing territorial disputes. Driven by self interest, both sides appear to have decided to put aside nationalist rivalries for now and focus on common concerns such as regional stability to further economic development and boost already robust trading relations.

Chinese President Hu Jintao's carefully orchestrated visit to Japan in May 2008 was the first by a Chinese leader to Japan in a decade. The warmth of the visit was in stark contrast to Jiang Zemin's 1998 visit—during which he criticized publicly Japanese officials for imperial Japan's war-time aggression—and the subsequent downturn in relations under former Prime Minister Junichiro Koizumi. Notably absent from the Chinese leader's statements was a call for Japan to apologize for historical grievances, and both sides emphasized a "forward-looking" friendship. The two leaders agreed to hold annual summits, cooperate on environmental technology, and enhance cultural exchanges. Days later, after China was struck by a devastating earthquake, Japan immediately offered condolences and pledged assistance. Sixty Japanese earthquake rescue experts then were dispatched to the hard-hit Sichuan province, the first foreign team that Beijing accepted.

The official reconciliation, however, may be challenged by sentiment among the Japanese public, some political groups, and the military. In early 2008, several packages of "gyoza" meat dumplings imported into Japan from China that contained a toxic pesticide sickened scores of people. Although Chinese and Japanese officials reportedly reacted quickly, the incident renewed long-standing concerns among the Japanese public about the safety and hygiene practices for Chinese products. Further, some conservative nationalist voices have criticized the government for being too "soft" on Beijing and practicing "kow-tow diplomacy." And despite official military-to-military contact in the form of reciprocal port calls, suspicion of Beijing's motives remains high among some military officials, who report periodic Chinese military activities around Japan's territory, including the incursion of two Chinese ships around a set of disputed islands in December 2008.

South Korea

The election of Lee Myung-bak as president of South Korea appeared at the outset to improve prospects for Seoul-Tokyo relations. After his election in December 2007, Lee indicated his desire to engage in more cooperation with Japan, in contrast to his predecessor Roh Moo-hyun, whose rhetoric against Japan many claimed precluded any meaningful engagement. Lee has said he would not emphasize history issues with Japan. However, in summer 2008 a long-standing dispute over the ownership of several small islands (known as Dokdo in Korean and Takeshima in Japanese) has flared anew after reports that Japan would refer to the islands as its territory in a handbook for teachers and textbook publishers. (The islands have been administered by South Korea since 1945.) This led South Korea to recall its ambassador to Japan and rebuke the Japanese ambassador in Seoul, as well as reject an offer for talks between the two foreign ministers at a regional forum in Singapore. Although both capitals have made some attempt to quell the controversy, the weakened political standing of both leaders limits their ability to take on an issue charged with nationalist tones. In addition, fundamental disagreements on a range of issues, including how to deal with North Korea's nuclear weapons, may challenge a full-scale revitalization of bilateral ties.

Military Issues[3]

Japan and the United States are military allies under a security treaty concluded in 1951 and revised in 1960. Under the treaty, Japan grants the United States military base rights on its territory in return for a U.S. pledge to protect Japan's security. In recent years Japan has edged closer to a more independent self-defense posture in both practice and in published security strategies. In December 2006, Japan's Defense Agency was formally upgraded to a ministry for the first time since World War II, giving the ministry more clout in budget and policy-making decisions.

Agreements to Deepen Cooperation

Under the Bush Administration, a series of Security Consultative Committee meetings (SCC, also known as the "2+2" meeting) of the Japanese and U.S. foreign and defense ministers outlined plans to expand the alliance beyond its existing framework. As U.S. personnel and facilities in Japan are realigned as part of the broader Pentagon strategy of deploying a more streamlined and mobile force, Japan is slated to take a more active role in contributing to global stability, primarily through increased coordination with the U.S. military. Key features of the arrangement include a reduction in the number of U.S. Marines in Japan, the relocation of a problematic air base in Okinawa, the deployment of an X-Band radar system in Japan as part of a missile defense system, expanded bilateral cooperation in training and intelligence sharing, and Japan's acceptance of a nuclear-powered aircraft carrier in the Yokosuka Naval Base.

Implementation of the plan to relocate 8,000 Marines to Guam and to replace the controversial Futenma Marine Air Station in Okinawa remains slow. Many of the agreement's most controversial elements are likely to face continued obstacles, particularly from local Japanese politicians in the areas identified to host new facilities and troops. U.S. officials say Japan will pay an estimated $26 billion overall for the realignment initiative. Some military officials in Japan are concerned that the high cost of the realignment could result in decreased Japanese capabilities because of budgetary restraints.

Loss of Momentum in 2007-2008

Political shifts in Japan since 2006 appear to have slowed some of the increased cooperation in the U.S.-Japan alliance. Although ties remain strong fundamentally, the Bush Administration shift on North Korean nuclear negotiations, the July 2007 House resolution criticizing the Japanese government for past "comfort women" policies, and the apparent decision not to consider exporting the F-22 to Japan may have undermined to some degree Japanese confidence in the robustness of the alliance.[4] Koizumi and Abe's platform of enhancing Japan's role in global affairs had been encouraged by U.S. officials who saw Japan's strategic interests aligning with their own. Implementation of the "2+2" agreements depends on Tokyo providing the necessary resources and political capital. The agreement signed by Hillary Clinton and her counterpart in February 2009 re-affirmed the timetable, but many obstacles remain. Because the realignment and transformation initiatives involve elements that are unpopular in the localities affected, successful implementation depends on leadership from the central government. If the ruling party continues to struggle to reestablish itself, details of the hard-fought agreements designed to sustain the alliance politically may falter.

A series of high-profile alleged crimes committed by U.S. military personnel in 2007-2008 sparked public anger about the troops' presence in Japan. Four Marines were accused of gang-raping a 19-year old in Hiroshima, another marine was accused of sexually abusing a 14-year old in Okinawa, and a sailor was charged with murdering a taxi driver in Yokosuka. U.S. officials, mindful of fall-out from a similar incident in 1995, in which three U.S. servicemen were convicted of raping a 12-year-old, cooperated with local Japanese authorities by handing over the suspects and, in the first two cases, decided to court-martial the marines when Japanese prosecutors dropped charges. The officials also announced they would undertake a review of sexual harassment training procedures for U.S. military personnel.

During the political maneuvering that followed the July Upper House elections, Japanese support of the U.S.-led Operation Enduring Freedom (OEF) in Afghanistan emerged as a key issue of contention. Although re-fueling operations were eventually resumed, the opposition parties succeeded in allowing the "Anti-terrorism Special Measures Law" authorization to expire, creating a gap in MSDF participation. Japanese participation is limited to activities related to provision of fuel and water to coalition forces. The opposition took a similar tactic for the renewal of host nation support funding. (See "Burden-Sharing Issues" section below.)

New International Security Partnerships

In early 2007, Japan signed a bilateral agreement with Australia that pledges cooperation on counterterrorism, maritime security, peace-keeping operations, and disaster relief. In October 2008, a similar pact was signed with India. The agreements, though short of a formal military alliances, may help to establish a framework of security cooperation among Japan, Australia, India, and the United States. Such partnerships adhere to the stated goal of "values-based diplomacy," in which Japan plans to strengthen ties with other democracies with similar political and economic freedoms. Continuing this trend, in September 2007 Japan joined a multinational naval exercise with the United States, Australia, Singapore, and India in the area west of the Malacca Straits. The exercise reinforced two interrelated trends in Asia-Pacific defense dynamics: the U.S.-led campaign of strengthening security ties among democratic allies and the strategic countering of Chinese military power. On the sidelines of the 2007 Asia Pacific Economic Cooperation (APEC) forum, Japan, Australia, and the United States held their first trilateral meeting.

Article 9 Restrictions

In general, Japan's U.S.-drafted constitution remains an obstacle to closer U.S.-Japan defense cooperation because of a prevailing constitutional interpretation of Article 9 that forbids engaging in "collective self-defense"; that is, combat cooperation with the United States against a third country. Article 9 outlaws war as a "sovereign right" of Japan and prohibits "the right of belligerency." Whereas in the past Japanese public opinion strongly supported the limitations placed on the Self-Defense Force (SDF), this opposition has softened considerably in recent years. Abe had indicated his intention to amend some of these restrictions by reinterpreting the right of collective self defense and, eventually, amending the constitution itself. (See "Constitutional Revision".) Since then, political will to advance the changes appears to have waned significantly. Since 1991, Japan has allowed the SDF to participate in non-combat roles in a number of United Nations peacekeeping missions and in the U.S.-led coalition in Iraq.

U.S. Bases on Okinawa

The reduction of marines on Okinawa seeks to quell the political controversy that has surrounded the presence of U.S. forces on the island for years. In early 2008, the charge that a U.S. Marine sexually abused a young Japanese girl renewed public outcry against the bases that had existed since the 1995 rape of a Japanese schoolgirl by American servicemen. Though constituting less than 1% of Japan's land mass, Okinawa currently hosts 65% of the total U.S. forces in Japan. Okinawan politicians have called for a renegotiation of the Japan-U.S. Status of Forces Agreement (SOFA) and a reduction in U.S. troop strength. The U.S. and Japanese governments oppose revising the SOFA, but have acknowledged the political demand to alleviate the burden of military presence in Okinawa. As part of the realignment of U.S. bases, U.S. officials agreed to move most aircraft and crews constituting the marine air station at Futenma to expanded facilities at Camp Schwab, located in Nago, a less-congested area of Okinawa. The agreement remains stalled, however, over a host of environmental, noise, and funding concerns.

Burden-Sharing Issues

The United States has pressed Japan to increase its share of the costs of American troops and bases. According to Pentagon reports, Japan has over the years provided up to$4 billion annually in direct and indirect Host Nation Support (HNS), which constitutes about 75% of the total cost of maintaining troops in Japan. In recent years, Japanese officials have reportedly suggested that HNS be reduced on grounds that Japan is now making a greater direct contribution to the alliance. Political divisions between the LDP-controlled Lower House and the DPJ-controlled Upper House in spring 2008 led to a delay in the implementation of a new agreement, which pledges to pay directly about 140 billion yen annually (about $1.4 billion) through FY2010 to defray the costs of stationing troops in Japan. The Upper House rejected the bill, citing opposition to paying for "recreational" activities by the U.S. military, but the approval by the more powerful Lower House went into effect after a month's delay. Japan pays for most of the salaries of about 25,000 Japanese employees at U.S. military installations.

Cooperation on Missile Defense

A U.S.-Japan program of cooperative research and development of anti-ballistic missiles began in 1999. The decision to acquire the ground-based U.S. Patriot Advanced Capability-3 (PAC-3) system and the ship-based U.S. Standard Missile-3 system was justified largely on the basis of North Korea's missile program. In December 2005, Japan's Defense Agency agreed that Japan will pay over $1 billion for the project over nine years. Following North Korean missile tests in July 2006, officials announced that the deployment of the PAC-3 system to Okinawa would accelerate. In December 2007, a Japanese destroyer successfully intercepted a missile in a test exercise near Hawaii.

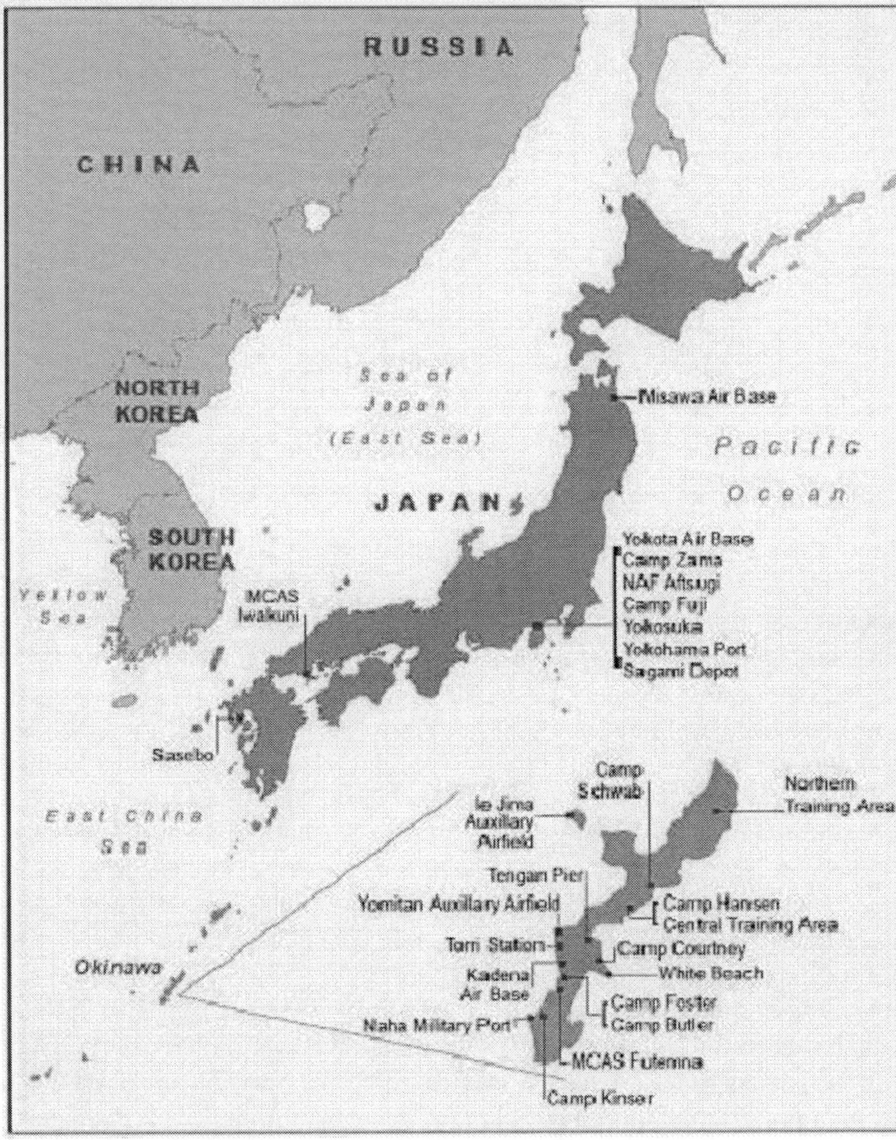

Source: Map Resources. Adapted by CRS.

Figure 2. Map of Military Facilities in Japan

ECONOMIC ISSUES[5]

Trade and other economic ties with Japan remain highly important to U.S. national interests and, therefore, to the U.S. Congress.[6] By the most conventional method of measurement, the United States and Japan are the world's two largest economies,[7] accounting for around 40% of world gross domestic product (GDP), and their mutual relationship not only has an impact on each other but on the world as a whole. Furthermore, their economies are intertwined by merchandise trade, trade in services, and foreign investments.

Table 1. U.S. Trade with Japan, Selected Years ($ billions)

Year	Exports	Imports	Balances
1995	64.3	123.5	-59.1
2000	65.3	146.6	-81.3
2003	52.1	118.0	-66.0
2004	54.4	129.6	-75.2
2005	55.4	138.1	-82.7
2006	59.6	148.1	-88.4
2007	62.7	145.5	-82.8
2008	66.6	139.2	-72.3

Source: U.S. Commerce Department, Census Bureau. FT900. Exports are total exports valued on a free alongside ship (f.a.s.) basis. Imports are general imports valued on a customs basis.

Overview of the Bilateral Economic Relationship

Although Japan remains important economically to the United States, its importance has slid as it has been edged out by other trade partners. Japan is the United States's fourth-largest merchandise export market (behind Canada, Mexico, and China) and the fourth-largest source for U.S. merchandise imports (behind Canada, Mexico, and China) the end of 2008. At one time Japan was the largest source of foreign direct investment in the United States, but by 2006 had fallen behind the United Kingdom. It was the eighth-largest target for U.S. foreign direct investment abroad as of the end of 2007. The United States remains Japan's largest export market and second-largest source of imports as of the end of 2008. The U.S. bilateral trade deficit with Japan reached a record $88.4 billion in 2006. In 2007, U.S. exports rose slightly, and imports declined; thus, the U.S. trade deficit with Japan decreased to $82.8 billion and to $72.3 billion in 2008. (See Table 1.)

Despite some outstanding issues, tensions in the U.S.-Japan bilateral economic relationship have been much lower than was the case in the 1970s, 1980s, and early 1990s. A number of factors may be contributing to this trend: Japan's economic problems in the 1990s and in the first few years of this decade changed the general U.S. perception of Japan as an economic "threat" to one of a country with problems; the rise of China as an economic power has caused U.S. policymakers to shift attention from Japan to China as a source of concern; the increased use by both Japan and the United States of the WTO as a forum for resolving trade disputes has depoliticized disputes and helped to reduce friction; and the emphasis in the bilateral relationship has shifted from economic to security matters.

However, the economic problems in Japan and United States associated with the credit crisis (both countries are now in recessions) and how the two countries deal with those problems will likely dominate the their bilateral economic agenda for the foreseeable future. In 2008, Japan's economy contracted 0.7%, declining 3.8% alone in the final quarter of 2008. The contraction has accelerated in 2009, as Japan's gross domestic product (GDP) declined 4.0% in the first quarter. Japan is experiencing its steepest recession since the end of World War II. Japan is also experiencing its highest unemployment rate in three years. This trend will likely curtail Japanese demand for imports. In addition, the value of the yen has hit 13-year highs in terms of the U.S. dollar, which will adversely affect Japanese exports to the

United States and other countries, contributing to the downturn in Japanese economic growth. (As of May 29, 2009, the exchange rate was $1=¥95.56.) The United States is the midst of a recession that will also likely affect trade flows in both directions.

Bilateral Trade Issues

Japan's Ban on U.S. Beef[8]

In December 2003, Japan imposed a ban on imported U.S. beef in response to the discovery of the first U.S. case of bovine spongiform encephalopathy (BSE or "mad cow disease") in Washington state. In the months before the diagnosis in the United States, nearly a dozen Japanese cows infected with BSE had been discovered, creating a scandal over the Agricultural Ministry's handling of the issue (several more Japanese BSE cases have since emerged). Japan had retained the ban despite ongoing negotiations and public pressure from Bush Administration officials, a reported framework agreement (issued jointly by both governments) in October 2004 to end it, and periodic assurances afterward by Japanese officials to their U.S. counterparts that it would be lifted soon.

In December 2005 Japan lifted the ban after many months of bilateral negotiations but reimposed it in January 2006 after Japanese government inspectors found bone material among the first beef shipments to have arrived from the United States after the ban was lifted. The presence of the bone material violated the procedures U.S. and Japanese officials had agreed upon that allowed the resumption of the U.S. beef shipments in the first place. The then-U.S. Secretary of Agriculture Johanns expressed regret that the prohibited material had entered the shipments.

In July 2006, Japan announced it would resume imports of U.S. beef from cattle 20 months old or younger. While praising the decision, some officials have called on Japan to broaden the procedures to include beef from older cattle. The first shipments arrived in August 2006.

Members of Congress have pressed Japan to lift restrictions on imports of U.S. beef further. On May 27, 2009, the Japan Ministry of Health, Labor, and Welfare and the Ministry of Agriculture, Forestry, and Fisheries reportedly were ready to ask the Food Safety Commission to determine whether it would relax restrictions and allow U.S. beef from cattle younger than 30 months to enter Japan, a decision that could take about six months to be rendered.[9]

U.S.-Japan FTA

With the conclusion of negotiations on a U.S.-South Korean free trade agreement (KORUS FTA) on April 1, 2007, and the formation of FTAs among other East Asian countries, interest seems to have increased in the possibility of a U.S.-Japan FTA. Japanese business leaders are concerned about being adversely affected by the trade preferences that South Korean exporters would gain under the proposed KORUS FTA. In May 2007, a Japanese government advisory panel recommended that Japan undertake the formation of an economic partnership agreement (EPA), Japan's version of an FTA, with the United States. During their late April 2007 summit meeting, President Bush and Prime Minister Abe touched on the issue. According to a White House fact sheet, they agreed to exchange information about one another's FTAs and EPAs with third countries. However, in a October 2, 2008 speech, Assistant USTR stated that she did not believe a U.S.-Japan FTA would occur in the near term primarily because of the stumbling block that would result over the issue of agricultural policy.[10]

Insurance

Market access in Japan for U.S. and other foreign insurance providers has been the subject of bilateral trade agreements and discussion for some time. Current U.S. concerns center around making sure that Japan adheres to its agreements with the United States, especially as Japan's domestic insurance industry and government regulations of the industry are restructured. Specifically, American firms have complained that little public information is available on insurance regulations, how those regulations are developed, and how to get approval for doing business in Japan. They also assert that government regulations favor insurance companies that are tied to business conglomerates—the keiretsu—making it difficult for foreign companies to enter the market.

The United States and Japan concluded agreements in 1994 and 1996 on access to the Japanese market for U.S. providers of life and non-life insurance and also on maintaining competitive conditions for foreign providers in the specialty insurance market—cancer insurance, hospitalization, nursing care, and personal accident insurance. U.S. and Japanese officials continue to meet under those two agreements, and U.S. providers have been able to expand their presence in Japan under them, according to the Office of the U.S. Trade Representative (USTR).

However, the United States has raised concerns about Kampo, the government-owned insurance company under the Japan Postal Service, which offers insurance services that directly compete with U.S. and other privately owned providers. The United States has also raised questions about the activities of regulated and unregulated insurance cooperatives, kyosai, claiming that these entities do not have to adhere to the same regulations that bind traditional private insurance companies, creating an unfair competitive advantage. A Japanese government privatization framework released in July 2006 generated statements from the American Chamber of Commerce in Japan and from the American Council of Insurers arguing that the privatization plan would allow Kampo to compete with foreign insurance providers by offering new products before it has been completely privatized. On October 1, 2007, the Japanese government began the privatization, a process that is expected to last ten years. U.S. industry and U.S. policymakers have indicated they will continue to monitor the privatization to make sure U.S. service providers are not placed at a competitive disadvantage in the Japanese market.

The Byrd Amendment

Japan, together with other major trading partners, challenged U.S. trade laws and actions in the World Trade Organization (WTO). For example, Japan and others challenged the so-called Byrd Amendment (which allows revenues from countervailing duty and antidumping orders to be distributed to those who had been injured). The WTO ruled in Japan's favor. In November 2004, the WTO authorized Japan and the other complainant-countries to impose sanctions against the United States. In September 2005, Japan imposed 15% tariffs on selected imports of U.S. steel products as retaliation, joining the EU and Canada. It is the first time that Japan had imposed punitive tariffs on U.S. products. In the meantime, a repeal of the Byrd Amendment was included in the conference report for S. 1932, the Deficit Reduction Act of 2005, that was signed by the President into law (P.L. 109-171) on February 8, 2006. The measure phases out the program over a period ending October 1, 2007.[11] Although Japan has praised the repeal of the Byrd Amendment, it criticized the delayed termination of the program and has maintained the sanctions on imports from the United States. Consequently, Japan announced in August 2006 that it would maintain the tariff sanctions until October 1, 2007. In August 2007, Japan notified the WTO that it would extend the sanctions for another year and did so again in August 2008.

WTO Dispute

On January 10, 2008, Japan requested permission from the WTO to impose sanctions on U.S. imports valued at around $250 million in retaliation for the failure of the United States to comply with a WTO Appellate Body decision against the U.S. practice of "zeroing" in antidumping duty determinations. On April 21, the WTO agreed to establish a dispute panel to hear the case and the panel is expected to issue its determination within 90 days.[12] However, on August 4, the WTO panel announced that a final ruling would not be issued until sometime in 2009.[13] The practice is one under which the U.S. Department of Commerce treats prices of targeted imports that are above fair market value as zero dumping margin rather than a negative margin. It results in higher overall dumping margins and U.S. trading partners have claimed and the WTO has ruled that the practice violates WTO rules.[14]

The Doha Development Agenda

Japan and the United States are major supporters of the Doha Development Agenda (DDA), the latest round of negotiations in the WTO. Yet, the two have taken divergent positions in some critical areas of the agenda. For example, the United States, Australia, and other major agricultural exporting countries have pressed for the reduction or removal of barriers to agricultural imports and subsidies of agricultural production, a position strongly resisted by Japan and the European Union. At the same time, Japan and others have argued that national antidumping laws and actions that member countries have taken should be examined during the DDA, with the possibility of changing them, a position that the United States has opposed.

In July 2006, WTO Director-General Pascal Lamy suspended the negotiations because, among other reasons, the major participants could not agree on the modalities that negotiators would use to determine how much they would liberalize their agricultural markets and reduce agricultural subsides. Negotiators had been meeting from time to time to try to resuscitate the talks. However, Lamy's attempt to hold a ministerial meeting to in December 2008 failed when the major parties to the negotiators could not resolve their differences over establishing modalities in agricultural and non-agricultural negotiations.

JAPANESE POLITICS[15]

Japan's political world is fixated around the coming national elections for Japan's Lower House of Parliament. Polls indicate the vote, which must be held by October, is likely to be closer than any previous one taken in decades. While many forecasters predict a muddled result in which no party has a clear victory, it is possible that the opposition Democratic Party of Japan (DPJ) could win, thereby assuming power. A DPJ victory would amount to a political earthquake in Japan, which except for a ten-month period in the 1990s has been ruled by the Liberal Democratic Party (LDP) since 1955. While most members of the DPJ are broadly supportive of the U.S.-Japan alliance and the general thrust of Japanese foreign policy, many features of the alliance may come under greater questioning if the DPJ won the Lower House.

Background—The Structural Debilities of Japan's Political System

In general, Japan's political peculiarities both constrain and enhance U.S. influence over Japanese policy. Compared to most industrialized democracies, the Japanese parliament is structurally weak, as is the office of the prime minister and his cabinet. Though former Prime Minister Koizumi (who served from 2001 to 2006) and his immediate predecessors increased politicians' influence relative to Japan's bureaucrats, with important exceptions Japan's policymaking process tends to be compartmentalized and bureaucratized, making it difficult to make trade-offs among competing constituencies on divisive issues. The result is often paralysis or incremental changes at the margins of policy, particularly during periods of weak premierships such as the one Japan has experienced for the past two to three years.

The Situation in May 2009

Political Turmoil Continues

For months, Japanese policymaking has been complicated – and in some cases, stalled – by two inter-related factors: divided government and a succession of weak LDP prime ministers. In March 2009, a third item was thrown into the mix: a political scandal involving Ichiro Ozawa, the leader of Democratic Party of Japan (DPJ), that led to his resignation two months later. All of these factors cloud the outcome of the next round of national elections, which must be held by October 2009.

The Japanese Diet has been divided since July 2007, when the opposition DPJ won national elections for the Upper House, marking the first time that the LDP had lost power in the less-powerful chamber of Japan's bicameral legislature. In an attempt to force early elections for the Lower House, the DPJ under its leader Ozawa has erected procedural obstacles to block or delay parts of the LDP's agenda, leading to the resignation of two LDP prime ministers since September 2007.

Aso has been a highly unpopular premier for much of his tenure; except for the initial period after the LDP selected him to be leader in September 2008, his disapproval ratings have been well over the 50% mark. Though Aso's poll numbers have risen somewhat following the Ozawa scandal and the unveiling of three successive economic stimulus packages cumulatively worth around 5% of Japan's annual GDP, they still top out in 30% range. Many polls indicate disapproval ratings twice that level. More troublingly for the LDP, Ozawa's resignation appears to have given the DPJ a popular boost.

Until the early spring of 2009, much of the political momentum had been favoring the DPJ, which for the first time was consistently besting the LDP in most opinion polls. However, in March, prosecutors arrested Ozawa's chief aide on charges of violating campaign contributions laws. Although Ozawa himself was not charged, the ensuing media coverage revived concerns within the DPJ and the general public about his leadership qualities. Following Ozawa's resignation in early May, the DPJ selected an Ozawa ally, former party leader Yukio Hatoyama, to be its president. He defeated another former leader, Katsuya Okada, who is seen by many as possessing a "cleaner" image. Polls taken after Hatoyama's selection indicated that the DPJ had once again overtaken the LDP, though not at the levels achieved before Ozawa's scandal. Ozawa remains as DPJ Deputy President in charge of election strategy. Okada is serving as DPJ Secretary General.

Possible Scenarios

With Lower House elections looming – at the latest, they must be held by October 2009 – Japanese politics have entered a fluid period, with a number of possible outcomes. One possibility is continued paralysis, particularly if the LDP wins the Lower House elections but loses its 2/3 majority (a 2/3 majority in the Lower House is needed to override an Upper House vote). A DPJ victory, while signifying the emergence of a true two-party system in Japan, could usher in a period of fundamental adjustment to policies that have remained static for decades under the LDP. Another possibility is the formation of a "Grand Coalition" between the LDP and the DPJ, an idea that Ozawa has flirted with from time to time. A fourth scenario is political realignment, in which members of either party defect to the other and/or form a new majority. Many observers predict that it will take multiple election cycles to produce a decisive victory for any political grouping. If true, then Japan is likely to experience months if not years of weak premierships.

The Democratic Party of Japan (DPJ)

Since its victory in the July 2007 Upper House election, the DPJ has emerged as a viable candidate to defeat the LDP. The DPJ was able to capitalize on widespread discontent with Abe the LDP by emphasizing economic and social security issues, and succeeded in winning over large numbers of voters from the rural areas of Japan, usually an LDP stronghold. A DPJ victory in 2009 would amount to a political earthquake in Japan, which except for a ten-month period in the 1990s has been ruled by the LDP since 1955. Ozawa has unveiled a highly populist policy blueprint that includes items such as providing income support to farmers and fishermen; abolishing certain provisional taxes; and reforming the national pension and healthcare systems. He would offset the over 18 trillion yen (over $160 billion) in revenue shortfalls by eliminating or trimming what he has called "wasteful" government programs that are funded through various "special accounts." Ozawa also has outlined measures to reduce bureaucrats' influence over politicians and has called for Japanese troops to participate in U.N. peacekeeping operations. Though Ozawa is not popular in opinion polls, he is respected in his party for his skills as a political tactician. Should Ozawa resign, there is no clear replacement, though former party leaders Yukio Hatoyama and Katsuya Okuda are often mentioned as the favorites.

The DPJ was formed in 1998 as a merger of four smaller parties and was later joined by a fifth grouping. The amalgamated nature of the DPJ has led to considerable internal contradictions, primarily between the party's hawkish/conservative and passivist/liberal wings. In particular, the issues of deploying Japanese troops abroad and revising the war-renouncing Article 9 of the Japanese constitution have generated considerable internal debate in the DPJ. The DPJ has been generally unified around the sense that Japan needs to become more of an equal partner in the U.S.-Japan alliance.

Constitutional Revision

Japan's constitution was drafted in 1946 by the U.S. Occupation authorities, who then imposed it on a reluctant Japanese legislature. Since the early 1990s, previously strong public opposition to revising the constitution has gradually weakened and public opinion polls now show widespread support for some sort of revision. In October 2005, the LDP released its long-awaited draft revision of the Japanese constitution. The most notable changes reduce many—though not all—of the provisions in the war-renouncing clause (Article 9) that set limits on Japan's military activities. After renouncing war and the "threat or use of force as a means of settling international disputes," the proposed revision explicitly states that Japan "shall maintain armed forces for self-defense" that operate under the prime minister and are subject to the Diet's approval and direction. The explicit mention of a military force is designed to rectify the disconnect between the current constitution—which says that "land, sea, and air forces, as well as other war potential, will never be maintained"—and the reality that Japan possesses a Self Defense Force. More importantly, the LDP's draft appears to allow Japan to participate in collective security arrangements by stating that the armed forces "may act in international cooperation to ensure the international community's peace and security."

Both the LDP and the DPJ are split—with the DPJ's internal divisions much deeper—between relatively hawkish and pacifist wings that appear to be sparring over the question of whether or not conditions (such as United Nations backing) should be attached to the right to join collective security arrangements. In other words, the issue is not whether, but how, Article 9 should be revised, a development that is due in part to increased concerns about North Korea and China. In March 2005, Japan's House of Representatives Research Commission on the Constitution, composed of representatives from various parties, released a report indicating that over two-thirds of members generally favor constitutional provisions allowing Japan to join U.N. collective security arrangements, stipulating the Self-Defense Forces' existence, and maintaining some portion of the war-renouncing clause of Article 9. A wide majority of the commission also favored allowing women to serve as emperor, establishing stronger privacy and environmental rights, creating a constitutional court, and revising Japan's federalist system.

Constitutional amendments must be approved by two-thirds of each chamber of the Diet, after which they are to be "submitted to the people" for majority approval. In May 2007, after over a year of debate, the Diet passed legislation detailing how a national constitutional referendum would be conducted. However, the bill was passed without any significant DPJ support. Indeed, the LDP-led coalition and the DPJ proposed separate referendum bills, dampening hopes for the two camps to cooperate on constitutional revision. Notably, according to the timetable outlined in the bill that passed, the soonest that a national referendum could be held would be three years after a referendum law is passed, i.e. 2010. Momentum behind constitutional revision was sapped by the LDP's loss in the July 2007 Upper House elections; many felt then LDP Prime Minister Shinzo Abe paid a political price for prioritizing constitutional and security reforms over the economic issues that were foremost in most voters' minds.

Japan's Demographic Challenge

Japan's combination of a low birth rate, strict immigration practices, and a rapidly-ageing population present policymakers with a significant challenge. Polls suggest that Japanese women are avoiding marriage and child-bearing because of the difficulty of combining career and family in Japan; the birthrate has fallen to 1.25, far below the 2.1 rate necessary to sustain a population size. Japan's current population of 128 million is projected to fall to about 100 million by mid-century. Concerns about a huge shortfall in the labor force have grown, particularly as the elderly demand more care. Japan's National Institute of Population and Social Security Research projects that the working-age population will fall from 85 million in 2005 to 70 million by 2030. Japan's immigration policies have traditionally been strictly limited, but policy adjustments have allowed for a larger foreign labor force. Over 68,000 foreign workers came to Japan in 2006 under a government-sponsored training program, in addition to 80,000 on an extended program.[16] With government encouragement, some private firms offer incentives to employees with children.

Selected Legislation

111th Congress

H.R. 44 (Bordallo). Seeks recognition of the loyalty and suffering of the residents of Guam who suffered unspeakable harm as a result of the occupation of Guam by Imperial Japanese military forces during World War II, by being subjected to death, rape, severe personal injury, personal injury, forced labor, forced march, or internment, as well as payments for death, personal injury, forced labor, forced march, and internment. Referred to Senate Committee on the Judiciary on March 5, 2009.

H.R. 423 (Mica). Seeks to provide compensation for certain World War II veterans who survived the Bataan Death March and were held as prisoners of war by the Japanese. Referred to House Subcommittee on Military Personnel on February 6, 2009.

110th Congress

H.R. 6497 (Hooley). Requires the payment of compensation to members of the Armed Forces and civilian employees of the United States who were forced to perform slave labor by the Imperial Government of Japan or by corporations of Japan during World War II, or the surviving spouses of such members, and for other purposes. Referred to the Committee on

Armed Services on July 15, 2008, and in addition to the Committees on the Judiciary, and Ways and Means, in each case for consideration of such provisions as fall within the jurisdiction of the committee concerned.

S. 3107 (Bingaman). Requires the payment of compensation to members of the Armed Forces and civilian employees of the United States who were forced to perform slave labor by the Imperial Government of Japan or by corporations of Japan during World War II, or the surviving spouses of such members, and for other purposes. Referred to the Committee on Finance on June 10, 2008.

H.R. 2886 (Knollenberg). To address the exchange-rate misalignment of the Japanese yen with respect to the United States dollar, and for other purposes. Referred to the Committee on Ways and Means on June 27, 2008, and in addition to the Committee on Financial Services, in each case for consideration of such provisions as fall within the jurisdiction of the committee concerned.

H.R. 1570 (Mica). Provides compensation for certain World War II veterans who survived the Bataan Death March and were held as prisoners of war by the Japanese. Referred to House Committee on Armed Services on March 19, 2007.

H.R. 3650 (Ros-Lehtinen). Provides for the continuation of restrictions against the government of North Korea unless the President certifies to Congress that the government of North Korea has met certain benchmarks, including releasing the 15 Japanese nationals recognized as abduction victims by the National Police Agency (NPA) of Japan. Referred to the House Committee on Foreign Affairs on September 25, 2007.

H.Res. 121 (Honda). Expresses the sense of the House of Representatives that the Government of Japan should formally acknowledge, apologize, and accept historical responsibility in a clear and unequivocal manner for its Imperial Armed Force's coercion of young women into sexual slavery, known to the world as "comfort women," during its colonial and wartime occupation of Asia and the Pacific Islands from the 1930s through the duration of World War II. Referred to the House Committee on Foreign Affairs on January 31, 2007.

H.Res. 508 (Saxton). Recognizes the strong security alliance between the government of Japan and the United States and expresses appreciation to Japan for its role in enhancing stability in the Asia-Pacific region and its efforts in the global war against terrorism. Passed/agreed to in House on September 5, 2007.

S. 1021 (Stabenow). Addresses the exchange-rate misalignment of the Japanese yen with respect to the United States dollar, and for other purposes. Referred to Senate Committee on Finance on March 28, 2007.

S. 1686, Sec. 6 (Landrieu). Establishes a United States-Japan Inter-parliamentary Group to meet once per Congress with representatives of the Diet of Japan for discussion of common problems in the interest of relations between the United States and Japan. Placed on Senate Legislative Calendar under General Orders on June 25, 2007.

S.Res. 399 (Brownback). Expresses the sense of the Senate that certain benchmarks must be met before certain restrictions against the government of North Korea are lifted, including that the government of North Korea has released or fully accounted to the satisfaction of the government of the United States and the government of the Republic of Korea for the whereabouts of the 15 Japanese nationals recognized as abduction victims by the National Police Agency (NPA) of Japan. Referred to the Committee on Foreign Relations on December 10, 2007.

End Notes

[1] This section was written by Emma Chanlett-Avery.

[2] For more information, see CRS Report RS22845, *North Korea's Abduction of Japanese Citizens and the Six-Party Talks*, by Emma Chanlett-Avery.

[3] For more information on the U.S.-Japan alliance, see CRS Report RL33740, *The Changing U.S.-Japan Alliance: Implications for U.S. Interests*, by Emma Chanlett-Avery.

[4] For more information on the F-22 issue, see CRS Report RS22684, *Potential F-22 Raptor Export to Japan*, by Christopher Bolkcom and Emma Chanlett-Avery.

[5] This section was written by William Cooper.

[6] For a more complete treatment of U.S.-Japan economic ties, see CRS Report RL32649, *U.S.-Japan Economic Relations: Significance, Prospects, and Policy Options*, by William H. Cooper.

[7] China's economy is now larger than Japan's by another method of measurement: purchasing power parity.

[8] For more information, see CRS Report RS21709, *Mad Cow Disease and U.S. Beef Trade*, by Charles E. Hanrahan and Geoffrey S. Becker.

[9] *International Trade Daily.* May 28, 2009.

[10] *International Trade Reporter.* October 16, 2008.

[11] For more information on the Byrd Amendment, see CRS Report RL33045, *The Continued Dumping and Subsidy Offset Act ("Byrd Amendment")*, by Jeanne J. Grimmett and Vivian C. Jones.

[12] *International Trade Daily.* April 21, 2008.

[13] *International Trade Reporter.* August 7, 2008.

[14] *International Trade Reporter.* January 17, 2008.

[15] This section was written by Mark Manyin and Emma Chanlett-Avery.

[16] "Foreign Labor Works for Japan," *Wall Street Journal Asia.* May 25, 2007.

In: Asian Economic and Political Issues, Volume 14
Editor: David A. Marek ISBN: 978-1-61728-019-1

Chapter 3

NORTH KOREA: ECONOMIC LEVERAGE AND POLICY ANALYSIS*

Dick K. Nanto and Emma Chanlett-Avery

SUMMARY

In 2009, the Democratic Peoples Republic of Korea (DPRK or North Korea) embarked on a course that includes a series of extremely provocative military actions, a shift in power toward the military, emphasis on ideological purity, rising criticism of the United States, and going forward with its nuclear and missile program in spite of sanctions and objections from much of the rest of the world. Two factors that seem to be operating to compel this more "aggressive" behavior by Pyongyang. The first is the apparent stroke by North Korea's leader, Kim Jong-il, in August 2008. The country appears to be preparing for succession, and in jockeying for position, the military seems to be gaining in policy precedence over the civilian side of government, and the military- first doctrine is prevailing over economic reform. The second factor has been the preparations for the 100th anniversary of the birth of Kim Il Sung, the founder of the DPRK, in 2012. By then the country wants to join the club of nuclear and space powers and to be an Asian tiger economy.

North Korea's dire economic straits provide one of the few levers to move the country to cooperate in attempts by the United States, China, South Korea, Japan, and Russia to halt and dismantle its nuclear program. These five countries plus North Korea comprise the "six parties" who are engaged in talks to resolve issues raised by the DPRK's development of a nuclear weapon. The Six-Party Talks are now stalled. Western leverage over the DPRK remains limited, but China, and to some extent Russia, are in a position to exert pressure on Pyongyang.

The economy of North Korea is of interest to Congress because it provides the financial and industrial resources for the Kim Jong-il regime to develop its military and to remain in

---

* This is an edited, reformatted and augmented version of a CRS Report for Congress publication, Report #RL32493, dated June 4, 2009.

power, constitutes an important "push factor" for potential refugees seeking to flee the country, creates pressures for the country to trade in arms or engage in illicit economic activity, is a rationale for humanitarian assistance, and creates instability that affects South Korea and China in particular. The dismal economic conditions also foster forces of discontent that potentially could turn against the Kim regime—especially if knowledge of the luxurious lifestyle of communist party leaders becomes better known or as poor economic performance hurts even the elite.

North Korea has extensive trading relationships with China and Russia and, until recently, with South Korea. U.S. and Japanese trade with North Korea since 2006 has been virtually nil except for U.S. aid deliveries. The DPRK has been running an estimated $1.5 billion deficit per year in its international trade accounts that it funds primarily through receipts of foreign assistance and foreign investment as well as through various questionable activities.

Following the DPRK's second nuclear test and subsequent actions, the focus in mid-2009 has been on negative incentives and increasing sanctions. The larger question, however, is how to move beyond tit-for-tat actions to a three-fold transformation of the DPRK: a transformation in its international relations, in the Stalinist methods by which Communist regime maintains its support, and in its moribund economy that cannot feed its own population.

MAJOR POINTS AND RECENT DEVELOPMENTS

- The DPRK or North Korea has embarked on a course that includes a major tightening of policies, a shift in power toward the military, emphasis on ideological purity, rising criticism of the United States, and going forward with its nuclear and missile program in spite of sanctions and objections from much of the rest of the world. On May 25, 2009, North Korea conducted its second test of a nuclear bomb and continues to test its arsenal of missiles. This holds significant implications for U.S. interests and goals in Asia. There are two factors that seem to be operating to compel this more "aggressive" behavior by Pyongyang. The first is the apparent stroke by North Korea's leader, Kim Jong-il, in August 2008. The country appears to be preparing for succession, and in jockeying for position, the military seems to be gaining in policy precedence over the civilian side of government, and the military-first doctrine is prevailing over economic reform. Leaders are leaning more toward nationalism, purity of thought, and loyalty both to the Communist party and to the party's ideals. South Korean intelligence reports that Kim Jong-il has designated his youngest son, Kim Jong-un, as his heir apparent (South Korea's Unification Ministry and the U.S. State Department, however, consider this chapter as "speculative."). Kim Jong-il may be allowing the provocative moves by the military to ensure their support of one of his young sons to succeed him, or the military may be preparing to install a new leader of their choice.
- The second factor in the aggressive military actions has been the preparations for the 100th anniversary of the birth of Kim Il Sung, the founder of the DPRK, in 2012. By then the country intends to become a recognized military and economic power.

Pyongyang apparently feels it has already attained the status of a politically, ideologically, and militarily powerful state, but it is not recognized by the world as a nuclear weapon state, and its missile delivery system is still under development. The military recognizes, however, that it needs the backing of an "economically powerful state" both to supply the army and to fulfill a lifelong "cherished desire" of Kim Il Sung. As a step in this process, in May 2009, the DPRK embarked on a 150-day campaign, a new "all-out assault for opening a great turnabout phase in the construction of an economically powerful state." The campaign calls for the people to rise up in unity, for socialist ideological purity, and to work harder to accomplish an upsurge in production.[1] The result of these two factors has been a series of policy pronouncements and military actions that have tightened the domestic orientation of the country and increasingly is isolating it from the rest of the world. North Korea also is threatening military action should its ships be searched under the Proliferation Security Initiative.

- **Recent Developments**: On March 17, North Korea detained American reporters, Laura Ling and Euna Lee, who are accused of "illegally" entering the country. On April 5, the DPRK tested a long-range missile (ostensibly to launch a satellite). On April 24, the United Nations tightened sanctions, and Pyongyang responded by expelling nuclear inspectors and effectively quitting the Six Party Talks on the DPRK's nuclear program. On May 8, a DPRK spokesman escalated its criticism of the United States by referring directly to the Obama Administration and U.S. "hostile policy toward the DPRK." At around that time, Ambassador Stephen Bosworth (the special envoy for North Korea) was leading an interagency delegation to Beijing, Seoul, Tokyo, and Moscow for consultations on North Korea issues. On May 14, Pyongyang announced it was nullifying contracts with South Korean companies in the Kaesong Industrial Complex. North Korea also has detained a Kaesong South Korean worker. On May 25, the DPRK tested a second nuclear weapon, and on May 25-26, tested five short-range missiles. On May 25, the United Nations Security council unanimously condemned North Korea's nuclear test as a clear violation of Security Council resolutions, and said it would begin work immediately on a new, legally binding resolution addressing the violations. On May 26, South Korea joined the U.S.-led Proliferation Security Initiative, and the DPRK responded by stating that it considered the action by South Korea a declaration of war and that it would respond with a military strike if any search and seizure of their vessels occurred. The DPRK subsequently indicated that it no longer is obligated to abide by provisions of the 1956 armistice following the Korean War barring either side from imposing a naval blockade, would not honor a North- South border in the Yellow Sea of its coast, nor would it respect the legal status of five islands on the South's side of the line. On June 2, South Korea's intelligence agency told lawmakers that Kim, Jong-un had been chosen as the successor to the ailing Kim Jong-il. On June 4, the two American reporters were put on trial.
- It is clear that the resurgence of the DPRK military in policymaking has nullified progress made under the Six-Party Talks and diminished the effectiveness of economic and diplomatic incentives and sanctions. These have been one of the few policy levers that countries could use to induce Pyongyang to abandon its nuclear

program. The basic contradiction in North Korea's current policy seems to be that it is unlikely to build a strong economy without access to capital, expertise, and imports of technology and certain raw materials from abroad, yet its military actions elicit condemnations and economic sanctions by other nations that only work to thwart its economic goals. Two keys in this process are actions by China and Russia, countries friendly to North Korea who joined in condemning the DPRK's May 25 nuclear test. Other than financial sanctions, economic sanctions appear to have had little effect on the Pyongyang regime because China, Russia, and other nations have traded with and provided assistance to the DPRK, and the Kim Jong-il regime seems willing to allow starvation rather than open the country to outsiders.

- The immediate response to North Korea's second nuclear test is centered on the United Nations. It appears that China and Russia may be willing to support stronger sanctions on the DPRK, since Pyongyang's actions are increasingly being perceived as being inimical to certain Chinese and Russian interests. The focus of U.N. action is likely to be on nonproliferation, the stopping of exports of nuclear and missile material, in tightening enforcement of previously announced sanctions, and measures to punish North Korea's elite. In addition to U.N. action, the United States may separately impose additional sanctions on the DPRK for U.S. currency counterfeiting operations run by the North Korean Government. The United States also could return the DPRK to the list of states that sponsor terrorism, although certain legal conditions would have to be met.
- The economy of the DPRK is in dire straits with a considerable share of its population on the edge of starvation and in need of outside food aid. In 2008, Pyongyang placed more emphasis on feeding its people, although it did without food aid and fertilizer from South Korea because Pyongyang would not request it, and South Korea placed conditions on providing the assistance.[2]
- Chinese investments and trade with the DPRK are helping the country to secure needed imports of energy, food, and machinery for factories. North Korea's trade deficit is being financed primarily through foreign aid, investments, and remittances from overseas workers, as well as through various illicit activities.
- Economic reforms ("adjustments") in the DPRK were gradually being implemented, but in 2009 were being reversed where possible. Without markets, however, there would be no means for North Koreans not receiving government food distributions to survive.
- A February 2007 Six-Party Agreement called for providing fuel and eventual normalizing of relations with the DPRK in response to specific actions by Pyongyang in regard to its nuclear program.[3]

NORTH KOREA'S "PLAN A" AND "PLAN B"

A source with close ties to the North Korean government has written that in 2009 Pyongyang has abandoned Plan A and turned to Plan B. Plan A called for the DPRK to consider exploring a shortcut to enhanced independence, peace and prosperity through rapprochement with the United States. This strategy obliged the Kim Jong-il administration to negotiate away its nuclear weapons program as part of a verified denuclearization of the Korean Peninsula in return for Washington's strategic decision to co-exist peacefully with Pyongyang. Plan A assumed the United States would cease its hostility toward the DPRK, conclude a peace treaty, and pledge in a verifiable way that it would not attack the DPRK with nuclear and conventional arms. It also assumed the United States would establish full relations with the DPRK, uphold its sovereignty and independence, lift sanctions, and provide it with fuel oil and light-water reactors.

Pyongyang apparently now has shifted to Plan B. This envisages the DPRK going it alone as a fully fledged nuclear weapon-armed state, with a military-first policy, and then growing into a mighty and prosperous country. It puts the policy of seeking reconciliation with the United States on the back burner and involves quitting the six-party talks, restarting nuclear facilities, and conducting additional nuclear and intercontinental ballistic missile tests. Under Plan B, the DPRK hopes to join all three elite clubs of the world by 2012 (centenary of the birth of Kim Il-sung, the nation's founder)—nuclear, space, and that of economic tigers—without seeking improved ties or a peace treaty with the United States.

Source: Kim Myong Chol, "Kim Jong-il shifts to plan B," *Asia Tiimes*, May 21, 2009, Online edition.

THE ISSUE, INTERESTS, AND POLICY

This chapter examines the economic side of U.S. leverage with North Korea. The security side is addressed in other CRS reports.[4] Here we examine the economy of North Korea[5] in the context of U.S. confrontation with that country over its nuclear weapon and missile programs. This chapter provides an overview of the North Korean economy, surveys its economic relationships with major trading partners, and examines various U.S. policy options.

The issue with respect to the economy of the Democratic People's Republic of Korea and its economic relations deals with what actions the United States could take that would lead to a verifiable halt to the DPRK's nuclear weapons program; the lessening of tensions between the DPRK and South Korea, Japan, and the United States; the prevention of proliferation nuclear weapons and missile material by North Korea; and the betterment of human rights and the standard of living of North Korean non-elites.

The year 2009 may turn out to be the tipping point in the quest by the DPRK to become a *de facto* nuclear-armed state, although its ability to deliver a nuclear weapon remains problematic. The DPRK has embarked on a course that includes a major shift in power toward the military, emphasis on ideological purity, rising criticism of the United States, a restart of its nuclear plant at Yongbyon, the test of a potential long-range ballistic missile in spite of sanctions and objections from much of the rest of the world, the capture of two American news reporters (trial set for June 4) and a South Korean worker from the joint Kaesong Industrial Complex,[6] and the test of its second nuclear weapon as well as short-range missiles. North Korea also has indicated that it would not return to the Six-Party Talks on denuclearization.

Following an apparent stroke by North Korea's leader, Kim Jong-il, in August 2008, the country appears to be preparing for succession and for the 100th anniversary in 2012 of the birth of Kim Il-sung, the nation's founder. In jockeying for position, the military and issues related to national security have taken policy priority over the civilian side of government and issues related to economics, international trade, and society at large. In addition, Pyongyang's leaders seem to be leaning more toward nationalism, purity of thought, and loyalty both to the Communist party and to the party's ideals. The result has been a policy shift that implies that the domestic issues are taking priority over foreign considerations leading to increased isolation from the rest of the world. Kim Jong-il reportedly has designated either his youngest son, Kim Jong-un, as his heir apparent.[7] Both South Korea's Unification Ministry and the U.S. State Department, however, consider the reported designation as "speculative."[8] As Kim Jong-il faces possible death, one prominent theory is that he is indulging hard-line elements in the armed forces in order to secure military backing for his chosen successor.[9] Another possibility is that the military is preparing to name its own leader to succeed Kim Jong-il.

Since Kim Jong-un in his mid-20s[10], if he becomes the successor to Kim Jong-il, he likely will undergo a period of grooming before actually assuming power. According to news reports, Kim Jong-il's brother-in-law, Jang Seong-taek, currently is running many of the day-to-day affairs of the DPRK on behalf of the ailing Kim Jong-il.[11] He may continue to do so through his membership on the National Defense Commission until Kim Jong-un is properly trained to take over leadership. the Commission currently is headed by Kim Jong-il, and Kim Jong-un reportedly has been appointed to this Commission. It is not clear whether the DPRK military and society will accept this "three generation succession," but North Korean diplomats reportedly have been told to "pay homage to Kim Jong-un," and some schoolchildren have been including his name in their songs.[12]

Little is know about Kim Jong-un except that he apparently attended the International School of Berne (Switzerland) under an alias during which time he learned English and associated with the children of U.S. diplomats. At the boarding school, he learned to play basketball and reportedly was a fan of the NBA and Michael Jordan. He returned to Pyongyang in his late teens.

North Korea at a Glance

Land Area: 120,540 sq km, slightly smaller than Mississippi

Population: 22.7 million (2009 est.) Head of State: Kim Jong-il

Capital: Pyongyang

Life expectancy: 63.8 years

GDP: CIA estimated $40 billion at purchasing power parity in 2008 or $26.2 billion at official exchange rate. Global Insight estimated $54.2 billion and $28.5 billion, respectively

GDP Per Capita: $1,700 (CIA) to $2,248 (Global Insight) at PPP in 2008

GDP Composition: agriculture: 30% industry: 39%, services: 3 1%

Exports: $1.9 billion (2007)

Export Commodities: minerals, metallurgical products, manufactures (including armaments), textiles, and fishery products

Imports: $3.2 billion c.i.f. (2007)

Import Commodities: petroleum, coking coal, machinery and equipment; textiles, grain

Sources: CIA, World Factbook; Global Insight. CRS calculations for trade.

Goals and Means

These developments hold significant implications for U.S. interests and goals in Asia. U.S. goals with respect to the DPRK have included (1) verifiable elimination of North Korea's nuclear weapons program; (2) the halt to DPRK nuclear or ballistic missile proliferation activities (particularly with Syria and Iran); (3) the reduction of tensions on the Korean Peninsula and between the DPRK and Japan, (4) the halt to DPRK-sponsored illicit activities (including counterfeiting of dollars and of products such as American cigarettes), and (5) better human rights and treatment of returned refugees in North Korea.

The Six-Party Agreement (United States, China, Russia, Japan, South Korea, and the DPRK) of February 13, 2007, included an economic incentive of heavy fuel oil and humanitarian food aid, as well as the prospect of the normalization of diplomatic relations between the DPRK and the United States and Japan in exchange for North Korea's freezing and allowing inspections of the activity at its Yongbyon nuclear reactor. By early 2009, the Yongbyon plutonium nuclear installation was about 80% dismantled. On June 26, 2008, President Bush had lifted the application of the Trading with the Enemy Act with respect to the DPRK[13] and in October 2008 had removed North Korea from its list of state sponsors of terrorism.[14] The progress being made under the Six Party Talks also enabled the United States to resume shipments of humanitarian aid to North Korea. A shipload of food and another of heavy fuel oil arrived in North Korea shortly after the announcement by President Bush of the above actions. These activities, as negotiated under the Six-Party Talks, have been halted since December 2008.

For the DPRK economy, the worst of the crisis reached in the mid-1990s seems to have passed, but the economy is still struggling and heavily dependent on foreign assistance to stave off starvation among a sizable proportion of its people. In a December 2008 report, the U.N. World Food Program (WFP) estimated total food production to be 4.21 million tons for the 2008/2009 marketing year (November 2008-October 2009), leaving the DPRK to face a cereal deficit of 836,000 tons, even with commercial imports (around 500,000 tons). This would leave insufficient food to feed almost 9 million people until the harvest in October 2009.[15] The potential starvation of a sizable part of North Korea's population provides some, but limited, leverage for the United States.

The only countries considered to have major influence in North Korea are China and Russia. Both issued strong statements condemning Pyongyang's second nuclear test. China arguably has the most influence, but even though China has not approved of many of North Korea's actions, it fears that instability in the DPRK will create a flood of refugees into its northern provinces. China's fear of a collapse of the regime is an incentive for it to ensure that the DPRK has sufficient energy and food for some minimal level of existence. Beijing is the host for the Six- Party Talks but faces conflicting goals. China needs stability in East Asia to continue its economic development and views the DPRK as a fellow communist state. Strategically, China would like to avoid an arms race in Northeast Asia and is leery of a reunified North and South Korea. The last thing China needs is for the alliance relationship between the United States and South Korea to be extended to the Yalu River bordering China.

Beijing seems to be more comfortable with an economically poor state with nuclear aspirations as a neighbor than a more independent, unified Korean state (possibly with nuclear weapons) that could go the way of the unified Germany and support the Western alliance. The North Korean nuclear problem, however, works against a major Chinese interest. It ensures that the United States will remain committed to its alliance relationships with Japan and South Korea and provides a rationale for a stronger U.S.-led antiballistic missile effort in East Asia. China's strategy also could backfire if a nuclear-armed DPRK compelled Japan[16] or South Korea to develop nuclear weapons of their own. The Economist Intelligence Unit sums up the situation as follows:

> North Korea's behavior is deeply embarrassing to the Chinese government. That China continues to extend vital diplomatic and material support to its unhinged neighbor— including by repatriating those refugees who manage to escape across the border—is hardly consonant with China's ambitions to be seen as a responsible global power. Moreover, North Korea's belligerence is having ripple effects that are profoundly contrary to China's strategic interests. The threat from North Korea could strengthen conservative governments in both Japan and South Korea, as well as reinforce both countries' alliances with the US. Lastly, if the threat from North Korea spurs Japan to abandon aspects of its pacifist constitution—or even to develop nuclear weapons—this would be a steep price to pay for preserving Chinese influence over half of the Korean peninsula.[17]

Pyongyang perceives its nuclear weapon and potential ballistic missile programs as a means to achieve two national goals: to gain stature in the world and to develop a credible deterrent against hostile military action. Without the DPRK nuclear program, North Korea would be a humanitarian aid "basket case" and a reclusive society that would be hard pressed to draw more world notice than countries such as Laos or Mongolia. Instead, North Korea is high on the world's security agenda, Pyongyang has become adept at using this attention to extract economic assistance and has used actions by other countries (such as sanctions or U.S. military exercises in the region) as propaganda tools to fuel nationalism and strengthen its regime. North Korea's leaders seem to be in a policy dilemma. They have pushed to become a nuclear power despite warnings not to do so even from China, their major ally. Yet North Korea's nuclear weapon development has become a rallying point for national pride and what they see as a military deterrent. Yet a January 2008 joint newspaper editorial by the Communist Party, military, and youth militia stated that "at present, no other task is more urgent or more important than solving the people's food problem and eating problem."[18] Pyongyang currently faces the archetypical economic trade-off between "guns and butter," but in their case the question is whether to retain the "guns" (nuclear weapons) or give them up in order to obtain "butter" (food imports). Apparently Pyongyang feels it can accomplish both goals, since it has designated 2012 to both become a nuclear and space power and to join the club of economic tigers of Asia.

As the DPRK goes through preparations for succession and the centennial year of 2012, the confluence of several forces is complicating matters. These include (1) the global financial crisis having reduced the ability of other nations to respond favorably to "extortion" by Pyongyang; (2) the grim economic situation faced by the North Korean people, although food prices are down from 2008 and scarcity does not impose hardship on the elites and Kim Jong-il's inner circle; (3) the deterioration in relations between South and North Korea and the hardening of policies by both sides having put the brakes on economic cooperation and raising the possibility of some limited military action by North Korea against the South (with retaliatory actions by the South); (4) an increase in China's exports to North Korea in 2008[19] despite the shrinkage in trade elsewhere in the world; (5) a tendency among the U.S. media to interpret North Korean actions as being primarily a test of the Obama Administration rather than considering the domestic North Korean factors driving the policies; and (6) the effect of actions in response to the DPRK's nuclear and missile tests on Iran in its nuclear program (Will such actions encourage or discourage Iran?).

U.S. interest in the moribund North Korea economy goes beyond the leverage that economic assistance provides in negotiations over Pyongyang's nuclear weapons. The economy provides the financial and industrial resources for Pyongyang to support its military and nuclear weapons program. It constitutes an important "push factor" for refugees seeking to flee the country. It creates pressure for the country to engage in illicit trade. When the economy is performing poorly, it diverts international food aid that could be used elsewhere and creates instability that raises the risk of desperate action by Pyongyang. Dismal economic conditions may foster forces of discontent in the DPRK that potentially could turn against the ruling regime of Kim Jong-il— especially if knowledge of the luxurious lifestyle of regime leaders and the higher standard of living in South Korea spreads or if the poor economic performance hurts even Pyongyang's elite. Despite over a decade of hardship, however, most dissatisfaction or opposition to the regime seems to be muted.

Conventional Wisdom and Considerations

Conventional wisdom with respect to North Korea includes the following considerations: (1) without stringent monitoring mechanisms, Pyongyang probably will cheat on any agreement; (2) the DPRK will renege on agreements for what seem to be superficial reasons, (3) Pyongyang's first priority seems to be regime survival; (4) North Korea regularly engages in illicit activity and may take actions opposed to normally accepted international law or standards of national behavior; (5) the DPRK likely will sell nuclear technology and missiles to countries not able to obtain them through other channels; (6) economic privation in North Korea mainly affects the population outside of the political and military elite, particularly in the countryside; (7) popular sentiment opposing the current regime, although reportedly on the rise, appears weak or suppressed sufficiently for Kim Jong-il or his successor to remain in power for an indefinite period of time; and (8) Pyongyang feels justified in its actions given what it perceives as "hostility" by the United States and South Korea and "broken promises" to build a light-water nuclear plant for the DPRK and to deliver energy and food aid.

Other factors to be considered include the following: (1) Japan would likely provide a large monetary settlement to Pyongyang in return for its years of occupation should a peace settlement be reached; (2) the border between China and North Korea is porous, particularly in the winter when the rivers are frozen and electricity so scarce that few lights operate at night; (3) centrally planned, communist economies that have been operating for several decades create distortions and consumer dissatisfaction that enable rapid transition to a market economy once those economies are liberalized; (4) economic reform and the opening of trade and investment in North Korea would likely induce large increases in production and economic well-being, but most DPRK production facilities are so lacking in new machinery and equipment that major investments would be needed to raise them to world standards; and (5) the level of distrust between the United States and the DPRK is deep and long-standing.

Strategy and Tools

The three legs of any grand strategy toward the DPRK include economic, diplomatic, and military means to accomplish U.S. goals and protect U.S. national interests. U.S. strategy may take both short- and long-term paths. A short-term strategy includes some tit-tor-tat—an immediate response to provocations by the DPRK—in order to affect the cost-benefit calculations by leaders in Pyongyang. Such responses would either increase the costs or decrease the benefits to the ruling regime stemming from the action in question, and arguably deter Pyongyang from similar actions in the future. Such sanctions have targeted the North Korean elite (as was done in freezing their bank accounts in Macao's Banco Delta Asia and restricting exports to North Korea of luxury goods) or North Korean companies (those involved in weapons sales, including small arms), and they have attempted to deprive the central government of revenues from illicit activities (particularly the sales of nuclear or missile-related items and from counterfeiting currency, drugs, and cigarettes). As of early June 2009, the United Nations was considering its immediate response to North Korea's second nuclear test. In the deliberations, it appears that China and Russia may be willing to support stronger sanctions on the DPRK, since Pyongyang's actions are increasingly being perceived as being inimical to certain Chinese and Russian interests.

A long-term strategy would be aimed at accomplishing a three-fold transformation in the DPRK: (1) a transformation in its relations with Western nations (to include the DPRK's perceived need for nuclear weapons to protect itself from hostile action by the United States), (2) a transformation in the basis of legitimacy of the ruling regime (to reduce the need to garner support through Stalinist tactics and by grandiose goals such as becoming a nuclear and space power), and (3) a transformation in the DPRK economy so that it no longer has to "extort" food and energy assistance in order to reduce starvation among its people.

In formulating U.S. policy,[20] what is not clear is whether current adverse North Korean policies will moderate after the succession crisis has passed. Will a new North Korean leader allow a return to the Six-Party Talks and release more market forces in the DPRK economy, or will the military-first campaign continue with even greater intensity under a new leader who likely will be under heavy influence by the military? Given the weaker power base of a young Kim successor to Kim Jong-il, it is possible that it will be easier for negotiators to deal with the father, Kim Jong-il, than with his son.[21] The 150-day campaign that began in May 2009 seems to be a somewhat desperate policy to increase production in view of the expected economic sanctions following the second nuclear test. The campaign is not likely to have a lasting impact on North Korean output, since the campaign relies primarily on more human effort. More work does not solve problems of antiquated machinery, insufficient supplies of electricity and raw materials, the lack of market incentives and market-based decision making, hunger among workers, and general inefficiencies caused by centralized planning. Still, the DPRK is likely to continue pushing toward its stated goal of becoming a newly industrialized country by 2012.

A problem in relations with the DPRK is that the arsenal of diplomatic weapons and incentives has diminished considerably. The United States and Japan have virtually no trade with North Korea, and Pyongyang is threatening to cut off more of South Korea's economic investments in the North. Humanitarian and economic assistance often do not reach the people most in need and reportedly are diverted to the military and party elites. The United States, however, does have financial clout in the world and no country, financial institution, or exporter would like to have to choose between its ties with the United States and those with the DPRK.

The tools that can be implemented to influence decision making in Pyongyang include positive and negative inducements, neither of which seem to work very well. Positive inducements consist primarily of economic and humanitarian assistance, diplomatic recognition, and increased economic and trade ties. North Korea also has been pressing for direct bilateral negotiations with the United States. Negative inducements toward North Korea include general economic sanctions, sanctions on particular companies, financial sanctions,[22] diplomatic isolation, actions to prevent sales of nuclear and missile technology and materials abroad, and the threat of military action.

The Six-Party Talks

Engagement with North Korea has been conducted under the Six-Party Talks plus bilateral discussions between Pyongyang and other nations. The talks (now suspended) include the United States, DPRK, China, Japan, South Korea, and Russia. This brings all major players to the table, exposes China and Russia to North Korean obstinacy, enables China and Russia to exert pressure on Pyongyang, and includes Japan and South Korea who have direct interests in a peaceful resolution of the problem and are likely to be the major providers of aid to the DPRK. The talks, however, rely heavily on China, and China has conflicting interests in the actual resolution of DPRK nuclear issue. (For discussion of the talks, see CRS Report RL33 590, *North Korea's Nuclear Weapons Development and Diplomacy*, and CRS Report RL33567, *Korea-U.S. Relations: Issues for Congress*, both by Larry Niksch.)

Table 1 summarizes the major negotiating priorities and bargaining chips for each side in the Six- Party Talks. Any policy package would have to address at least some of the priorities of each nation.

The highest priority for the United States, Japan, and Russia reportedly is for North Korea to scrap its nuclear weapons program in a manner that is verifiable. Japan also is concerned about North Korean missiles (which have been fired over Japan) and a full accounting for the abduction of its citizens. In addition, the United States, China, Russia, and Japan seek a stop to weapons proliferation, while Japan also seeks normalization of relations with the DPRK, and South Korea seeks a framework for rapprochement, possible reunification with the North, less military tension along the demilitarized zone (DMZ), and access to cheap labor and markets in the North.

Pyongyang's primary goals appear to include (1) preservation of communist rule under Kim Jong-il and his successor, (2) obtaining a security guarantee that would preclude a possible preemptive attack by the United States or its allies or attempt at regime change, (4) maintaining key elements of its nuclear weapons programs, (3) establishing diplomatic relations with the United States and Japan, (4) reunification with the South on its own terms, and (5) obtaining economic assistance for its ailing economy while maintaining its *juche* philosophy.

Table 1. Major Priorities and Bargaining Chips by Country in the Six-Party Talks with North Korea

Country	Priority	Bargaining Chips
United States	Complete, verifiable, and irrevocable scrapping of nuclear weapons; non-proliferation; human rights; peace treaty	Guarantee security and regime, economic aid, normalized diplomatic and trade relations
North Korea	Guarantee security and regime survival; establish diplomatic relations with the U.S. and Japan; reunification with South Korea on own terms; peace treaty; obtain food aid	Scrap nuclear weapons and missiles, reduce tensions along DMZ, allow economic cooperation
South Korea	Set framework for peaceful resolution and prosperity on the peninsula; reunification; access to North Korean labor and markets, non-nuclear Korean peninsula; human rights; peace treaty	Economic support, energy, business investment and technology
Japan	Scrap nuclear weapons program and missiles; resolve abductions of Japanese citizens	Normalized diplomatic relations, economic support
China	Non-nuclear Korean peninsula, non-proliferation; continued influence on peninsula, weakening U.S. alliance with Japan and with South Korea; peace treaty	Economic support, alliance support
Russia	Scrap N. Korean nuclear weapons; non-proliferation; promote stability in N.E. Asia	Buffer diplomacy, energy assistance, business investment

Source: Adapted from: *The Seoul Economic Daily, 22* August 2003, cited in Hong Soon-Jick, "North Korean Nuclear Crisis: Prospects and Policy Directions," *East Asian Review*, Vol. 15, No. 3, Autumn 2003, p. 31.

North Korea claims that the reasons for its nuclear program are to deter an attack by the United States and to use the bombs if South Korea starts a war or to devastate Japan in order to prevent the United States from participating in such a war.[23] The nuclear program also enables it to gain international prestige, to exercise a degree of hegemony over South Korea, and to extract economic assistance from other countries. Pyongyang is unlikely to abandon this nuclear program without significant changes to the underlying reasons for the program's existence. Its fear of being attacked had been exacerbated by its inclusion in the "axis of evil," the Bush doctrine of preemptive strikes, the U.S.-led invasion of Iraq,[24] and the death of Saddam Hussein. They apparently see nuclear weapons as an insurance policy against attempts at regime change by the West. Also, Pyongyang apparently has observed that once a country becomes a recognized nuclear power, the United States becomes more friendly with it. Pakistan, India, and China are cases in point.

Policy Options

Major U.S. policy options, given the above interests, goals, assumptions, and strategies with respect to the DPRK, include the following.

- Continue current policies with respect to the DPRK. These include (1) targeted economic sanctions and diplomatic isolation both bilaterally and through the United Nations; (2) diplomatic engagement through bilateral and plurilateral meetings under the aegis of the Six-Party Talks and related meetings; (3) keeping North Korea from joining international financial institutions; (4) international efforts to counter trafficking by North Korea in illegal drugs, counterfeit currency, or other contraband; (5) non-proliferation efforts, including the Proliferation Security Initiative; and (6) maintenance of U.S. military forces in South Korea and Japan and continued development of a missile defense system for East Asia.
- Intensify negative pressures on the DPRK: tighten and provide for closer monitoring of U.N. and U.S. sanctions; (e.g., freeze assets of and sanction certain North Korean companies and individuals; ban certain North Koreans from traveling abroad; tighten a ban on imports of luxury goods into the DPRK); impose sanctions on the DPRK for counterfeiting U.S. currency; return the DPRK to the list of sponsors of terrorism (although certain legal conditions would need to be met)[25] induce China to use its extensive influence with and exports to North Korea to punish it for its nuclear test and to bring Pyongyang back to the Six-Party Talks; stop providing protection for North Korean ships from Somali pirates; invoke provisions of U.N. Security Council resolution 1718 passed after the 2006 test that authorizes the United States and other nations to halt and inspect shipping into and out of North Korea for contraband missile parts or nuclear materials. (This sanction has not been enforced, partly because of concerns that it could escalate hostilities with North Korea.)
- Negative pressures also may include weakening the hold by Pyongyang on the daily lives of its citizens and support of Kim Jong-il by fostering alternative centers of power, facilitating the transition to a market economy, and increasing information flows into the country. Negative pressure may include a major campaign of soft power to include admittance of more North Korean refugees into the United States, funding exchanges and visits by North Korean cultural shows and dance groups to the United States, and having the World Food Program provide North Koreans with food that is more identifiable as originating abroad. (South Korea has found a secret weapon that has been a hit with North Koreans: South Korean "Choco Pies," a snack consisting of two large round cookies covered with chocolate with a filling of marshmallow in between (much like an Oreo cookie). They were so popular in the lunches provided to Kaesong Industrial Complex workers in North Korea that they were making their way into black markets in the surrounding area and causing alarm among North Korean authorities.[26])
- Wait and see if Pyongyang is serious about not participating in the Six-Party Talks and trying to join the nuclear, space, and economic tiger club by 2012, but continue to monitor the situation and quietly take prudent countermeasures through the United Nations and with China until the DPRK's succession question is settled. Not give

Pyongyang one thing that it desires—world attention and over-reacting by governments thereby providing propaganda material and support for the ruling regime. Coordinate policy thrusts with South Korea and Japan (who are pressing for stronger sanctions), then with China, Russia, and others. Under specific conditions, offer to hold bilateral talks in the context of the Six-Party Talks and reaffirm the position that the United States is willing to normalize relations; sign a peace treaty; give some energy, food, and technical assistance for complete abandonment of nuclear weapons, and eventually to allow the DPRK to join the International Monetary Fund and Asian Development Bank.

Legislation

The 111th Congress, is considering the following legislation:[27]

- S. 6 (Reid). Restoring America's Power Act of 2009. Sense of Congress that Congress should enact, and the President should sign, legislation to restore and enhance the national security of the United States by (among others) reducing the threat posed by unsecured nuclear materials and other weapons of mass destruction and effectively addressing the security challenges posed by Iran and North Korea.
- S. 837 (Brownback). North Korea Sanctions Act of 2009. A bill to require that North Korea be listed as a state sponsor of terrorism, to ensure that human rights is a prominent issue in negotiations between the United States and North Korea, and for other purposes.
- H.Res. 309 (Peter King). Expressing the sense of the House of Representatives that North Korea should immediately stop any hostile rhetoric and activity towards the Republic of Korea and engage in mutual dialogue.
- H.R. 485 (Ros-Lehtinen). Security through Termination of Proliferation Act of 2009. States that specified U.S. sanctions with respect to Iran, North Korea, or Syria shall remain in effect until the President certifies to the appropriate congressional committees that such country has verifiably dismantled its weapons of mass destruction programs.
- H.R. 1980 (Ros-Lehtinen). North Korea Sanctions and Diplomatic Nonrecognition Act of 2009. To continue restrictions against and prohibit diplomatic recognition of the Government of North Korea, and for other purposes.
- H.R. 2290 (Sherman). International Uranium Extraction and Milling Control Act of 2009. To provide for the application of measures to foreign persons who transfer to Iran, Syria, or North Korea certain goods, services, or technology that could assist Iran, Syria, or North Korea to extract or mill their domestic sources of uranium ore.
- H.R. 2346 (Obey). Supplemental Appropriations Act, 2009.[28] Among its provisions, it rejects a request for $34.5 million in Department of Energy nonproliferation funds to dismantle nuclear facilities in North Korea and rejects $95 million requested for energy assistance to North Korea in the foreign assistance accounts. House bill provides $18 million for development assistance to North Korea in the Economic Support Fund. Passed House and Senate and on May 21, 2009, went to conference.

THE DEVELOPMENT OF U.S. POLICY

The White House, State Department, Defense Department, Treasury, the Special Envoy for North Korea, and others are formulating the Obama Administration's policy toward the DPRK. It is clear, however, that in early 2009 relations with the DPRK have deteriorated, primarily because of North Korea's succession crisis and second nuclear test but also because the push has ended for some success at the end of the Bush Administration. Pyongyang also seems to have escalated its negative actions because it perceived that neither the Obama Administration nor the new South Korean President seemed to be "taking the bait" and reacting to the increasingly confrontational actions by Pyongyang.

As the George W. Bush Administration drew to a close, it showed a new willingness to negotiate directly with the DPRK, although it maintained the umbrella of the Six-Party Talks. The February 13, 2007 Six-Party Agreement included a provision that North Korea freeze its nuclear installations at Yongbyon and invite back the International Atomic Energy Agency to monitor the freeze. North Korea also was to discuss with the other six parties "a list of all its nuclear programs, including plutonium extracted from used fuel rods" from the five megawatt reactor (which North Korea claims to have reprocessed into nuclear weapons-grade plutonium). In exchange, South Korea was to provide financing for 50,000 tons of heavy oil to be shipped to the North. The DPRK and the United States also were to start talks "aimed at resolving bilateral issues and moving toward full diplomatic relations" and the United States was to settle the Banco Delta Asia issue.[29] Under the Agreement, North Korea and Japan also were to "start bilateral talks" toward normalization of relations on the basis of settlement of "outstanding issues of concern" (which Japan interprets as requiring a settlement of the issue of North Korea's kidnapping of Japanese citizens).

The February 2007 Agreement represented a clear change in strategy by the United States and other parties to the talks. For the first time, the Banco Delta Asia action was linked by the United States to the Six-Party Talks and nuclear issues. In essence, the United States agreed to see that the Banco Delta issue was settled before Pyongyang would have to take action to invite International Atomic Energy Agency inspectors back into the country and to shut down its nuclear plant. For the DPRK, this meant that the $25 million in frozen funds from Banco Delta accounts would be released first. This was done. The Agreement also implied that a strategy of regime change appeared to be off the table. The question now is whether the DPRK will live up to its commitments under the Agreement and what leverage the United States, China, and other participants have to ensure Pyongyang's compliance.

As a result of the February 2007 Six-Party Agreement, the United States began to provide fuel and food aid and held out the prospect of eventual normalization of relations with the DPRK in response to specific disclosure and other actions by Pyongyang in regard to its nuclear program. [30] On June 26, 2008, President Bush announced the lifting of the application of the Trading with the Enemy Act (TWEA) with respect to the DPRK and notified Congress of his intent to rescind North Korea's designation as a State Sponsor of Terrorism.[31]

What is evident from the experience of the past seven years is that Pyongyang's stalling and the United States' refusal to negotiate bilaterally (even under the umbrella of the Six-Party Talks) provided time for Pyongyang to continue to develop nuclear bombs.[32] Pyongyang's tactics seem to have been to continue to escalate its nuclear program and then to pause and let the world grow accustomed to this new level before moving to a new level.

Currently, however, it appears that the Pyongyang has given the military the green light to attain recognized nuclear power status by the year 2012 even in the face of economic and diplomatic sanctions and the possibility of triggering military action by other countries.

After North Korea's 2006 nuclear test, it became evident that even China opposed the path Pyongyang was taking. Following the nuclear test, the United States took the issue to the United Nations. The resulting U.N. Security Council Resolution 1718 (October 14, 2006) called on North Korea to abandon its nuclear and missile programs and imposed several sanctions. The resolution imposed an arms embargo on North Korea, banned trade in materials related to ballistic missiles or weapons of mass destruction, and barred exports of luxury goods to the DPRK. It also froze funds and other financial assets owned by people connected with North Korea's unconventional weapons program and banned travel by such people. China and Russia supported this resolution. Japan responded by curtailing imports from and travel to North Korea, banned North Korean ships from entering its ports, and prohibited exports of 24 luxury products to the DPRK. In tightening sanctions following the April 5, 2009, long-range missile test, China also cooperated to a certain extent.

It appears, however, that despite deep privation and negative growth during the mid-1990s, economic sanctions have had little effect on Pyongyang's behavior in ways that would achieve U.S. ends. The ruling elite and military have first priority on scarce food and other supplies. The Kim regime allots economic privileges to its insiders. Peasants may starve, but ranking communist party members live in a separate world of relative luxury.[33] The poor economic conditions also do not appear to have materially undermined the Kim regime. Experts consider internal dissident forces too weak and Kim's control over his military too strong for a domestic *coup* to occur.[34] Pyongyang has taken halting steps toward opening its economy to international investment and has allowed more private markets, but these are similar to policies nearly all centrally planned economies are taking, and China and Russia have been recommending that North Korea adopt them also. As part of the tightening of policy in 2009, Pyongyang is clamping down on many of the private markets, although the "cat has already been let out of the bag." As long as the central government is unable to provide food and necessities through its ration system, non-elites in North Korea have no choice but to engage in private market activity. The alternative is starvation.

Irrespective of whether the U.S. economic sanctions worsened North Korea's economy, the poor state of the North Korea's agriculture and industries has indirectly affected U.S. national interests. It has necessitated humanitarian aid and has generated a deficit in trade that Pyongyang has attempted to fill by dealing in illegal drugs and missiles. Food scarcity also has pushed numerous refugees into China and South Korea.

OVERVIEW OF THE DPRK ECONOMY

The North Korean economy is one of the world's most isolated and bleak.[35] It was completely bypassed by the Asian "economic miracles" of the past three decades that brought modern economic growth and industrialization to South Korea, Taiwan, Singapore, and Hong Kong, as well as rapid growth and trade liberalization to China, Thailand, Malaysia and other Asian nations. The "Stalinist" North Korean economy can be characterized by state ownership of means of production; centralized economic planning, the lack of basic freedoms necessary for a market economy (such as freedom of movement and of commerce), political repression; and an emphasis on military development (military first policy). The economic system is designed to be self-reliant and closed. The irony of the situation is that the longer the economy tries to remain self-sufficient, the poorer its performance and the more dependent the country becomes on the outside world just to survive.

During the 1990s, as many as two million people starved to death. Major portions of the North Korean population survived primarily through transfers of food and other economic assistance from abroad. The worst of the food crisis has passed, but shortages still exist, and the country depends on staples from China, and, when allowed, from the U.N. World Food Program[36] as well as fertilizer from South Korea (when it was being delivered).

During the 1990s, the inefficiencies of North Korea's centrally planned economy, especially its promotion of state-owned heavy industries, along with high military spending—about 15-25% of GDP—joined with drought and floods to push the economy into crisis.[37] In addition, the collapse of the Soviet bloc meant the loss of Russian aid, export markets, and cheap oil. Trade with the former Soviet Union dropped from as much as $3.58 billion in 1999 and has recovered to only $230 million (mostly petroleum) by 2005.[38] This added to disastrous domestic economic conditions in North Korea.[39] Food has been so scarce that North Korean youth are shorter than those in other East Asian nations.[40] Since 1998, the military reportedly has had to lower its minimum height requirement in order to garner sufficient new recruits. Life expectancy has been contracting. With the help of the WFP, which had been feeding more than a quarter of North Korea's 23 million people, chronic malnourishment among children reportedly fell from 62% in 1998 to about 37% in 2004. About one-third of mothers were considered to be both malnourished and anemic.[41] The Food and Agriculture Organization of the United Nations estimated that 7.6 million North Koreans were undernourished in the 2002-2004 period.[42] North Korea refers to this period of hardship as the "arduous march," an apparent comparison to the "long march" in Chinese revolutionary history. In January 2006, Pyongyang ordered the WFP to stop food deliveries to the DPRK, but limited food assistance (about 75,000 tons annually) was resumed after an agreement in May 2006.[43] Over the winter of 2007-2008, the abnormally dry and cold weather reportedly combined with severe flooding during the summer of 2007 seriously affected the crop growth.[44] In a December 2008 report, the WFP estimated total food production to be 4.21 million tons for the 2008/2009 marketing year (November 2008-October 2009), leaving the DPRK to face a cereal deficit of 836,000 tons, even with commercial imports (around 500,000 tons). Food assistance requirements to feed almost 9 million people were estimated at 800,000 tons until the next harvest in October 2009.[45]

An extensive analysis of the famine in the 1 990s concludes that the "ultimate and deepest roots of North Korea's food problems must be found in the very nature of the North Korean economic and political system."[46] Since 2002, Pyongyang has allowed some reforms that may ease the economic pressures over the long term. In a sense, these reforms legitimized what was already occurring following the collapse of the centrally planned economy.[47] The Kim regime refuses to call the economic measures "reforms," but as will be discussed later in this chapter, that in essence is what they are. North Korea prefers to characterize the reforms as "utilitarian socialism." This includes the introduction domestically of market economy elements (called the July 1, 2001 measures) and in the international arena, the pursuit of normalization of relations with countries that have traditionally been hostile toward their country.

The DPRK's gross national product in 2008 in purchasing power parity prices (PPP)—prices adjusted to international levels—has been estimated at $40 billion (CIA estimate) to $54 billion (Global Insight estimate). This amounts to national income of about $1,700 to $2,248 per capita in PPP values or roughly in the range of that of Zimbabwe, Uzbekistan, Bangladesh, or the Sudan. This is considerably lower than that of China ($6,000),[48] Indonesia ($3,900), or Japan ($38,455). It is also dramatically lower than South Korea's $26,000 in PPP values or $18,933 at market prices.[49] According to the Bank of Korea, in market prices, North Korea's GDP in 2007 was an estimated $25.6 billion compared with $888 billion for South Korea. Global Insight, an econometric consulting firm, estimated North Korea's GDP in 2006 at $22.9 billion ($23.9 billion in 2007).[50] A remarkable fact is that in the post-Korean War and into the mid-1970s, living standards were higher in North Korea than in either South Korea or China. Now, North Korea is far behind its rapidly growing neighbors.

As shown in Figure 1, growth in estimated real gross domestic product (GDP) in the DPRK was dropped into the negative for most of the 1 990s before beginning to recover in 1999. In 2004 to 2006, growth has been continuing at about 2%, up slightly from earlier years. In 2006, the economy shrank by 1.3% and continued to decline in 2007 by an estimated 2.9%. In essence, the economy appears to have recovered moderately after the 1 990s but has contracted again over 2006-2007. In 2008, the economy seems to have weathered the global financial crisis with positive growth that is expected by Global Insight (an economic consulting firm) to continue at about 2% per year to 2011.

It should be noted that various scholars and government officials produce a variety of estimates of North Korean growth rates and GDP. Some estimates show gradual recovery, but others argue that real per capita GDP has been stagnant or even declining over the past decade. One problem is that estimates of inflation are difficult to obtain and are inherently unreliable. The reason is that there is no systematic method of collecting data, and even if there were, households in different sectors of the economy often pay different prices for the same commodities—particularly staples that have been distributed through official channels to some but must be purchased in markets by others. Rice, for example, may be sold in an official market for one price, sold in an irregular market for another, or distributed as a ration to certain households basically for free. Another problem is that officials who report data often are under pressure to meet certain targets. Unlike in the West where data may be "sugar coated" to make them more palatable, in the DPRK, the underlying statistics often are "rubberized." They may be stretched or compressed according to official expectations.

Another problem with North Korean data is that there is a huge difference between the official exchange rate and the free market rate. This problem is avoided in PPP estimates that compare purchasing power and adjust for exchange rate differences. In estimates of GDP expressed in dollars, however, the exchange rate is used to convert North Korean won to U.S. dollars. Tourists can exchange dollars to won at about 140 won per dollar, but the black market rate is about 4,300 won per dollar.[51]

What can be said for certain is that a sizable part of the DPRK population lives on the edge of existence. In few countries today does a small decline in GDP or summer flooding cause massive starvation and growth stunting as it does in the DPRK. Also, despite the threat of imprisonment for crossing the border into China and being repatriated to North Korea, a large number of refugees still attempt to flee the economic and political conditions in the country.

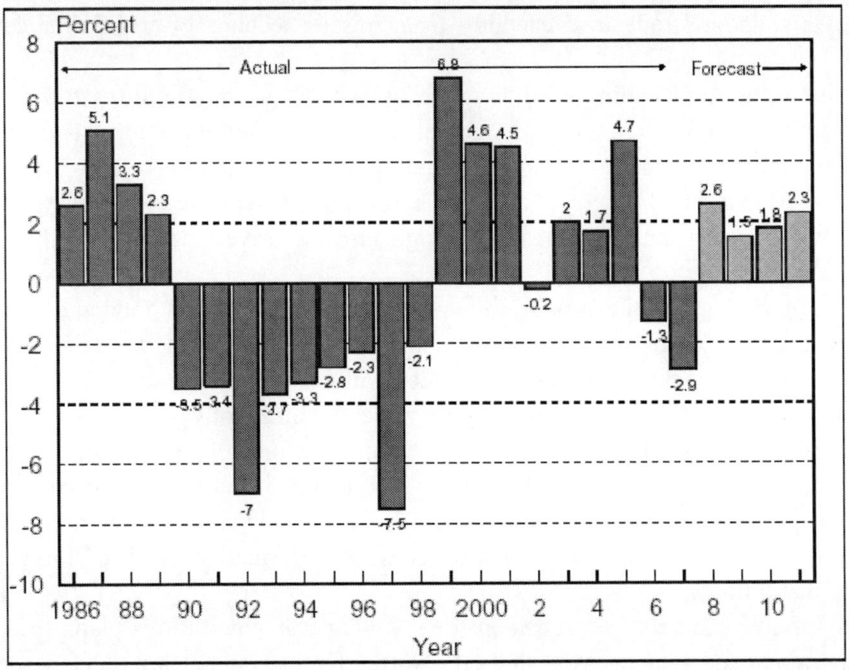

Source: Congressional Research Service with data from Global Insight (based on Bank of Korea data).

Figure 1. Estimated Real Annual Growth in North Korea's GDP, 1986-2011

In this land of scarcity, consumer necessities have been rationed and used to reward party loyalists. Under Pyongyang's economic reforms, this system appears to be phasing out, but beginning in the fall of 2005, North Korea has backtracked on many of its economic reforms by forbidding private sales of grains and reinstituting a centralized food rationing system. Pyongyang also reportedly closed its food markets but then opened consolidated markets that carried food and other items.

The combination of a weak economy unable to provide basic food and necessities and a ruling regime intent on maintaining its power has created economic divisions within society. North Korea reportedly officially classifies its citizens into three ranks and fifty-one categories based on their ideological orientation. However, in actuality, the economy has created five classes of people. The official categories are used to allocate rations for daily necessities, jobs, and housing.[52] The *de facto* categories have resulted from the intrusion of market forces and trading on the official class divisions.

The top class consists of the elite who claim the first rewards from society. They are the party cadres who are leaders in the military and bureaucracy and who enjoy privileges far above the reach of the average household. While starvation haunts the provinces, many of the privileged class live in Pyongyang (where provincial North Koreans cannot enter without special permission); some drive foreign cars, acquire imported home appliances, reside in apartments on a lower floor (so they do not have to climb too many stairs when the electricity is out), and buy imported food, medicines, and toiletries at special hard currency stores.[53] The elite have a strong vested interest in maintaining the current economic system, despite its problems. Their incomes originate from the treasury, from foreign investors (mostly South Korean), remittances from ethnic Koreans in Japan (although these have been curtailed), and the country's shadowy trade in everything from missile technology to fake banknotes and narcotics.[54]

After the elites surrounding Kim Jong-il, the second group comprises business traders with access to foreign capital and international transactions; the third consists of "organized thugs" who make their money through public trading and markets. The fourth class is composed of urbanites and others who scrape by on government rations, while the fifth class is farmers who support their way of life through farming private plots and selling goods in markets.[55]

Despite hushed grumbling about economic deprivation, forced food deliveries to the central government, a rationing system with insufficient stocks to deliver, and new prohibitions on markets that are difficult to understand and rationalize, dissent in North Korea remains stifled. Support for the ruling regime appears sufficiently strong—even among the lower classes of people—although this support is often enforced by severe squashing of even the slightest hint of dissent. Even suspicious comments in casual conversations may be reported to the authorities. The country is far from developing a middle class with independent economic means, personal sources of information, and a thirst for more democratic institutions.

In 2007, South Korea's new President Lee Myung-bak stated in his plan, "Vision 3000: Denuclearization and Openness," that if North Korea denuclearizes and opens, his administration will help to make North Korea's national income $3,000 per person within ten years. The plan, however, does not provide an alternative if North Korea does not denuclearize[56] and has been shelved for now.

Juche Philosophy and the Military

The Pyongyang regime has pursued a policy of self-sufficiency and isolation from the world economy that they call *juche* or self-reliance. *Juche* goes beyond economics as it has been used since the 1950s to perpetuate power by the central government and to build an aura of the supernatural around their supreme leaders Kim—both father and son.[57] Although the regime does not emphasize the connection, the current system of dynastic succession with a paramount father figure also harkens back to Confucianism and the powerful dynastic tradition that united the Korean peninsula for hundreds of years.

The economic practice of *juche* has minimized international trade relations, discouraged foreign direct investment, and fostered what it considers to be core industries—mostly heavy manufacturing. While promoting such heavy industry, for most of the post-Korean War period, Pyongyang has emphasized the parallel development of military strength.

Current head of state, Kim Jong-il (often referred to as "Dear Leader"), has given highest priority to the military. This military-first policy places the army ahead of the working class for the first time in the history of North Korea's so-called revolutionary movement.[58] Under Kim Il-sung (Kim Jong-il's father), the *juche* ideology placed equal emphasis on political independence, self- defense, and economic self-support capabilities. Kim Jong-il, however, insists that North Korea can be a "country strong in ideology and economy" only when its military is strong.[59] The country, therefore, has been developing its industries within the context of a military-industrial complex with strong links between heavy industry and munitions production. Some of North Korea's munitions industries (manufacturing dual use products) are virtually indistinguishable from those supplying civilians.[60]

In 1998 at the 10th Supreme People's Assembly, the military's National Defense Commission arguably eclipsed the Politburo as the supreme national decision making body in North Korea. In the years since, the term "military-first politics" has been used to signify the privileged status the Korean People's Army holds and to stress the ascendant position of the military relative to the power of the Korean Workers' Party, the traditional center of the DPRK's decision making.[61] Of course, the ultimate decision maker in Pyongyang is the Dear Leader, Kim Jong-il, who is Chairman of the National Defense Commission.

North Korea claims to spend about 15% of its GDP on national defense. In 2006, Pyongyang's defense budget was an estimated $2.3 billion to maintain its 1.1 million member military.[62] South Korea estimated the North's military expenditures at $5 billion in 2003. In 2005, North Korea stated that the defense budget was 15.9% of its total annual budget,[63] but others had put the figure at 27.2% in 2003. Even a defense budget of $2.3 billion, however, implies an expenditure of $2,090 per member of the military, a woefully small amount. This implies that the tug of war between "guns and butter" within the North Korean regime must be quite intense given the scarcity of resources throughout the country even though the military does operate businesses that bring in additional revenues.

The heavy weight of the military in Pyongyang's decision making may help explain what to outsiders seem to be inexplicable actions by the North Korean government. For example, almost immediately after negotiators had issued the September 19, 2005, Six-party Statement in which North Korea ostensibly committed itself to abandoning all nuclear weapons and existing nuclear programs, Pyongyang began backtracking and within two months announced a boycott of future Six-Party Talks.[64] It also may help explain North Korea's carrying out its nuclear tests despite being warned not to do so by the United States, China, and other nations. Progress in the six-party talks under which North Korea shut down its Yongbyon nuclear reactor as required in phase I of the February 13, 2007 agreement arguably represented a defeat for the military, but the restart of Yongbyon and nuclear tests in 2009 indicate a strong resurgence by military interests.[65]

When *juche* is combined with central planning, a command economy, and government ownership of the means of production, economic decisions that in a market economy would be made by private business and farmers have to go through a few elite in Pyongyang. These decisionmakers may or may not understand advances in agronomy or manufacturing and tend to be motivated by non-economic factors, such as maintaining political power or avoiding blame for initiatives gone awry. Farming methods based partly on crop rotation or new varieties of rice, for example, may be viewed as too risky.[66] Foreign investment also is hindered partly because the regime abhors being "exploited" by capitalists who seek to make profits on their business ventures in North Korea and partly because of their deep-seated mistrust of Westerners, Japanese, and South Koreans.

Industrial Sectors

North Korea's industrial sectors are shifting rapidly. At the end of World War II, the DPRK represented the industrialized part of the Korean peninsula. Under Japanese colonialism, heavy industry, water power, and manufacturing were concentrated in the North, while agriculture flourished in the less mountainous South. Even in 1990, 49% of the North Korean economy was in mining, manufacturing, and construction, while 23% was in services (including government and utilities) and 27% in agriculture. In recent years, however, the DPRK's non-military industries have almost collapsed. By 1997, mining, manufacturing, and construction had dropped from 49% to 32% of the economy but in 2003 had risen somewhat to 36%. In 2003, services had risen to 37% of the economy, while agriculture has remained fairly constant at 27%. In 2007, mining, manufacturing, and construction were making a slow recovery to 40% of the economy. Services had gained slightly to 39%, and agriculture had declined to 21% of GDP. (See Figure 2.) Some of the most advanced industries in North Korea are associated with its military, and in 2008, about $250 million in goods were produced in the Kaesong Industrial Complex by South Korean firms using North Korean labor.[67]

The drop in the share of manufacturing in GDP has come about largely because of the rapid decline in production from factories, not because of large absolute increases in services or agricultural production. One report indicated that in 2003 factories were running at about 30% of their capacity. The economy lacks food for workers, raw materials, energy, and foreign currency to buy new equipment and imported inputs into the manufacturing process.[68] Much industrial capital stock is nearly beyond repair as a result of years of underinvestment and shortages of spare parts. Recently, the government has emphasized earning hard currency, developing information technology, addressing power shortages, and attracting foreign aid, but it appears unwilling to do so in any way that jeopardizes its control.

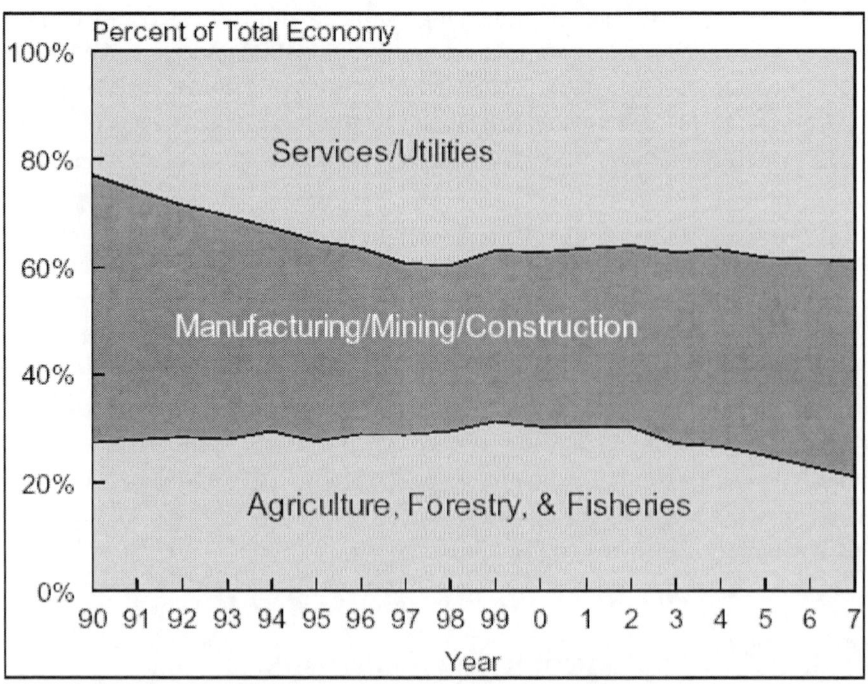

Source: Congressional Research Service with Data from Bank of Korea.

Figure 2. North Korea's Industrial Sectors

North Korea's mining sector is recovering somewhat. In 2008, 28% of China's imports from North Korea were in mineral fuels ($208 million, mostly coal), and 28% were ores ($213 million, mostly iron, zinc, precious metal, lead, and molybdenum).[69] North Korea is rich in minerals and ores.[70] The regime looks askance, however, at exporting ores or commodities that were typical of "economic imperialism" during the colonial era when the foreign companies "exploited" the resources of less developed economies.

The DPRK leadership, in their joint editorial at the beginning of 2008, however, emphasized the need for rebuilding the national economy, particularly mining and the metal, chemical, and light industries. They noted the construction of a large-scale hydroelectric power plant completed in 2007 and set out the goal of constructing an economically powerful state by 2012.[71]

As has been previously noted, the agricultural sector also is in dire straits. The economy depends heavily on collective farms that have been devastated by drought or floods, lack of fertilizers and other inputs, antiquated farming methods, and a lack of incentives for private production. In recent years, there has been a new emphasis on fishing—using both traditional methods and new aquaculture technology. The lack of fertilizer deliveries from South Korea in 2008 had a large effect on agricultural production.

The increase in the service sector is typical of industrializing countries, but in North Korea's case, much of it is because of the relative decline of the manufacturing sector. For a country undergoing economic stress, service sector freelancing often is employment of last resort for urban dwellers.

Economic Reforms and Free Trade Zones

As with other isolationist economies in the contemporary world of globalization and interlinked societies, North Korea has been plagued with the negative effects of its attempts at self sufficiency: technological obsolescence, uncompetitive exports, economic privation, and lack of foreign exchange. Much of the reforms, however, have been from the "bottom up" by necessity as the central government faltered on its ability to deliver food and basic necessities through its distribution system. These difficulties, together with advice from China and Russia, have compelled the Pyongyang regime to allow some economic reforms.[72] To the extent possible, they are allowing reforms in the Chinese sequence with economic reforms preceding political reforms while eschewing the Russian model of political reform preceding and concurrent with economic reforms.[73] The DPRK also has been examining the Vietnamese model of development and *do moi* (reform). Kim Jong-il reportedly prefers the Vietnamese style of gradual economic reform rather than the abrupt Chinese style.[74]

The reforms began in July 2002 when Pyongyang announced a series of measures that some had hoped would mark the beginning of the end of the Stalinist controls over the economy and the onset of more use of the market mechanism to make economic decisions, particularly production and consumer purchases. Although the government has dubbed the reforms an "economic adjustment policy,"[75] in the manufacturing sector, in particular, the actions appear to be a desperate attempt to revive the moribund economy. The reforms also dovetail with North Korea's "military first" policy. As Kim Jong-il has given first priority to the military, the rest of the population has suffered.[76] This, in turn, has raised pressures on Pyongyang to increase the productivity of its economic system.

The adjustments (reforms) featured an end to the rationing system for daily commodities (except for food), a huge increase in prices of essentials and in wages, a major devaluation of the currency (official exchange rate), abolishment of the foreign exchange coupon system, increased autonomy of enterprises, authorization of the establishment of markets and other trading centers, and a limited opening of the economy to foreign investment. Prices still remain under centralized control but at levels closer to those existing in peasant (free) markets. North Korea has not abandoned the socialist planned economy, but it has been compelled to "adjust" certain aspects of it.

Under the initial reforms, overall prices increased by 10 to 20 times. Government prices for many essential items, however, rose by much more. The price for rice rose by 550 times, for corn 471 times, for diesel oil 38 times, and for electricity 60 times. Wages also were raised but not enough to keep pace with skyrocketing consumer prices. Wages rose by 18 times for laborers and 20 times for managers.[77] Even though not all workers received the promised wage increases, the price and wage reforms caused households to face rampant consumer inflation, and many people ended up worse off financially than before the reforms.

In North Korean factories, reforms include greater control over prices, procurement, wages, and some incentives to increase profits in order to distribute them based on individual performance. The regime also is looking to implement reforms in agriculture similar to those implemented in China (along the lines of the rural household contract system). In the mid-1990s, North Korea's agricultural work squads had already been reduced in size. Now they are moving toward family oriented operations with farmers allowed to retain more of any production exceeding official targets.

Although small farmers' markets have long existed in North Korea, Pyongyang did not legalize such farmers' markets until June 2003. This followed the formal recognition of commercial transactions between individuals and the 1998 revision to the constitution that allowed individuals to keep profits earned through legitimate economic activities.[78] Now free markets and shopping centers that use currency, not ration coupons, are spreading. The Pyongyang Central Market, for example, became so crowded that a new, three-story supermarket had to be built. Pyongyang's Tongil market with its lines of covered stalls stocked with items such as fruit, watches, foreign liquor, clothes, Chinese-made television sets, and beer from Singapore also is bustling with sellers and consumers reminiscent of those in other Asian countries.[79] Visitors to Pyongyang in late 2006 indicated that the market was thriving with all types of products and shoppers driving European cars.[80]

The North Korean population is gradually becoming re-accustomed to operating in open markets. This has raised fears by the DPRK regime of encroachment by capitalism into their socialist economic system. On August 26, 2007, Kim Jong-il announced that "markets have become anti- socialist, Western-style markets." This has led to a steady stream of government edicts restricting market activity across the country. At first, authorities prohibited women under the age of 40 from selling goods in Pyongyang markets. Then on December 1 the authorities banned women under the age of 49 from running businesses in Pyongyang. (Since males are officially required to be at their assigned workplaces, women generally run the businesses.) Certain products, such as videos of South Korean dramas, movies, and other so-called non-socialist elements are also banned from central markets.[81]

Enforcement of the new regulations at first was spotty, but in late 2007, it appears to have become more strict. According to news reports, policing is also being conducted by central government security agencies, organizations that normally deal with issues such as intelligence gathering and sedition.[82] The extent of the Kim regime's attempts to control the development of a market economy can be illustrated by the increased difficulty of acquiring travel permits for persons suspected of being wholesale merchants intending to carry goods from one place to another. This crackdown on travel also is affecting normal tourist and family trips. Corruption, however, allows some businesses to continue, as certain officials reportedly are receptive to bribes. Secret peddling on streets and other banned activity also continues out of sight of the authorities (particularly by young and nimble traders).[83]

Foreign Investment

North Korean economic reforms also include opening certain areas to foreign investment. Under the Joint-Operation Act of 1984 to 1994, there were 148 cases of foreign investment worth about $200 million into North Korea. Of these 148 cases, 131 were from pro-North Korean residents of Japan. In 1991, Pyongyang opened the Rajin-Sonbong free trade zone and established the Foreigner Investment Act. To 1997, some 80 investments totaled $1.4 million. Other areas receiving foreign investment include Nampo, Pyongyang, Kosung-gun, Shimpo, Wonsan, and Mt. Kumkang. Foreign companies in North Korea include 50 South Korean companies (e.g., Hyundai, daewoo, Taechang, LG, Haeju, and G-Hanshin), DHL, ING Bearing Bank; Japan's Hohwa, Saga, and New Future Ltd. companies; Taiwan's JIAGE Ltd., and the China Shimyang National Machinery Facility Sales Agency Corporation.[84] The U.N. Development Programme is promoting the Tumen River Valley Development Project which aims to develop business based on transit transportation, tourism, and commissioned processing trade.[85] Mt. Kumkang has been developed with the cooperation of South Korea's Hyundai corporation into a tourist destination for South Koreans and a venue for reunions of families separated by the DMZ. As relations with South Korea soured and a tourist there was shot operations at Mt. Kumkang have ceased.

According to data compiled by the United Nations Conference on Trade and Development (UNCTAD) since 1987, the DPRK had a cumulative $1.56 billion in foreign direct investment (FDI) as of the end of 2006. Annual FDI flows have been sporadic, even negative in some years, but since 2003, they have been rising. (See Figure 3.) In 2007, both South Korea and China increased their investments in North Korea.

The industrial sector is receiving some help from Chinese investments and from South Korean firms operating in the Kaesong Industrial Complex. It also is able to attract a limited amount of foreign investment from other nations. For example, in January 2008, Orascom Telecom, the fourth-largest Arab phone operator based in Cairo, Egypt,[86] announced that its subsidiary in North Korea (CHEO Technology—25% owned by the state-owned Korea Post and Telecommunications) had received a license to be the first provider of mobile telephone services throughout the country. The company is to invest up to $400 million in network infrastructure over the first thee years and to provide service to Pyongyang and other major cities within one year.[87]

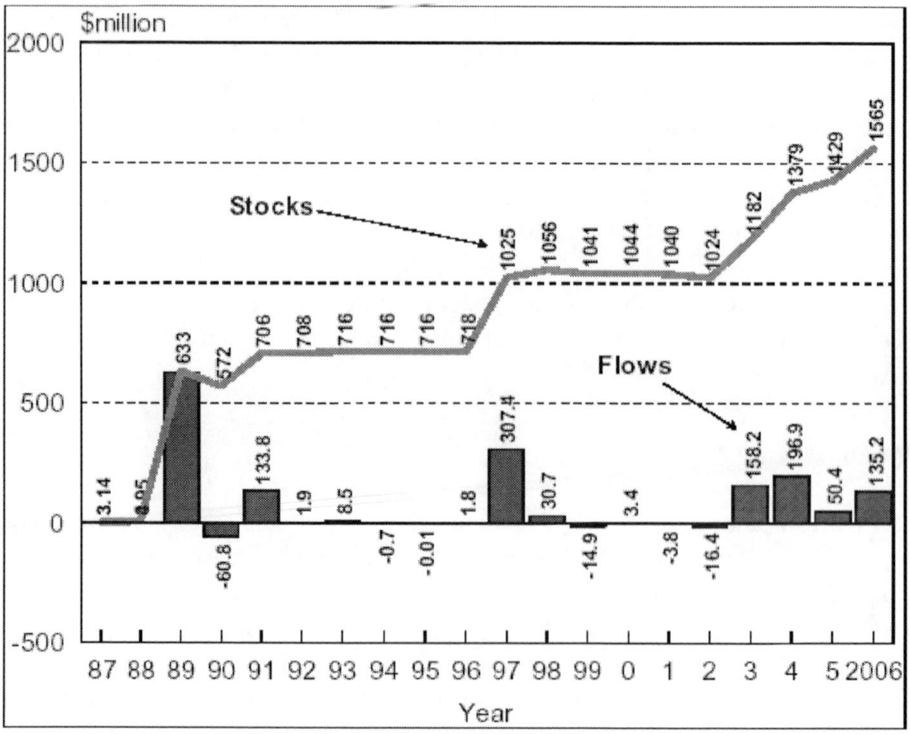

Source: United Nation Conference on Trade and Development, FDI database.

Figure 3. Foreign Direct Investment Flows and Stocks in the DPRK, 1987-2006

Since 2000, the DPRK has attempted to emulate China's highly successful free trade zones (FTZ) by establishing the Sinuiju Special Administrative Region (SAR) on the northwestern border with China and Kaesong (Gaesong) Industrial Complex along the border with South Korea. Since being established in 2002, the development of the Sinuiju SAR has been stymied partly because of the arrest by Beijing of Chinese businessman Yang Bin, a Chinese-Dutch entrepreneur who was named as its governor, on charges of illegal land use, bribery and fraud. After Kim Jong-il's visit to China in 2006, Sinuiju appears to be receiving new attention. Foreign currency management groups reportedly are moving in, and ordinary citizens are being replaced by residents of Pyongyang and other areas.[88]

Kaesong Industrial Complex[89]

The most significant effort at creating free-trade zones is the Kaesong Industrial Complex (KIC), although North Korea in 2009 has threatened to shut it down. Some South Korean companies already are moving out of the complex.[90] Until 2009, this joint effort between the North and South was developing rapidly, despite tensions over North Korea's testing of ballistic missiles and a nuclear weapon. The KIC is managed by South Korea's Hyundai Asan and Korea Land Corporation. Located just over the border 43 miles north of Seoul on the route to Pyongyang, this 810-acre complex aims to attract South Korean companies, particularly small and medium sized enterprises, seeking lower labor and other costs for their manufactured products and who may not be able to establish subsidiaries in China or other countries. As of December 2008, 93 companies had begun operations in Kaesong. They were employing 38,931 North Korean personnel and 1,055 South Korean personnel.[91] To be completed in three stages, the first stage (2002-2007) had 3.3 million square meters of a total of 66 million square meters being constructed or under construction in 2006. Hyundai Asan and the Korea Land Corporation plan to eventually attract 300 businesses in the first stage, 700 in the second, and 1,000 businesses in the third stage with an estimated total of 300,000 workers. Of the $374 million initial cost for the first stage, $223 million was to be provided by the South Korean government. In December 2006, the Korea Electric Power Corporation connected North and South Korea by a 100,000 kilowatt power- transmission line for use by the companies in the KIC.

The initial 15 companies operating in Kaesong and their products included Living Art (kitchenware), Shinwon (apparel), SJ Tech (semiconductor component containers), Samduk Trading (footwear), Hosan Ace (fan coils), Magic Micro (lamp assemblies for LCD monitors), Daewha Fuel Pump (automobile parts), Taesung Industrial (cosmetics containers), Bucheon Industrial (wire harness), Munchang Co. (apparel), Romanson (watches, jewelry), JY Solutec (automobile components and molds), TS Precision Machinery (semiconductor mold components), JCCOM (communication components), and Yongin Electronics (transformers, coils).[92]

In 2006, the KIC produced some $7.5 million worth of goods each month.[93] In September 2007, monthly production had reached $17.1 million. In 2008 yearly production reached about $250 million or about $20.8 million per month. The major products include textiles, chemical products, metals and machinery, and electric and electronic products.[94]

Kaesong developed partly from South Korea's sunshine policy of economic engagement with the North. The KIC serves both geopolitical and economic purposes. Geopolitically, it provides a channel for rapprochement between North and South Korea, a bridge for communication, a method of defusing tensions, and a way to expose North Koreans to outside ideas and ways of doing business. Economically, the KIC provides small- and medium-sized South Korean firms with a low-cost supply of labor for manufacturing products, provides jobs for North Korean workers, and provides needed hard currency for Pyongyang. Although KIC operations continued even after the North Korean nuclear test in 2006, its status in 2009 is in doubt.

A controversial issue has arisen with respect to the KIC and the proposed South Korea-U.S. Free- trade Agreement (FTA). South Korea had requested that products exported from the complex be considered to have originated in South Korea in order to qualify for duty free status under the proposed FTA. Such a provision had been included in other South Korean FTAs.

The language of the proposed Korea-United States FTA (signed but not yet approved by Congress) does not provide for duty-free entry into the United States for products made in Kaesong. Annex 22-B to the proposed FTA, however, provides for a Committee on Outward Processing Zones (OPZ) to be formed and in the future to designate zones, such as the KIC, to receive preferential treatment under the FTA. Such a designation apparently would require legislative approval by both countries.

Other issues raised by the KIC have been the conditions for North Korean workers, whether they are being exploited,[95] as well as the hard currency funds the industrial complex provides for the ruling regime in Pyongyang. South Korean officials, as well as other analysts, point out that average wages and working conditions at Kaesong are far better than those in the rest of North Korea. The monthly minimum wage is $50 ($57.50 including the cost of social insurance). General workers receive $50, team leaders receive $52-$55, and heads of companies receive $75 per month. After the government, takes its share of the wages, the workers receive about $37 per month. Workers also receive overtime pay. [96]

The North Korean government derives hard currency from several sources in the KIC project, including leasing fees and its taxes and fees deducted from the wages of North Korean workers. The wages are first paid in hard currency to a North Korean government agency that takes a certain percentage before paying the North Korean workers in won. The government collects about $20 per month (in social insurance taxes plus its cut of wages) for each of the 10,000 workers now at Kaesong. Its monthly take from wages, therefore, would amount to approximately $200,000 per month or $2,440,000 over a year. One estimate is that Pyongyang has earned a total of about $20 million from the Kaesong Industrial Complex.[97]

Investment from China

China has a direct interest in economic reform and recovery in the DPRK. Chinese business interests with support from Beijing are beginning to invest widely in the North Korean economy. Unlike, South Korean investors, Chinese are allowed to invest in enterprises fully integrated into the DPRK economy. They also have provided machinery and equipment to existing North Korean factories.

Chinese investment in mineral extraction in the DPRK seems to represent an easing the DPRK constitutional ban against "cultural infiltration (Article 41). This has been interpreted to include international economic integration and globalization.[98] However, Pyongyang seems to be treating investment from China as being "not contaminated" relative to those from South Korea or other nations. South Korean investments are carefully walled off from the average North Korean citizen, whereas China has been able to invest in production facilities in various locations.

According to Chinese sources, from January to October 2006, the Chinese side approved 19 new investments in the DPRK, with negotiated investment of $66.67 million. Cumulative investment up to the end of October 2006 included Chinese government approval of 49 investments in the DPRK with negotiated investment of $135 million.[99] These figures seem understated. Since 2006, Chinese investments have increased significantly. The projects of the investment covered such fields as food products, medicine, light industry, electronics, chemical industry and minerals.

Major Chinese investments involving mining and minerals in the DPRK include the following:[100]

- China Tonghua Iron and Steel Group has invested 7 billion yuan (approximately $875 million) in developing the DPRK's Musan Iron Mine. Two billion yuan (approximately $250 million) is to be used for the preliminary construction of communication facilities and cables from Tonghua, China, to the DPRK's Musan area; 5 billion yuan (approximately $625 million) is to be used mainly on technology and equipment in developing the mine as well as in Musan's overall planning.) This mine is the largest open-cut iron mine in Asia with verified iron- rich ore reserves reaching seven billion tons.

- On October 20, 2007, China's Tangshan Iron and Steel Company (China's third largest steel company) and the DPRK's Department of Foreign Economic Cooperation and Taep'ung International Investment Group signed a letter of cooperation intent. The two sides are to cooperate on the DPRK Kimch'aek Metallurgy Park Project, and the DPRK So'ngjin Iron, Steel, Coal, and Electricity Project. Tangshan is to build a steel smelting plant in the DPRK with an annual steel output of 1.5 million tons. It is to be jointly funded by the DPRK side and is to involve joint development and utilization of nearby iron ore.
- The China Iron and Steel Group reportedly is ready to develop a molybdenum mine in the DPRK with a goal of producing more than 10,000 tons of molybdenum concentrate per year.
- China and the DPRK have signed a "PRC-DPRK Inter-Governmental Agreement on Joint Development of Offshore Oil" to pursue joint energy projects.
- China's Jilin Province also has cooperated with the Hyesan Youth Copper Mine (containing the largest copper deposit in Asia), Manp'o Zinc and Lead Mine, and the Hoeryo'ng Gold Mine in the DPRK. One project is to transmit electricity from Jilin's Changbai County to the DPRK in exchange for the gold, copper, and other ores. The joint project is to install power transmission facilities with an estimated total investment of 220 million yuan ($27.5 million).
- China's Heshi Industry and Trade Company along with the International Mining Company have set up a joint venture with the DPRK's So'gyo'ng 4 Trade Company called the "DPRK-China International Mining Company." The Chinese side is to provide equipment and capital, while the DPRK side is to contribute mineral resources and the existing facilities.
- In October 2005 China Minmetals also signed with the DPRK side an "Agreement on Establishing A Joint Venture in Coal Industry in the DPRK," which called for establishing a joint venture with the DPRK at the Ryongdu'ng Coal Mine.
- On August 23, 2004, China's Zhaoyuan Shandong Guoda Gold Stockholding Company and the DPRK Committee for the Promotion of External Economic Cooperation agreed to establish a joint venture mining company to mine the gold in the DPRK's Mt. Sangnong and to ship all the mined gold concentrate to Zhaoyuan for smelting. The DPRK's Sangnong Gold Mine is estimated to have at least 150 tons of mineable gold. However, due to a shortage of capital and backward technology, it has been in a state of semi-stoppage of production. Guoda is to provide equipment and technology and is to ship the mineral ores by sea to Zhaoyuan for smelting.

International Trade

Despite North Korea's isolation and emphasis on *juche*, it does trade with other countries. According to trade statistics compiled by the International Monetary Fund, the DPRK had at least some trade with 80 of the 182 countries or customs territories that report their trade data to the Fund. [101] For Pyongyang, the foreign economic sector plays an important role in that it allows the country to import food, technology, and other merchandise that it is unable to produce in sufficient quantities at home. Since North Korea does not export enough to pay for its imports, it generates a deficit in reported merchandise trade that must be financed by other means. Pyongyang has to find sources of foreign exchange—other than from its overtly traded exports— to pay for the imports. Experts point out that the DPRK has used its military threat to "extort" aid and other transfers from the United States, Japan, South Korea, and the humanitarian agencies. This, along with various illicit activities, has helped Pyongyang to finance a surfeit of imports.

Detailed data on the country's external economic relations suffer from reliability problems similar to those associated with the domestic economy. The foreign economic data on actual commercial transactions, however, tend to be more accurate since they also are reported by trading partner countries and are compiled by the International Monetary Fund and United Nations. Individual countries, for example, report on their imports from and exports to North Korea. These mirror statistics, however, differ from North Korea's actual annual numbers because of differences in data gathering methods, coverage, timing, and reporting. Countries also may misreport trade with the Republic of Korea as trade with the Democratic People's Republic of Korea. Detailed and reliable data on trade in military equipment and illegal drugs also are notoriously difficult to obtain and to verify. [102]

South Korea also compiles statistics on trade with North Korea that differ from its data reported to the United Nations. South Korea considers trade with the North as inter-Korean trade, not foreign trade. The trade figures that South Korea reports to the IMF for its commercial transactions with the North are considerably lower than the figures that it reports as inter-Korean trade [usually available from the Korea Trade-Investment Promotion Agency (KOTRA)]. The inter-Korean trade data reported by South Korea also include more detail on non-transactional trade (mostly foreign aid) with North Korea. IMF data also differ somewhat from those reported by data vending companies (such as Global Trade Atlas and Global Insight). This chapter uses a combination of trade totals (mirror statistics) from the IMF, partner country data from the Global Trade Atlas, intra-Korean trade from South Korea's KOTRA, and references some estimates of total trade from Global Insight.

The DPRK's policy of *juche*, its suspicion of foreign countries, and the collapse of its industrial production, has resulted in a minimal level of commercial relations with other nations in the world. This trade has been rising in recent years, although much of this increase can be attributed to investments by South Korea and China in DPRK mining and manufacturing. As shown in Table 2, in 2007 North Korea exported an estimated $1,854 million in merchandise (down from $2,048 million in 2006) while importing $3,242 million (up from $2,962 million in 2006) for a merchandise trade deficit of $1,388 million. Judging by trade with China and South Korea, total trade in 2008 appears to have risen. Imports from China, in particular, rose 46% from $1,393 million in 2007 to $2,033 million in 2008. In recent years, North Korea's exports to and imports from China and South Korea have risen. South Korea and China account for 73% of North Korean exports and 75% of North Korean imports. Economic sanctions imposed by Japan have reduced that bilateral trade to almost nothing.

Table 2. Estimated North Korean Trade by Selected Trading Partner, Selected Years, 2000-2008 ($ in millions)

				North Korean Exports					
	2000	**2001**	**2002**	**2003**	**2004**	**2005**	**2006**	**2007**	**2008**
World	1,307	1,148	1,278	1,251	1,524	1,683	2,048	1,854	n.a.
China	37	167	271	395	586	499	468	584	754
Japan	257	226	235	174	164	132	78	0	0
S. Korea	152	176	272	289	258	340	520	765	930
Russia	8	17	11	3	5	7	20	34	14
India[a]	20	3	5	1	4	8	9a	41a	n.a.
Thailand	19	24	45	57	91	133	148	34	29
Germany	25	23	29	24	22	45	17	16	21
				North Korean Imports					
	2000	**2001**	**2002**	**2003**	**2004**	**2005**	**2006**	**2007**	
World	1,859	3,083	1,970	2,049	2,615	3,093	2,962	3,242	n.a.
China	451	573	468	628	799	1,081	1,232	1,393	2,033
Japan	207	1,066	133	92	89	62	44	9	8
S. Korea	273	227	370	435	439	715	830	1,032	890
Russia	38	62	69	111	205	206	190	126	97
India	173	162	182	157	121	55	105	660	n.a.
Thailand	189	106	172	204	239	207	216	184	48
Germany	53	80	139	71	68	63	63	34	31
Balance of Trade	**-552**	**-1,935**	**-692**	**-799**	**-1,090**	**-1,410**	**-914**	**-1,388**	**n.a.**

Table 1 Source: S. Korean data from S. Korea, Unification Ministry. World trade data from U.N. COMTRADE Database, accessed via U.S. Department of Commerce, Trade Policy Information System, August 2008. Country data from Global Trade Atlas and U.N. COMTRADE Database. World trade totals mirror data derived from U.N. reporter country trade with North Korea plus inter-Korean trade reported by South Korea and adjusted Indian data for 2006 and 2007.

Note: n.a. = not available

a. Data for Indian imports from North Korea seem in error. (Items such as electrical machinery and parts, in particular, likely actually were imported from South Korea.) After comparing reported Indian data with that for China, 2006 imports by India from North Korea of $475 million were reduced to $9 million, and 2007 imports of $173 million were reduced to $41 million.

North Korea's major trading partners have been China, South Korea, Japan, Russia, Germany, Thailand and India (as well as Brazil, Singapore, and Hong Kong). As shown in Figure 4 and Table 2, North Korea's major import sources have been China, South Korea, Russia, Japan, and Thailand. Germany and India also are major suppliers. Major imports by North Korea include machinery, minerals, plant products, and chemical products.[103] In particular, imports of energy materials and foods reflect Pyongyang's attempts to remedy these fundamental shortages.

Despite current tensions over Pyongyang's nuclear program, imports appear to be growing and are estimated to have exceeded their peak in 2001 when a large shipment of food aid from Japan (mainly rice valued at high Japanese prices) artificially increased the import total. Fuel imports from China, food imports from various countries, and supplies of material and components for assembly in the Kaesong Industrial Complex account for most of the increases. Imports from the United States and Japan have been virtually nonexistent. It is apparent that China and South Korea have become the largest sources of imports for the DPRK.

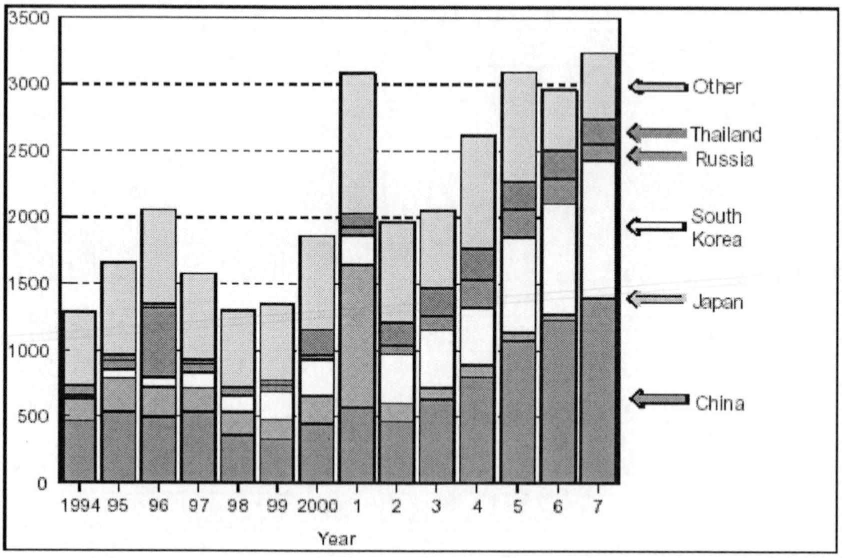

Source: Data from U.N. COMTRADE Database, Global Trade Atlas, and (South) Korea Unification Ministry.

Figure 4. North Korean Imports of Merchandise by Major Country of Source, 1994-2007

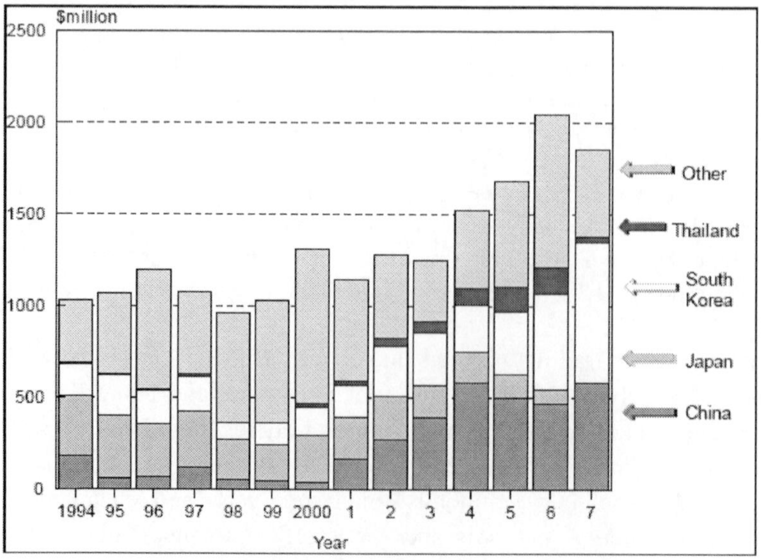

Source: Data from U.N. COMTRADE Database, Global Trade Atlas, and (South) Korea Unification Ministry.

Figure 5. North Korean Exports of Merchandise by Major Country of Destination, 1994-2007

Major export markets for the DPRK have been China, Thailand, and South Korea (primarily because of production from South Korean factories in the Kaesong Industrial Complex). (See Figure 5 and Table 2.) In Europe, Germany has been North Korea's major trading partner, and in Latin America, Brazil is developing as a market for North Korea's exports. Since 2003, exports to Japan have declined—due to trade sanctions and friction over the DPRK's admitted kidnappings of Japanese citizens. North Korea's major exports include ores, coal, animal products, textiles, machinery, electronic products, and base metals.

A recent remarkable development has been North Korea's increase in exports of primary products (such as fish, shellfish and agro-forest products) as well as mineral products (such as base metallic minerals). Pyongyang reportedly has imported aquaculture technology to increase production of cultivated fish and agricultural equipment to increase output of grains and livestock. It also has imported equipment for its coal and mineral mines. Much of the coal and mineral exports have resulted from partnering with Chinese firms through which the Chinese side provides modern equipment in exchange for a supply of the product being mined or manufactured. The production from the Kaesong Industrial Complex also has become significant. North Korean imports from South Korea and China both exceeded $1 billion in 2006, and North Korean exports to South Korea reached $765 million and to China $582 million.

Meanwhile, traditional exports of textiles and electrical appliances have been declining. This reflects North Korea's unstable power supply, lack of raw materials and components imported from abroad, and the need to ship finished goods to China or another third country for final inspection. This diminishing ability of North Korea to provide a reliable manufacturing platform for the least complicated assembly operations without help from foreign investors does not bode well for the country's future ability to generate the exports necessary to balance its trade accounts.

In considering additional economic sanctions on North Korea, one possible action would be to ban DPRK exports of small arms and ammunition. Data on such trade are available to a certain extent, but such exports are likely to be under-reported in official statistics. Some such transactions, however, are revealed in the import data of various countries.

Table 3 shows imports of small arms and ammunition by trading partner countries from North Korea from 2001 to 2007. The total reported transactions has been about $5.2 million over the seven years. The importers have included countries from Latin America, Europe, Southeast Asia, and the Middle East.

OTHER SOURCES OF FOREIGN EXCHANGE

North Korea's annual merchandise trade deficit of about $1 billion implies that Pyongyang must either be receiving imports without immediate payment required (aid and capital flows) or be generating foreign exchange through some means—either legal or illegal. Legal means include borrowing, foreign investments, foreign aid, remittances from overseas North Korean workers, selling military equipment not reflected in trade data, and by selling services abroad. Illegal methods include the counterfeiting of hard currency, illegal sales of military equipment or technology, sales of illegal drugs, or by shipping illegal cargo between third countries. The country also can dip into its foreign exchange reserves.[104]

Table 3. Imports by Country of Small Arms and Ammunition from North Korea (In Dollars)

Importer	2001	2002	2003	2004	2005	2006	2007	Total
9302—Revolvers & Pistols, Designed to Fire Live Ammo								
Guatemala	30,268	73,901	0	0	0	0	0	104,169
9303—Sport Shotguns & Rifles Etc, Very Pistols, Etc.								
Indonesia	17,600	0	0	0	0	0	0	17,600
Luxembourg	0	0	1,562	0	0	0	0	1,562
9304—Arms Nesoi, Other Than Side Arms and Similar Arms								
Bolivia	0	0	0	910	0	0	0	910
Denmark	5,557	0	0	0	0	0	0	5,557
Ethiopia	0	0	0	0	364,414	0	0	364,414
Germany	6,000	0	0	0	0	0	0	6,000
Madagascar	447	0	0	0	0	0	0	447
Mexico	0	0	2,397	0	121,383	0	0	123,780
9305—Parts & Accessories of Arms of Headings 9301 to 9304								
Guatemala	3,027	7,392	0	0	0	0	0	10,419
9306—Bombs, Grenades, etc.; Cartridges, etc. and Parts								
Australia	0	0	0	0	0	3,910	0	3,910
Brazil	0	0	0	0	0	0	45,500	45,500
Czech Republic	0	0	0	0	0	0	0	1,380
Germany	2,000	0	0	0	0	0	0	2,000
Indonesia	675,882	0	0	0	0	0	0	675,882
Wallis and Futuna	0	2,231	0	0	0	0	0	2,231
9307—Swords, Cutlasses, Bayonets, & Similar Arms & Parts								
Ghana	0	0	0	0	23,127	0	0	23,127
United Arab Emirates	0	0	0	0	802,975	3,059,141	0	3,862,116
Total	740,781	83,524	3,959	910	1,311,899	3,063,051	45,500	5,251,004

Source: Congressional Research with Data from United Nations COMTRADE Database.

Note: The categories are by four-digit Harmonized System codes and description. A "Very pistol" is a flare gun

Legal Sources of Funds

North Korea is able to borrow on international capital markets. As of the fourth quarter of 2007, the country had loans from foreign located banks that report to the Bank of International Settlements (BIS) of $50 million (down from $116 million at the end of 2006 and $121 million at the end of 2005, $81 million in 2004, and $190 million in 2003). The amount of loans for 2007 is a relatively small amount, only about $2 per capita. Total liabilities to BIS banks (including those located in North Korea) came to $1,532 million for the fourth quarter of 2007 (up considerably from $489 million in first quarter 2007). Most of these liabilities appear to be export credits. North Korea also had deposits of $388 million in BIS banks at the end of 2007.[105]

International bond issues are not a major source of funds for North Korea. In May 2003, the country issued ten-year bonds—the first since 1950—but since its sovereign securities are not rated by major Western credit rating agencies, the issue has generated little interest on international financial markets and is aimed at domestic investors. Pyongyang claims that a million people had signed up to receive the bonds, but many speculate that the deductions from the salaries of North Korean purchasers in amounts equivalent to four months' wages to buy the bonds is not voluntary.[106] North Korea does not pay interest on the bonds. Rather the government holds a lottery in which the winners receive monetary prizes greater than the foregone interest on the bonds.[107]

Although North Korea is not a major recipient of foreign direct investment (FDI), in 2007, the stock of foreign direct investment in the DPRK was $1,378 million. The inflow that year was $53 million, up from the outflow of $105 million in 2006, and the inflow of $50 million in 2005, but less than the $197 million in 2004, and $158 million in 2003.[108] The FDI comes mainly from South Korea and China. North Korea's free trade zones, particularly the Kaesong Industrial Complex, however, are attracting more foreign direct investment, although the future of Kaesong is now in question.

A major source of funding for imports into the DPRK has been foreign aid or direct government transfers. Both developmental and humanitarian aid and past assistance under KEDO (Korean Peninsula Energy Development Organization, created under the 1994 Agreed Framework, but construction was terminated in 2003) to build two light water nuclear reactors and provide heavy fuel oil have enabled imports into North Korea without financing from Pyongyang.

North Korea also receives funds in the form of official development assistance (ODA) from aid donor nations, multilateral development banks, and other organizations; other official flows; and private flows. The Organisation for Economic Co-operation and Development (OECD) compiles these data from its member nations plus 12 others and from multilateral agencies. The OECD data, however, do not include reporting from South Korea (Seoul considers transactions with the North as intra-country, not as foreign), China, or Russia (not members of the OECD). As shown in Table 4, in 2004, net total receipts for North Korea came to $1,529.6 million from donors, primarily because of a $1.15 1.1 million receipt from France, $142.3 million from the United Kingdom, and $56.5 million from the United States. In 2005, however, the net total dropped to $148.7 million as the dispute over North Korea's nuclear program escalated, fell further to $59.6 million in 2006 as North Korea made significant repayments of previously received funds, and rose to $178.1 million in 2007. Of this amount, $102 million came from the Netherlands.

As shown in Table 5, much of the total receipts by North Korea came in the form of official development assistance. In recent years, the country has received between $55 and $265 million in net official development assistance (ODA) from the countries and agencies that report such data to the OECD (does not include Russia, China, and South Korea). In 2004, total net ODA was $160.8 million, in 2005 was $86.8 million, in 2006 was $54.5 million, and in 2007 was $97.6 million. The major donors have been the multilateral agencies, European Community, the United States, Sweden, Norway, and Australia. In 2008, the United States provided the DPRK with $$93.7 million in food aid and $106.0 million in fuel oil for a total of $199.7 million.[109]

The United States also has paid North Korea to search for remains of American servicemen missing from the Korean War. In 2003, it paid $2.1 million to conduct four searches.[110]

Table 4. North Korea: Total Net Receipts by Major Source/Donor (Excluding Russia, South Korea, and China), 2001-2007 ($ millions)

	2001	2002	2003	2004	2005	2006	2007
U.S.	0.3	131.2	42.9	56.5	6.9	0.4	32.5
Germany	34.1	35.0	11.8	54.2	6.5	3.2	1.2
France	12.8	-656.4	447.7	1,151.1	6.2	-16.9	0.3
Netherlands	0.1	0.6	0.8	0.5	0.65	101.8	102.0
Australia	4.8	5.4	2.1	3.9	5.3	4.5	6.6
Norway	7.9	5.5	9.5	5.6	5.3	3.8	4.4
Sweden	3.4	4.3	4.9	46.2	59.4	-74.8	8.6
Switzerland	6.1	2.1	4.0	3.9	4.2	7.0	5.9
UK	1.1	-15.9	44.8	142.3	0.2	..	1.2
Canada	1.5	0.2	2.1	-1.4	1.6	-1.6	14.8
Multilateral	65.0	40.1	51.7	47.5	41.5	23.3	27.0
—of which EC	40.3	61.2	30.9	31.4	19.4	12.1	16.6
WFP	0.6	0.1	3.2	7.5	8.4	1.8	1.0
UNTA	2.6	2.5	1.8	2.5	3.03	2.01	3.4
UNICEF	2.6	2.5	1.8	2.5	3.03	2.01	3.4
Arab Agencies	14.5	2.2	7.9	1.3	-0.4	-1.7	-0.2
Total	218.6	-440.2	593.4	1,529.6	148.7	59.6	178.1

Source: Organisation for Economic Cooperation and Development. *Source OECD, International Development Statistics,* online database. http://stats.oecd.org.

Note: Data are from OECD members, multilateral agencies, and 12 other reporting nations excluding South Korea, China, and Russia. UNTA = U.N. Transitional Authority. WFP = U.N. World Food Program. EC = European Community. Total Receipts include Official Development Assistance + Other Official Flows + Private Flows.

Table 5. North Korea: Net Official Development Assistance by Major Source/Donor (Excluding Russia, South Korea, and China), 2001-2007 ($ in millions)

	2001	2002	2003	2004	2005	2006	2007
U.S.	0.3	131.2	42.9	56.0	7.9	0.4	32.5
Germany	27.0	33.2	7.2	7.5	5.2	2.9	1.4
France	0.3	0.5	-0.4	-0.5	-0.4	0.6	0.3
Australia	4.6	2.0	2.1	3.3	4.6	2.7	6.6
Norway	2.5	3.6	4.4	5.6	5.3	3.8	4.7
Sweden	3.4	4.3	4.9	5.4	5.5	5.1	7.8
Switzerland	4.5	3.4	4.0	3.9	4.2	6.0	5.9
European Community	40.3	61.2	30.9	31.4	19.4	12.1	16.6
Multilateral Agencies (not EC)	1.8	3.1	4.0	1.1	2.7	1.7	10.4
Non-DAC	0.4	1.87	1.4	11.1	5.9	2.3	-0.5
Total	117.6	265.2	131.0	160.8	86.8	54.5	97.6

Source: Organisation for Economic Cooperation and Development, Development Statistics database.

Note: Non-DAC=Non-OECD Development Assistance Committee, such as Thailand and Poland.

As indicated in Table 6, since 1991, the South Korean government has provided a total of $3,337.0 million in assistance to the DPRK. Of this, $2,221.99 million was humanitarian assistance (food aid, fertilizer, or assistance provided through non-governmental organizations). Total assistance reached a high of $635.43 million in 2007 but dropped to $159.36 million in 2008 as deliveries of food and fertilizer were halted. South Korean civilian organizations also have provided assistance to North Korea ($71 million in 2003).[111]

As shown in Table 7, in addition to humanitarian assistance, South Korea has provided $1,115.01 million in economic and other assistance to the DPRK since 1991. This has taken the form of road and rail construction, business subsidies, development of the Kaesong Industrial Complex, tours of Kumgang Mountain, family reunions, and other. The road and rail assistance was mainly for connecting the Kaesong Industrial Complex located across the demilitarized zone in North Korea to South Korea. Also related to Kaesong was much of the aid to ROK businesses as well as direct expenditures to develop the industrial complex. Not included in South Korean assistance to the DPRK are the wages of North Korean workers in Kaesong or other internal business transactions.

Table 6. South Korean Total and Humanitarian Assistance to the DPRK ($ millions)

Year	Total Assistance	Total Humanitarian	Food Aid	Fertilizer	Assistance through NGOs
1991	3.02		-	-	-
1992	0.71		-	-	-
1995	236.60		236.60	-	-
1996	9.82		3.76	-	3.07
1997	0.00		-	-	20.05
1998	0.03		-	-	14.26
1999	28.88		-	28.53	-
2000	178.00	163.10	76.69	83.42	2.99
2001	170.72	90.29	14.68	49.47	26.14
2002	254.57	175.37	84.63	66.60	24.14
2003	343.25	256.93	159.21	70.13	27.59
2004	326.75	196.31	98.25	84.46	13.60
2005	596.35	357.26	193.79	123.44	40.03
2006	393.49	226.65	10.65	125.66	90.34
2007	635.43	395.71	157.34	103.49	134.88
2008	159.36	54.11	3.91	0.00	50.20
Total	3,337.00	2,221.99	1,039.51	735.19	447.29

Source: Republic of Korea (South Korea) government and Korean EX-IM Bank, via South Korea Ministry of Unification.

Note: NGO=Non-governmental Organization. Total Assistance = Humanitarian + Economic + Other Assistance

Table 7. South Korean Economic and Other Assistance to the DPRK ($millions)

Year	Road and Rail	Mt. Kumgang Tours	Aid to ROK Business	Kaesong Industrial Complex	Family Reunions	Other
1991						
1992	-	-	-	-	0.71	-
1995	-	-	-	-	-	-
1996	-	-	-	-	-	6.06
1997	-	-	-	-	-	-
1998	-	-	-	-	0.01	0.02
1999	-	-	-	-	0.35	-
2000	12.89	-	0.44	-	2.75	1.81
2001	69.6	34.86	0.83	-	1.20	0.08
2002	53.5	26.71	2.20	-	20.56	0.37
2003	94.09	5.03	10.66	-	3.47	0.66
2004	96.55	6.20	27.78	6.00	3.68	3.83
2005	193.17	0.01	28.62	25.65	16.67	15.00
2006	93.06	1.28	50.16	80.75	15.91	16.02
2007	68.33	0.50	60.95	82.89	30.8	131.13
2008	14.38	1.52	9.79	52.22	19.00	58.54
Total	695.57	76.11	191.45	247.5	115.12	236.55

Source: Republic of Korea (South Korea) government and Korean EX-IM Bank, via South Korea Ministry of Unification.

Another major source of income for certain North Korean families has been in remittances from overseas Koreans, particularly those who live in Japan.[112] Most of the North Koreans in Japan either remained there after World War II or are descendants of those people. Some had been forcibly brought there to work in coal mines or factories during the 50-year Japanese occupation of Korea. Currently, of the approximately 650,000 ethnic Koreans who live in Japan, an estimated 56,000 to 90,000 are from the North Korean area, and many are reported to be actively involved in supporting the Pyongyang regime. Ethnic Koreans in Japan work in a variety of businesses and occupations, but they face discrimination in Japanese society and are known for operating pachinko (pinball) parlors and other enterprises providing entertainment and night life as well as being involved with Japan's *yakuza* or gangsters. Many of these, as well as managers of North Korean-related credit unions, regularly have sent remittances to relatives or associates in North Korea. One unusual method of smuggling money to North Korea has been to hide 10,000 yen bills (worth roughly $90 each) under expensive melons being shipped to Kim Jong-il as gifts.[113]

Given the decade of stagnation (1992-2002) of the Japanese economy and rising tensions between Japan and North Korea, these remittances have reportedly been declining. A 2003 Japanese newspaper report placed the amount at between $200 million and $600 million per year, but that figure could be exaggerated.[114] In testimony before parliament, Japan's Finance Minister stated that in Japan's FY2002, $34 million had been sent from Japan to North Korea through financial channels that required reports to the Japanese government.[115] Recent Japanese sanctions include a lowering of the amount on remittances to North Korea that require reporting from 30 million to 10 million yen (. from reported to April, following North

Korea's rocket launch, Japan imposed fresh sanctions including reducing the amount of remittance to North Korea subject to reporting to the Japanese government from more than 30 million yen ($300,000) to more than 10 million yen ($100,000). Anecdotal evidence indicates that considerable amounts of currency from Japan are simply carried by individuals on ships or sent through China and not reported. Japan, however, has tightened inspections of North Korean ships and curtailed operations of ferry boats traveling between the two countries.[116] Remittances by North Koreans living in South Korea and China also are reportedly growing. These could amount to around $6 million per year from 6,000 (of 10,000) refugees in South Korea and some more from the 100,000 refugees living in China.[117]

In summary, the DPRK's net total receipts plus remittances, aid and investments from South Korea, and special food and fuel assistance in connection with negotiations over Pyongyang's nuclear program, constitute most of the overt resource inflows that North Korea has received each year over and above its export earnings. These have amounted to perhaps $700 million on net per year. North Korea must finance the remainder of its trade deficit—about $300 million—by other means. It appears that these other means have included exports of military equipment and illicit activity.

Illegal or Questionable Sources of Funds[118]

Data on North Korean sales of military equipment abroad is understandably murky, but the country is thought to have sold hundreds of ballistic missiles to Iran, Iraq, Syria, Pakistan, and other nations in the past decade to earn foreign currency.[119] The interdiction by Spain of an unmarked vessel in December 2002 containing parts for 12 to 15 Scud missiles (valued at about $4 million each) bound for Yemen from North Korea is one example of such arms sales.[120] In testimony in 2003 before the House Committee on International Relations, the Undersecretary of State for Arms Control and International Security pointed out that North Korea possesses Scud and No-Dong missiles and is developing the Taepo-Dong 2. He stated that the country is by far the most aggressive proliferator of missiles and related technologies to countries of concern. These sales are one of the North's major sources of hard currency.[121] According to a U.S. military officer quoted in the Japanese press, North Korea exported $580 million worth of ballistic missiles to the Middle East in 2001.[122] Between 1998 and 2001, North Korea is estimated to have exported some $1 billion in conventional arms to developing nations. [123] In a 2009 article, the *Wall Street Journal* quotes analysts as saying that North Korean sales of short- and medium-range missile systems remain among North Korea's largest export earners, part of an arms trade that generates $1.5 billion annually.[124] This is likely to be an overstatement, since it exceeds the total deficit in North Korea's annual deficit in trade of about $1 billion.

With respect to illegal drug trade, officials from the U.S. military command in Seoul reportedly said that North Korea is earning between $500 million and $1 billion annually from the narcotics trade.[125] North Korea is thought to produce more than 40 tons of opium per year which would make it the world's third-largest opium exporter and sixth-largest heroin exporter. The regime also is accused of trafficking in methamphetamine stimulants. U.S. counter-narcotics officials are reported to have said that since 1976, there have been at least 50 arrests or drug seizures involving North Koreans in more than 20 countries. Japanese authorities say that nearly 50% of illegal drug imports into Japan come from North Korea.[126] According to the U.S. State Department, although such reports have not been conclusively verified by independent sources, defector statements have been consistent over years and occur in the context of regular narcotics seizures linked to North Korea. The State Department's *International Narcotics Control Strategy Report* for 2007 stated its view is "that it is likely, but not certain, that the North Korean government has sponsored criminal activities in the past, including narcotics production and trafficking, but notes that there is no evidence for several years that it continues to traffic in narcotics." During 2006, the Japanese media reported that drug trafficking occurred along the DPRK-PRC border with Japanese criminal figures traveling to the border area to purchase methamphetamine for smuggling back to Japan.

According to the State Department, in March 2006, a new decree warned citizens, state factories and groups in the DPRK to "... not sell, buy, or use drugs illegally" and that "organizations, factories and groups should not illegally produce or export drugs." Punishment is severe, up to death, and the family members and shop mates of offenders face collective responsibility and punishment with the perpetrator.[127]

In a blatant incident in May 2003, the Australian navy and special forces commandeered a North Korean ship (Pong Su) off the country's southern coast that allegedly was moving 110 pounds of almost pure heroin valued at $50 million. The ship apparently picked up the heroin elsewhere in Asia and took a circuitous route to Australia.[128]

Allegations also have been made that North Korea engages in counterfeiting operations, particularly of U.S. $100 notes. It is believed that the country has earned $15 million to $20 million per year in counterfeiting,[129] but it is not clear that North Korea currently engages in counterfeit currency production, although such notes still reportedly circulate. In June 2009, the United States reportedly was considering new sanctions on North Korea for U.S. currency counterfeiting operations run by the North Korean government.[130] Also, North Korean General O Kuk-ryol, who recently was promoted to the country's National Defense Commission and who reportedly is in charge of arranging the succession of Kim Jong-il's third son, Kim Jong-un, was identified by U.S. and foreign intelligence sources as a key figure in the covert production and distribution of high-quality counterfeit $100 bills.[131]

In the opinion of a North Korean expert at Seoul's Sejong Institute, "North Korea's economy had received a death sentence long ago, but it keeps afloat thanks to international aid and the country's trading in weapons and illicit goods."[132]

Since late 2005, the United States has taken several measures to reduce illicit financial activities by North Korea. On June 28, 2006, President Bush issued Executive Order 13382 (Blocking Property of Weapons of Mass Destruction Proliferators and Their Supporters).[133] On October 21, 2005, pursuant to Executive Order 13382, the U.S. Treasury designated eight North Korean entities as proliferators of weapons of mass destruction and their delivery vehicles. The action prohibited all transactions between the designated entities and any U.S. person and froze any assets the entities may have had under U.S. jurisdiction.[134]

On September 15, 2005, the U.S. Treasury designated Banco Delta Asia SARL as a "primary money laundering concern" under Section 311 of the Patriot Act because it represented an unacceptable risk of money laundering and other financial crimes. Treasury stated that "Banco Delta Asia has been a willing pawn for the North Korean government to engage in corrupt financial activities through Macau.... "[135] On March 14, 2007, the Treasury finalized its rule against Banco Delta Asia, barring the bank from accessing the U.S. financial system, but allowing the $25 million in North Korean funds held to be released.

U.S.-DPRK Trade Relations

U.S. trade with the DPRK is quite limited. The United States does not maintain any diplomatic, consular, or trade relations with North Korea, and the country does not have normal trade relations (most favored nation) status. This means that North Korean exports are subject to the relatively high tariffs existing before World War II in the United States. For example, women's blouses of wool or cotton carry a 90% import duty if from North Korea but are duty free if from free-trade agreement countries, such as Canada, Israel, or Mexico, or are subject to 9 to 10% duty if from most other nations. As a communist nation, North Korea also does not qualify for duty- free treatment of certain products that are imported from designated developing countries under the generalized system of preferences program.[136]

The United States, moreover, maintains various economic sanctions on North Korea because the country is considered a threat to national security, is a communist state, and it proliferates weapons of mass destruction.[137] In June 2008, however, the Bush Administration announced that it was lifting restrictions under the Trading with the Enemy Act and was starting the process to remove the DPRK from the list of State Sponsors of Terrorism. Other sanctions, including U.N. sanctions imposed following North Korea's nuclear test, still remain in place. The United States resumed shipments of food and heavy fuel oil to North Korea as humanitarian aid but subsequently halted them. Travel to and trade with North Korea in other than dual-use goods are allowed if overarching requirements are met, and there are no restrictions on the amount of money Americans may spend in the DPRK. The sanctions related to the proliferation of weapons of mass destruction generally target the offending entities. North Korean assets in the United States frozen prior to June 19, 2000, remain frozen. North Korea is on the most restricted list of countries for U.S. exports (Country Group E list) of items such as computers, software, national security-controlled items, items on the Commerce Control List,[138] and service or repair of such items. Economic sanctions on North Korea, however, are essentially unilateral by the United States. Most other nations (except Japan) allow relatively free trade in non-sensitive goods with the DPRK.

In October 2007, President Bush reportedly approved the lifting of some sanctions imposed on the DPRK under an act governing human trafficking. This easing allowed the United States to provide assistance in educational and cultural exchanges to the extent that the aid doesn't damage its national interest.[139] In February 2008, the New York Philharmonic Orchestra performed in Pyongyang.[140]

The United States uses trade with North Korea as leverage and to send a message of disapproval for various activities by Pyongyang. As the Six-Party nuclear talks have progressed, however, the United States has expressed its willingness begin discussions to normalize relations with the DPRK, has removed it from the terrorism list,[141] and has indicated its willingness to negotiate a peace treaty to formally end the Korean Conflict. The way also could be opened for North Korea's admission to membership in international financial institutions (such as the World Bank, International Monetary Fund, and Asian

Development Bank). This would allow the DPRK to receive development assistance that would help finance additional imports from countries such as the United States.

Table 8 shows U.S. merchandise exports, imports, and trade balances with North Korea since 1990. Imports have been zero or relatively low with a peak of $1,495,000 in 2004. Almost all of these imports from North Korea were organic chemicals and woven apparel. A possible concern is that imports of books, newspapers, and manuscripts have dropped to zero. For a country with great strategic importance to the United States, information on North Korea is not flowing directly into the U.S. market. U.S. exports at $23,750,000 in 2004 rose from $32,000 in 1990 to $25,012,000 in 2002 and to $52 million in 2008. However, much of this has been food and energy assistance provided as part of North Korea's process of denuclearization. The small annual surplus in U.S. trade with North Korea arises primarily from food and energy assistance that has been provided to the DPRK.

According to the U.S. Department of Commerce, the United States has no direct investment in North Korea.[142] An American company interested in doing business in North Korea, particularly establishing a company, likely would work through an overseas subsidiary. Some American business executives with the U.S. Chamber of Commerce in South Korea, for example, reportedly travel to North Korea for business purposes,[143] and some U.S. enterprises reportedly are working as subcontractors in the development of North Korea's Kaesong industrial complex.[144]

Table 8. U.S. Merchandise Exports, Imports, and Trade Balances with North Korea, 1990-2007 ($ in thousands)

Year	U.S. Exports	U.S. Imports	Balance
1990	32	0	32
1991	484	10	474
1992	83	0	83
1993	1,979	0	1,979
1994	180	0	180
1995	11,607	0	11,607
1996	541	0	541
1997	2,409	0	2,409
1998	4,454	0	4,454
1999	11,265	29	11,236
2000	2,737	154	2,583
2001	650	26	624
2002	25,012	15	24,997
2003	7,977	0	7,977
2004	23,750	1,495	22,255
2005	5,757	3	5,754
2006	3	0	3
2007	1,728	0	1,728
2008	52	0	52

Source: U.S. Department of Commerce through World Trade Atlas.

North-South Korean Economic Relations

Economic relations have been a major route for opening relations between North and South Korea. Seoul has a major stake in relations with the DPRK and the outcome of the current Six- Party Talks.[145] It seeks a "soft landing" for the current standoff over the North's nuclear program—one that will lead to a lessening of tensions and steady integration of North Korea's economy into the global economic and financial system. As with other countries divided by ideology and a history of hostilities as "pawns" on the chess board of the Cold War, the two halves of the peninsula face numerous issues to be resolved before they can normalize relations— let alone contemplate reunification.

South Korea has much to gain from rapprochement with the North. Its strategy has been to use its economic leverage and family reunions (families separated by the division of the Korean Peninsula) to open channels with the North Korean people while maintaining a credible military deterrent to overt hostile action by Pyongyang. South Korea recognizes that essentially it has won the Cold War on the Korean peninsula, but it recoils at the prospect of funding economic rehabilitation in the DPRK as West Germany did with East Germany. Seoul also recognizes that its economic ties are gradually shifting from reliance on the American market to greater integration with China, Japan, and other countries of Asia. Its labor costs are rising, and many of its companies are remaining competitive only by manufacturing in China and other low-wage markets. For them, the prospect of abundant cheap labor just a short distance to the north is appealing and perhaps an alternative to cheap labor in China.

In 2008, total merchandise trade between North and South Korea was $1,820 million, up from $1,797.9 million in 2007, $1,349.7 million in 2006, and more than triple the $403.0 million just seven years earlier. South Korean exports, which had reached $1,032.6 million in 2007, fell to $890 million in 2008. South Korean imports from North Korea rose to $930 million, up from $765.3 million in 2007. Much of the increase in exports has been in the form of food and industrial goods. In 2006, $419.3 million in South Korean exports to the North were actually South Korean aid shipments.

The major items purchased by South Korea from the North include food/aquatic/forestry products, textiles, steel/metal products, and electronics. The major South Korean exports to North Korea include chemicals, textiles, machinery, steel/metal products, and food/forestry products.

As indicated in Table 6 and Table 7 above, South Korea also provides the DPRK with humanitarian and economic assistance. Since 1991, this has amounted to a total of $3,337.00 million with $2,221.99 million in humanitarian assistance and $1,115.01 million in economic and other assistance. Since 2008, this assistance has largely come to a stop.

Since 1992, particularly under the Sunshine Policy of former South Korean President Kim Dae Jung and under the Policy for Peace and Prosperity of former President Roh Moo-hyun, Seoul has permitted its corporations to pursue business interests in North Korea. In 2003, the government allowed activities by 89 companies including 35 involved in contract processing (assembly, sewing, or other processing done under contract) by North Koreans.[146] The companies included Daewoo (jackets, bags), Samsung Electronics (communications center, switchboard), Samcholi Bicycle, Green Cross (medicine), International Corn Foundation (corn seeds), Hyundai (Mt. Kumkang tourism, development), and Hanshin Co.

(glass). The Korea Electronic Power Corporation's work on the construction of a light water nuclear power plant under the U.S.-North Korean 1994 Agreed Framework has been halted.[147] One global strategy of South Korean businesses is to develop processing sites in North Korea to take advantage of low labor costs there; in some cases, labor costs are competitive with those in China. The two countries also have taken some halting steps toward linking their economic systems. In addition to the business relationships, since September 2002, the two countries have been reconnecting the Gyeongui (Seoul-Sinuiju) and Donghae (East Sea) railway lines and adjacent highways.

As discussed in the section above on Economic Reforms and Free Trade Zones, the focus of North-South economic cooperation now is the Kaesong Industrial Complex (KIC). Managed by South Korea's Hyundai Asan and Korea Land Corporation and located just over the border in North Korea, this 810 acre complex already has attracted small and medium sized enterprises from South Korea. The KIC accounts for much of the increased commercial trade between the North and the South. In 2008, the KIC produced some $20 million worth of goods each month. [148]

It provides small- and medium-sized South Korean firms with a low-cost supply of labor for manufacturing products, provides jobs for North Korean workers, and provides needed hard currency for Pyongyang.

North Korea depends more on South Korea in international trade than South Korea does on the North. North Korea accounts for less than 1% of total South Korean exports, while North Korean exports to South Korea account for more than a third of total North Korean exports. South Korea has access to global markets for many of its world class industries (automobiles, semiconductors, consumer electronics, etc.), while North Korea faces restricted markets for its limited array of exports.

In his inaugural speech on February 25, 2008, President Lee Myung-bak indicated that South Korea attitude toward inter-Korean relations should be pragmatic, not ideological. He reiterated his plan to provide assistance in order to raise the per capita income of North Korea to $3,000 within ten years if Pyongyang denuclearizes.[149]

CHINA-DPRK ECONOMIC RELATIONS

China remains the DPRK's chief ally. In addition to sharing its status as one of the last communist regimes in the world, China views the Korean peninsula as vital to its strategic interests. Beijing values North Korea as a buffer between the democratic South Korea and the U.S. forces stationed there, as a rationale to divert U.S. and Japanese resources in the Asia Pacific toward dealing with Pyongyang and less focused on the growing military might of China, and as a destination for Chinese foreign investment and trade. Beijing arguably has more influence in Pyongyang than any other nation.

Cooperation between the two countries is extensive but often strained. In 1961, China and the DPRK signed a mutual defense pact, but recently a Chinese official reportedly said that they are not "well informed of the internal situation of the North Korean military" and that the DPRK "does not listen to what China has to say."[150] (This presumably referred to Pyongyang's missile and nuclear tests.) Also with respect to North Korean refugees, their first destination is usually northeastern China. According to Human Rights Watch, China labels

North Korean bordercrossers as illegal economic migrants, rather than refugees or asylum seekers, and usually sends them back to North Korea.[151]

China also is hosting and facilitating the ongoing Six-Party Talks that seek a resolution to the North Korean nuclear problem.

In August 2001, Chinese President Jiang Zemin visited Pyongyang and promised increased humanitarian and economic assistance. In April 2004, Kim Jong-il visited Beijing to discuss food aid and nuclear issues.

According to Jane's Information Group, several issues have arisen to cause friction in the SinoNorth Korean relationship. These include

- Chinese exasperation at the DPRK's failure to reform its economy;
- Pyongyang's prevarication over the nuclear and peace treaty issues and the consequent dangerous stimulus this provides to proliferation in the region;
- The nuclear standoff with the United States and Pyongyang's possession of nuclear weapons;
- Growing economic and political rapport between Pyongyang and Taipei;
- The North Korean refugee problem on the China-DPRK border;

Table 9. South Korean Merchandise Trade with North Korea, 1990-2007 ($ in thousands)

Year	South Korean Imports	South Korean Exports	Total Trade	Balance
1990	12,278	1,188	13,466	-11,090
1991	105,719	5,547	111,266	-100,172
1992	162,863	10,563	173,426	-152,3
1993	178,167	8,425	186,592	-169,742
1994	176,298	18,249	194,547	-158,049
1995	222,855	64,436	287,291	-158,419
1996	182,400	69,639	252,039	-112,761
1997	193,069	115,270	308,339	-77,799
1998	92,264	129,679	221,943	37,415
1999	121,604	211,832	333,436	90,228
2000	152,373	272,775	425,148	120,402
2001	176,170	226,787	402,957	50,617
2002	271,575	370,155	641,730	98,580
2003	289,252	434,965	724,217	145,713
2004	258,000	439,000	697,000	181,000
2005	340,300	715,500	1,055,800	375,200
2006	519,563	830,198	1,349,761	310,635
2007	765,346	1,032,550	1,797,896	267,204
2008	930,000	890,000	1,820,000	-40,000

Sources: South Korea Ministry of Unification, KOTRA.

- Pyongyang's missile testing, prompting Japan to acquire a Theater Missile Defense system, with Taiwan wishing to be included;
- North Korea's construction of underground missile sites close to the Chinese border; and
- North Korea's cavalier attitude towards business. (China occasionally suspends shipments of humanitarian aid to the DPRK because Pyongyang regularly 'forgets' to return Chinese railroad rolling stock.)[152]

In 2006, Pyongyang's missile and nuclear tests severely strained relations between China and the DPRK. Beijing had warned the DPRK not to conduct either of the tests and "lost face" when Pyongyang went ahead with them anyway. As a result, for the first time China agreed to UN resolutions imposing sanctions on the DPRK[153] and also took measures to halt banking transactions with North Korean entities and to curtail shipments of petroleum. China, however, did not agree to conduct inspections of shipments along its borders with North Korea. Some analysts indicate that Pyongyang may be growing weary of its lop-sided relations with Beijing and may be attempting to become more independent. Pyongyang may view nuclear weapons as a "trump card to intimidate China as much as the United States."[154] After North Korea's long-range missile test in April 2009, China agreed to stronger U.N. sanctions on three North Korean companies. After North Korea's second nuclear test in May 2009, China issued a strong statement of condemnation and apparently has been cooperating in developing a U.N. Security Council resolution addressing the issue.

Since the collapse of the Soviet Union, China has been the DPRK's largest trading partner and supplier of concessional assistance (through subsidized trade and direct transfers). As an export market and source of imports, however, North Korea plays a relatively minor role for China. In 2007, the DPRK ranked 64th among China's export markets—smaller than Peru, Egypt, or Hungary. As a source of imports, North Korea ranked 70th—below Gabon, Yemen, or Belgium. Table 10 shows China's merchandise trade with the DPRK.

Table 10. China's Merchandise Trade with the DPRK, 1995-2008 ($ in millions)

Year	China's Imports	China's Exports	Total Trade	China's Balance
1995	63.609	486.037	549.646	422.428
1996	68.638	497.014	565.652	428.376
1997	121.610	534.411	656.021	412.801
1998	51.089	356.661	407.750	305.572
1999	41.722	328.634	370.356	286.912
2000	37.214	450.839	488.053	413.625
2001	166.797	570.660	737.457	403.863
2002	270.863	467.309	738.172	196.446
2003	395.546	627.995	1,023.541	232.449
2004	582.193	794.525	1,376.718	212.332
2005	496.511	1,084.723	1,581.234	588.212
2006	467.718	1,231.886	1,699.604	764.168
2007	581.521	1,392.453	1,973.974	810.932
2008	754.045	2,033.233	2,787.278	1,279.188

Sources: Chinese (PRC excluding Hong Kong) data as supplied by World Trade Atlas.

China is a major source for North Korea of imports of petroleum. According to Chinese data, exports to the DPRK of crude oil reached $414 million and shipments of oil (not crude) totaled $120 million. Total exports of mineral fuel oil of $585 million accounted for 29% of all Chinese exports to the DPRK. China, however, does not appear to be selling this oil to North Korea at concessionary prices. In 2008, the average price for Chinese exports of crude oil to North Korea was $0.78 per kilogram, while it was $0.71 for such exports to the United States, $0.66 for South Korea, $0.81 for Japan, and $0.50 for Thailand.[155]

China also provides aid directly to Pyongyang. By bypassing the United Nations, China is able to use its assistance to pursue its own political goals independently of the goals of other countries. It is widely believed that Chinese food aid is channeled to the military. This allows the World Food Program's food aid to be targeted at the general population without risk that the military-first policy or regime stability would be undermined by foreign aid policies of other countries.[156]

In November 2003, China reportedly transferred responsibility for securing its border with North Korea from the police to its army.[157] Many of China's two million ethnic Koreans live along this border, and it is a favorite crossing point for refugees from North Korea. In 2006, China built a 20-kilometer long fence along its border with North Korea. It is located primarily along areas where the Yalu River dividing the two countries is narrow and the river banks low.[158] Much of China's trade with the DPRK goes through the port of Dandong on the Yalu River. In 2002, 40% of Chinese exports to and 11% of its imports from North Korea passed through Dandong.[159]

China's major imports from North Korea include mineral ores, mineral fuels (coal), woven apparel, fish and seafood, iron and steel, and wood. China's major exports to North Korea include mineral fuels and oil, meat, electrical machinery, machinery, plastic, man-made filament, vehicles, and iron and steel. (See section of this chapter on foreign investments for activity by Chinese firms in the DPRK.)

Japan-DPRK Economic Relations

Japan's economic relations with North Korea have declined sharply as tension over Pyongyang's nuclear and missile programs has spiked, and there has been no resolution of the Japanese abducted by North Korea's intelligence agency. North Korea's May 2009 test of a nuclear device reinforced existing trends in DPRK-Japan economic relations. Although the Japanese government was reportedly considering a complete economic embargo on North Korea in the wake of the most recent test, the impact is considered largely symbolic because of the already drastically reduced trade.

After North Korea test launched several missiles in July 2006 and then detonated a nuclear device in October 2006, Japan imposed strict unilateral sanctions, causing bilateral trade to plummet. Japan banned imports and most North Korean nationals from entering Japan, prohibited all North Korean ships from entering Japanese ports, and outlawed the export of "luxury goods" to North Korea, including caviar, jewelry, liquor, and any food known to be favored by North Korean leader Kim Jong-il. Tokyo has also ceased sending any humanitarian aid to North Korea, and has refused to provide economic or energy assistance until their concerns with Pyongyang are resolved.

Table 11. Japan's Merchandise Trade with the DPRK, 1994-2007 ($ in millions)

Year	Japan's Imports	Japan's Exports	Total Trade	Japan's Balance
1994	328.313	171.092	499.405	-157.221
1995	338.073	253.798	591.871	-84.275
1996	290.745	226.480	517.225	-64.265
1997	301.796	178.942	480.738	- 122.854
1998	219.489	175.137	394.626	-44.352
1999	202.564	147.839	350.403	-54.725
2000	256.891	206.760	463.651	-50.131
2001	225.618	1,064.519	1,290.14	838.901
2002	235.840	132.645	368.485	-103.195
2003	174.390	91.445	265.835	-82.945
2004	164.299	88.743	253.042	-75.556
2005	132.277	62.505	194.782	-69.772
2006	77.776	43.8 16	12 1.592	-33.96
2007	0.000	9.331	9.331	9.331
2008	0.000	7.663	7.663	7.663

Source: Japanese data as supplied by World Trade Atlas.

This pattern is a reversal of earlier economic relations. Although Japan and North Korea have never established official diplomatic relations, the two nations maintained significant economic ties for well over a decade. From the end of the Cold War, Japan was second only to China among North Korea's top trading partners. Bilateral trade declined considerably in the 1980s, but the drop was attributed primarily to the steep overall downturn of the North Korean economy as much as the state of bilateral relations. Before relations deteriorated, Japanese leaders made several efforts to normalize relations with North Korea, promising considerable economic assistance to the country. Since 2002, however, North Korea's provocative missile and nuclear device tests, along with the issue of Japanese citizens kidnapped by North Korean agents in the 1970s and 1980s, has stalled any further diplomatic progress and retarded economic relations. From 2001-2005, Japan's share of North Korean trade declined as China, South Korea, and Russia expanded trade with Pyongyang.

As indicated in Table 11, by 2008, total trade between Japan and the DPRK had fallen to $8 million from $1,290 million in 2001. In 2007, Japan had no imports from the DPRK and reported exports of $8 million.

Before Japan stopped importing from North Korea, seafood made up almost half of the North's exports to Japan, followed by electrical machinery, aluminum and articles thereof, mineral fuels, and apparel. North Korean clams and *matsutake* mushrooms are particularly prized in the Japanese market. Japan sent items such as vehicles, electrical machinery, boilers/reactors, manmade filaments, wool, and articles of iron or steel to North Korea. Some Japanese lawmakers have argued that Japan should expand the ban on imports from North Korea to cover exports as well.

Japan's food aid to North Korea has also dwindled as relations soured. The pattern of Japanese aid reflects developments in the political relationship between Tokyo and Pyongyang: shipments began in 1995 and 1996 when relations warmed, were temporarily suspended periodically as tensions mounted, and eventually ceased altogether in late 2004 because of disagreement over the abduction issue. Between 1995 and 2004, Japan provided 1.2 million metric tons of humanitarian food aid to North Korea, mostly through the United Nations World Food Program.[160]

A group of pro-Pyongyang ethnic Koreans living in Japan known as the Chosen Soren (Chongryun in Korean) in the past provided North Korea with additional funds in the form of cash remittances and, possibly, facilitated illicit trade such as drug trafficking and counterfeiting. Although the exact amount of remittances is unknown, the total appeared to be in the neighborhood of $100 million per year but declined sharply since the early 1 990s. A series of scandals involving ethnic Korean banks in Japan revealed that money was illegally channeled to North Korea through the network of Chosen Soren-affiliated credit unions. Following the missile tests in 2006, Japan froze fund transfers and overseas remittances by 15 groups and one individual suspected of links to North Korean weapons programs, and established rules that require financial institutions to report to the Japanese government remittances overseas of more than 300 million yen.

RUSSIA-DPRK ECONOMIC RELATIONS

Russian reforms and the end of the Cold War greatly reduced the priority of the DPRK in the strategy of Russian foreign policy. Following Soviet support of North Korea in the Korean War, the USSR provided assistance to Pyongyang that helped equip its military and create its heavy industrial sector. In 1998, at the peak of the bilateral relationship, about 60% of North Korea's trade was with the Soviet Union. Much of the trade was in raw materials and petroleum that Moscow provided to Pyongyang at concessional prices. Relations between the two cooled in the 1990s as Russia recognized South Korea, announced that trade with North Korea was to be conducted in hard currencies, and opted out of its bilateral defense agreement.[161]

Recently, overall relations between Russia and North Korea have been improving. Russia is upgrading its railway connections with the DPRK and has been participating in an ambitious plan to build a trans-Korean railway. As is the case with China and South Korea, Russia is critical to North Korean security, since Russia shares a border with the DPRK, and Russian cooperation would be necessary to enforce any security guarantee. As fuel aid from abroad has decreased, moreover, North Korea has turned again toward Russia as a source of supply.

An observer of Russia-DPRK relations views Russian policy toward North Korea as an important component of Moscow's general strategy toward what it considers the critically important Asia- Pacific region. Russia's strategic course includes a calculating and pragmatic approach toward North Korea and the Korean Peninsula in general. Moscow has gained unique and exclusive communications capabilities with Pyongyang based on the development of trust between the leadership of the two states at the highest political levels.[162]

This observer also points out that the perspective of Russia on the North Korea nuclear issue does not fully coincide with that of the United States. While Moscow has insisted on a denuclearized Korean peninsula and the irreversible dismantlement of North Korea's nuclear weapons and nuclear development programs, it also firmly supports the peaceful resolution of the issue. Russia is a participant in the Six-Party Talks. Moscow apparently has concluded that the Kim Jong-il regime does not face impending collapse, and therefore, outside pressure and economic sanctions intended to bring about regime change work only to increase tensions and the probability of a military confrontation. Russia also does not favor a Korean Peninsula unified by military force with American help. This would put U.S. forces on the Russia-Korean border. Rather, Russia supports a unified Korea that would maintain friendly relations with all countries, including Russia, and opposes foreign interference in the unification process.[163]

As is the case with China, Russia also is concerned that economic hardships in the DPRK push refugees across the border into Russian territory. Moscow also supported U.N. Security Council Resolutions in 2006 that condemned North Korea's missile and nuclear tests. This has cooled the relationship to some extent. Russia also condemned the May 2009 nuclear test.

The DPRK's trade with Russian lags behind what it has been in the past. In 2008, North Korea ranked 107th among Russia's sources of imports (below Jamaica and Ghana) and 92nd in terms of markets for Russian exports (below the Virgin Islands and Gibraltar). The increasing volume of Russian mineral fuel exports to the DPRK has moved Russia past Japan, Germany, and Thailand to become North Korea's third largest trading partner.

Major Russian exports to the DPRK include mineral fuels, wood pulp, machinery, non-rail vehicles, iron and steel, and wood. Russian exports of mineral fuels have been declining from a peak of $224.4 million in 2005 to $73.5 million in 2007 and $41.6 million in 2008. Major Russian imports from North Korea include machinery, electrical machinery, glass, and plastics.

In December 2006, Russia reportedly agreed to write off some 80% of the $8 billion in debt owed it by the DPRK. North Korea had borrowed the funds in the 1960s to build power plants. This opened the way for Russia to engage in more economic cooperation with the DPRK.[164]

Table 12. Russia's Merchandise Trade with the DPRK, 1994-2006 ($ in millions)

Year	Russia's Imports	Russia's Exports	Total Trade	Balance
1994	44.00[a]	52.00[a]	96.00[a]	8.00[a]
1995	15.00[a]	70.00[a]	85.00[a]	55.00[a]
1996	347.00[a]	525.00[a]	872.00[a]	178.00[a]
1997	16.790	72.449	89.239	55.659
1998	8.463	56.497	64.960	48.034
1999	7.208	48.507	55.715	41.299
2000	7.633	35.631	43.264	27.998
2001	14.664	56.099	70.763	41.435
2002	10.317	47.404	57.721	37.087
2003	2.903	112.343	115.246	109.440
2004	4.575	204.665	209.240	200.090
2005	6.862	224.402	231.264	217.540
2006	20.076	190.563	210.639	170.487
2007	33.539	126.068	159.607	92.529
2008	13.519	97.005	110.524	83.486

Sources: Russian data as supplied by World Trade Atlas.

a. 1994-96 data from International Monetary Fund. Direction of Trade Statistics

POSSIBLE ECONOMIC INCENTIVES

Normalizing Diplomatic Relations

Normalization of diplomatic relations with the DPRK would apply to the United States, Japan, and South Korea. North Korea already has diplomatic relations with China, Russia, and the European Union (including an embassy in London). Associated with normalizing relations would be a peace treaty formally ending the Korean War. For Japan, the DPRK would have to resolve certain issues, including a full accounting of the status of kidnapped Japanese citizens, North Korea's missile firings over Japan, and incursions by suspected DPRK espionage and drug- running ships into Japanese waters. Upon conclusion of these normalization talks, Japan is likely to offer $5 billion to $10 billion to North Korea in compensation for its occupation.[165]

Normalizing diplomatic relations allows countries to communicate with each other in a more direct fashion, enables diplomats to gather information directly, and provides more interaction on a personal level. Normalized relations can help to overcome the Pyongyang propaganda machine both within the DPRK and on the world stage. Normalization, however, can imply that the United States is willing to tolerate conditions in North Korea. This may be unacceptable to some. Absent normalized relations, Washington could seek a relationship similar to that with Cuba. Even without diplomatic ties, the U.S. mission in Havana is attached to that of Switzerland and maintains a staff similar in size to a regular embassy. (North Korea has been a member of the United Nations since 1991 and has representatives in New York.) Japan has initiated talks with Pyongyang that could lead to normalized relations, and South Korea has been seeking diplomatic ties and possibly some form of reunification in the future. In 2007, bilateral talks between Japan and the DPRK on normalization were stymied by the abduction issue, but they have resumed in 2008.

Negotiating a Trade Agreement

After normalization, the United States could negotiate a trade agreement with the DPRK that would cover goods, services, and investments and could be modeled after the 2001 bilateral trade agreement concluded between the United States and the Socialist Republic of Vietnam.[166] Upon implementation of the trade agreement, each country would accord the other normal trade relations (most favored nation) status. The immediate effect would be to allow North Korean exports to the United States to enter at the lower rates of duty accorded to nearly all other nations of the world. The trade agreement also could cover investment and other U.S. interests.

Although the DPRK's market currently is small, eventually it could re-industrialize and become a larger economic player in the region. Liberalization of North Korean trade and investment relations, moreover, can work through the economy in the same way that it did in China and Russia by exposing the public to the benefits of increased wealth. The major negative to establishing trade with North Korea is that, unless it is part of a larger package that includes other concessions, the United States could be viewed as exchanging an important bargaining chip for minimal gain.

Easing U.S. Sanctions

The United States could ease economic sanctions on North Korea if the country resolves the issues that caused the sanctions to be imposed initially. Since North Korea's other trading partners have more liberal trade with North Korea, it is mainly American companies and traders that are impacted by the sanctions. Pyongyang can spend its available foreign exchange in any of a number of world markets—in China, Russia, South Korea, Europe, or elsewhere. Moreover, as North Korea opens its economy, U.S. businesses would be able to decide whether or not to invest there based on their own economic interests and not because they are hindered from doing so by U.S. law.

Allowing the DPRK to Join International Financial Institutions (IFIs)

The United States could stop blocking the DPRK from joining the major IFIs, particularly the Asian Development Bank, World Bank, and International Monetary Fund.[167] Pyongyang is particularly interested in joining the Asian Development Bank, but IFI procedures require membership first in the International Monetary Fund. The IMF requires certain economic data which the World Bank or Asian Development Bank needs to evaluate projects and loan requests. Membership in IF Is requires that a country establish data gathering and reporting mechanisms as well as open their country to visits, surveys, or assessments by the IFI. As an incentive, a special fund could be set up in the World Bank or Asian Development Bank to assist North Korea in its economic transition. This fund could be financed by Japan or South Korea in conjunction with their normalization of relations with the DPRK.

Fuel and Food Aid

The Bush administration resumed shipping fuel and food aid on a humanitarian basis to the DPRK. South Korea also has resumed shipments of fuel, but it has insisted that food and fertilizer aid be sent only if requested by North Korea.

Products from the Kaesong Industrial Complex

When South Korea was negotiating the proposed Korea-U.S. Free Trade Agreement (signed but not yet approved by Congress), they asked that products from the Kaesong Industrial Complex in North Korea be included under the FTA and be accorded duty-free entry into the United States. The resulting FTA language, however, does not provide for duty-free entry into the United States for products made in Kaesong. Annex 22-B to the proposed FTA, however, does provide for a Committee on Outward Processing Zones (OPZ) to be formed and to designate zones (such as the Kaesong Industrial Complex) to receive preferential treatment under the FTA. Such a designation apparently would require legislative approval by both countries.

End Notes

[1] "Magnificent Gunshots of 150-Day Battle Have Sounded—All Forward in an All-Out Assault," *Minju Joson*, May 5, 2009, Electronic edition (in Korean). Translated by Open Source Digest, Document KPP20090505051002. DPRK Cabinet Paper Editorializes on Commencement of '150-Day Battle.'

[2] The extent that Pyongyang has reversed policies of allowing economic interaction with the South was indicated by the reported execution in late 2008 of Choe Sung-chol, a party official who played a key role in North-South relations. When South Korea cut off deliveries of food and fertilizer to the North, Pyongyang held him accountable for the unwanted impact from the country's dependence on the capitalist South. He was punished for "planting fantasies about South Korea in North Korean society."

[3] For details on the Six-Party Talks, see CRS Report RL33590, *North Korea's Nuclear Weapons Development and Diplomacy*, and CRS Report RL33567, *Korea-U.S. Relations: Issues for Congress*, both by Larry A. Niksch.

[4] See CRS Report RL34256, *North Korea's Nuclear Weapons: Technical Issues*, by Mary Beth Nikitin, CRS Report RL33590, *North Korea's Nuclear Weapons Development and Diplomacy*, by Larry A. Niksch, and .CRS Report RS21473, *North Korean Ballistic Missile Threat to the United States*, by Steven A. Hildreth.

[5] Information on the DPRK's economy is scanty and suspect. The closed nature of the country and the lack both of a comprehensive data-gathering structure and a systematic reporting mechanism make quantitative assessments difficult. Still, sufficient information is available to provide a sketch of the North Korean economy that has enough details to address different policy paths.

[6] Choe, Sang-hun, "North Korea says it will try 2 Americans," *International Herald Tribune*, May 15, 2009. Note: The United States is working through the Swedish embassy in Pyongyang for release of the two reporters. Sweden , represents U.S. interest in North Korea.

[7] Kim Hyun, "Spy Agency Confirms N.K. Leader's Third Son as Successor: Lawmakers," *Yonhap (Seoul)*, June 2, 2009, p. Reprinted in Open Source Center #FEA20090603861068.

[8] Kim Hyun, "Kim's failing health prompting N. Korean power transfer to son," *Yonhap*, June 4, 2009.

[9] Economist Intelligence Unit ViewsWire, *North Korea politics: Nuclear threat*, May 27, 2009.

[10] Some in the North Korean military have begun to refer to Kim Jong-un as the "36 year-old young General," an apparent attempt to add 10 years to his age. Moon Sung Hwee, "Kim Jong Woon Mentioned By Name," *Daily NK*, June 4, 2009.

[11] David E. Sanger, Mark Mazzetti and Choe Sang-hun , "North Korean Leader Is Said to Pick a Son as Heir," *New York Times*, June 2, 2009, Internet edition.

[12] Kim Hyun, "Spy Agency Confirms N.K. Leader's Third Son as Successor: Lawmakers," *Yonhap (Seoul)*, June 2, 2009, p. Reprinted in Open Source Center #FEA20090603861068.

[13] U.S. Department of State. "North Korea: Presidential Action on State Sponsor of Terrorism (SST) and the Trading with the Enemy Act (TWEA)." Fact Sheet, June 26, 2008. This began the clock on a 45-day period of prior notification of Congress (ending August 11) for delisting North Korea as a state sponsor of terrorism.

[14] Merle D. Kellerhals Jr., *U.S. Removes North Korea from State Sponsors of Terrorism List; North Korea agrees to comply with nuclear verification requirements*, America.gov, October 14, 2008.

[15] U.N. World Food Program. 8.7 Million North Koreans Need Food Assistance, December 10, 2008.

[16] CRS Report RL34487, *Japan's Nuclear Future: Policy Debate, Prospects, and U.S. Interests*, by Emma Chanlett-Avery and Mary Beth Nikitin.

[17] Economist Intelligence Unit ViewsWire, *North Korea politics: Nuclear threat*, May 27, 2009.

[18] Full text of North Korea's 2008 New Year's joint editorial, BBC Monitoring Asia Pacific. London. January 2, 2008. p. 1.

[19] In 2008, China's exports to the DPRK increased by 46% from $1,392 million to $2,033 million.

[20] In June 2009, Deputy Secretary of State Steinberg led a delegation visiting Japan, South Korea, and China to consult with governments there on the challenges faced in dealing with North Korea's missile and nuclear program. The delegation included Special Envoy for North Korea Stephen Bosworth, Under Secretary of the Treasury for Terrorism and Financial Intelligence Stuart Levey, Assistant Secretary of Defense for Asia and Pacific Security Affairs Wallace Gregson, and Senior director for Asian Affairs on the National Security Council Jeffrey Bader.

[21] Kang Hyun-kyung, "N. Korea's Next Leader Is Eager English Learner," *Korea Times*, June 3, 2009.

[22] U.S. sanctions are designed to negatively affect the Pyongyang leadership and not cause additional hardship for the common people. For a review of sanctions, see Karin Lee and Julia Choi, *North Korea: Unilateral and Multilateral Economic Sanctions and U.S. Department of Treasury Actions, 1955-April 2009,* National Committee on North Korea, Updated April 28, 2009. 89 pp.

[23] Jane's Information Group. Armed Forces, Korea, North. Jane's Sentinel Security Assessment, March 4, 2003.

[24] Laney, James T. and Jason T. Shaplen. "How to Deal With North Korea," *Foreign Affairs*, March/April 2003. p. 20-21.

[25] Jon Herskovitz, "U.S. Might Impose Counterfeiting Sanctions on North Korea," *Reuters*, June 4, 2009.

[26] "N.Koreans Love Choco Pie," *Chosen Ilbo*, May 23, 2009, English Internet edition.

[27] Major congressional actions with respect to security and human rights aspects of U.S.-DPRK relations are included in CRS Report RL33567, *Korea-U.S. Relations: Issues for Congress*, by Larry A. Niksch; CRS Report RL34256, *North Korea's Nuclear Weapons: Technical Issues*, by Mary Beth Nikitin; and CRS Report RL30613, *North Korea: Terrorism List Removal*, by Larry A. Niksch.

[28] For information on North Korea in the FY2009 Spring Supplemental Appropriations for Overseas Contingency Operations (H.R. 2346), see CRS Report R40531, *FY2009 Spring Supplemental Appropriations for Overseas Contingency Operations*, coordinated by Stephen Daggett and Susan B. Epstein.

[29] On September 15, 2005, the U.S. Treasury designated Banco Delta Asia SARL as a "primary money laundering concern" under Section 311 of the Patriot Act because it represented an unacceptable risk of money laundering and other financial crimes. Treasury stated that "Banco Delta Asia has been a willing pawn for the North Korean government to engage in corrupt financial activities through Macau.... " On March 14, 2007, the Treasury finalized its rule against Banco Delta Asia, barring the bank from accessing the U.S. financial system, but allowing the $25 million in North Korean funds held to be released.

[30] For details on the Six-Party Talks, see CRS Report RL33590, *North Korea's Nuclear Weapons Development and Diplomacy*, and CRS Report RL33567, *Korea-U.S. Relations: Issues for Congress*, both by Larry A. Niksch.

[31] U.S. Department of State. "North Korea: Presidential Action on State Sponsor of Terrorism (SST) and the Trading with the Enemy Act (TWEA)." Fact Sheet, June 26, 2008. This began the clock on a 45-day period of prior notification of Congress (ending August 11) for delisting North Korea as a state sponsor of terrorism.

[32] For details, see CRS Report RL34256, *North Korea's Nuclear Weapons: Technical Issues*, by Mary Beth Nikitin.

[33] BBC Monitoring, Asia Pacific. Former Bodyguard of North Korean Leader Interviewed, October 13, 2003, p. 1.

[34] The only significant power base that might challenge the regime is the military. Since Kim Jong-il became Chairman of the National Defence Commission, however, he has promoted 230 generals. Most of the army's 1,200-strong general officer corps owe their allegiance to him. Jane's Information Group, "Internal Affairs, Korea, North," *Jane's Sentinel Security Assessment*. June 10, 2003.

[35] For an in-depth study of the North Korean economy, see Marcus C. Noland, *Avoiding the Apocalypse: The Future of the Two Koreas*, Institute for International Economics, 2000.

[36] In January 2008, a program for recovery assistance for vulnerable groups in the DPRK lasting from April 2006 to May 2008 had appealed for $102,234,076 and had received 56% of the income against that appeal. The largest donors were South Korea, Russia, Switzerland, Germany, and Australia. World Food Program. Resourcing Update, Project No. 10488.0, January 15, 2008.

[37] Officially, in 2009, 15.8% of the DPRK's $3.7 billion budget was allocated for national defense. Some South Korean analysts argue that the actual figure is higher. U.S. Embassy, Seoul, Economic Section, "DPRK Finance Minister Kim Announces National Budget to Increase 7 Percent in 2009," *North Korea Economic Briefing,* May 21, 2009.

[38] Data from Global Insight. Subscription database.

[39] Global Insight. Korea, North: Economic Trends: Economic Growth: Background. March 4, 2003.

[40] Chao, Julie. Economic Devastation Visible in Pyongyang. Korea Is like a Land Time Forgot, and Crisis with U.S. Isn't Helping. *The Austin American Statesman*, May 3, 2003. P. A17.

[41] Watts, Jonathan. Where Are You, Beloved General? In a Land Where Paranoia, Propaganda, and Poverty Are the Norm, an Albino Raccoon Reassures North Koreans That Good Times Are Ahead. *Mother Jones*, Vol. 28, No. 3, May 1, 2003. p. 52.

[42] Food and Agriculture Organization. Food Security Statistics. Online at http://www.fao.org/statistics/faostat/foodsecurity/Files/NumberUndernourishment_en.xls.

[43] U.N. World Food Programme. WFP Set to Resume Operations in North Korea, Press Release, May 10, 2006.

[44] Kim, Hyung-jin. North Korea Winter Threatens Food Supply, Associated Press, Seoul, March 3, 2008.

[45] U.N. World Food Program. 8.7 Million North Koreans Need Food Assistance, December 10, 2008.

[46] Stephan Haggard and Marcus Noland. *Famine in North Korea, Markets, Aid, and Reform* (New York: Columbia University Press, 2007). P. 3.

[47] Georgy Toloraya. The Economic Future of North Korea: Will the Market Rule? Korea Economic Institute, Academic Paper Series, Volume 2. No 10, December 2007.

[48] A recent World Bank Study indicates that China's PPP values should be reduced by about 40% for 2005 and subsequent years. World Bank. *2005 International Comparison Program, Preliminary Results*, December 17, 2007.

[49] PPI figures are from the World Bank. *World Development Indicators.*

[50] Global Insight (subscription service), "North Korea, Economic Growth: Outlook," updated July 23, 2008.

[51] Global Insight (subscription econometric forecasting service), "North Korea." (Updated February 2009).

[52] South Korea. Ministry of Unification. *North Korea Today*, August 14, 2001 (Internet edition).

[53] UN World Food Programme. World Hunger—Korea (DPR). Available at http://www.wfp.org/country_brief/indexcountry.asp?country=408.

[54] Desperate Straits, Special Report (1). *The Economist*, May 3, 2003 (U.S. Edition).

[55] Class Divergence on the Rise as Market Economics Spread in DPRK, Institute for Far Eastern Studies, North Korea Brief. September 21, 2007. Cited in NAPSNet, September 21, 2007.

[56] Analysis team of the Daily NK. Lee Myung-Bak's Administration: A Breakthrough in North Korea's Opening, *The Daily NK* (Internet edition), December 12, 2007.

[57] See, for example: Natural Wonders Prove Kim Jong-il's Divinity: North Korean Media, Agence France Presse. May 3, 2003.

[58] British Broadcasting Corporation. N. Korea: Paper Supports Leader Kim Jong-il's Military-first Ideology, April 26, 2003. Reported by BBC from KNCA News Agency (Pyongyang).

[59] Toyama, Shigeki. Expert on Kim Chong-il's "Military-First Politics," South-North Issues, Tokyo Gunji Kenkyu (in Japanese, translated by FBIS), August 1, 2002. P. 108-117.

[60] Nam, Woon-Suk. Guidelines of Economic Policies. KOTRA, January 9, 2001.

[61] Gause, Ken E. *North Korean Civil-military Trends: Military-first Politics to a Point.* Army War College, September 2006. P.

[62] The International Institute for Strategic Studies. *The Military Balance, 2006.* London, Routledge, 2006. P. 276. Also, *The Military Balance, 2007*, p. 357. Note: in the 2008, edition of the *Military Balance*, the DPRK's defense budget is listed as "definitive data not available."

[63] "DPRK Allocates 15.9 Percent of State Spending for Military." *People's Daily Online*, April 12, 2005.

[64] Asia: The deal that wasn't; North Korea. *The Economist.* London: September 24, 2005. p. 81.

[65] For a description of decisionmaking in the DPRK, see Former DPRK Diplomat's Book on DPRK National Strategy, Inner Circle Politics (2). Open Source Center document KPP20070918037001. August 20, 2007. (Translated by Open Source Center from Korean)

[66] Current experiments in agriculture are directed from Pyongyang with seven major tasks that include replacing chemical fertilizers with organic and microbial ones. See Yonhap News. N. Korea Eyes China as a Model for Development. May 11, 2004.

[67] Republic of Korea, Ministry of Unification, *Inter-Korean Relations in 2008*, Seoul, Korea, February 2009.See CRS Report RL34093, *The Kaesong North-South Korean Industrial Complex*, by Dick K. Nanto and Mark E. Manyin.

[68] Former North Korean Professor Interviewed on Pyongyang's Economic Reform. *Choson Ilbo*, April 14, 2003. Translated and reported by BBC Worldwide Monitoring, April 18, 2003.

[69] Global Trade Atlas using Chinese data.

[70] Shanghai Northeast Asia Investment & Consultancy Company. *A Study Report on the DPRK Mineral Resources.* Shanghai Northeast Asian Forum website, in Chinese, December 7, 2007. Reported by Open Source Center, document #KPP20080123032002.

[71] Pak, Yo'n. Basic Spirit That Runs Consistently in This Year's Joint Editorial, *Rodong Sinmun*, in Korean, January 4, 2008. Translated by Open Source Center, document #KPP20080104053004.

[72] Mika Marumoto, "North Korea and the China Model: The Switch from Hostility to Acquiescence," *Academic Paper Series, On Korea,* Korea Economic Institute, vol. 1 (2008), pp. 98-117.

[73] For a history of DPRK reforms in light of interaction with China, see Mika Marumoto. North Korea and the China Model: The Switch from Hostility to Acquiescence . Korea Economic Institute. Academic Paper Series, Vol. 2, No. 5, May 2007.

[74] The DPRK Learns Vietnam, *Kookmin Ilbo*, Seoul, October 25, 2007. CanKor Report #296. DPRK-Vietnamese Relations, November 1, 2007. Jung Sung-ki. Kim Jong-il Interested in Vietnamese-style Reform Policy, *Korea Times.* October 28, 2007.

[75] Hong, Ihk-pyo. A Shift Toward Capitalism? Recent Economic Reforms in North Korea. *East Asia Review*, vol. 14, Winter 2002. Pp. 93-106.

[76] In January 2007, the communist party's central committee reportedly asked families to "voluntarily" offer food to the army, since the food shortage in the people's army was severe. Yang, Jung A. Citizens Exploited as the Nation Cannot Produce its Own Income. *The Daily NK* (Internet edition), January 24, 2007.

[77] Hong, Ihk-pyo, A Shift Toward Capitalism?, *East Asia Review*, Winter 2002. Pp. 96.

[78] Jeong, Chang-hyun. Capitalist Experiments Seen Expanding into DPRK. *Joong Ang Ilbo*, October 19, 2003. Translated in CanKor #160 by Canada-DPR Korea e-clipping Service, April 13, 2004.

[79] Lintner, Bertil. North Korea, Shop Till You Drop, *Far Eastern Economic Review*, May 13, 2004. P. 14-19.

[80] Pritchard, Charles L. Siegfried S. Hecker, and Robert Carlin. News Conference: Update from Pyongyang, sponsored by the Korea Economic Institute, held at the National Press Club, Washington, DC, November 15, 2006.

[81] Institute for Far Eastern Studies. *State of the Market in the DPRK*, North Korea Brief No. 07-12-5-1. Posted December 11, 2007.

[82] Han Young Jin. Even the National Security Agency Participates in the Control of the Jangmadang. The Daily NK (electronic version). December 26, 2007.

[83] Good Friends: Centre for Peace, Human Rights and Refugees, *North Korea Today*, No. 103, December 2007.

[84] KOTRA, North Korea, Status of Induced Foreign Capital.

[85] K. Park. A Report on Visit to Rajin-Seonbong Region, January 4, 2001. KOTRA,

[86] Orascom also reportedly is investing $115 million in a North Korean cement manufacturer for a 50% stake in the firm.

[87] Arab Firm Earns First Mobile License In DPRK. *Yonhap*, January 30, 2008.
[88] Institute For Far Eastern Studies. Interest Revived in the Sinuiju Special Administrative Region. Reported by Nautilus Institute, Policy Forum Online 06-25A, March 30, 2006.
[89] For details, see CRS Report RL34093, *The Kaesong North-South Korean Industrial Complex*, by Dick K. Nanto and Mark E. Manyin
[90] "Tenant Companies Are Moving Out of Kaesong," *Hankyoreh* , June 3, 2009, Open Source Document ID: KPP20090604049004.
[91] Republic of Korea. Ministry of Unification. Inter-Korean Relations in 2008. February 2009.
[92] Republic of Korea. Ministry of Unification. Gaeseong Industrial Complex Project—Status and Tasks, June 2005.
[93] South Korea to Continue "Utmost Efforts" for Inter-Korean complex—Minister. Yonhap News Agency. Reported by BBC Monitoring Asia Pacific. London, December 8, 2006.
[94] Republic of Korea. Ministry of Unification. Key Statistics for Gaeseong Industrial Complex. September 30, 2007.
[95] Rights Body Criticizes South Korea Over Refugee Protection, Inter-Korean Complex. Yonhap News Agency, Seoul. Reported by BBC Monitoring Asia Pacific. London, January 12, 2007.
[96] South Korea Considers Expanding Joint Industrial Complex in North. Yonhap News Agency, Seoul. Reported by BBC Monitoring Asia Pacific. London, July 26, 2006. Ministry of Unification (South Korea). The Gaesong Industrial Complex. Status of North Korean Workers. November 14, 2006. Online at http://www.unikorea.go.kr/english/EUP/ EUP0201R.jsp.
[97] CRS Report RL33435, *The Proposed South Korea-U.S. Free Trade Agreement (KORUS FTA)*, by William H. Cooper and Mark E. Manyin.
[98] See Eberstadt, Nicholas. *The North Korean Economy, Between Crisis and Catastrophe* (New Brunswick, NJ, Transaction Publishers, 2007). p. 227.
[99] Embassy of the People's Republic of China in the Democratic People's Republic of Korea. A brief account of the economic and trade relations between China and the DPRK. Online at http://kp.china-embassy.org/eng/zcgx/jmwl/ t306852.htm.
[100] Shanghai Northeast Asia Investment & Consultancy Company. *A Study Report on the DPRK Mineral Resources*. Shanghai Northeast Asian Forum website, in Chinese, December 7, 2007. Reported by Open Source Center, document #KPP20080123032002.
[101] International Monetary Fund. *Direction of Trade Statistics*. It should be noted that countries occasionally misreport trade with South Korea as trade with the DPRK.
[102] For a report on DPRK statistics, see Mika Marumoto, *Project Report: DPRK Economic Statistics Project* , March 2009, http://uskoreainstitute.org/research/projects/index#dprkSTATS.
[103] (South) Korea Trade-Investment Promotion Agency.
[104] For an examination of North Koreas external relations, see Stephan Haggard and Marcus Noland, North Korea's External Economic Relations, Peterson Institute for International Economics Working Paper No. WP07-7, August 2007.
[105] Data are from Joint BIS-IMF-OECD-WB External Debt Hub at http://devdata.worldbank.org/sdmx/jedh/ jedh_home.html.
[106] Gittings, Danny. Kim Can't Kill the Free Market. *The Wall Street Journal (Brussels)*, May 30, 2003. p. A11.
[107] DPRK Holds Annual Lottery for Government Bond Repayments. Institute for Far Eastern Studies, *NK Brief* No. 08-1-3-2, January 3, 2008.
[108] United Nations Conference on Trade and Development. *World Investment Report, 2007*. New York, United Nations, FDISTAT database showing Major FDI Indicators.
[109] CRS Report R40095, *Assistance to North Korea*, by Mark E. Manyin and Mary Beth Nikitin.
[110] U.S. to Pay N. Korea for MIA Search. Associated Press. July 15, 2003. For details on U.S. assistance to North Korea, see CRS Report RS21834, *U.S. Assistance to North Korea: Fact Sheet*, by Mark E. Manyin.
[111] Republic of Korea, Ministry of Unification. Inter-Korean Relations on the Occasion of the 4th Anniversary of the June 15 Joint Declaration. June 18, 2004. p. 9.
[112] For details, see CRS Report RL32137, *North Korean Supporters in Japan: Issues for U.S. Policy*, by Emma Chanlett-Avery. DPRK workers also are countries such as those in the Middle East, China, and Russia.
[113] Melons Used to Smuggle Cash to N Korea. Japan Today News (Online), January 1, 2003.
[114] Remittance Law Reinterpreted Cash Transfers to Pyongyang May Be Suspended as Deterrent. *The Daily Yomiuri* (Tokyo), May 19, 2003. p. 1.
[115] Japanese Finance Minister Says "At Least" 34m US Dollars Sent to North Korea. Financial Times Information, Global News Wire—Asia Africa Intelligence Wire. June 6, 2003.
[116] See, for example, Masaki, Hisane. N Korea's Missiles Met by Japanese Sanctions, *Asia Times Online*, July 6, 2006.
[117] "Refugees' Remittances to N.Korea 'Growing'," *Chosun Ilbo*, February 10, 2009, english.chosun.com.
[118] For details, see CRS Report RL33885, *North Korean Crime-for-Profit Activities*, by Liana Sun Wyler and Dick K. Nanto.
[119] Asano, Yoshiharu. N. Korea Missile Exports Earned 580 Mil. Dollars in '01. *Daily Yomiuri*, May 13, 2003.
[120] Solomon, Jay. U.S. Debates North Korean Exports, *Asian Wall Street Journal*, May 5, 2003. p. A1.

[121] Testimony of John R. Bolton, Under Secretary for Arms Control and International Security, U.S. Department of State. U.S. House Committee on International Relations, June 4, 2003.

[122] Asano, Yoshiharu. N. Korea Missile Exports Earned 580 Mil. Dollars in '01. *Daily Yomiuri*, May 13, 2003. Pearson, Brendan. Illicit Boost for N Korea Economy. *Australian Financial Review*, May 14, 2003. p. 12.

[123] CRS Report RL33696, *Conventional Arms Transfers to Developing Nations, 1998-2005*, by Richard F. Grimmett. p. 53. This figure is rounded to the nearest $100 million.

[124] Jay Solomon, "Tests Point to Spread of Weapons Trade," *The Wall Street Journal*, May 28, 2009, p. A6.

[125] Paddock, Richard C. and Barbara Demick. N. Korea's Growing Drug Trade Seen in Botched Heroin Delivery, *Washington Post*, May 21, 2003. Also see CRS Report RL33885, *North Korean Crime-for-Profit Activities*, by Liana Sun Wyler and Dick K. Nanto.

[126] Kim, Ah-young, Halt North Korea's Drug Habit; a Narcotic State, *International Herald Tribune*, June 18, 2003. p. 8.

[127] U.S. Department of State. *International Narcotics Control Strategy Report, 2007*. March 2007.

[128] Struck, Doug. Heroin Trail Leads to North Korea. *Washington Post Foreign Service*, May 12, 2003. p. A01.

[129] For details, see CRS Report RL33324, *North Korean Counterfeiting of U.S. Currency*, by Dick K. Nanto.

[130] Jon Herskovitz, "U.S. Might Impose Counterfeiting Sanctions on North Korea," *Global Security Newswire by National Journal Group*, June 4, 2009.

[131] Bill Gertz, "Exclusive: N. Korea general tied to forged $100 bills," June 2, 2009, On-line edition.

[132] Choe, Sang-Hun. N. Korea Sees Sanctions Amid Tough Times. Associated Press Online, June 12, 2003.

[133] Available at http://www.whitehouse.gov/news/ releases/2005/06/ 20050629.html.

[134] U.S. Department of the Treasury. Treasury Targets North Korean Entities for Supporting WMD Proliferation. Press Release JS-2984, October 21, 2005.

[135] U.S. Department of the Treasury. Treasury Designates Banco Delta Asia as Primary Money Laundering Concern under USA PATRIOT Act. Press Release JS-2720, September 15, 2005.

[136] See CRS Report RL33663, *Generalized System of Preferences: Background and Renewal Debate*, by Vivian C. Jones, *Generalized System of Preferences*, by William H. Cooper.

[137] See CRS Report RL31696, *North Korea: Economic Sanctions*, by Dianne E. Rennack.

[138] http://w3.access.gpo.gov/bis/ear/ear_data.html

[139] Yoon, Won-sup. US Eased Sanctions on North Korea in 2007, *Korea Times*, February 12, 2008.

[140] Daniel J. Wakin. North Koreans Welcome Symphonic Diplomacy. *New York Times*, February 27, 2008. p. 1.

[141] The North Korean Counterterrorism and Nonproliferation Act (H.R. 3650, Ros-Lehtinen, Ileana) provides for the continuation of restrictions against the government of North Korea (imposed as a result of the DPRK being deemed a supporter of international terrorism) unless the President certifies to Congress that North Korea has met certain benchmarks respecting: (1) missile or nuclear technology transfers; (2) support of terrorist groups and terrorist activities, (3) counterfeiting of U.S. currency, (4) release of South Korean POWs, Japanese journalists, and Kim Donk-Shik; and (5) Bureau 39's closure.

[142] U.S. Bureau of Economic Analysis. U.S. Direct Investment Abroad Detail for Historical-Cost Position and Related Capital and Income Flows, 2001. *Survey of Current Business*, September 2002, p. 94.

[143] Meeting with President of the American Chamber of Commerce and CRS analysts, April 7, 2003, Washington, DC.

[144] Koo, Kyung-hee. U.S. Enterprises Participate in Developing the Gaeseong Industrial Complex. KOTRA-North Korea Team. January 30, 2004. Reprinted in *KOTRA Bulletin*, February 11, 2004.

[145] The Six-Party Talks are made up of representatives from the United States, Japan, North Korea, South Korea, Russia, and China.

[146] Speech by Minister Jeong Se-hyun on the 34th Anniversary of the Ministry of Unification. *Korean Unification Bulletin*, No. 53, March 2003.

[147] In March 1996, KEPCO was designated the prime contractor for the construction of two 1,000MW light water nuclear reactors in North Korea for KEDO (Korean Peninsula Energy Development Organization). It broke ground near Sinpo in August 1997. By the end of 2001, the project was 16% completed with some 1,200 workers employed. For details on the Agreed Framework, see CRS Report RL33590, *North Korea's Nuclear Weapons Development and Diplomacy*, by Larry A. Niksch. For the approval list, see KOTRA, Companies Approved for South-North Korean Economic Cooperation.

[148] South Korea to Continue "Utmost Efforts" for Inter-Korean complex—Minister. Yonhap News Agency. Reported by BBC Monitoring Asia Pacific. London, December 8, 2006.

[149] Inauguration Speech of President Lee Myung-bak, February 25, 2008. On website of the South Korean Ministry of Foreign Affairs and Trade. http://www.mofat.go.kr/index.jsp.

[150] Chu, Wan-chung. These Days, North Korea Does not Even Listen to China. *Chosun Ilbo*, August 7, 2006. Reprinted by BBC Monitoring Asia Pacific, August 10, 2006.

[151] CRS Report RS22973, *Congress and U.S. Policy on North Korean Human Rights and Refugees: Recent Legislation and Implementation*, by Emma Chanlett-Avery. Human Rights Watch. China: Protect North Korean Refugees, March 9, 2004. James D. Seymour. China: Background Paper on the Situation of North

Koreans in China, A Writenet Report by commissioned by United Nations High Commissioner for Refugees, Protection Information Section, January 2005.

[152] Jane's Information Group, *op. cit.*

[153] See UN Security Council Resolution 1718, October 14, 2006.

[154] Kahn, Joseph. China May Press North Koreans. *The New York Times*, October 20, 2006. p. A1.

[155] Average price calculated by World Trade Atlas using Chinese trade statistics.

[156] Babson, Bradley O. *Towards a Peaceful Resolution with North Korea: Crafting a New International Engagement Framework* Paper presented at a conference sponsored by the American Enterprise Institute, Korea Economic Institute, and Korea Institute for International Economic Policy, Washington, DC, February 12-13, 2004.

[157] Foley, James. China Steps Up Security on North Korean Border. *Jane's Intelligence Review*, November 1, 2003.

[158] China Erects Massive Fence on N. Korean Border After Test. *World Tribune.com,* October 25, 2006. Schafer, Sarah. Threatening the Whole World, on China's Border with North Korea, Local Villagers Fear the Fallout from Pyongyang's Nuclear Aspirations, *Newsweek*, October 12, 2006. (Internet edition).

[159] Lee, Chang-hak. China's Trade with N.K. Via Dandong Exceeds US $200 million. KOTRA, February 21, 2003.

[160] CRS Report RL31785, *Foreign Assistance to North Korea*, by Mark E. Manyin.

[161] Lunev, Stanislav. New Era in Russian-North Korean Relations. Newsmax.com, August 23, 2000.

[162] Vorontsov, Alexander. *Current Russia—North Korea Relations: Challenges and Achievements*. The Brookings Institution Center for Northeast Asian Policy Studies, February 2007, 24 p.

[163] *Ibid.*

[164] Russia to Forgive Most of N. Korea's Debt. The Chosun Ilbo (digital version), January 5, 2007.

[165] See CRS Report RL32161, *Japan-North Korea Relations: Selected Issues*, by Mark E. Manyin.

[166] The White House, George W. Bush. "Presidential Proclamation: To Implement the Agreement Between the U.S. and Socialist Republic of Vietnam on Trade Relations," June 1, 2001.

[167] For information on requirements to join the International Monetary Fund, see Primorac, Marina. How Does a Country Join the IMF? *Finance & Development*, June 1991, vol. 28, Issue. 2; pp 34-5.

In: Asian Economic and Political Issues, Volume 14 ISBN: 978-1-61728-019-1
Editor: David A. Marek

Chapter 4

SRI LANKA: BACKGROUND AND U.S. RELATIONS*

K. Alan Kronstadt and Bruce Vaughn

SUMMARY

Sri Lanka, an island nation in the Indian Ocean, is a constitutional democracy with a relatively high level of development. Political, social, and economic development has, however, been seriously constrained by ethnic conflict between the majority Sinhalese and minority Tamil ethnic groups. Since 1983, a separatist war costing at least 70,000 lives has been waged against government forces by the Liberation Tigers of Tamil Eelam (LTTE), a rebel group that sought to establish a separate state or internal self-rule in the Tamil-dominated areas of the North and East. The United States designated the LTTE as a Foreign Terrorist Organization in 1997. Open fighting in this conflict came to a close with the defeat of LTTE field forces and the combat death of their leader Velupillai Prabhakaran in May 2009. The government now faces the challenge of consolidating peace with the Tamil community now that LTTE forces have been defeated. Sri Lanka also suffered a huge natural disaster in December 2004. A massive tidal wave killed up to 35,000 citizens in Sri Lanka's worst-ever natural disaster.

The current state of affairs in Sri Lanka presents the United States and the international community with several key challenges. Chief among these is how to help the government of Sri Lanka to win the peace now that it has won the war against LTTE forces in the field. Many observers feel that the manner in which the post conflict period is addressed will have a great impact on the degree to which the grievances of the Tamil minority can be put to rest. A policy that would address these grievances is perceived by many to be more likely to avert a resurgence of conflict than one that ignores or exacerbates them. Another key challenge is how to recast foreign aid to assist those in need and those displaced by the civil war.

Political rivalry between the Sri Lankan Freedom Party (SLFP) and the United National Party (UNP) has long hindered peace efforts. The United People's Freedom Alliance, a

---

* This is an edited, reformatted and augmented version of a CRS Report for Congress publication, Report #RL31707, dated June 4, 2009.

coalition of the SLFP and the staunch Marxist People's Liberation Front (JVP), won a slim majority in 2004 parliamentary elections and defeated the UNP to replace its then-Prime Minister Ranil Wickremesinghe with perceived hardliner Mahinda Rajapaksa, who himself went on to win the presidency in a narrow 2005 electoral victory. Rajapaksa stabilized his position by enticing the defection of several UNP and Muslim party parliamentarians in early 2007, but his government has faced constant pressure from the JVP and from hard-line Buddhist-nationalist parties that are part of the ruling coalition. Meanwhile, the LTTE suffered a major schism in 2004 when a top commander in the East known as Colonel Karuna broke away with up to 6,000 cadres and began collaborating with government forces.

The ethnic violence of mid-2006 was followed by a major government military offensive in 2007 and Colombo's formal withdrawal from the ceasefire agreement in January 2008, which culminated in the military defeat of the LTTE in May 2009. U.S. policy supports peaceful efforts to reform Sri Lanka's democratic political system in a way that provides for full political participation of all communities; it does not endorse the establishment of another independent state on the island. Since Sri Lankan independence in 1948, the United States has provided more than $3.6 billion in assistance funds, about two-thirds of this in the form of food aid. Direct non-food aid for FY2007 is estimated at $9.4 million. Serious human rights problems in Sri Lanka are blamed on all major parties to the ethnic conflict and have led to some limited U.S. and international aid sanctions.

This chapter provides historical, political, and economic background on Sri Lanka and examines U.S.-Sri Lankan relations and policy concerns. Congressional interest in Sri Lanka has focused on renewed and serious violent ethnic conflict in a quarter-century-old civil war, an attendant humanitarian emergency, and efforts to revive a moribund peace process. A new key challenge for the international community is how to assist Sri Lanka to effectively consolidate peace with the Tamil minority now that open fighting in the civil war is over. Human rights, and U.S. appropriations for food, economic, and military assistance are further congressional interests. A Congressional Caucus on Sri Lanka and Sri Lankan Americans was established in 1998. U.S. attention to Sri Lanka in the late 20th century focused mainly on efforts to resolve the country's ethnonational conflict, which centered on an armed struggle between majority Buddhist Sinhalese and a Hindu Tamil minority clustered in the island's north and east. During this time Washington largely deferred to India as the major external actor in Colombo.

Most Recent Developments

A "growing and grave humanitarian crisis" developed during the last phase of the civil war between Sri Lankan government forces and the LTTE.[1] Large numbers of civilians became trapped with the remnants of the LTTE forces in a shrinking pocket that ended along a coastal strip of land in northeastern Sri Lanka. President Barack Obama pointed out on May 13, 2009, that these people have "little access to food, water, shelter and medicine. This has led to widespread suffering and the loss of hundreds if not thousands of lives."[2] These civilians were finally freed when LTTE resistance collapsed in May 2009.

Government forces reportedly shelled the LTTE position on April 21, 2009, leading to the mass exodus of some 100,000 civilians that had reportedly been forced to remain as "human shields" with the LTTE forces. Reports suggest that 6,500 to 7,000 died from January to May 2009, but the government barred journalists and aid workers from the area, so estimates are difficult to confirm.[3]

Renewed shelling of the LTTE-held position on May 9 and 10 killed hundreds to over a thousand civilians, including many children, and wounded over one thousand civilians. There was little medical attention available for those wounded in the rebel-held area. On May 12 it was reported that the only medical facility available in the LTTE enclave was shelled, killing 49 and wounding over 50 people.[4] Continued shelling on May 12 and 13 prevented a Red Cross ferry from delivering food and evacuating the wounded.[5] The military denied that it was shelling the LTTE position despite credible reports that it was responsible. The government and the LTTE both accused each other of being responsible for the shelling.[6]

It remains to be seen if those elements of the LTTE that managed to escape the closing net of the military forces of the government of Sri Lanka will regroup given that their leader, Velupillai Prabhakaran, was evidently killed in the fighting. Sir Lanka's Tamil minority community's views toward the government may be adversely affected by the apparent lack of concern over civilian casualties in this closing phase of the conflict.

How the government of Sri Lanka handles the post-conflict humanitarian crisis with the Tamil minority that constitute 12.6% of Sri Lanka's population will likely have a great impact on its ability to heal the wounds caused by the civil war and bring the Tamil and Sinhalese communities together. United Nations (U.N.) Chief Ban Ki-moon reportedly believes that a full and fair integration of the Tamil minority into Sri Lanka is key to a process of national reconciliation. Should the government fail to convince Sri Lankan Tamils that it is making a sincere effort to aid the estimated 300,000 Internally Displaced Persons (IDPs), many of whom are in need of food, water, and sanitation, it will likely find it harder to truly bring peace to the nation.[7]

The United States and Sri Lanka

In the leadup to the defeat of the LTTE, U.S. policy called for an end to hostilities and a pause to the fighting on humanitarian grounds. It had also sought to urge the Government of Sri Lanka to allow international observers into the area of conflict.[8] In addition, the United States supported the U.N. Secretary General's call for U.N. staff to be allowed into the conflict zone and to allow the United Nations and International Committee of the Red Cross staff to access sites where IDPs were being processed and where they were coming across the front lines of the fighting.[9] It was reported in February that the Tokyo Co-Chairs (a donor group consisting of Norway, Japan, the United States, and the European Union) jointly expressed their concern over the plight of civilians caught in the conflict.[10] The United States had urged the LTTE, which is listed by the United States as a terrorist group, to surrender to a third party and has stated that "the international community should be prepared to play a role to end the fighting."[11] It was reported that the U.S. sought to delay a $1.9 billion International Monetary Fund loan to Sri Lanka to apply pressure on Colombo to increase aid to civilians caught in the conflict. It was also reported that the U.S. Embassy in Colombo rejected such assertions.[12]

The United States also believes that "addressing good governance, decentralization, and poverty in the south, as well as key democratic and economic opportunities for Tamils and Muslims, especially in the east, is necessary to solidify support for peace and eliminate the rhetoric of extreme elements."[13]

Recent Congressional Interest

In March 2009, several Members of Congress wrote a letter to Secretary of State Hillary Clinton to express their concern over the situation in Sri Lanka. The group "strongly encourage active U.S. leadership to bring about a long-delayed political settlement to the conflict that will guarantee Tamils full political rights and participation in their governance, and an end to the longstanding ethnic discrimination.... Until the ethnic conflict is substantively addressed, there will not be an enduring end to the conflict."[14] Other Members were reportedly more supportive of the Sri Lankan government's position that the war against the LTTE should be brought to a conclusion reportedly out of concern that the LTTE could regroup and/or escape if pressure on it was lifted.[15] On May 19, 2009, several Senators joined Senators John Kerry and Richard Lugar in stating that the government of Sri Lanka "has a chance to forge a long-term political solution, one that acknowledges the legitimate aspirations of all Sri Lankans, including Sinhalese, Tamils, and other groups. This means taking steps towards reconciliation and justice, including the devolution of power to local bodies as provided for by the constitution of Sri Lanka."[16]

HISTORICAL SETTING

Once a port of call on ancient maritime trade routes, Sri Lanka is located in the Indian Ocean off the southeastern tip of India's Deccan Peninsula. The island nation was settled by successive waves of migration from India beginning in the 5th century BCE. Indo-Aryans from northern India established Sinhalese Buddhist kingdoms in the central part of the island. Tamil Hindus from southern India settled in the northeastern coastal areas, establishing a kingdom in the Jaffna Peninsula. Beginning in the 16th century, Sri Lanka was colonized in succession by the Portuguese, Dutch, and English, becoming the British crown colony of Ceylon in 1815. In the late 19th century, Tamil laborers were brought from India to work British tea and rubber plantations in the southern highlands. Known as Indian Tamils, the descendants of these workers currently comprise 5% of Sri Lanka's population and are clustered in the south- central "tea country." Descendants of earlier Tamil arrivals, known as Sri Lankan or Ceylon Tamils, constitute up to 12% of the country's population and live predominantly in the North and East. Moorish and Malay Muslims (largely Sunni) account for another 8% of the population. The majority of Sri Lankans (about three-quarters) are ethnic Sinhalese, most of them Buddhist.[17] In 1972, Ceylon was renamed Sri Lanka ("resplendent land"), as it was known in Indian epic literature.

Although Ceylon gained its independence from Britain peacefully in 1948, succeeding decades have been marred by ethic conflict between the country's Sinhalese majority clustered in the densely populated South and West, and a largely Hindu Tamil minority living in the northern and eastern provinces. Following independence, the Tamils—who had attained educational and civil service predominance under the British—increasingly found themselves discriminated against by the Sinhalese-dominated government, which made Sinhala the sole official language and gave preferences to Sinhalese in university admissions and government jobs. The Sinhalese, who had deeply resented British favoritism toward the Tamils, saw themselves not as the majority, however, but as a minority in a large Tamil sea that includes 60 million Tamils just across the Palk Strait in India's southern state of Tamil Nadu.

Sri Lanka in Brief

Population: 20.9 million; *growth rate*: 1.0%

Area: 65,610 sq. km. (slightly larger than West Virginia)

Capital: Colombo

Head of Government: President Mahinda Rajapaksa (Sri Lankan Freedom Party)

Ethnic Groups: Sinhalese 74%; "Sri Lankan"Tamils 12%; "Indian" Tamils 5%; Moors 7%

Languages: Sinhala (official and national language) 74%; Tamil (national language) 18%; English widely used

Religions: Buddhist 69%; Muslim 8%; Hindu 7%; Christian 6%; unspecified 10% (2001 census)

Life Expectancy at Birth: female 77 years; male 73 years

Literacy: female 90%; male 95%

Gross Domestic Product: 2.5% growth projected for 2009. per capita GDP in purchasing power parity projected to be $4,873 in 2009.

Inflation: 6.3% estimate for 2009

Destination of Exports: U.S. 21.3%, U.K. 11.7%, India 6.6%, Germany 5.0%, Italy 4.6%.

Sources: CIA *World Factbook*; U.S. Commerce Department; Government of Sri Lanka, Economist Intelligence Unit; Global Insight, Military Balance

Political Setting

The Democratic Socialist Republic of Sri Lanka has a working multi-party democratic system despite relatively high levels of political violence. The country's political life has long featured a struggle between two broad umbrella parties—the Sri Lanka Freedom Party (SLFP) and the United National Party (UNP)—both dominated by prominent family clusters. Since independence, the two parties have frequently alternated in power. In the simplest terms, the SLFP may be viewed as more Sinhala nationalist, statist, and social democratic, while the UNP may be viewed as more Western-oriented, liberal, and open to free market economics.[18] Initially, Sri Lanka followed the Westminster parliamentary model. In 1978, however, the UNP instituted a strong executive presidential system of government. Under this French-style system, the popularly elected president has the power to dissolve the 225-

member unicameral parliament and call new elections, as well as to appoint the prime minister and cabinet. The Colombo government has operated a Secretariat for Coordinating the Peace Process.[19]

Chandrika Kumaratunga—longtime leader of the SLFP and daughter of two former prime ministers—was re-elected to a second six-year term in December 1999, three days after she lost vision in one eye in a Tamil separatist suicide bombing that killed 26 people. Although Kumaratunga's People's Alliance (PA) coalition went on to win a narrow victory in the 2000 parliamentary elections, a year later she was forced to dissolve parliament and call for new elections in order to avoid a no-confidence vote. In the resulting 2001 parliamentary elections, the UNP won 109 seats (to 77 for the PA) and formed a majority coalition—called the United National Front (UNF)—with the much smaller Tamil National Alliance and the Sri Lanka Muslim Congress. Prime Minister Ranil Wickremesinghe pledged to open talks with the Tamil rebels and to resuscitate the ailing Sri Lankan economy.[20]

2003 Political Crisis

A year-long political crisis began in November 2003, when President Kumaratunga suspended Parliament, declared a state of emergency, and dismissed key ministers responsible for peace talks with the LTTE. Kumaratunga's ongoing feud with then-Prime Minister Wickremesinghe—she believed his conciliatory approach toward the rebels was allowing them to consolidate their positions and rearm—likely spurred her surprise move.[21] The shakeup undermined existing peace efforts by the prime minister and cast doubt on his ability to follow through on peace negotiations with the LTTE. Kumaratunga's ensuing February 2004 dismissal of Parliament, and the LTTE's claim that this was a "grave setback" to negotiations, cast a further pall on the future of the peace process.

2004 Parliamentary Elections

As UNP leader Wickremasinghe, who served as prime minister from 2001 to 2004, was relatively more open to talks with the Tamil rebels, his bitter personal rivalry with President Kumaratunga reportedly hampered progress in peace negotiations. An April 2004 national election was held to restore the Parliament dissolved by Kumaratunga. In those polls, the United People's Freedom Alliance (UPFA) coalition, composed of the populist SLFP and the staunch Marxist-Leninist, Sinhalese nationalist People's Liberation Front (JVP), took a plurality of the seats in parliament and so ousted the UNP. The UPFA won 105 seats and nearly 46% of the vote as compared to the UNP, which won 82 seats and about 38% of the vote. The UNP's defeat was attributed in part to a perception among voters that too many concessions were being made to the LTTE in peace negotiations. An EU Election Observation Mission noted some problems with the conduct of the 2004 polls, but called them a "vast improvement" in comparison to past exercises.[22] The December 2004 tsunami killed up to 35,000 Sri Lankans and devastated much of the coast.

Table 1. Selected 2004 Parliamentary Election Results

Party/Coalition	Total votes won	Percentage of total vote	Total seats won	Percentage change from previous Parliament
United People's Freedom Alliance (mainly the Sri Lankan Freedom Party and the Janatha Vimukthi Peramuna or People's Liberation Front)	4,223,970	45.6	105	+12
United National Front (mainly the United National Party)	3,504,200	37.8	82	-27
Tamil National Alliance (backed by Tamil separatists)	633,654	6.8	22	+22
Jathika Hela Urumaya (JHU or National Heritage Party, led by Buddhist monks)	552,724	6.0	9	+9
Sri Lanka Muslim Congress	186,876	2.0	5	—
Other	136,353	1.5	2	-15
Total	9,262,732	—	225	—

Source: International Foundation for Election Systems

2005 Presidential Election

A November 2005 presidential poll saw SLFP stalwart Mahinda Rajapaksa barely defeat Wickremasinghe in an election marked by an LTTE-engineered boycott affecting much of the Tamil community (the LTTE was accused of using intimidation tactics to enforce the boycott). The United States expressed "regret" that many Tamil voters were deprived of the opportunity to make their views known and it condemned LTTE "interference in the democratic process."[23] Unlike Rajapaksa, Wickremasinghe was not beholden to Sinhala nationalist parties, and many analysts believe he would have won the election with the votes of a large majority of Tamils.[24]

Separatist-related violence escalated during 2006 and, as the October date for renewed peace negotiations approached, President Rajapaksa sought to find common ground with the country's main opposition UNP. A resulting three-page memorandum of understanding signed by Rajapaksa and opposition leader Wickremesinghe gave the peace process a boost with the two leaders agreeing to adopt a bipartisan approach to conflict resolution. The pact represented a rare expression of political unity, especially among the fractious Sinhalese of the country's Sinhala-dominated South.[25] Rajapaksa also at this time constituted an All Party Representative Committee (APRC) as part of an effort to create constitutional proposals that would represent a political consensus on power-sharing between the island's majority and minority ethnic communities.

After the October peace talks with the rebels talks failed to make progress, President Rajapaksa changed his political strategy and in January 2007 was able to secure a simple (113-seat) parliamentary majority for his coalition by offering ministerial positions to lure 19 parliamentarians from the UNP and another 6 from the Muslim Congress into defection from the opposition benches. The cross-overs put a damper on bipartisanship in Colombo by spurring the UNP's withdrawal from the APRC and served to further deepen the SLFP-UNP rift. The adjustment did, however, ease Rajapaksa's previous dependence on his hard line and oftentimes unpredictable Marxist JVP and Buddhist JHU allies, potentially making a deal with the rebels more attainable. The JHU, in particular, has been at the forefront of a resurgent Sinhalese Buddhist nationalism that adamantly opposed Tamil autonomy in the North and that has played a role in some human rights violations.[26] By the end of 2007, some senior members of Rajapaksa's cabinet were openly calling for a blanket ban on the LTTE and a formal end to the 2002 truce.[27] JVP leaders, convinced that a UNP administration would only deepen the country's woes, rejected opposition efforts to bring down the SLFP-led coalition government.[28] The Rajapaksa government vowed to hold local-level elections by the end of 2007 as part of a controversial devolution plan. However, the preference of President Rajapaksa and his party was to devolve power at the district level only, not at a higher level as demanded by the Tigers.

LTTE Schism

The LTTE experienced its own instability and factional disagreements in the lead up to its defeat in May 2009. In March 2004 there was a major rupture within the LTTE ranks: Vinayagamoorthi Muralitharan, alias Colonel Karuna (who, as Special Commander, Batticaloa-Amparai District, was in charge of the LTTE's military operations in the Eastern Province) split with the Northern command of the LTTE headed by the supreme commander of the LTTE (Veluppillai Prabhakaran) and took an estimated 6,000 soldiers with him. Colonel Karuna then called for a separate truce with the government. Factional fighting ensued between Karuna's splinter group and the Northern faction of the LTTE, resulting in Prabhakaran's reassertion of control over the eastern areas where Karuna had previously operated. The Karuna faction's ongoing influence did much to damage the longstanding LTTE claim to be the sole representative of Sri Lanka's Tamil people.

After the 2004 schism, Colonel Karuna and those loyal to him apparently fought in cooperation with government forces.[29] Karuna himself was arrested in London in November 2007 while traveling on a forged passport possibly supplied by the Colombo government.[30] The Karuna group (along with the LTTE and sometimes government forces) is widely accused of abusing human rights in the course of its struggle, especially through the recruitment of child soldiers. The United States has called on Colombo to exert control over paramilitary groups such as Karuna's that are believed to commit human rights abuses against the Sri Lanka people.[31]

Ethnic Conflict and Civil War

A combination of communal politics (as practiced by both Sinhalese and Tamil political leaders) and deteriorating economic conditions created deep schisms in Sri Lankan society through the early decades of independence. By the 1970s, the government was facing Tamil unrest in the North and East, while the Sinhalese Marxist JVP waged a terrorist campaign against Tamils in the central and southern regions. Periodic rioting against Tamils in the late 1970s and early 1980s, culminating in the devastating communal riots of 1983, spawned the creation of several militant Tamil groups that sought to establish by force a Tamil homeland to include the Northern and Eastern provinces. The Liberation Tigers of Tamil Eelam, led by its charismatic founder and chief strategist Velupillai Prabhakaran, was established in 1976 and emerged as the strongest and best organized of these groups.

A full-scale separatist war broke out in the North following July 1983 riots in which several thousand Tamils were killed in retaliation for the slaying of 13 Sinhalese soldiers by separatist Tamil militants. More than two decades of ensuing war have claimed some 70,000 lives and displaced hundreds of thousands of people. Each of four major attempts at a peaceful settlement ended in failure and further violence. A ceasefire agreement (CFA) brokered by the Norwegian government in February 2002 was formally abrogated by the Colombo government in January 2008. The government then sought a military solution that proved successful with the defeat of LTTE forces in May 2009.

Parties to the Military Conflict

Sri Lankan Security Forces

The Sri Lankan military, with a budget believed to exceed $1 billion in 2007, is comprised of about 151,000 active personnel. The quality of equipment (mostly outdated Soviet- and Chinese-made weaponry) and training has generally been poor. Morale has suffered with a past inability to decisively defeat a long-running insurgency and with sometimes embarrassing tactical level defeats at the hands of tenacious Tamil Tiger forces. Beginning in 2002, the Colombo government focused on efforts to improve its defense capabilities. Morale was also bolstered, likely contributing to battlefield successes in 2006 and 2007, which themselves further burnished the military's self-image. Over the decades of Sri Lankan independence, the country's military has become increasingly dominated by ethnic Sinhalese, meaning that in much of the northern and eastern provinces it is now widely regarded as a foreign force. This perception is reinforced by reported human rights abuses against civilians in these Tamil-dominated areas, a problem that the Colombo government has with only mixed success sought to address.[32]

The Sri Lankan army is armed with 62 tanks, 217 armored personnel carriers, and 157 towed artillery tubes. The navy operates 123 patrol and coastal combatants, most of them inland and riverine, but also possesses 2 missile boats, along with a very modest amphibious capability. The air force flies 2 fighter/ground attack squadrons—one notable for its 4 MiG27s, another made up of 10 Israeli-made Kfir jets—as well as 14 Russian-made Hind and attack helicopters and 28 American-made Bell utility helicopters. Paramilitary forces include a 30,000-person active police force and a 13,000-person home guard.[33]

The Tamil Tigers

During the last phase of open fighting LTTE forces were estimated at up to 7,000-15,000 armed combatants, with roughly half of them trained in combat. The actual number may have been considerably lower, especially given significant battlefield losses in 2007. Arms include long-range artillery, mortars, antiaircraft weaponry, and captured armored vehicles. A small but effective naval contingent, known as the Sea Tigers, includes speedboats, fishing vessels, mini-subs of indigenous construction, and underwater demolition teams. The LTTE air wing also reportedly constructed an airstrip at Iranamadu in the North and had acquired at least two light aircraft to go along with a few pre-existing helicopters and gliders.[34]

The LTTE's weapons reportedly were obtained through illegal arms markets in Burma, Thailand, and Cambodia, and from captured Sri Lankan forces. Financial support for the LTTE reportedly comes from the worldwide diaspora of some 600,000-800,000 Tamil émigrés (especially the Tamils in Canada and Western Europe), as well as from smuggling and legitimate businesses. There are numerous reports that the government of North Korea has provided arms and possibly training to Tiger forces.[35] The LTTE has been criticized for alleged campaigns to extort and coerce funds from overseas Tamils, especially in Canada and Britain. International efforts to restrict financial flows to terrorist groups have contributed to a reported 70% decline in overseas fund-raising by the LTTE. It was estimated that the Tigers were able to raise $200-300 million per year from various licit and illicit businesses.[36]

The United States designated the LTTE as a Foreign Terrorist Organization under U.S. law in 1997. The European Union followed suit in 2006, thus depriving the rebels of funds collected from members and supporters in Europe. The move also made untenable the position of Norwegian and Danish truce monitors who could no longer maintain neutrality.

The U.S. Federal Bureau of Investigation has listed the Tamil Tigers "among the most dangerous and deadly extremists in the world," crediting the rebels with inventing the suicide belt and perfecting the use of suicide bombers, murdering some 4,000 people since 2006, and being the world's only terrorist organization to assassinate two world leaders.[37]

The LTTE was a prolific employer of suicide bombing, with one report calling it responsible for fully half of all suicide attacks worldwide in the early years of this century.[38] Tamil Tiger suicide bombers are believed responsible for the assassination of numerous Sri Lankan political leaders, including Sri Lankan President Ranasinghe Premadasa in May 1993, and many moderate Tamil leaders who opposed the LTTE. Former Indian Prime Minister Rajiv Gandhi—whose efforts to assist Colombo in enforcing a peace accord with the Tamils in 1987 ended in the deaths of about 1,200 Indian troops—was assassinated in May 1991 by a suspected LTTE suicide bomber.

Current Challenges and Imperatives

With the field forces of the LTTE defeated, the government of Sri Lanka faces the immediate challenges of rounding up remaining LTTE cadres and dealing with the humanitarian situation concerning the plight of the internally displaced persons in the area of conflict. It also faces a longer-term challenge that may hold the key to resolving tensions between the majority Sinhalese and minority Tamil communities. This challenge is how to address Tamil concerns and achieve the effective reintegration of the Tamil people into the Sri Lankan nation. To achieve this, Sri Lanka will reportedly focus on relief, rehabilitation, resettlement, and reconciliation.[39] Focus will likely be on relief in the immediate post-conflict phase.

IDPs

A key concern for the international community in the closing phase of the war and in the immediate post conflict phase has been how to obtain unfettered access to provide assistance to the estimated 300,000 IDPs in government run camps in war torn Tamil areas. The government of Sri Lanka allowed Secretary General Ban Ki-moon and a number of journalists some access during the secretary's visit in May 2009. Secretary General Ban called on the international community to fund the Common Humanitarian Action Plan which will seek to address the needs of those affected by the war. Providing adequate care for these IDPs and effectively returning them to their home areas is a key concern.

Reintegration

U.N. Secretary General Ban Ki-moon called on Sri Lanka to heal its wounds and "unite without regard to religious or ethnic identity" during his May 2009 visit to war torn areas of Sri Lanka.[40] He also called on the government of Sri Lanka to undertake visible confidence building measures to signal good intentions to the Tamil minority. These could be a meaningful step to begin the process of a reconciliation. His mission to Sri Lanka was reportedly focused on humanitarian relief, reintegration, reconstruction and finding an equitable political solution.[41]

The issue of whether or not alleged war crimes will be pursued is a potential area of friction between the government of Sri Lanka and elements in the international community. The Office of the U.N. High Commissioner for Human Rights, Navi Pillay, called for a war crimes inquiry in Sri Lanka. Many in the international community were appalled by reports of both the use of civilians as human shields by the LTTE and the indiscriminate shelling of civilians in LTTE held areas by government forces in the closing phase of the war. Ms. Pillay stated "independent and credible international investigation into recent events should be dispatched to ascertain the occurrence, nature and scale of violations of international human rights and international humanitarian law."[42]

The U.N Human Rights Council passed a resolution on May 27 that was in the view of Human Rights Watch "deeply flawed" because it ignored calls for an international inquiry into alleged abuses of human rights. Human Rights Watch Advocacy Director Juliette de Rivero stated "The Human Rights Council did not even express its concern for the hundreds of thousands of people facing indefinite detention in government camps."[43]

DECEMBER 2004 INDIAN OCEAN TSUNAMI[44]

The tsunami (tidal wave) that devastated much of coastal South and Southeastern Asia on December 26, 2004, hit Sri Lanka particularly hard some 90 minutes after its launch by an earthquake centered west of Sumatra, Indonesia. The massive wave caused some 35,000 deaths, fully or partially destroyed at least 100,000 homes, and displaced nearly 600,000 Sri Lankans in the country's worst-ever natural disaster. The island's east coast was most affected and there was some evidence that the tsunami weakened the LTTE through the destruction of many of its naval assets and the loss of at least 1,000 of its cadres.[45] The Sri Lankan navy also saw significant damage to some of its southern coastal facilities. The single most costly event in terms of human lives was the complete destruction of a train traveling along a coastal railroad track. More than 2,000 people died in this single incident.[46] Fortunately, a projected outbreak of disease following the tsunami never materialized.

President Bush expressed condolences to the Sri Lankan people over the "terrible loss of life and suffering," and the U.S. government moved quickly to provide assistance to those nations most affected.[47] USAID oversaw a total of about $135 million in relief and reconstruction aid for Sri Lanka, devoted especially to the provision of emergency relief supplies, transitional housing, livelihoods restoration, and psychological and social support.[48]

There were hopes that the human costs of the disaster would bring about an opportunity to reinvigorate the stalemated peace process, but negotiations on how to disburse relief aid reflected existing political obstacles. After much wrangling, in June 2005 the Colombo government and the LTTE reached an agreement to share some $3 billion in international tsunami aid under a Post-Tsunami Operational Management Structure (PTOMS). However, the agreement was challenged in court and was never implemented, leaving both parties more distrustful than before. In the words of one analysis, "Protracted negotiations about the institutional arrangements for delivering tsunami assistance to the North-East mirrored earlier peace talks and exposed the deep underlying problems of flawed governance, entrenched positions, and patronage politics."[49]

Economic Issues

The civil war in Sri Lanka has hindered Sri Lanka's economic as well as its political development. Real GDP growth is expected to decline to 2.5% in 2009. Projections are predicting increased growth in 2010 of up to 5.7%. Much of this increase is expected to come from an improved security situation.[50] Inflation fell to a five-year low in April 2009. Sri Lanka has a significant fiscal deficit which is thought to be more than 8% of GDP in 2008. Balance of payments are under stress and the country had, as of May 2009, foreign exchange reserves of approximately six weeks of imports. The government has been in negotiations with the IMF for an emergency loan of $1.9 billion to avert default on debt service obligations.[51] It is reported that Sri Lanka's debt service will total $900 million in 2009.[52]

Sri Lanka's poor economic situation may give the international donor community some leverage over Sri Lankan post-conflict policies towards the Tamil minority. This leverage is in the view of some offset to a large extent by the popularity of the Rajapaksa government's persecution of the war against the LTTE within the Sinhalese community and by support from other segments of the international community. The Sri Lankan shares market rose 2.54% on May 28, 2009, to reach its highest close since September 2008 on the news that U.N. Human Rights Council passed a resolution which was viewed as marking international acceptance of Sri Lanka's war against the LTTE.[53]

Formerly a colonial economy based on plantation crops (tea, rubber, coconut, sugar, and rice), modern Sri Lanka's manufactured products now account for about four-fifths of the country's exports, including garments, textiles, gems, as well as agricultural goods. Tourism and repatriated earnings of Sri Lankans employed abroad are important foreign exchange earners. The first country in South Asia to liberalize its economy, Sri Lanka began an ongoing process of market reform and privatization of state-owned industries in 1977. Many observers attribute the ability of the national economy to thrive even in the midst of civil war to these successful reforms. Privatization efforts have slowed in recent years, however. Since 2001, both tourism and investor confidence, previously on the rebound, were negatively affected by major LTTE terrorist attacks and renewed political instability. Sri Lanka's entire economy has also suffered as a result of a recent prolonged drought (the worst in two decades), related hydroelectric power shortages, and the worldwide economic downturn around the turn of the century.

In November 2006, the Colombo government issued a discussion draft of its 10-year development framework, *Mahinda Chintana [Mahinda's Thoughts]: Vision for a New Sri Lanka*. According to a January 2007 World Bank report,

> The vision sets out ambitious growth targets (over 8% by 2010) aimed at reducing poverty incidence to 12% of the population by 2015 (from 23% in 2002). The rapid growth scenario assumes the continuation of a favorable external environment and implies improved security conditions. A key target is to raise total investment from 28-30% of GDP in 2006 to 34% in 2010, with the largest contribution coming from the public sector. Public sector savings (currently negative) are expected to contribute 5 percentage points of GDP to gross domestic savings by 2010. FDI is projected at around 2% of GDP (compared to less than1% in the past decade).[54]

The war negatively impacted the economy, especially by reducing investor confidence and by damaging the vital tourism sector. The civil war placed a heavy burden on the country's economy, as well as hindering its future potential. Defense expenditures as a percentage of GDP have doubled since 1980. Aside from defense spending, other costs of the war include damage to infrastructure and expenditures for humanitarian relief. Several analyses have asserted that annual growth rates over the past 24 years could have been 2-3 percentage points higher in the absence of protracted ethnic conflict. International donors say the Mahinda plan for poverty reduction is dependent upon peace.[55]

With its location on major sea-lanes, excellent harbors, and high educational standards, Sri Lanka has long been viewed as a potential regional center for financial and export-oriented services. For decades, Sri Lanka has invested heavily in education, health, and social welfare, maintaining high living standards compared to much of South Asia. The U.N. Development Program ranked Sri Lanka 99th out of 177 countries on its 2007/2008 human development index (between Azerbaijan and Maldives), down from 93rd the previous year, but still higher than any other South Asian country.

U.S. RELATIONS AND POLICY CONCERNS

The White House issued a statement on April 24, 2009, that expressed "deep concern" for the plight of civilians caught in the final stages of the conflict between the LTTE and Sri Lankan military forces. The statement also called on the government of Sri Lanka to stop shelling civilians in the "safe zone" and to allow international aid workers and the media access to civilians that had escaped the area of fighting. The statement further made the observation that "it would compound the current tragedy if the military end of the conflict only breeds further enmity and ends hopes for reconciliation."[56]American policy toward Sri Lanka has focused on U.N. and international efforts to address humanitarian needs, has urged the government of Sri Lanka to allow access to both the ICRC and U.N. representatives to the former conflict area, and has observed that the end of the conflict represents an opportunity to seek reconciliation and build a democratic and tolerant Sri Lanka.[57]

According to the U.S. State Department, a history of cordial U.S.-Sri Lanka relations has been based in large part on shared democratic traditions. U.S. policy supports efforts to reform Sri Lanka's democratic political system in a way that provides for full political participation of all communities; it does not endorse the establishment of another independent state on the island. The United States and Sri Lanka signed a new Trade and Investment Framework Agreement (TIFA) in 2002. However, the political instability of subsequent years set back the time frame for any possible Free Trade Agreement (FTA), and relevant negotiations were put on hold pending positive developments in peace negotiations. The United States also maintains a limited military-to-military relationship with the Sri Lanka defense establishment.

During a May 2007 visit to Colombo, the lead U.S. diplomat for the region, Assistant Secretary of State for South and Central Asia Richard Boucher, outlined key U.S. concerns about "the way things have been heading" in Sri Lanka. First among these was the negative impact that armed ethnic conflict was having on the people, both directly through terrorism and human rights abuses, and indirectly by harming the country's economy. In the area of human rights, Secretary Boucher placed special emphasis on the increased incidence of abductions and unlawful killings, as well as on widespread reports of government attempts to intimidate the press. He acknowledged that the government of President Rajapaksa had voiced a commitment to upholding human rights, but said "a lot more needs to be done" both in dealing with the behavior of government security forces and in controlling "paramilitaries" (often a euphemism for the Karuna faction, which broke away from the LTTE in 2004). He conveyed to Sri Lankan political leaders of all stripes the U.S. position that consensus through the All Parties Representative Committee—"a consensus that identifies for the Tamil community their role in the island, their place, their control over various levels of government and their own lives"—represented the best basis for future progress toward conflict resolution.[58]

In August 2007 testimony before the House Foreign Affairs Committee, a State Department official offered that

> Sri Lanka's long-standing ethnic conflict, fragile peace process, and deteriorating human rights conditions continue to cause concern for the United States and the international community.... Our top policy priorities for Sri Lanka remain restoration of good governance and respect for human rights leading to an eventual negotiated settlement. We believe that finalizing a credible devolution of power proposal, together with ending human rights violations and improving government accountability, are essential steps toward a lasting peace.[59]

He went on to review the ways in which the United States is supporting peace efforts, including through the four-member Tokyo Conference mechanism, through USAID projects to promote inter-ethnic dialogue, and by helping to fund humanitarian relief programs overseen by Save the Children, the U.N. Children's Fund, the World Food Program, and the International Committee of the Red Cross.

The U.S. State Department first designated the LTTE as a Foreign Terrorist Organization in 1997.[60] In 2003, then-Deputy Secretary of State Richard Armitage reiterated that

> if the LTTE can move beyond the terror tactics of the past and make a convincing case through its conduct and its actual actions that it is committed to a political solution and to peace, the United States will certainly consider removing the LTTE from the list of Foreign Terrorist Organizations, as well as any other terrorism-related designations.[61]

The LTTE rejected calls that it renounce violence, saying it could do so only when the aspirations of the Tamil people are met by a political settlement. The U.S.-led global anti-terrorism campaign, which reportedly has resulted in the international withholding of several billion dollars from the LTTE and made it more difficult for the group to acquire weapons, was a likely factor in the rebels' decision to enter into peace negotiations in late 2001.[62]

Trade, Investment, and Aid

U.S. Trade and Investment

The United States is by far Sri Lanka's most important trade partner, accounting for more than one-quarter of the country's total exports. During Prime Minister Wickremasinghe's 2002 visit to Washington, the United States and Sri Lanka signed a new Trade and Investment Framework Agreement (TIFA) to establish "a forum for Sri Lanka and the United States to examine ways to expand bilateral trade and investment." The agreement

> creates a Joint Council to enable officials to consider a wide range of commercial issues, and sets out basic principles underlying the two nations' trade and investments relationship." The Council also will "establish a permanent dialogue with the expectation of expanding trade and investment between the United States and Sri Lanka.[63]

The U.S. government continues to urge Colombo to curb its large budget deficit, simplify the tax code, and expand the tax base. It further urges the removal of non-tariff barriers and restrictive, even discriminatory, import fees and levies to facilitate greater trade.[64] The violent ethnonational conflict has precluded most major U.S.-Sri Lanka economic initiatives since 2006.

U.S. Assistance

The State Department's FY2009 request for Sri Lanka included $6.5 million in Development Assistance, $4 million for the Economic Support Fund, $900,000 for Foreign Military Financing, $600,000 for International Military Education and Training, $350,000 for International Narcotics Control and Law Enforcement, and $650,000 for Nonproliferation, Antiterrorism, Demining and Related Programs.[65]

U.S. assistance to Sri Lanka is currently focused on providing emergency relief assistance and assisting the potential return of IDPs to their homes. As of April 10, 2009, USAID and State Humanitarian Assistance, including the Bureau of Population, Migration and Refugees, had provided a total of $58 million in assistance in FY2008 and FY2009 for the complex emergency in Sri Lanka. These programs were focused on humanitarian access and protection, health, shelter, water-sanitation-hygiene, food assistance, and emergency relief commodities.[66] There will likely be a need for demining assistance in areas that have witnessed fighting in addition to the need to provide shelter for IDPs and assist in their return home.[67]

Direct U.S. non-food aid included more than $14.5 million for FY2006 and an estimated $9.4 million in FY2007 (see Table 2). About half of this was aimed at supporting the peace process through democracy and governance programs. When funding for disaster relief, Food for Peace, and U.S. disbursements to the International Committee of the Red Cross and the U.N. High Commissioner for Refugees are included, total U.S. humanitarian assistance to Sri Lanka exceeded $26 million in FY2007. Other U.S. aid to Sri Lanka has focused on increasing the country's economic competitiveness; creating and enhancing economic and social opportunities for disadvantaged groups; promoting human rights awareness and enforcement; providing psychological counseling to communities in the conflict zones; tsunami recovery efforts, and demining (the FY2006 total included a significantly boosted demining fund).

From 2003 to 2005, USAID ran a two-year program intended to generate greater support for a negotiated peace settlement to end the long-standing ethnic conflict. About three-quarters of the FY2007 aid was to be used to support democracy, economic growth, and humanitarian assistance in Sri Lanka. USAID works to "foster political reconciliation" and participates in "joint reconstruction programs [with the Colombo government] that foster economic reintegration as well as social reconciliation."[68] The Administration's FY2008 request also included a modest, but unprecedented INCLE program that would use $350,000 in U.S. aid to support law enforcement reforms in Sri Lanka.

Security Relations

The United States and Sri Lanka have maintained friendly military-to-military and defense relations. According to the U.S. State Department, senior Sri Lankan military officers continue to strongly support U.S. strategic goals and programs, and Sri Lanka continues to grant blanket over flight and landing clearance to U.S. military aircraft, and routinely grants access to ports by U.S. vessels. Modestly funded U.S. military training and defense assistance programs have in recent years assisted in professionalizing the Sri Lankan military and provided the country with basic infantry supplies such as boots, helmets, radios, flack vests, and night vision goggles, along with maritime surveillance and interdiction equipment for the navy and communications and mobility equipment to improve the army's humanitarian and U.N. peacekeeping missions.[69]

The United States and Sri Lanka inked an Acquisition and Cross-Services Agreement in March 2007. The pact, which creates a framework for increased military interoperability, allows for the transfer and exchange of numerous logistics, support, and re-fueling services during joint operations or exercises. A U.S. official visiting Sri Lanka during that month called it a "very routine" and "fairly modest" barter arrangement that the United States has with 89 other countries, and he emphasized that it has no wider applications beyond logistics.[70]

Table 2. Direct U.S. Assistance to Sri Lanka, FY2000-FY2008 (in millions of dollars)

Program or Account	FY 2000	FY 2001	FY 2002	FY 2003	FY 2004	FY 2005	FY 2006	FY 2007	FY 2008 (est.)	FY 2009 (Req.)
CSH	0.7	0.3	0.3	0.3	0.3	0.3	—	—	—	-
DA	3.7	3.4	5.2	6.2	4.8	6.8	3.7	3.5	5.2	4.0
ESF	—	—	3.0	4.0	12.0	9.9	4.0	3.0	—	-
FMF	—	—	—	—	2.5	0.5	1.0	1.0[a]	0.4[a]	.9
IMET	0.2	0.3	0.3	0.3	0.6	0.5	0.5	0.5	0.6	.6
INCLE	—	—	—	—	—	—	—	—	0.2	.4
NADR	—	—	—	2.4	1.8	2.7	3.6	1.4	1.1	.7
TI	—	—	—	—	—	—	1.7	—	—	-
Subtotal	**4.6**	**4.0**	**8.7**	**13.1**	**21.8**	**20.7**	**14.5**	**9.4**	**7.5**	**6.6**
Food Aid[b]	—	13.9	8.7	3.1	3.6	10.8	8.9	14.0	—	-
Total	**4.6**	**17.9**	**17.4**	**16.2**	**25.4**	**31.5**	**23.4**	**23.4**	**7.5**	**6.6**

Sources: U.S. Departments of State and Agriculture; U.S. Agency for International Development.. Columns may not add up due to rounding.

Abbreviations:

CSH: Child Survival and Health

DA: Development Assistance

ESF: Economic Support Fund

FMF: Foreign Military Financing

IMET: International Military Education and Training

INCLE: International Narcotics Control and Law Enforcement

NADR: Nonproliferation, Anti-Terrorism, Demining, and Related (mainly humanitarian demining assistance, but includes modest anti-terrorism assistance to be increased in FY2008)

TI: Transition Initiatives (temporary development programs for post-conflict states)

a. An amendment to the Consolidated Appropriations Act, 2008 (P.L. 110-161) halted FMF funding, the issuance of defense export licenses, and the transfer of military equipment or technology to Sri Lanka unless the Secretary of State certifies to Congress that the Colombo government has undertaken a series of actions related to human rights protection in Sri Lanka. The provision does not apply to assistance for maritime and air surveillance and communications.

b. P.L. 480 Title II (grants), Section 416(b) of the Agricultural Act of 1949, as amended (surplus donations), and Food for Progress. Food aid totals do not include freight costs.

In November 2007, the United States provided Sri Lanka with a radar-based maritime surveillance system and several advanced inflatable boats under Section 1206 of the National Defense Authorization. The Commander of the U.S. Pacific Command, Adm. Robert Willard, visited Sri Lanka in mid-January to meet with his naval counterparts there and review ongoing maritime cooperation. Adm. Willard noted for Sri Lankan officials that improvements in human rights protection could lead to enhanced U.S.-Sri Lanka cooperation.[71]

Geopolitical Context

Some see the West's ability to pressure the Sri Lankan government as limited due to China's growing involvement in the country.[72] It has been reported that China's aid to Sri Lanka has increased dramatically since 2005. In the view of some analysts and observers, China is seeking to gain influence with the Sri Lankan government as part of a "string of pearls" naval strategy to develop port access in the northern reaches of the Indian Ocean.[73] Indian defense planners are reportedly particularly concerned with Chinese efforts to develop ports in the region.[74] India is home to some 60 million Tamil people and it has raised concerns over the treatment of Tamils in Sri Lanka. China is reportedly investing significantly in the development of a port in Hambantota, Sri Lanka on the country's southeastern coast. China is also reportedly helping to develop port facilities in Gwadar, Pakistan; Chittagong, Bangladesh; and Sittwe, Burma.[75] Colombo was also reportedly upset with Western calls for a truce in the lead up to their defeat of the LTTE in May 2009. Rajapaksa stated "They are trying to preach to us about civilians. I tell them to go and see what they are doing in Iraq and Afghanistan."[76]

Human Rights Concerns

Internally Displaced Persons

Large numbers of people were displaced, and many of them were wounded, during the closing phase of the civil war in 2009. These people were added to others who were already displaced from their homes as a result of previous fighting. Providing these people with basic needs until they can be returned to their homes will likely be a large challenge for the government and one with which the international community could help. As fighting in the Sri Lanka's East and North intensified in 2006 and throughout 2007, several hundred thousand civilians were displaced from their homes. The great majority of these are Tamils and Muslims. One report had intense March 2007 battles in Batticaloa creating about 95,000 new internally displaced persons (IDPs) in just one week. Another report had fighting between government forces and the rebels forcing more than 20,000 Sri Lankans to flee their homes in the latter months of 2007.[77] International human rights groups urged all parties to the conflict to protect civilians and allow access by humanitarian aid agencies, which are often blocked from entering conflict zones.[78] The United Nations counts more than 300,000 people as having remained in a state of "protracted displacement" for two decades.[79]

Human rights abuses in Sri Lanka largely have been associated with ethnic conflict and civil war. In the summer of 2007, tens of thousands of Sri Lankans took to the streets of Colombo in antigovernment protests organized by the opposition UNP. The demonstrators called for new national elections, an end to rife corruption, and swift action against human rights violators.[80] Some analysts see occasional large-scale and apparently arbitrary Sri Lankan government detentions—including a December 2007 sweep in and near the capital during which more than 2,500 Tamils were rounded up and questioned for links to the LTTE—doing great damage to its credibility.[81] Nongovernmental Sri Lankan organizations regularly document the scope of the country's humanitarian crisis.[82]

International human rights groups have issued numerous reports echoing these concerns.[83] On the issue of religious freedom in Sri Lanka, the State Department reported in September 2007 that,

> The constitution accords Buddhism the "foremost place," but Buddhism is not recognized as the state religion. The constitution also provides for the right of members of other faiths to freely practice their religion. While the Government publicly endorses this right, in practice there were problems in some areas.[84]

Such perceived problems included proposed anti-conversion laws, and legal restrictions and sporadic attacks on Christian churches. The U.S. government found no change in the status of respect for religious freedom in Sri Lanka in 2007. With regard to human trafficking, the State Department's latest annual report (issued in June 2007) determined that Colombo "does not fully comply with the minimum standards for the elimination of trafficking; however, it is making significant efforts to do so," and it placed Sri Lanka on the "Tier 2 Watch List" for its "failure to provide evidence of increasing efforts to address trafficking over the previous year, especially in its efforts to punish trafficking for involuntary servitude."[85]

During his August 2007 visit to Sri Lanka, a top U.N. humanitarian official noted that dozens of aid agency staff had been reported killed on the island since January 2006, and he identified Sri Lanka as one of the most dangerous countries in the world for humanitarian workers. Colombo condemned the remarks, calling them a contribution to forces devoted to discrediting the Sri Lankan government.[86] The worst such attack in recent years involved the August 2006 murder of 17 local aid workers employed by a French nongovernmental organization operating near Trincomalee. Colombo vowed to pursue a full investigation of the massacre, but much suspicion fell upon government security forces themselves as being complicit, given that such an attack was seen to serve no tactical purpose for the Tigers. One year later, with no arrests made in the case and rights groups demanding swifter government action, a top Colombo official appeared to lay blame on the French NGO, itself, for sending its employees into a known combat zone.[87]

In August 2007, New York-based Human Rights Watch issued a sharp critique of Sri Lanka's worsening human rights situation, focusing particular attention on a "dramatic increase" in abuses by government forces since 2006 and on Colombo's alleged responsibility for "unlawful killings, enforced disappearances, and other serious human rights violations," most of them affecting members of the country's Tamil and Muslim minorities. The Sri Lankan government rejected most of the allegations as baseless and unsubstantiated, saying that its largely successful efforts to resolve issues such as disappearances and internal displacement had been ignored.[88] London-based Amnesty International has called on the U.N. Human Rights Council (UNHRC) to address a growing number of reported human rights violations by all parties to the conflict, including failures to protect civilians, attacks on journalists, and a "persistent climate of impunity" that it said required systematic monitoring and urgent investigations.[89]

Child Abductions

Over the course of Sri Lanka's decades-long civil war, thousands of children have been abducted and forcefully recruited as soldiers. The U.N. Children's Fund had confirmed more than 6,400 child abductions in Sri Lanka's North and East provinces as of early 2007, the great majority of these perpetrated by the LTTE.[90] The Karuna faction has come under especially harsh criticism for involvement in child abductions and forced recruitments. Elements of Sri Lankan military and police forces are accused of assisting in such abductions. Colombo has responded to criticisms from international human rights groups by flatly denying any government complicity or "willful blindness" toward forced recruitments.[91]

"Disappeared" Persons

As in many ethnic conflicts, Sri Lanka's civil war has led to the "disappearance" of many thousands of people. According to one report, more than 1,000 people are believed to have been "disappeared" during the year ending June 2007.[92] One nongovernmental report acknowledged severe abuses by the LTTE while also accusing the Colombo government of "using extra-judicial killings and enforced disappearances as part of a brutal counter-insurgency campaign" and predicted that such tactics would lead to "further embitterment of the Tamil population and a further cycle of war, terrorism, and repression."[93]

Annex One: Civil War Timeline

The Norwegian-brokered peace effort, which began in 1999, produced notable success after then-Prime Minister Wickremasinghe revived the process upon taking office in late 2001. A permanent ceasefire agreement (CFA) was reached in February 2002 and, despite incidents of alleged violations, was for several years generally observed by both sides. In addition, confidence-building measures called for under the ceasefire were implemented. A Sri Lanka Monitoring Mission (SLMM) comprised of members from Nordic countries was created to investigate reported violations of the CFA. In April 2002, LTTE leader Prabhakaran emerged from hiding for his first press conference in 12 years and made the unprecedented suggestion that the LTTE would be willing to settle for less than full Tamil independence. Five months later, Sri Lanka lifted its 1998 ban on the LTTE, a move which the Tigers had demanded as a pre-condition for peace talks. However, Buddhist clerics and their political party, the JHU, have staunchly and consistently opposed negotiating with the LTTE.[94]

Peace Talks Progress, 2002-2003

In September 2002, at a naval base in Thailand, the Colombo government and the LTTE held their first peace talks in seven years. The meeting, which resulted in an agreement to establish a joint task force for humanitarian and reconstruction activities, was deemed successful by both sides. On the third day, the LTTE announced that it would settle for "internal self-determination" and "substantial regional autonomy" for the Tamil population rather than full independence—a major shift in the rebels' position. A second round of talks brought another breakthrough when the two sides agreed on a framework for seeking foreign aid to rebuild the country (officials estimated that repairing the war-damaged infrastructure in the island's northeast could cost as much as $500 million).[95] A multilateral "donor conference" in Oslo in late November brought numerous pledges of external assistance, with the United States promising to "play its part" toward implementation of a peace plan.[96]

In what appeared to be yet another meaningful breakthrough, talks in the final month of 2002 ended with the issuance of a statement that "the parties have agreed to explore a solution founded on the principle of internal self-determination in the areas of historical habituation of the Tamil-speaking peoples, based on a federal structure within a united Sri Lanka."[97] This language marked a significant concession from both parties: the Colombo government for the first time accepted the idea of federalism and the rebels, in accepting a call for *internal* self-determination, appeared to have relinquished their decades-old pursuit of an independent Tamil state.

A fifth round of negotiations took place in Berlin in February 2003, but made no notable progress. Renewed armed conflict had the potential to disrupt the engagement: the meetings began only hours after three LTTE rebels incinerated themselves at sea when Norwegian truce monitors boarded their weapons-laden craft. Although an apparent violation of the ceasefire, the incident did not derail the peace process; it did, however, serve to erode international confidence, especially among potential donor nations. The United States called the Tigers' arms smuggling effort "highly destabilizing" and urged the LTTE to "commit itself fully to peace and desist from arms resupply efforts."[98]

Talks in Japan in March 2003 produced no major breakthroughs on political or human rights issues. A Japanese participant suggested that the promise of major external assistance—anticipated at some $3 billion over three years—is all that kept the disputing parties at the negotiating table.[99] As with earlier talks, violence again threatened to derail the process: On March 10, 2003, a Sri Lankan Navy vessel sank what the Colombo government described as an attacking Tiger boat, killing 11. The Tigers condemned the attack, claiming that their unarmed "merchant vessel" was not a threat. Norwegian truce monitors criticized both sides while refraining from ruling who was at fault.[100]

In the spring of 2003 the Colombo government said it was considering holding an island-wide non-binding referendum to endorse its current peace negotiations with Tamil rebels. A public opinion poll found that 84% of all Sri Lankans believed peace could be achieved through dialogue, including more than 95% of Tamils.[101] Yet the LTTE pulled out of the peace negotiations in April, just days before a seventh round of peace talks was set to begin in Thailand. The Tigers issued a statement protesting their exclusion from a scheduled June 2003 donor conference in Japan and expressing unhappiness with slow progress in efforts to improve the quality of life for the country's Tamil minority.[102]

In September 2003, Norway and Japan led an effort to revitalize the peace process and prevent its devolution back into further conflict. These initiatives followed a meeting of the Tigers with constitutional experts in Paris, a meeting that was part of the Tigers' effort to respond to a Sri Lankan government proposal for an interim administration in the northeast of Sri Lanka (a major concession by the government to Tiger demands which were a prerequisite for further talks).[103] For their part, the LTTE had previously made the key concession that it would settle for an autonomy agreement rather than its previous goal of a separate state. Despite such concessions by both sides, a peace agreement was not guaranteed. The LTTE indicated that it would once again seek secession and an independent state if substantial autonomy was not achieved through the negotiation process.[104]

The Colombo government was at that time split between a more conciliatory faction represented by President Chandrika Kumaratunga and a more hard line faction represented by the JVP. The UNP opposition was regarded as the major party most willing to negotiate with the LTTE in order to end the conflict. Many observers believed this was due to the fact that a large portion of UNP political support comes from Sri Lanka's business classes, whose success in turn depends on limiting the impact of uncertainty and instability which the conflict creates.

It was hoped that the LTTE would respond to the government's offer and rejoin peace negotiations by the end of September 2003. An earlier proposal for an interim administration was rejected by the LTTE. The government continued having difficulty making offers as some observers noted that a constitutionally viable solution would require the consent of the more hard line faction in the government led by the JVP, which was on record as opposed to further concessions to the LTTE.[105]

The international community made an effort to support the dialogue process by offering inducements for peace. The international donors conference held in Tokyo in June 2003 obtained aid pledges for Sri Lanka totaling $4.5 billion (nearly one-quarter of the package was pledged by Japan). Some 51 nations and 20 international institutions participated in the conference, though it was boycotted by the LTTE.[106] At the same time, the World Bank approved a loan of $125 million to assist Sri Lankan poverty reduction and reconstruction in the northeast, and to support the peace process.[107] Then-U.S. Deputy Secretary of State Armitage expressed support for the peace process at the Tokyo conference by asking the LTTE to end its boycott of the talks and offering $54 million in U.S. aid.[108] Yet both the government and the rebels remained intransigent in their positions, and the LTTE refused to rejoin Norwegian-sponsored peace negotiations.

Peace Process Stalemated, 2004-2005

Despite international inducements, the peace process remained deadlocked for more than two years, with the LTTE continuing to insist on interim self-rule in the Tamil northeast as the basis of resumption of negotiations. The government expressed a desire that the LTTE restate its willingness to explore a federal solution to the conflict, and Colombo also requested that discussion of an Interim Self Governing Authority (ISGA) be part of a comprehensive peace discussion and not a precondition of such negotiations. Moreover, divisions within both the government and the LTTE cast pervasive doubt on the eventual outcome of the peace talks.

The crisis continued beyond the April 2004 elections and was exacerbated in 2005 by a number of factors, including tensions between the SLFP and its JVP coalition partners over the privatization of the university educational system and the petroleum sector; the possibility of a joint government-LTTE distribution mechanism for foreign aid (to LTTE controlled areas) in response to the December 2004 Indian Ocean tsunami; and the prospect of a peace agreement that would grant greater autonomy to the Tamil-controlled North and East. The JVP strongly opposed each of these options and made numerous threats to withdraw from the United People's Freedom Alliance, a move that would deprive the ruling coalition of its parliamentary majority.[109]

Following the mid-2004 LTTE schism there were numerous instances of political and military operatives being killed by each side as they struggled for power in the East. The

LTTE accused Colonel Karuna and those loyal to him of cooperating with Sri Lankan Army (SLA) paramilitaries and special forces in raids and targeted killings of forces under their command, which the SLA denied. Karuna later withdrew to a fortified base in the jungles of eastern Sri Lanka where his forces were able to repel LTTE attacks.[110] During the first half of 2005 there were several reported instances of serious ceasefire violations. First was the February death of a high-level LTTE political officer, followed by an increase in targeted, politically-motivated killings throughout the eastern provinces.[111]

April 2005 saw a much-publicized incident when a Sea Tiger unit attacked a Sri Lankan Navy vessel carrying a peace monitor, slightly wounding him. This led to a formal censure of the LTTE by the ceasefire monitoring group, the Sri Lanka Monitoring Mission (SLMM), and marked a particularly brazen attack as the Sri Lankan Navy vessel was flying the SLMM flag to indicate that monitors were aboard.[112] By the middle of 2005, politically-motivated killings reportedly were taking one life per day and, following the LTTE's August 2005 assassination of Foreign Minister Lakshman Kadirgamar, an ethnic Tamil, Parliament passed a state of emergency regulation that has been renewed every month since.[113]

Civil War Resumes in 2006

The narrow November 2005 election victory of perceived hardliner President Rajapaksa led to a further escalation of violence between government security forces and LTTE cadres. One month later, a pro-LTTE Tamil National Alliance parliamentarian was assassinated inside a government high security zone in the eastern town of Batticaloa. In February 2006, Colombo and the LTTE voiced renewed commitment to the CFA and violence waned until April, when an explosion at a Sinhalese market in Trincomalee led to a limited backlash against Tamils. Shortly after, an LTTE suicide bomber attacked a major army compound in Colombo, killing eight soldiers and seriously wounding the army's top general. The government retaliated with air strikes on Tiger positions. In June 2006, an LTTE suicide bomber succeeded in killing the army's third highest-ranking general in a suburb of Colombo. Mutual animosities intensified.

A dramatic surge in violence in early August 2006 was sparked by a water dispute: the Sri Lankan military had moved to reopen a sluice gate in Tiger-controlled territory after negotiations failed to resolve the quarrel (in closing the gate, LTTE forces had cut water supplies to thousands of mostly Sinhalese farmers south of Trincomalee). Rather than employ a small force for the operation, the government launched large-scale airstrikes on nearby Tiger positions in tandem with a ground offensive. The LTTE's political wing called the attacks a "declaration of war."[114] The four Tokyo Donor countries (including the United States) issued a statement calling on both sides to immediately end hostilities and re-engage negotiations, but the LTTE said that Colombo's military operations made further talks impossible.

By the late summer of 2006, the Sri Lankan army was pressing a major offensive in the area around the Tiger stronghold of Trincomalee, the LTTE was declaring that the ceasefire appeared to have ended, and human rights groups were demanding that both sides allow humanitarian supplies to reach civilians who had been trapped in the crossfire and who were unable to obtain food and other basic commodities. Hundreds of thousands of these civilians were displaced by the fighting. Battles in August became so fierce that more than 800 rebels and security personnel were reported killed in one week alone. Under heavy air bombardment, the Tigers retreated from their positions near the strategic Trincomalee harbor in September, while their naval forces lost a series of fierce battles off the northern Jaffna Peninsula.[115] In displacing the Tigers from Trincomalee's environs, the government carried out the first major seizure of enemy territory by either side since the 2002 ceasefire.

In a now-weakened position, the LTTE changed course and agreed to engage in new and unconditional negotiations with Colombo. Some observers opined that, as in the past, dwindling financial resources were a primary motive for the government's decision to re-engage the peace process as called for by international aid providers.[116] A new round of talks was set for October 2006 in Oslo, Norway, even as the government's ongoing military offensives brought fierce battles in both the North and East. Possible overconfidence in the army ranks may have led to serious reversals during the course of the month as their units were repulsed around Jaffna at considerable cost.[117] The Tigers also retaliated with a series of suicide attacks, including a truck bombing that left 99 Sri Lankan sailors and civilians dead in the north-central city of Harbrane; and the detonation of "suicide boats" that left a sailor and 15 rebels dead near the Sri Lankan Navy Headquarters in Galle, a major tourist destination some 70 miles south of Colombo.

In the lead up to October peace talks, President Rajapaksa moved to establish a common negotiating position that would include the country's main opposition UNP. A resulting pact was widely hailed as a rare expression of political unity, especially in the country's Sinhala-dominated South.[118] However, and despite low expectations, the talks were a conclusive failure: The government rejected a key rebel demand to reopen the strategically vital A-9 highway that crosses LTTE-controlled territory leading to Jaffna, and the two sides failed even to agree on a timetable for future meetings. Renewed exchanges of artillery fire began hours after the talks adjourned.[119]

Fighting continued during the final months of 2006. LTTE leader Prabhakaran blamed President Rajapaksa for the conflict's resurgence and he called the CFA "defunct." The U.S. State Department expressed being "disturbed" by such claims, and it condemned the Tigers for "fueling violence and hostility," and urged both sides to honor the CFA and return to negotiation.[120] The LTTE disregarded the admonition and declared a renewed struggle for independence. Tiger cadres subsequently attempted to assassinate the defense secretary—who is also President Rajapaksa's brother—by bombing his motorcade, but he escaped unharmed.

Government Military Successes in 2007

Government forces took control of the LTTE's eastern stronghold of Vakarai in January 2007, resulting in up to 20,000 more internally displaced persons (another 15,000 Tamil civilians were described as being "trapped" by the fighting). From Colombo's perspective, the "liberation" of Vakarai saved these civilians from being used as "human shields" by the rebels.[121] Although the Norwegian government insisted that its effort to end the civil war had not failed—and the British government offered to play a greater role in the peace process, including a willingness to talk directly with the terrorist-designated LTTE—there developed a growing consensus among independent observers that full-scale civil war had returned to the island.

By March 2007, the government was claiming to have completely cleared LTTE forces from the island's east coast. Later that month, Tiger rebels launched an unprecedented air attack, using two crude planes to bomb an air force base adjacent to Colombo's main airport. Although damage reportedly was light, the ability of the Tigers to penetrate Sri Lankan air defenses and return safely to their base 250 miles away was a major embarrassment to the

Colombo government. Further Tiger air raids in April—one killing at least six soldiers at the main army base in Jaffna, another destroying fuel facilities in Colombo—spurred acute security concerns among commercial airline companies serving the island, and caused analysts to identify an even greater threat perception among residents of the southern provinces.[122]

The Tigers appeared to have been evicted from their last major bastion in the Eastern Province in July 2007 and the Colombo government claimed to be in full control of the region for the first time in 13 years. Following its military victories in the East, the government vowed to devote more than $50 million toward infrastructure programs designed to win hearts and minds in the region and to establish a credible civil administration there by holding local elections before 2008.[123] The LTTE responded to government declarations with threats to cripple the country's economy with attacks on military and economic targets. The Rajapaksa government asserted openness to resuming negotiations with the rebels even as it pressed ahead with military operations in the North.

An October 2007 attack by 21 rebel "suicide commandos" caused serious damage to the Anuradhapura air force base in the Northwest province and was a major embarrassment for government and military officials. Eight Sri Lanka air force planes were reported destroyed, including an expensive surveillance platform. Fourteen soldiers died battling the rebel force. Retaliatory government air strikes on LTTE training camps reportedly killed dozens of rebels in the country's north. Still, the Anuradhapura attack was viewed as a stunning short-term psychological victory for the rebels which served to boost their morale following debilitating military losses of the previous summer.[124]

Colombo was not deterred, however, and pressed ahead with offensive military operations. Among those killed in November 2007 government airstrikes was S.P. Tamilselvan, the leader of the Tigers' political wing widely believed to be Prabhakaran's topmost deputy. This was followed by the violent death of the purported chief of the Tigers' intelligence wing, alias "Colonel Charles," in a January 2008 government military ambush on his vehicle at the island's far northern tip. Some observers view these apparent targeted killings as further evidence of a new government intent to decisively defeat the rebels through use of force.[125] Sri Lankan military officials claim that their operations in the latter months of 2007 destroyed about half of the Tigers' forces and that the "remaining 3,000" were in complete disarray and near to final defeat.[126]

During a March 2007 visit to Washington, Sri Lankan Foreign Minister Rohitha Bogollagama told Secretary of State Condoleezza Rice that Colombo was committed to a negotiated solution to the conflict and to constitutional reforms that would enable an enduring settlement and address the "concerns of the minorities."[127] President Rajapaksa himself repeatedly insisted that military operations were aimed only at combating terrorism. His government claimed to seek only a "negotiated and sustainable" settlement through the All Party Representative Committee. Yet, in late December 2007, the Sri Lankan president reportedly stated that military victories "will surely pave the way to push the LTTE to seek a political solution to the problem."[128]

Faced with a choice between scaling back army operations and resuming peace negotiations or pressing ahead with military offensives, President Rajapaksa appears to have concluded the Tigers could be decisively defeated on the battlefield. The risk of alienating key hard-line coalition supporters likely played a central role in this calculation.[129] Thus, despite heavy material and political costs—including the alienation of more negotiation-minded political allies, severe economic damage, cuts in foreign aid, and censure from foreign governments and international human rights groups—Rajapaksa decided to pursue an all-out effort to defeat the LTTE by use of force.[130]

Increased strife has been costly for Sri Lanka on the world stage. In May 2007, the British government cited human rights concerns in suspending about $3 million in debt relief aid to Colombo. In the same month, a U.S. official cited like concerns in explaining why Millennium Challenge Corporation (MCC) funding has not been forthcoming, saying the island's security circumstances continued to preclude finalizing a compact under that program (Sri Lanka subsequently was "deselected" for MCC eligibility). The United States and other international donors suspended aid or withheld new commitments for similar reasons in 2007. President Rajapaksa has responded with defiance, saying his country is not dependent on foreign aid and can go it alone, if necessary. Defense Secretary Gotabaya Rajapaksa, the president's brother, has decried the "international bullying" on human rights.[131]

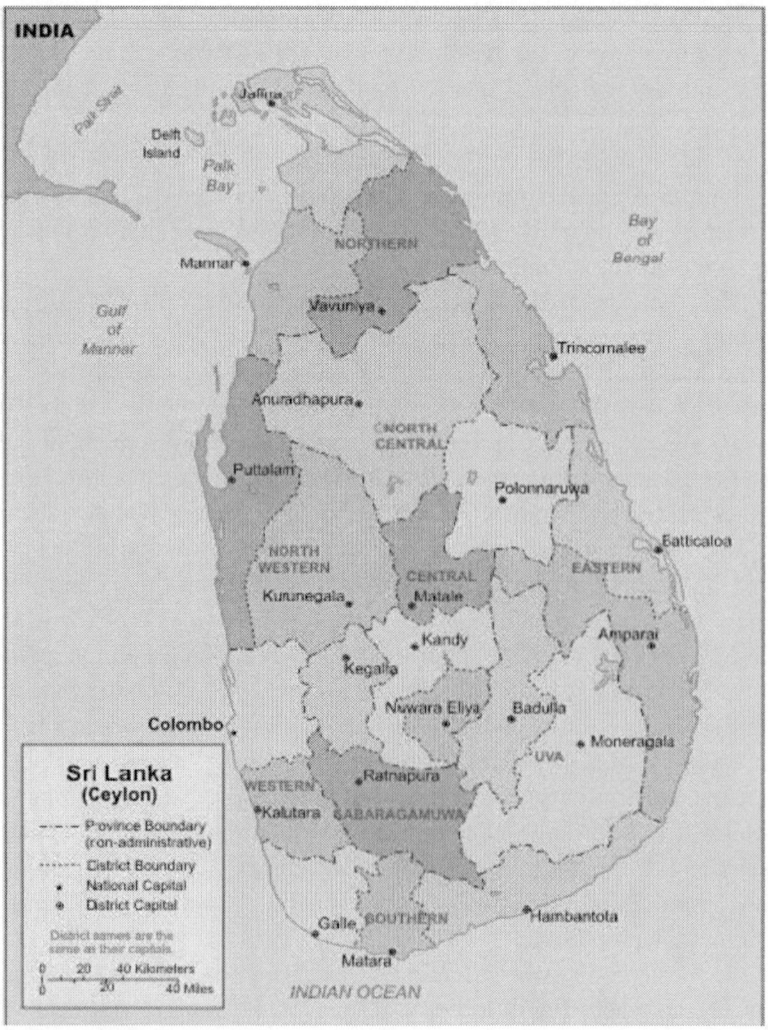

Source: Map Resources. Adapted by CRS.

Figure 1. Map of Sri Lanka

End Notes

[1] "Statement by Ambassador Susan Rice, U.S. Permanent Representative to the United Nations," *Federal News Service,* April 30, 2009.
[2] "Statement by the President on the Situation in Sri Lanka," Office of the Press Secretary, The White House, May 13, 2009.
[3] Krishan Francis, "Hundreds are Killed in Sri Lanka Attack," *The Washington Post,* May 11, 2009.
[4] Ravi Nessman, "Doctor Says 49 Killed in Sri Lanka Hospital Attack," *Associated Press*, May 12, 2009
[5] "50 Die in Attack on Sri Lankan War Zone Hospital," *Associated Press,* May 13, 2009.
[6] "Sri Lanka: Country Report," The Economist Intelligence Unit, April, 2009.
[7] Gerard Aziakou, "UN Chief to Visit Sri Lanka Conflict Zone," *Agence France Presse*, May 22, 2009.
[8] "Call for an End to Hostilities in Sri Lanka," Office of the Spokesman, U.S. Department of State, April 16, 2009. http://srilanka.usembassy.gov.
[9] "State Department Conducts Daily Press Briefing," *US Fed News,* April 23, 2009.
[10] "Statement of the Tokyo Co-Chairs," US Embassy Colombo, February 4, 2009. http://www.usembasssyblogspot.com
[11] "US Urges Tamil Tigers to Surrender, Aid for Sri Lankan Refugees," *Voice of America,* April 25, 2009.
[12] "Talks Still on with Sri Lanka on Bailout Package," *Agence France Presse*, May 1, 2009.
[13] "Sri Lanka: Program Overview," State Department, Congressional Budget Justification Document, 2008.
[14] "Support Humanitarian Relief and a Political Settlement in Sri Lanka," Hon. James Moran, Member of Congress, March 6, 2009. "US Congress Letter to Secretary of State Hillary Clinton," Ilankai Tamil Sangam, March 11, 2009.
[15] "Sri Lanka's Ambassador to U.S. Briefs United States Congressmen," *Colombo Times*, April 28, 2009.
[16] "Kerry, Lugar, Brown, Brownback, Leahy Mark the End to Sri Lanka's Civil War," United States Senate Committee on Foreign Relations, May 19, 2009.
[17] U.S. Department of State, "Background Notes: Sri Lanka," November 2007, at http://www.state.gov/r/pa/ei/bgn/5249.htm.
[18] David Rampton and Asanga Weilikala, "The Politics of the South," Asia Foundation Sri Lanka Strategic Conflict Assessment 2005 Series, 2005, at http://www.asiafoundation.org/pdf/SL_Politics_of_the_South.pdf.
[19] See http://www.peaceinsrilanka.org.
[20] "New Sri Lanka Premier Sworn In Pledging Peace," *Reuters*, December 9, 2001.
[21] "Woman Behind Sri Lanka's Turmoil," *Christian Science Monitor*, November 7, 2003.
[22] See http://ec.europa.eu/external_relations/human_rights/eu_electionfinal_%20report04.pdf.
[23] Adam Ereli, "Sri Lanka - Presidential Election," State Department Press Statement, November 18, 2005.
[24] Chandra de Silva, "Sri Lanka in 2005," *Asian Survey* 46, 1, January 2006, p. 116.
[25] "S. Lanka Parties in Unity Pact Ahead of Peace Talks," *Reuters*, October 23, 2006.
[26] "Buddhist Nationalism Behind Sri Lanka's Violent Surge," *Christian Science Monitor*, June 18, 2007.
[27] "Ban LTTE, End Truce," *Daily News* (Colombo), December 29, 2007.
[28] "JVP Won't Support Govt Ouster,"*Daily News* (Colombo), August 31, 2007.
[29] See "Colonel's Control," *Outlook* (Delhi), March 27, 2007.
[30] "Tamil Warlord Entered UK on Forged Passport," *Guardian* (London), December 21, 2007.
[31] See http://www.state.gov/p/sca/rls/rm/2007/84701.htm.
[32] "Executive Summary: Sri Lanka," *Jane's Sentinel Security Assessment - South Asia*, April 26, 2007; "Armed Forces: Sri Lanka," *Jane's Sentinel Security Assessment - South Asia*, July 25, 2007.
[33] *The Military Balance 2007* (Institute for International and Strategic Studies, London, 2007).
[34] "Kumaratunga's Dilemma on Joint Mechanism," *Asian Tribune*, April 23, 2005.
[35] See CRS Report RL30613, *North Korea: Terrorism List Removal*, by Larry A. Niksch.
[36] "Expert Criticizes Canada for Not Banning LTTE," *Island* (Colombo), September 15, 2003; Human Rights Watch, "Tamil Tigers Extort Diaspora for 'Final War' Funds," March 15, 2006; "Feeding the Tiger," *Jane's Intelligence Review*, September 1, 2007; "LTTE Crippled Financially, Fund Raising Activities on Decline," *Press Trust of India*, October 22, 2007; "Sri Lanka rebel Arms - Buying Goes Global," *Associated Press*, November 5, 2007.
[37] "Taming the Tamil Tigers," January 10, 2008, at http://www.fbi.gov/page2/jan08/tamil_tigers011008.html.
[38] Cited in "Suicide Bombing Masters: Sri Lankan Rebels," *New York Times*, January 14, 2003.
[39] "Durable Political Solution Key to Development in Post-Conflict Sri Lanka-Ban," *States News Service*, May 24, 2009.
[40] Gerard Aziakou, "UN Chief Visits Conflict Zone," *Mail & Guardian*, May 23, 2009.
[41] "Durable Political Solution Key to Development in Post-Conflict Sri Lanka-Ban," *States News Service*, May 24, 2009.
[42] "Inquiry into Alleged Abuses Crucial for Sri Lanka's Recovery – UN Rights Chief," *States News Service*, May 26, 2009.

[43] "Sri Lanka: UN Rights Council Fails Victims: Member States Ignore Need for Inquiry into Wartime Violations," *Human Rights Watch*, May 27, 2009.

[44] See also CRS Report RL32715, *Indian Ocean Earthquake and Tsunami: Humanitarian Assistance and Relief Operations*, by Rhoda Margesson et al.

[45] Chandra de Silva, "Sri Lanka in 2005," *Asian Survey* 46, 1, January 2006, p. 116.

[46] "Sri Lanka: Railroad Line Closed by Tsunami Reopened" *Associated Press*, February 21, 2005.

[47] "Bush Sends Condolences to Asia, Offers Aid," *Associated Press*, December 27, 2004.

[48] See http://www.usaid.gov/press/releases/2008/pr080118.html.

[49] Jonathan Goodhand and Bart Klem, "Aid, Conflict, and Peacebuilding in Sri Lanka 2000-2005," Asia Foundation Sri Lanka Strategic Conflict Assessment 2005 Series, 2005, at http://www.asiafoundation.org/pdf/full_sr_report.pdf.

[50] "Sri Lanka Country Report," *The Economist Intelligence* Unit, May 2009.

[51] Claire Innes, ""Key Interest Rate Cut to Two-Year Low in Sri Lanka," *Global Insight*, May 21, 2009.

[52] Claire Innes, "U.S. Rules Out IMF Loan Programme for Sri Lanka as Humanitarian Crisis Deepens," *Global Insight*, May 15, 2009.

[53] "Sri Lanka Shares Up 2.5% on UN Resolution," *Reuters*, May 28, 2009.

[54] See http://siteresources.worldbank.org/SRILANKAEXTN/Resources/SLDFReport2007Final.pdf.

[55] "Sri Lanka: Executive Summary," Global Insight, May 14, 2003; "Sri Lanka Development Hostage to War, Say Donors," *Reuters*, January 29, 2007.

[56] "Statement on Continuing Conflict in Sri Lanka," Office of the Press Secretary, The White House, April 24, 2009.

[57] "State Department Daily Press Briefing," State Department Press Release, May 21, 2009.

[58] See http://www.state.gov/p/sca/rls/rm/2007/84701.htm.

[59] Statement of Steven Mann, Principal Deputy Assistant Secretary of State for South and Central Asian Affairs, August 1, 2007, at http://www.internationalrelations.house.gov/110/man080107.htm.

[60] See the FTO list at http://www.state.gov/s/ct/rls/crt/2006/82738.htm.

[61] "Transcript: Armitage Says U.S., Other Nations Have Role in Ending Sri Lankan Conflict," U.S. Department of State *Washington File*, February 14, 2003.

[62] "U.S. Seeks to Allay Sri Lanka Fears on Rebel Ban," *Reuters*, April 19, 2002; "Smiles That Conceal the Worries - Sri Lanka's Civil War," *Economist* (London), July 20, 2002.

[63] "Trade and Investment Framework Agreement Between the U.S. and Sri Lanka," at http://www.slembassyusa.org / investment/tifa.html.

[64] Richard Boucher, "Remarks to the American Chamber of Commerce Colombo, Sri Lanka," U.S. Department of State, June 1, 2006.

[65] "Sri Lanka: Program Overview," State Department, Congressional Budget Justification Document, 2008.

[66] Bureau for Democracy, Conflict, and Humanitarian Assistance (DCHA), Office of U.S. Foreign Disaster Assistance (OFDA), U.S. Agency for International Development, Fact Sheet #4, FY 2009, April 10, 2009.

[67] "Sri Lankan Ambassador to U.S. Briefs U.S. Congressmen," *Colombo Times,* April 28, 2009.

[68] See http://www.state.gov/documents/organization/60655.pdf.

[69] See annual Congressional Budget Justifications at http://www.state.gov/s/d/rm/rls/cbj.

[70] "U.S. & Sri Lanka Sign Mutual Services Pact," U.S. Embassy Colombo Press Release, March 5, 2007; "Sri Lanka: Development and Domestic Prosperity," March 9, 2007, at http://www.state.gov/p /sca/rls/rm/2007/82035.htm.

[71] See http://srilanka.usembassy.gov.

[72] Sujan Dutta, "USA, India Engaging with Sri LankaAmid Growing China Role," *BBC News*, March 11, 2009.

[73] Michael Richardson, "Full Steam Ahead for Naval Might," *The Straits Times*, January 15, 2009.

[74] India and China continue to have unresolved border disputes that date back to their 1962 border war, and broader rivalries over influence in the region.

[75] "Chinese Billions Helping Lanka Ward Off Western Peace Efforts," *Asian News International*, May 2, 2009.

[76] Nicolas Revise, "Bitter With West, Sri Lanka Turns East for Cash and Support," *Agence France Presse*, May 3, 2009.

[77] "UN Warns of Sri Lanka Food Crisis," *BBC News*, March 20, 2007; http://hrw.org/english/docs/2007/12/07/slanka17509.htm. At the end of 2007, the United Nations reported that most of the more than 200,000 refugees from spring fighting around Batticaloa had been able to return to their homes.

[78] See, for example, an Amnesty International press release at http://web.amnesty.org/library/print/ENGASA370092007.

[79] UNHCR press release at http://www.unhcr.org/news/NEWS/469789cd4.html.

[80] "Thousands Protest in Sri Lanka," *Associated Press*, July 26, 2007.

[81] See, for example, B. Muralidhar Reddy, "Colombo Crackdown," *Frontline* (Chennai), January 4, 2008.

[82] See, for example, Center for Policy Alternatives, "Policy Brief on Humanitarian Issues," December 2007, at http://www.cpalanka.org/Policy_Brief/Brief_on_Humanitarian_Issues.pdf.

[83] See http://www.amnesty.org/en/region/asia-and-pacific/south-asia/sri-lanka and http://hrw.org/englishwr2k7/ docs/ 2007/01/11/slanka14837.htm.
[84] See http://www.state.gov/g/drl/rls/irf/2006/71444.htm.
[85] See http://www.state.gov/g/tip/rls/tiprpt/2007/82807.htm.
[86] "Sri Lanka Anger at UN Aid Claims," *BBC News*, August 10, 2007.
[87] "Sri Lanka Slides Back Into Civil War," *Jane's Terrorism and Security Monitor*, January 17, 2007; "Sri Lanka Blames Aid Group in Killings," *Reuters*, August 13, 2007.
[88] Human Rights Watch, "Return to War: Human rights Under Siege," August 6, 2007, at http://hrw.org/reports/2007/ srilanka0807; "HRW Report Based On Unsubstantiated, Outdated Information," *Daily News* (Colombo), August 8, 2007.
[89] Amnesty International Public Statement, September 4, 2007.
[90] See http://www.unicef.org/infobycountry/files/Sri_Lanka_DU_7Mar07.pdf.
[91] Human Rights Watch press releases at http://hrw.org/english/docs/2006/11/28/slanka14678.htm and http://hrw.org/ english/docs/2007/01/24/slanka15141.htm. "HRW Allegations Baseless - Peace Secretariat," *Daily News* (Colombo), January 27, 2007.
[92] Amnesty International press release at http://web.amnesty.org/library/print/ENGASA370132007.
[93] International Crisis Group, "Sri Lanka's Human Rights Crisis," June 14, 2007, at http://www.crisisgroup.org/ home/ index.cfm?id=4896.
[94] "Sri Lanka Lifts Ban on Tigers Ahead of Thai Talks," *Agence France Presse*, September 4, 2002.
[95] "Sri Lankans in Reconstruction Talks," *BBC News*, November 18, 2002. Large numbers of Tamil refugees began returning to the war-torn region after the 2002 ceasefire ("100,000 Refugees Return to Sri Lanka," *Associated Press*, September 20, 2002).
[96] "Transcript: U.S. Prepared to 'Play Its Part' to Further Peace in Sri Lanka," U.S. Department of State Washington File, November 25, 2002.
[97] "Sri Lanka to Explore a New Government," *New York Times*, December 6, 2002.
[98] "Sri Lankan Peace Talks Start in Berlin," *Reuters*, February 7, 2003; "Suicide Bomb Blunts Sri Lanka's Peace Momentum," *Agence France Presse*, February 10, 2003; "U.S. Criticizes Tamil Tiger Smuggling," *BBC News*, February 12, 2003.
[99] "Sri Lanka Negotiators Leave Japan With Little Progress, But Cash Hopes Alive," *Agence France Presse*, March 22, 2003.
[100] "Sri Lanka Monitors Chide Both Sides Over Sea Clash," *Reuters*, March 17, 2003.
[101] "Sri Lanka Ponders Peace Vote," *BBC News*, April 4, 2003; "Overwhelming Support for Peace Talks - Poll," *Daily News* (Colombo), March 24, 2003.
[102] "Sri Lanka's Tamil Tigers Pull Out of Peace Talks," *Reuters*, April 23, 2003.
[103] "Norway to Make Fresh Bid to Revive Sri Lanka Peace Process," *Agence France Presse*, September 3, 2003.
[104] "Sri Lanka to Explore a New Government," *New York Times*, December 6, 2003.
[105] "Sri Lanka Peace," Voice of America Federal News Dispatch, June 20, 2003.
[106] See the Tokyo Conference Declaration at http://www.mofa.go.jp/region/asia-paci/srilanka/conf0306/ declaration.html.
[107] "World Bank Gives $125 Million," *Agence France Presse*, June 18, 2003.
[108] "U.S. Asks Tamil Tigers to Resume Talks with Sri Lankan Government," *BBC Monitoring South Asia*, June 13, 2003.
[109] "JVP Threatens to Bring Down Lanka Govt. Over LTTE Tsunami Deal," *Hindu* (Chennai), April 20, 2005.
[110] Press Trust of India, March 21, 2005.
[111] "Batticaloa LTTE Leader Killed," *Hindu* (Chennai),February 7, 2005.
[112] "Tamil Tiger 'Breached Ceasefire,'" *BBC News*, April 8, 2005.
[113] "Sri Lanka: Political Killings Escalate," Human Rights Watch, August 16, 2005.
[114] "Strategic Questions in Sri Lanka," *BBC News*, August 4, 2006.
[115] "Fighting Escalates in Northern Sri Lanka," *Associated Press*, August 17, 2006; "Sri Lanka Battles a Weakened Tamil Tigers," *Christian Science Monitor*, September 5, 2006.
[116] "Lack of Cash Pushes Sri Lanka to Peace Talks: Analysts," *Agence France Presse*, September 13, 2006.
[117] "Tigers Strike Back," *Outlook* (Delhi), October 14, 2006; "Sri Lanka Clashes Kill 129 Troops," *BBC News*, October 12, 2006.
[118] "S. Lanka Parties in Unity Pact Ahead of Peace Talks," *Reuters*, October 23, 2006.
[119] "Heavy Shelling In North Sri Lanka After Talks Fail," *Reuters*, October 30, 2006.
[120] Daily Press Briefing, November 28, 2006.
[121] "Sri Lanka Says Captures Tiger Lines, Kills 30 Rebels," *Reuters*, January 16, 2007; "Forces Liberate Vakarai Civilians," *Daily News* (Colombo), January 20, 2007.
[122] "Sri Lankan Separatists Take Fight to the Air," *Christian Science Monitor*, March 28, 2007; "Airlines Cancel Sri Lanka Flights," *BBC News*, April 30, 2007.
[123] "With Tanks, Jets, Sri Lanka Fetes Fall of Rebel East," *Reuters*, July 19, 2007.

[124] "Sri Lanka Rebel Attack Further Detailed,"*Associated Press*, October 24, 2007; "Despair in the Air," *Frontline* (Chennai), November 3, 2007.
[125] See, for example, Ajai Sahni, "Shattered Haven," *Outlook* (Delhi), November 8, 2007.
[126] "Sri Lanka Army Chief Says Rebel Force Halved, Bases Surrounded," *Daily News* (Colombo), December 31, 2007.
[127] See Embassy of Sri Lanka Press Release, March 16, 2007, at http://www.slembassyusa.org/press_releases/spring_2007/fm_says_sl_16mar07.html.
[128] "Negotiated End to Conflict Govt's Aim," *Daily News* (Colombo), September 27, 2007; "Sri Lanka Open to 'Negotiated' Solution to Conflict," *Agence France Presse*, October 13, 2007; "Military Victories Will Pave the Way to Political Solution - President," *Daily News* (Colombo), December 27, 2007.
[129] "Sri Lanka's President Poised Between War and Peace," *Financial Times* (London), January 9, 2007.
[130] "Back to the Gun," *India Today* (Delhi), May 28, 2007.
[131] "Sri Lanka President Shuns Aid Suspension by UK, US," *Reuters*, May 16, 2007; "Aid Weapon Used Against Sri Lanka," *Financial Times* (London), May 22, 2007; "Sri Lanka Accuses 'Bullying' West," *BBC News*, June 12, 2007.

In: Asian Economic and Political Issues, Volume 14 ISBN: 978-1-61728-019-1
Editor: David A. Marek

Chapter 5

TAIWAN'S POLITICAL STATUS: HISTORICAL BACKGROUND AND ONGOING IMPLICATIONS*

Kerry Dumbaugh

SUMMARY

In 1979, official U.S. relations with Taiwan (the Republic of China) became a casualty of the American decision to recognize the government of the People's Republic of China (PRC) as China's sole legitimate government. Since then, U.S. unofficial relations with Taiwan have been built on the framework of the Taiwan Relations Act (P.L. 96-8) and shaped by three U.S.-China communiqués. Under these agreements, the United States maintains its official relations with the PRC while selling Taiwan military weapons and having extensive economic, political, and security interests there. But developments in both the PRC and Taiwan political systems mean U.S. officials continually are facing new policy choices. These developments include ongoing transformations in both Taiwan's and the PRC's political systems, economic and trade cycles and, in 2008, a renewal of the long-stalled contacts, talks, and agreements between the two sides. This chapter, intended as a background overview, briefly summarizes U.S. political history with Taiwan and discusses the complications it has for current U.S. policy and for congressional actions. For analysis of current developments in Taiwan and their implications for U.S. policy, see CRS Report R40493, *Taiwan-U.S. Relations: Developments and Policy Implications*, by Kerry Dumbaugh.

FROM THE MAINLAND TO TAIWAN

With the victory of Mao Tse-tung and his Communist Party military forces on mainland China in 1949, the remnants of the government of America's former World War II ally, the

* This is an edited, reformatted and augmented version of a CRS Report for Congress publication, Report #RS22388, dated June 4, 2009.

Republic of China (ROC) led by Generalissimo Chiang Kai-shek, fled to the island of Taiwan off the south China coast. For the next thirty years, both regimes claimed legitimacy as the sole legal government of the Chinese people. In Beijing on October 1, 1949, a victorious Mao proclaimed the creation of the People's Republic of China (PRC). Meanwhile, Chiang Kai-shek established a temporary capital for his government in Taipei, Taiwan, declaring the ROC still to be the legitimate Chinese government-in-exile and vowing that one day he would "retake the mainland" and drive out communist forces.[1]

The United States initially appeared reluctant to support the ROC's claim of legitimacy, and there is evidence that President Harry Truman was prepared to abandon Chiang's government on Taiwan and deal with Mao's PRC regime.[2] But that U.S. position quickly evaporated with North Korea's surprise invasion of South Korea on June 25, 1950. Within a week, President Truman ordered U.S. air, naval, and ground forces to go to South Korea's aid and ordered the U.S. 7th fleet to prevent any attack on Taiwan, saying that "determination of the future status of Formosa [the island's designation as a Japanese colony] must await the restoration of security in the Pacific ..."[3] U.S. support for the ROC was solidified when Chinese Communist forces entered the Korean War in support of North Korea in October-November 1950. As a result, in April 1951, the United States resumed direct military assistance to the ROC government on Taiwan, and in 1954 the United States and Chiang's government signed the U.S.-ROC Mutual Defense Treaty, making the two governments allies once again. This remained the situation for three decades: Taiwan and China remained officially at war; the United States continued to support the ROC claim as the legitimate government of all China, refused to recognize the legitimacy of the PRC, and maintained a defense alliance with the ROC government on Taiwan; and for much of this time, the ROC government continued to represent China in the United Nations and other international organizations.[4]

OFFICIAL U.S. RECOGNITION OF PRC IN 1979

In the 1950s and 1960s, the U.S.-ROC Mutual Defense Treaty allowed U.S. forces to use Taiwan as a forward base against Sino-Soviet communism in Asia. But after President Nixon's diplomatic opening to Beijing in 1971-72 and the major pullback of U.S. forces in Asia under the guidelines of the "Nixon doctrine," U.S. officials began to view Beijing more as a strategic asset against the Soviet Union than as an adversary to be confronted in the Taiwan Strait.[5] The Nixon overtures resulted in the so-called "Shanghai Communiqué" of 1972 (the first of three U.S.-China communiqués) which set the stage for the reversal of U.S. post-WWII China policy.

Official U.S. recognition of PRC legitimacy did not come until 1979, after the Carter Administration made a surprise announcement on December 15, 1978, that the United States would sever official relations with the ROC government on Taiwan and recognize the PRC government in Beijing on January 1 of the new year.[6] In the Joint Communiqué on Establishing Diplomatic Relations that announced the change, the United States *acknowledged* (an important distinction in future debate on the U.S. "one-China" policy) that both the PRC and ROC governments claimed there was only one China and that Taiwan was a province of it.[7] As part of the process of recognizing the PRC government, U.S. officials also notified the ROC government (Taiwan) that the United States intended to terminate, effective January 1, 1980, its military obligations toward Taiwan under the 1954 U.S.-ROC Mutual Defense Treaty. In a unilateral statement released on December 16, 1978, the United States declared that it "continues to have an interest in the peaceful resolution of the Taiwan issue and expects that the Taiwan issue will be settled peacefully by the Chinese themselves."[8]

In an important historical side-note, President Carter's unilateral decision to terminate the U.S.-ROC Mutual Defense Treaty in accordance with the treaty's terms (which permitted either party to terminate it with one year's notice) resulted in a landmark lawsuit over congressional constitutional prerogatives that went all the way to the Supreme Court. The suit, brought by Senator Barry Goldwater, alleged that the Senate's constitutional role in approving treaties required President Carter to consult the Senate before ending a treaty. (The constitution is silent on how U.S. treaties can be terminated.) After decisions and reversals in Federal District Court, the District of Columbia Court of Appeals in 1979 issued a ruling which among other things stated that the President did not have to seek congressional approval before ending the U.S.-ROC Mutual Defense Treaty. Senator Goldwater appealed to the U.S. Supreme Court, which on December 13, 1979, denied his appeal, leaving the appellate court's ruling standing.

The Taiwan Relations Act (P.L. 96-8)

While the record shows that the 96th Congress in 1979 clearly concurred with the strategic imperative of normalizing relations with the PRC, many Members were unhappy with what they saw as the Carter Administration's minimal proposals for continued dealings with the ROC government on Taiwan. In particular, some were concerned that the package of legislation the White House submitted to Congress to govern future unofficial relations with Taiwan—the "Taiwan Enabling Act"—did not go far enough in protecting either Taiwan or U.S. interests. Congressional debate on the legislation in 1979 was extensive and complicated. The end result was passage of a much amended version of the Administration's proposal—the Taiwan Relations Act (TRA—P.L. 96-8)—which remains the domestic legal authority for conducting unofficial U.S. relations with Taiwan today.[9] Much of the TRA deals with the logistics of U.S.-Taiwan relations: the establishment of the American Institute in Taiwan (AIT) as the unofficial U.S. representative for diplomatic interactions with Taiwan, including details about its staffing, functions, and funding.[10] Of particular relevance for long-term U.S. policy are Section 2 (b) and Section 3 of the TRA, dealing with U.S. strategic interests in and arms sales commitments to Taiwan; and Section 4, allowing for the continued application of existing U.S. laws and treaties with Taiwan in the absence of official diplomatic ties.

Infrastructure of U.S.-Taiwan Relations under the TRA

The dissolution of U.S. diplomatic relations with Taiwan placed Taiwan into a unique legal no-man's land that the TRA was designed to redress. One set of considerations involved how Taiwan – essentially rendered a legal "non-state" by the severing of relations – was to be treated under U.S. law after 1978. Many of these issues are addressed in Section 4 of the

TRA, which specifies that in matters of U.S. law, Taiwan is to be treated in a manner consistent with the way that "foreign countries, nations, states, governments, or similar entities" are treated, irrespective of other provisions in U.S. law concerning the requirements of maintaining diplomatic relations. The TRA specifically includes in this treatment the maintenance of all treaties (agreements between sovereign states); the continuation of "the ownership of or other rights or interests in properties, tangible and intangible, and other things of value" owned by the governing authorities on Taiwan prior to December 31, 1978; immigration laws; and the capacity of Taiwan to sue and be sued in U.S. courts.

In another key issue, the severing of diplomatic relations with Taiwan left both the Taiwan and U.S. governments with no practicable official way of managing programs, transactions, financial arrangements, consular services, or other relations with each other. Sections 6 through 9 of the TRA, then, established a non-profit, tax-exempt corporation separate from the U.S. government – the American Institute in Taiwan (AIT) – to handle those issues with Taiwan that would have been conducted by U.S. government authorities such as the State Department if diplomatic relations existed. The AIT is funded through an annual U.S. government appropriation and has offices in Taiwan (in Taipei and Kaohsiung) as well as in Washington, DC (headquartered in Arlington, Virginia). In providing for staffing for the AIT, Section 11 of the TRA states that U.S. government officers or employees may separate from the U.S. government in order to take a position with AIT. Upon completion of their service with AIT, such U.S. government employees are entitled to return to comparable positions in the U.S. government with no loss of "attendant rights, privileges, and benefits ... "[11] The title of the head of the U.S. AIT is "Director."

The TRA provided for a comparable "Taiwan Instrumentality" in Section 10, authorizing the President to extend similar privileges and immunities to Taiwan officers of this instrumentality as Taiwan extended to AIT officials. Originally established as the Coordination Council for North American Affairs, (or CCNAA), the Taiwan office in Washington, DC, has been known as the Taipei Economic and Cultural Representative's Office (TECRO) since 1994. In addition, TECRO oversees twelve other offices throughout the United States, known as Taiwan Economic and Cultural Offices (TECO); these are in Atlanta, Boston, Chicago, Guam, Honolulu, Houston, Kansas City, Los Angeles, Miami, New York, San Francisco, and Seattle. The title of the head of TECRO is "Representative." AIT and TECRO officials operate on behalf of their governments in dealing with each other's governments.

U.S. Arms Sales Commitments to Taiwan

Although it is a common American misperception that the TRA mandates the United States to defend Taiwan in case of attack, nothing in the TRA specifically obligates the United States to come to Taiwan's defense or to resort to military conflict on Taiwan's behalf. Section 2 of the TRA speaks in broad terms about U.S. interests in peaceful resolution to the Taiwan question, saying that any forceful resolution would be of "grave concern to the United States," and further states that U.S. policy is to "maintain the capacity of the United States to resist ... coercion" in addressing the Taiwan issue. Section 3 provides for the sale of U.S. defense articles and services to Taiwan, but it is non-specific about the nature of these articles. It merely calls for "such defense articles and services ... as may be necessary to enable Taiwan to maintain a sufficient self-defense capability." Section 3 gives Congress a role in determining what needs Taiwan may have.

Much of the U.S. debate on Taiwan arms sales since the TRA was enacted has involved differing judgments—often between Congress and the White House—about what should be the capabilities and quantities of the "necessary" articles and services provided for in Section 3 of the TRA.[12] A more recent U.S. debate has evolved since 2001, after Taiwan itself began to appear increasingly hesitant (for domestic political reasons) to invest in some of the weapons systems that the United States offered for sale under the TRA. This latter development – undoubtedly unforeseen at the time of the TRA's enactment– raises potentially consequential questions for Congress about how, or even if, the United States can honor its commitments under Section 3 of the TRA if Taiwan seems unwilling to participate meaningfully in expanding or at least in maintaining its own self-defense capacity, particularly in the face of significant and ongoing military improvements in the PRC.[13]

Strategic Ambiguity

After normalization of Sino-U.S. relations and the severing of the U.S.-ROC military alliance, the PRC was largely satisfied with U.S. "one-China" formulations alluding to Taiwan's political status. But upon Congress' passage of the TRA, PRC leaders objected strenuously to the act's provision for continued U.S. arms sales to Taiwan, regarding it as a violation of U.S. commitments to end its military alliance with Taipei. After two years of bilateral tensions, a U.S.-PRC joint communiqué—the third and final Sino-U.S. communiqué since Nixon's opening to China in 1972—addressed this point on August 17, 1982. In that communiqué, the PRC cited it had a "fundamental policy" of striving for a peaceful solution to the Taiwan question, while Washington stated that the United States did not –

> seek to carry out a long-term policy of arms sales to Taiwan, that its arms sales to Taiwan will not exceed, either in qualitative or quantitative terms, the level of those supplied in recent years since the establishment of diplomatic relations between the United States and China, and that it intends to reduce gradually its sales of arms to Taiwan.[14]

The three U.S.-PRC communiqués and the 1979 Taiwan Relations Act for decades served as the framework by which U.S. officials balanced two competing policy objectives—widely referred to as U.S. "strategic ambiguity" about Taiwan. On the one hand were three communiqués in which U.S. policymakers recognized the legitimacy of the PRC government, appeared to acknowledge there was only "one China," and suggested an eventual ending point to U.S. weapons sales to Taiwan. On the other was the TRA in which the United States established a statutory framework for maintaining extensive unofficial contacts with Taiwan and which committed the United States to providing weapons for Taiwan's defense against what most saw as Taiwan's only potential enemy—the PRC. "Strategic ambiguity" remained the basis of U.S. Taiwan policy throughout the 1980s and well into the 1990s, and many observers give it much of the credit for helping to facilitate U.S.-China relations, preserve U.S.-Taiwan contacts, and protect Taiwan's own political and economic interests.

POLICY IMPLICATIONS AND ISSUES FOR CONGRESS

Despite the policy framework of the TRA and the three communiqués, Taiwan continues to be a particularly complex issue for U.S. policy and a recurring issue for Congress. Some of these complicating factors are old issues arising from the political compromises that the 1979 normalization process demanded—notably, the "one-China" formulation, U.S. security interests in and arms sales to Taiwan, and the U.S. position on Taiwan's status in key international organizations. Other complications are the result of changing political trends, particularly in Taiwan, that have presented increasing challenges for the policy framework. These issues crop up periodically in congressional debate in ways that occasionally prompt comment from U.S. government officials.

One such recurring issue concerns the U.S. position on Taiwan's membership in international organizations, such as the World Health Organization and the United Nations. The policy parameters in Section 4(d) of the Taiwan Relations Act make the following specific pronouncement on this point: "Nothing in this Act may be construed as a basis for supporting the exclusion or expulsion of Taiwan from continued membership in any international financial institution or any other international organization." But nuance has crept into this TRA formulation in subsequent U.S. Administrations. In his "three no's" statement of June 30, 1998, for example, President Bill Clinton said "... we don't believe that Taiwan should be a member of any organization for which statehood is a requirement." Some claim that this phraseology is a misinterpretation of the relevant provision in the TRA.

Another such issue concerns the U.S. "one China" policy formulation. Although the United States has never repudiated and in fact has continued forcefully to restate that commitment, purists can argue that the U.S. iterations of the "one China" policy over the years have departed from the original formulation in subtle but significant ways. The first two joint communiqués, below, address the "one China" issue in a similar manner, in contrast to the third communiqué, which injects more nuance into the formulation:

- "The United States acknowledges that all Chinese on either side of the Taiwan Strait maintain there is but one China and that Taiwan is a part of China. The United States Government does not challenge that position." – *The Joint U.S.-China Communiqué, Shanghai, February 1972*
- "The Government of the United States of America acknowledges the Chinese position that there is but one China and Taiwan is part of China." – *The Joint Communiqué on the Establishment of Diplomatic Relations Between the United States of America and the People's Republic of China, January 1, 1979*
- "In the Joint Communiqué [of January 1, 1979]... the United States of America ...acknowledged the Chinese position that there is but one China and Taiwan is part of China.... The United States Government attaches great importance to its relations with China, and reiterates that it has no intention of infringing on Chinese sovereignty and territorial integrity, or interfering in China's internal affairs, or pursuing a policy of 'two Chinas' or 'one China, one Taiwan.'" – *The U.S.-China Joint Communiqué, August 17, 1982.*

Enacted between the second and third communiqué, the Taiwan Relations Act of 1979 leaves the "one China" question unaddressed. But language in the Conference Report suggests that the 96th Congress wanted to emphasize the "one China" formulation contained in the first two communiqués. As the Conference Report states: "[The U.S. Administration] has acknowledged the Chinese position that Taiwan is a part of China, but the United States has not itself agreed to this position." Subsequent iterations by a series of U.S. Administrations concerning U.S. policy on Taiwan almost always have adhered to bare-bones statements, with each being parsed and dissected meticulously by the parties involved for any hidden nuance or perceived change.[15]

A third issue is the question of U.S. arms sales to Taiwan, for which the TRA makes provision. Despite the 1982 communiqué in which the United States expressed intent to reduce and eventually end annual arms sales to Taiwan, such sales not only have continued but in some years have increased substantially—notably, with the George W. Bush Administration's April 2001 weapons sale package to Taiwan that included, among other systems, four decommissioned Kidd-class destroyers, 12 anti-submarine warfare P-3 aircraft, and eight diesel submarines. This sale was surpassed in size and value only by the 1992 sale of 150 F-16 aircraft to Taiwan by the George H. W. Bush Administration.

Debate also regularly recurs over what the United States should do if the PRC uses force against Taiwan. Some observers focus on the lack of any mandate in the TRA for U.S. military intervention, while others point out that the TRA bases the entire foundation of U.S.-PRC official relations on the premise that Taiwan's future will be resolved peacefully.[16] Some believe that the potential for U.S. military conflict with China over Taiwan has grown given the PRC's military build-up opposite Taiwan, Beijing's refusal to renounce using force against the island, and intermittent but troubling U.S.-PRC naval encounters in the western Pacific. Others suggest the potential for conflict has been minimized given the growing rapprochement and cross-strait ties between the PRC and Taiwan that have occurred in 2008 and 2009 under Taiwan President Ma Ying-jeou.

The biggest complicating factor for U.S. policymakers today may come from Taiwan's own political circumstances, which have changed dramatically since Congress passed the 1979 TRA.[17] Under the authoritarian rule of Chiang Kai-shek's Nationalist Party (also known as the KMT), Taiwan's political decisions were predictable, closely aligned with U.S. interests, and dependent largely on U.S. support. But several decades of political reforms have made Taiwan politics today not only more democratic and more nationalistic, but more fluid and harder to predict.

Given the historical record and with continuing transformations in both the PRC and Taiwan political systems, U.S. officials may be facing new and more difficult policy choices concerning Taiwan in the coming years. While many consider Taiwan's continuing democratic maturation, most recently demonstrated by the 2008 presidential election, to be a validation of U.S. goals for the spread of democratic values, that democratization also further emphasizes the unique and delicate challenges for U.S. policy that Taiwan poses. The U.S. government continues to embrace the efficacy of the fundamental U.S. policy framework on Taiwan—defined by one observer as "one-China, peaceful resolution, U.S. arms sales, the Taiwan Relations Act, and the three communiqués." But other observers, including some Members of Congress, appear critical of what they see as excessive U.S. secretiveness and substantive "inflexibility" on Taiwan issues.

Criticism has been leveled especially at the secretive set of "Taiwan Guidelines"—a lengthy and closely held State Department memo written in 1979-1980 purporting to govern what U.S. officials can and cannot do or say with respect to Taiwan after the severance of official U.S.- Taiwan relations.[18] Under the "Guidelines," for instance, the U.S. government maintains that senior U.S. officials are unable to have any contact with senior Taiwan officials, and that Taiwan officials cannot be received in U.S. government buildings, because the United States does not recognize the government in Taiwan as the legitimate Chinese government. The full "Guidelines" reportedly are extremely confidential even within the U.S. government apparatus, although officials in relevant U.S. government departments are reminded of their basic premises periodically in an abbreviated memo. Reportedly, the only official modification of the "Guidelines" since their original inception occurred during the Clinton Administration in 1993-1994, the principal change being the initiation of U.S. high-level engagement with Taiwan for economic entities.[19] The only public issuance of these modifications appears to have been given in the 1994 testimony of Winston Lord, Assistant Secretary of State for East Asia, before the Senate Foreign Relations Committee.[20]

As of the date of this chapter, evidence suggests that the administration of President Barack Obama will continue to pursue the overall policy direction toward the PRC and Taiwan that past U.S. administrations have followed. But within this broad framework, it still is unclear what shading, if any, the Administration may give to the U.S. policy direction or whether administration officials will undertake another Taiwan policy review to respond to new developments.

Some Members of Congress and former U.S. government officials, for instance, have suggested that there is room for more flexibility on the logistics of daily U.S. interaction with Taiwan. In this view, the United States could ease the constraints on U.S. interaction with Taiwan and make clear that routine practical interactions – such as higher-level working visits, permitting Taiwan officials to enter the premises of the State Department and the National Security Council, or more routine treatment of requests for U.S. visits by senior Taiwan officials – have no implications for the U.S. "one China" policy. A few have taken the notion of flexibility even farther, arguing that the United States should scrap the "one China" policy altogether, despite the potentially grave costs to U.S.-China relations, and establish diplomatic relations with Taiwan.

Reflecting these views, Members of Congress in recent years have introduced a number of measures calling for changes or for greater flexibility in U.S. policy on Taiwan. Measures introduced in the 110th and 111th Congresses as of this writing include:

- Establishing diplomatic relations with Taiwan: H.Con.Res. 18 (Representative John Linder, introduced January 9, 2009); H.Con.Res. 73 (Representative Thomas Tancredo, introduced February 16, 2007);
- Lifting current restrictions on U.S. interactions with Taiwan officials: H.Con.Res. 136 (Representative Steve Chabot, introduced May 1, 2007); S.Con.Res. 48 (Senator Tim Johnson, introduced October 2, 2007);
- Supporting Taiwan's membership in international organizations: H.Con.Res. 250 (Representative Scott Garrett, introduced November 8, 2007);
- Requiring Senate confirmation of the Director of the American Institute in Taiwan: H.R. 1390 (Representative Thomas Tancredo, introduced March 7, 2007);

- Prohibiting funding to implement the "Taiwan Guidelines": House Amendment 372 to H.R. 2764 (Representative Thomas Tancredo, introduced June 21, 2007).

End Notes

[1] It is crucial to note that at this time and for most of the next 53 years, both the PRC and the ROC claimed Taiwan as a province of China. Taiwan's provincial capital remained at Taichung.

[2] On January 5, 1950, for example, President Truman announced the United States "would not provide military aid or advice to [Chiang's] Chinese forces" on Taiwan. On June 7, 1950, Secretary of State Dean Acheson said in a news conference that while the United States did not support transferring Chinese representation in the United Nations to the PRC, it would not use its U.N. Security Council veto to block a move to do so.

[3] "Statement by the President on the Situation in Korea," June 27, 1950. http://www.trumanlibrary.org/publicpapers/ viewpapers.php?pid=800 President Truman's reference to "Formosa" uses the name by which Taiwan was known under Japanese sovereignty (China ceded Taiwan's sovereignty to Japan under the 1895 Treaty of Shimonoseki).

[4] The ROC was a founding member of the U.N. in 1945 as well as a permanent member of the U.N. Security Council. In the 1960s, countries sympathetic to the PRC began introducing regular resolutions in the General Assembly to remove Taiwan from that body and seat the PRC as the representative of China. U.S.-led actions successfully blocked these resolutions until October 25, 1971, when two-thirds of the members of the General Assembly passed Resolution 2758, withdrawing recognition from the ROC and recognizing the PRC as the sole legitimate government of China. Taiwan's government has reapplied for U.N. membership and/or observer status since 1991—unsuccessfully until April 29, 2009, when the WHO invited Taiwan to attend its May 18-27, 2009 meeting as an observer.

[5] President Nixon first used the PRC's formal name in his "State of the World" report to Congress on Feb. 25, 1971, (Jones, DuPre, ed., *China: U.S. Policy Since 1945*, Congressional Quarterly Inc., 1980, pp. 321-322); National Security Advisor Henry Kissinger left for his first, secret trip to China on July 9, 1971; Nixon made his historic visit to China on February 21, 1972.

[6] In recognizing the legitimacy of the PRC government, the United States fulfilled 3 conditions that Beijing had consistently placed on normalization of relations: withdrawal of all U.S. military forces from Taiwan; severing of diplomatic relations with Taiwan; and termination of the U.S.-Taiwan defense treaty.

[7] Widely and over-simply referred to as the "one China policy," this and other "one-China"-like statements for decades have been parsed and dissected by each involved government for every conceivable nuance. The various iterations of "one-China" policy formulations can be found in CRS Report RL30341, *China/Taiwan: Evolution of the "One China" Policy—Key Statements from Washington, Beijing, and Taipei*, by Shirley A. Kan.

[8] Jones, DuPre, ed., p. 342.

[9] For more detailed discussions of congressional actions at the time, see "Congress and U.S. policy in Asia: New relationships with China and Taiwan," in *Congress and Foreign Policy—1979*, House Committee on Foreign Affairs, U.S. Government Printing Office, Washington D.C. 1980, pp. 54-71; Wolff, Lester L. And Simon, David L., eds., *Legislative History of the Taiwan Relations Act*, American Association for Chinese Studies, Jamaica, New York, 1982; Jones, DuPre, ed., *China: U.S. Policy Since 1945*, Congressional Quarterly Inc., 1980.

[10] See the American Institute in Taiwan (AIT) website at http://www.ait.org.tw/en/.

[11] Taiwan Relations Act, P.L. 96-8, Section 11 (2).

[12] CRS Report RL30957, *Taiwan: Major U.S. Arms Sales Since 1990*, by Shirley A. Kan.

[13] In a 2005 speech to the U.S.-Taiwan Business Council-Defense Industry Conference 2005, Ed Ross, Director of DOD's Defense Security Cooperation Agency, strongly criticized Taiwan's foot-dragging on passage of a defense budget that would allow purchases of U.S. weapons, saying it was reasonable in such a situation to question the level of U.S. commitment to Taiwan's self-defense. Agence France-Presse, "Pentagon official warns Taiwan on defense spending," September 21, 2005.

[14] While the 1982 communiqué was being negotiated, the Taiwan government presented the United States with six points it proposed be used as guidelines in conducting U.S.-Taiwan relations. According to former Ambassador John Holdridge, the United States agreed to these points—the so-called "six assurances." The six points included assurances that the United States would not set a date for termination of arms sales to Taiwan, would not alter the terms of the Taiwan Relations Act, and would not pressure Taiwan to negotiate with China or act as mediator between Taiwan and China. See CRS Report 96-246, *Taiwan: Texts of the Taiwan Relations Act, the U.S. - China Communiques, and the "Six Assurances"*, by Kerry Dumbaugh, for text of the "six assurances."

[15] The convoluted evolution of "one-China" policy statements among all three governments can be found in CRS Report RL30341, *China/Taiwan: Evolution of the "One China" Policy—Key Statements from Washington, Beijing and Taipei*, by Shirley A. Kan.

[16] Section 2(b)(3) of the TRA states that it is U.S. policy "to make clear that the United States decision to establish diplomatic relations with the [PRC] rests upon the expectation that the future of Taiwan will be determined by peaceful means."

[17] See CRS Report R40493, *Taiwan-U.S. Relations: Developments and Policy Implications*, by Kerry Dumbaugh.

[18] According to one former U.S. government official interviewed on July 5, 2006, much pertaining to the "Guidelines" is simply commonly understood practice—such as that high State Department and other senior U.S. government officials cannot go to Taiwan.

[19] Some observers point out that the Taiwan Guidelines seem to have been bent on at least two other occasions without official modification—when U.S. Trade Representative Carla Hills, a cabinet officer, went to Taiwan in December 1992 to discuss U.S.-Taiwan trade ties, and when Taiwan President Lee Teng-hui in 1995 became the first Taiwan president since 1979 permitted to make a landmark "unofficial" visit to the United States.

[20] Hearing on Taiwan Policy, Senate Foreign Relations Committee/East Asian and Pacific Affairs, September 27, 1994.

In: Asian Economic and Political Issues, Volume 14
Editor: David A. Marek
ISBN: 978-1-61728-019-1

Chapter 6

AFGHANISTAN: GOVERNMENT FORMATION AND PERFORMANCE*

Kenneth Katzman

SUMMARY

The central government's limited writ and widespread official corruption are helping sustain a Taliban insurgency, and have fed pessimism about the Afghanistan stabilization effort. However, ethnic disputes remain confined largely to political debate and competition, enabling President Hamid Karzai to focus on trying to build Afghan institutions, and on his bid for re-election in presidential elections slated for August 20, 2009. Karzai has faced substantial loss of public confidence, in large part due to widespread official corruption, but his opponents—divided by ethnicity and personal ambition—were unable to form a strong electoral coalition as the presidential election registration process closed on May 8, 2009.

At the same time, U.S. officials have been shifting away from reliance on building the central government and toward promoting local governing bodies and security initiatives. That trend is to accelerate, according to the Obama Administration's review of U.S. strategy, the results of which were announced on March 27, 2009. The core of the new strategy is a so-called "civilian surge" that will virtually double, to about 900, the number of U.S. civilian personnel to deploy to Afghanistan to help build its governing and security institution, and to increase economic development efforts. The Administration also says it will develop "metrics" by which to judge the performance and legitimacy of the Afghan government, including its efforts to curb official corruption, although the Administration and many in Congress appear reluctant to tie any U.S. funds or other activities to Afghanistan's performance on such metrics. The review did not emphasize building democracy in Afghanistan, although that goal appears implicit within its recommendations.

* This is an edited, reformatted and augmented version of a CRS Report for Congress publication, Report #RS21922, dated June 5, 2009.

POST-TALIBAN POLITICAL TRANSITION AND POLITICAL LANDSCAPE

In addition to supporting Afghanistan's holding of democratic elections and urging adherence to international standards of human rights, U.S. policy has been to extend the authority and encourage the reform of Afghanistan's central government. The policy has been predicated on the observation that weak and corrupt governance is causing some Afghans to acquiesce to, or even support outright, Taliban insurgents as providers of security and impartial justice. The United States provides about 27,000 forces to a 61,000 troop NATO-led coalition there; another 14,000 U.S. troops continue the original post-September 11 counter-terrorism mission in Afghanistan. An additional 21,000 U.S. forces are in the process of flowing to Afghanistan, as announced in the context of the March 27, 2009 presentation of the Obama Administration strategy review on Afghanistan and Pakistan.

Although democracy promotion, per se, was not a major feature of the Obama Administration strategy announcement, Afghanistan has taken significant steps toward democracy since the fall of the Taliban in November 2001. Karzai's is the first fully elected government in Afghan history, although there were parliamentary elections during the reign of King Zahir Shah (the last were in 1969, before his reign was ended in a 1973 military coup). Presidential, parliamentary, and provincial elections, and adoption of a constitution were part of a post-Taliban transition roadmap established by a United Nations-sponsored agreement of major Afghan factions signed in Bonn, Germany on December 5, 2001, ("Bonn Agreement"),[1] after the Taliban had fallen. The political transition process is depicted in the table below.

Elections have not produced complete harmony among Afghanistan's many communities. Since its formation in late 2001, Karzai's government has come to be progressively dominated by ethnic Pashtuns, who are about 42% of the population and traditionally have governed Afghanistan. A table on major Pashtun clans is provided below, as is a map showing the distribution of Afghanistan's various ethnicities.

Of the major security ministries and organizations, only the National Directorate for Security (NDS, the Intelligence directorate) is still headed by a non-Pashtun (Amrollah Saleh, a Tajik). Adhering to a tacit consensus, the other security ministries (Defense, Interior) tend to have non-Pashtuns in key deputy or subordinate positions. One prominent example is the defense ministry, in which the chief of staff is a Tajik (Bismillah Khan), who reports to a Pashtun Defense Minister (Abdul Rahim Wardak). On the other hand, Afghanistan's non-Pashtun communities have said that they will not react violently to their progressive diminution in the upper levels of government, but would keep their competition peaceful.

Some believe that assisting the transition to democracy are traditional Afghan patterns of authority and decisionmaking, which in many cases have democratic and representative elements. Some of these processes, such as the *loya jirga*, or traditional Afghan assembly consisting of about 1,000 delegates from all over Afghanistan, have been used in the post-Taliban period. Others note that, at the local level, *shuras*, or *jirgas* (consultative councils) composed of local notables, are key mechanisms for making authoritative local decisions. Afghans turn often to these local mechanisms to adjudicate disputes rather than use the national court system. Some estimates say that 80% of cases are decided in the informal justice system.

Karzai and His Opponents

It is the National Assembly (parliament)—particularly the 249 seat elected lower house *(Wolesi Jirga, House of the People*—that is the key institution for the ethnic minorities to exert influence. To the chagrin of many Afghans who want to build a democratic Afghanistan governed by technocrats and newly emerging political figures, many seats in the lower house are held by personalities and factions prominent in Afghanistan's recent wars, and many of these are non-Pashtuns who inhabit the north and the west, and Kabul city. The lower house is divided into three roughly equal coalitions—pro-Karzai deputies, ethnic minority and other some Pashtun "opposition" figures, and "independents" of varied ethnicities. The factions in the lower house are not strictly organized according to Afghanistan's 90 registered political parties.

Karzai has not formed his own party, but his core support in the *Wolesi Jirga* consists of former members of the hardline conservative Pashtun-based Hizb-e-Islam party; and supporters of Abd-i-Rab Rasul Sayyaf—a prominent Islamic conservative *mujahedin* party leader.[2] Another base of Karzai's support in parliament is the contingent from Qandahar (Karzai's home province) and Helmand provinces, including several Karzai clan members. One clan member in the body is his cousin Jamil Karzai, and another is relative by marriage Aref Nurzai. Karzai's elder brother, Qayyum, was in the lower house representing Qandahar until his October 2008 resignation due to health reasons, although Qayyum continues to represent his brother informally domestically and abroad, including at 2008 and 2009 meetings to explore negotiated settlements with "moderate" Taliban figures. Also pro-Karzai are former Pashtun militia and Taliban leaders, including Hazrat Ali (Nangarhar Province), who had gained fame for leading the Afghan component of the failed assault on Osama bin Laden's purported redoubt at Tora Bora in December 2001; Pacha Khan Zadran (Paktia) who, by some accounts, helped Osama bin Laden escape Tora Bora; and Mullah Abdul Salam ("Mullah Rocketi"), from Zabol. (Salam has filed to run for president in 2009.)

The Opposition

The "opposition" is led by ethnic minorities (Tajik, Uzbek, and Hazara) who were in an alliance against Taliban rule that was called the "Northern Alliance." Leaders of these groups, and particularly Tajiks, view as a betrayal Karzai's firing of many of the non-Pashtuns from the cabinet—such as former Foreign Minister Dr. Abdullah Abdullah (Tajik, dismissed in 2006). However, as noted above, the bloc says its disputes with Karzai will remain political and peaceful, and members of the bloc meet occasionally with Karzai to discuss issues and negotiate understandings.

In April 2007, *Wolesi Jirga* Speaker Yunus Qanooni and former Afghan president Burhanuddin Rabbani (both, like Abdullah, are prominent ethnic Tajik Northern Alliance figures and former associates of the legendary *mujahedin* commander Ahmad Shah Masood) organized a broader (it includes some Pashtuns) opposition bloc called the "United Front" (UF). Joining the bloc were both of Karzai's vice presidents, and some Pashtuns prominent in the Soviet-occupation era such as Sayed Muhammad Gulabzoi (Khost Province) and Nur ul-Haq Ulumi, who chairs parliament's defense committee. The UF advocates amending the constitution to give more power to parliament and to empower the elected provincial councils (instead of the President) to select governors and mayors. Fearing Pashtun consolidation, the

UF has been generally opposed to Karzai's overtures to Taliban fighters to end their fight and join government—an initiative that is now backed by the Obama Administration as a means of combating the Taliban insurgency. Yet the UF is not always cohesive, as has been shown in the context of the 2009 presidential elections (discussed below).

Even before the formation of the UF, the lower house opposition first showed its strength in March 2006, following the December 19, 2005 inauguration of parliament, by requiring Karzai's cabinet to be approved individually, rather than *en bloc*, increasing opposition leverage. However, Karzai rallied his support and all but 5 of the 25 nominees were confirmed. One of those defeated was a female nominee for Minister of Women's Affairs, leaving Afghanistan without any women ministers. (The post had been held by a female since it was established in 2002.) In May 2006, the opposition compelled Karzai to change the nine-member Supreme Court, the highest judicial body, including ousting 74-year-old Islamic conservative Fazl Hadi Shinwari as chief justice. Parliament approved his new Court choices in July 2006, all of whom are trained in modern jurisprudence.

In May 2007, the UF achieved a majority in parliament to oust Karzai ally Rangin Spanta as Foreign Minister. Karzai refused to replace him, instead seeking a Supreme Court ruling that Spanta should remain, on the grounds that his ouster was related to a refugee issue (Iran's expulsion of 100,000 Afghan refugees), not a foreign policy issue. The Court has, to date, supported Karzai, and Spanta remains Foreign Minister, although the UF continues to challenge his legitimacy.

Karzai and the UF have often battled for the support of the many "independents" in the lower house. Among them are several outspoken women, intellectuals, and business leaders, such as the 39 year-old Malalai Joya (Farah Province), a leading critic of war-era faction leaders. In May 2007 the lower house voted to suspend her for this criticism for the duration of her term. She continues to legally challenge the expulsion but, to date, remains barred. Others in this camp include Ms. Fauzia Gailani (Herat Province); Ms. Shukria Barekzai, editor of *Woman Mirror* magazine; and Mr. Ramazan Bashardost, a former Karzai minister who champions parliamentary powers and has established a "complaints table" outside the parliament building to highlight and combat official corruption. U.S.-based International Republican Institute (IRI) has helped train the independents; the National Democratic Institute (NDI) has assisted the more established factions.

Karzai has relatively fewer critics in the 102 seat *Meshrano Jirga (House of Elders),* partly because of his bloc of 34 appointments (one-third of that body). He engineered the appointment of an ally as Speaker—Sibghatullah Mojadeddi—a noted Islamic scholar and former *mujahedin* party leader who headed the post-Communist *mujahedin* government for one month (May 1992).[3] He has since 2003 headed an effort to reconcile with Taliban figures (Peace and Reconciliation Commission, or "PTSD" program). Karzai also appointed Northern Alliance military leader Muhammad Fahim to the body, perhaps to compensate for his removal as Defense Minister, although he resigned after a few months and later joined the UF. (He is now Karzai's primary running mate in the 2009 elections.) There is one Hindu, and 23 women; 17 are Karzai appointees and 6 were selected in their own right.

The upper house tends to be more Islamist conservative than the lower house, advocating a legal system that accords with Islamic law, and restrictions on press and Westernized media broadcasts. In late 2008, the body approved a resolution opposing a U.S.-Afghan plan to establish local security organs to help keep Taliban infiltrators out of Afghan communities.

The plan, now termed the "Afghan Public Protection Force," is being tested in Wardak provinces south of Kabul (see below).

On less contentious issues, the executive and the legislature have worked well. During 2008, parliament passed a labor law, a mines law, a law on economic cooperatives, and a convention on tobacco control. It also confirmed several Karzai nominees, including the final justice to fill out the Supreme Court. In 2009, as discussed further below, the National Assembly approved a Shiite Personal Status Law. Both houses of parliament, whose budgets are controlled by the Ministry of Finance, are staffed by about 275 Afghans, reporting to a "secretariat." There are 18 oversight committees, a research unit and a library.

Government Performance[4]

U.S. policy has been to help expand Afghan institutions and to urge reforms such as merit-based performance criteria and weeding out of the rampant official corruption. Afghan ministries are growing their staffs and technologically capabilities, although they still suffer from a low resource and skill base, and corruption is fed in part by the fact that government workers receive very low salaries. The anti-corruption and governmental performance aspect of U.S. policy is to be enhanced as a result of the Obama Administration's strategy review, as announced March 27, 2009, which concluded that more needed to be done to promote the legitimacy and effectiveness of the Afghan government at both the Kabul and local levels. As a consequence of the review, the Administration plans to send about 430 U.S. civilian personnel—and many additional civilians from partner countries will join them—to advise Afghan ministries, and provincial and district administrations.

The Administration also plans to develop metrics to assess progress in building Afghan governance; the proposed metrics are, according to Undersecretary of Defense Michelle Flournoy, to be briefed to Congress in May 2009. Some in Congress have said they oppose firm conditionality of any U.S. aid to Afghanistan on Afghanistan's performance on such metrics, or linkage to any timelines of progress in the U.S. stabilization effort.

There has also been a growing perception that Karzai's government is weak in its administrative ability. The former U.S. Ambassador to Afghanistan, Zalmay Khalilzad, who is of Afghan origin (a Pashtun) is reported as of May 2009 to be negotiating with Karzai about becoming a strong chief executive officer if Karzai is re-elected; these talks came after Khalilzad declined to run against Karzai in the upcoming election. The Obama Administration did not take a firm position on the Khalilzad idea during Karzai's May 2009 visit to the United States, but some are said to believe that a high ranking position for Khalilzad in the Afghan government could further confuse the channels of communication between the Obama Administration and the Karzai government. (Khalilzad's political activities in Afghanistan are discussed further below.)

Regional Strongmen

The Obama Administration review did not specifically outline any new measures to sideline regional strongmen. Karzai has at times indulged and at other times move against regional strongmen, but he has been hesitant to confront them outright to the point where their followers go into armed rebellion. His choice of Muhammad Fahim, the military chief of the

Northern Alliance/UF faction, as first Vice Presidential running mate in the August 2009 elections is likely to reignite concerns that Karzai continues to rely on faction leaders and refuses to modernize his governing approach. Karzai argues that these faction leaders have significant followings and that compromises with them is needed to keep the government intact as he focuses on fighting "unrepentant" Taliban insurgents.

In 2008, some observers cited Karzai's handling of prominent Uzbek leader Abdurrashid Dostam as evidence of political weakness. Dostam is often referred to as a "warlord" because of his command of partisans in his redoubt in northern Afghanistan (Jowzjan and Balkh provinces), and he is widely accused of human rights abuses of political opponents in the north. To try to separate him from his militia, in 2005 Karzai appointed him to the post of chief of staff of the armed forces. On February 4, 2008, Afghan police surrounded Dostam's villa in Kabul in response to reports that his followers attacked and beat an ethnic Turkmen rival, but Karzai did not order his arrest for fear of stirring unrest among Dostam's followers. To try to resolve the issue without stirring unrest, in early December 2008 Karzai purportedly reached an agreement with Dostam under which he resigned as chief of staff and went into exile in Turkey in exchange for the dropping any case against him.[5] Dostam continues to be consulted by leading Afghan politicians.

Karzai also has weakened prominent Tajik political leader, former Herat governor Ismail Khan, by appointing him Minister of Energy and Water. On the other hand, some say the province has now been infiltrated by Taliban—at least in Pashtun areas of the province and neighboring provinces—because the strong hand of Khan is no longer governing there. Others say that some strong governors, such as Ghul Agha Shirzai of Nangarhar, continue to siphon off customs duties at border crossings, undermining the revenue flow to the central government.

In February 2007, both houses passed a law giving amnesty to so-called "warlords." Karzai altered the draft to give victims the right to seek justice for any abuses; Karzai did not sign a modified version in May 2007, leaving the status unclear.

Official Corruption

During the Bush Administration, U.S. officials generally refrained from publicly criticizing Karzai when, in the interests of political harmony, he has purportedly tolerated corruption. However, President Obama and his senior aides, including the special representative for Afghanistan and Pakistan Ambassador Richard Holbrooke, have been somewhat more publicly critical of Karzai's shortcomings than were Bush Administration officials. The Obama Administration strategy review highlights the need to reduce official corruption and says that some of the Administration's forthcoming "metrics" will help determine performance toward that end.

Partly as a result of what many Afghans view as a "predatory" central government, some Afghans—and many international donors—are said to be losing faith in the government and in Karzai's leadership. Some observers, such as former Coordinator for Counter-Narcotics and Justice Reform Thomas Schweich, in a July 27, 2008 *New York Times* article, have gone so far as to assert that Karzai, to build political support, is deliberately tolerating officials in his government who are allegedly involved in the narcotics trade. The *New York Times* reported allegations (October 5, 2008) that another Karzai brother, Qandahar provincial council chief Ahmad Wali Karzai, has protected narcotics trafficking in the province. Another brother, Mahmoud Karzai, has apparently grown wealthy through real estate and auto sales ventures in Qandahar and Kabul, purportedly by fostering the impression he can influence his brother, President Karzai. Mahmoud Karzai held a press conference in Washington, D.C. on April 16, 2009 denying allegations of corruption against him.

Observers who follow the issue say that most of the corruption takes place in the course of performing mundane governmental functions, such as government processing of official documents, in which processing services routinely require bribes in exchange for action.[6] In other cases, Afghan security officials are said to sell U.S./internationally provided vehicles, fuel, and equipment to supplement their salaries. Several high officials, despite very low official government salaries, have acquired ornate properties in west Kabul since 2002. Other observers who have served in Afghanistan say that Karzai has appointed some provincial governors to "reward them" and that these appointments have gone on to "prey" economically on the populations of that province. Transparency International, a German organization that assesses governmental corruption worldwide, ranked Afghanistan in 2008 as 176th out of 180 countries ranked in terms of government corruption. Because of the corruption, only about 10% of U.S. aid is channeled through the Afghan government, although Special Representative for Afghanistan and Pakistan Richard Holbrooke said in May 2009 that empowering Afghan governance requires raising that to about 40% or 50%. Currently, the Ministry of Health, and the Ministry of Rural Rehabilitation and Development, and a few others qualify to have U.S. funds channeled through them.

To try to address the criticism, in August 2008 Karzai, with reported U.S. prodding, set up the "High Office of Oversight for the Implementation of Anti-Corruption Strategy" with the power to investigate the police, courts, and the attorney general's office, and to catalogue the overseas assets of Afghan officials. Karzai himself declared his assets on March 27, 2009. In October 2008, Karzai replaced the ministers of Interior, of Education, and of Agriculture with officials, particularly the new Interior Minister (former Soviet-era official Muhammad Hanif Atmar) believed to be dedicated to reform of their ministries and weeding out of official corruption. However, Atmar's appointment incurred further UF concern because Atmar, a Pashtun, replaced a Tajik (Zarrar Moqbel) in that post. Some press reports in March 2009 suggested that the United States and Britain were urging Karzai to appoint Atmar as a "chief of staff" or similar position to be able to monitor government corruption at high levels. In his public appearances during his visit to the United States in May 2009, Karzai repeatedly stressed what he said were efforts by him and his government to remove corrupt officials and combat official corruption.

Some of Karzai's anti-corruption steps have been recommended in studies within the State Department, the Afghan government, and the U.N. Office of Drugs and Crime which is responsible for assisting Afghanistan on counter-narcotics. The Afghan government committed itself to anti-corruption efforts in the so-called "Afghanistan Compact" adopted at an international meeting in London on February 1, 2006, and it ratified the U.N. Convention Against Corruption in August 2008.

Increasing Focus on Local Solutions and Governance

In part to address the flaws of the Afghan central government, U.S. policy shifted somewhat in 2008 toward promoting local security and governance solutions. The Afghan government asserts that it itself is promoting local governance as the next stage in Afghanistan's political and economic development. A key indicator of this Afghan shift came in August 2007 when Karzai placed the selection process for local leaders (provincial governors and down) in a new Independent Directorate for Local Governance (IDLG)—and out of the Interior Ministry. The IDLG, with advice from India and other donors, is also in the process of empowering localities (Afghanistan has 22,000 villages) to decide on development priorities. About 30,000 total positions in Afghanistan are to be elected, under the local governance programs advanced by the IDLG. These are mostly community development councils that are helping to decide on development priorities for international donors. The IDLG does not envision that the local leaders being elected will conflict with any district leaderships elected when Afghanistan finally does hold (still delayed) district elections. Some accounts say that the efforts to expand local governance has been hampered by corruption and limited availability of skilled Afghans.

Provincial Governors

Many believe that the key to effective local governance is the appointment of competent governors. In March 2008 Karzai replaced the weak and ineffective governor of Helmand - Asadullah Wafa - with Gulab Mangal, who is from Laghman Province and who the U.N. Office of Drugs and Crime (UNODC) said in an August 2008 report is taking relatively effective action to convince farmers not to grow crops other than poppy. A subsequent UNODC report in February 2009 said his efforts are likely to result in a reduction of cultivation in Helmand in 2009. However, there are reports Karzai wants to replace him with the former governor, Sher Mohammad Akhundzadeh, who is accused of human rights abuses when he was governor during 2002-2005 but who remains powerful in the province. The UNODC report said that improving governance in some provinces had contributed to the increase to 18 "poppy free" provinces (out of 34), from 13 in the same report in 2007. Ghul Agha Shirzai has been effective in curbing cultivation in Nangarhar, although Shirzai reportedly has also not remitted all the customs duties collected at the Khyber Pass/Torkham crossing to the central government. Another four provinces might move into that category in 2009, according to UNODC.

Governing Qandahar is a sensitive issue in Kabul because of Karzai's active interest in his home province. The governor of Qandahar was changed (to former General Rahmatullah Raufi, replacing Asadullah Khalid) after an August 7, 2008 Taliban assault on the Qandahar prison that led to the freeing of several hundred Taliban fighters incarcerated there. Karzai changed that governorship again in December 2008, naming Canadian-Afghan academic Tooryalai Wesa as governor, perhaps hoping that his ties to Canada would assuage Canadian reticence to continuing its mission in Qandahar beyond 2011.

Local Security Programs

The IDLG is also the chief implementer of the "Social Outreach Program" which provides financial support (about $125 – 200 per month) and other benefits to tribal and local leaders in exchange for their cooperation with U.S./NATO led forces against the Taliban insurgency. The civilian aspects of the program are funded partly by USAID.

A more widely debated security aspect of the program is the Afghan Public Protection Force, referred to above. Afghan officials say it is not a resurrection of the traditional tribal militias ("*arbokai*") that provided local security—and often clashed with each other—before and during Afghanistan's recent wars, but that the local forces formed under the program are under the authority of the Interior Ministry. U.S. commanders say U.S. weapons will not be provided to the militias, only training, but some weapons may come from the Afghan government. The security components of the program are partially funded with DoD funds (the Commanders Emergency Response Program or CERP). The program has begun in Wardak province, although reportedly with halting cooperation from some tribal leaders in furnishing recruits for the program, and will also be implemented in Kapisa, Ghazni, and Lowgar in early 2009. Special Representative for Afghanistan and Pakistan Richard Holbrooke told observers in Washington D.C. in April 2009 that the "jury is still out" on the pilot program.

Some see the shift toward new local militias as a reversal of the 2001-2007 programs to disarm militias nationwide. The upper house of parliament passed a resolution in November 2008 opposing the formation of local militias. In March 2009 press interviews, Karzai indicated that the program might not be effective in increasing local security.

Overall Human Rights Issues

The Obama Administration review did not specifically delineate a U.S. policy on Afghanistan's human rights practices, although this issue could be deemed addressed implicitly by the Administration's statement that policy is intended to make the Afghan government more "accountable." On human rights issues, the overall State Department judgment is that the country's human rights record remains poor, according to the Department's report for 2008 (issued February 25, 2009). The security forces are widely cited for abuses and corruption, including torture and abuse of detainees.

There has been some backsliding in recent years on media freedoms, which was hailed during 2002-2008 as a major benefit of the U.S. effort in Afghanistan. A press law was passed in September 2008 that gives some independence to the official media outlet, but also contains a number of content restrictions, and requires that new newspapers and electronic media be licensed by the government. Prior to the new law, Afghanistan's conservative Council of Ulema (Islamic scholars) has been ascendant. With the Council's backing, in April 2008 the Ministry of Information and Culture banned five Indian-produced soap operas on the grounds that they are too risque, although the programs were restored in August 2008 under a compromise that also brought in some Islamic-oriented programs from Turkey. At the same time, there have been a growing numbers of arrests or intimidation of journalists who criticize the central government or local leaders. On the other hand, freedoms for women have greatly expanded since the fall of the Taliban with their elections to the parliament (numbers in the table below), their service at many levels of government, including a governorship (Bamiyan Province), and their growing presence in the judiciary (67 female judges), the press, and the private sector. Wearing the *burqa* (head-to-toe covering) is no longer required but many women still wear it.

The September 2008 International Religious Freedom report says the Afghan government took limited steps during the year to increase religious freedom. Still, members of minority religions, including Christians, Sikhs, Hindus, and Baha'i's, often face discrimination; the

Supreme Court declared the Baha'i faith to be a form of blasphemy in May 2007. In October 2007, Afghanistan resumed enforcing the death penalty after a four-year moratorium, executing 15 criminals. One major case incurring international criticism has been the January 2008 death sentence, imposed in a quick trial, against 23-year-old journalist Sayed Kambaksh for allegedly distributing material critical of Islam. On October 21, 2008, a Kabul appeals court changed his sentence to 20 years in prison; a judgment upheld by another court in March 2009. He still might receive a Karzai pardon.

A positive development is that Afghanistan's Shiite minority, mostly from the Hazara tribes of central Afghanistan (Bamiyan and Dai Kundi provinces) can celebrate their holidays openly, a development unknown before the fall of the Taliban. Some Afghan Shiites follow Iran's clerical leaders politically, but Afghan Shiites tend to be less religious and more socially open than their co-religionists in Iran. The Minister of Justice is a Shiite, the first of that sect to hold that post.

The Afghan government tried to further accommodate Shiite demands in 2009 by enacting (passage by the National Assembly and signature by Karzai in March 2009) a "Shiite Personal Status Law," at the request of Shiite leaders. The law was intended to provide a legal framework for members of the Shiite minority in family law issues. However, the issue turned controversial when international human rights groups and governments—and Afghan women in a demonstration in Kabul—complained about provisions that would appear to sanction marital rape and which would allow males to control the ability of females in their family to go outside the home. President Obama publicly called these provisions "abhorrent." In early April 2009, taking into account the outcry, Karzai sent the law back to the Justice Ministry for review, saying it would be altered if it were found to conflict with the Afghan constitution. On April 19, 2009, Karzai said on CNN that his government's review of specific provisions of the law, which was long and highly detailed, had been inadequate, and Karzai reiterated during his U.S. visit in May 2009 that the controversial provisions would be removed. Revised legislation will have to again go through the full legislative process. There was further unrest among some Shiite leaders in late May 2009 when they learned that the Afghan government had dumped 2,000 Iranian-supplied religious texts into a river when an Afghan official complained that the books insulted the Sunni majority.

Afghanistan was again placed in Tier 2 in the State Department's June 4, 2008, Trafficking in Persons report for 2008 on the grounds that it does not fully comply with minimum standards for the elimination of trafficking in persons. However, the report says it is making significant efforts to do so, including by establishing anti-trafficking offices in the offices of the Attorney General in all 34 provinces.

Funding Issues

USAID has spent about $440 million (FY2002-2008) to build democracy in Afghanistan, and an additional $68 million to promote "rule of law," and to assist Afghanistan's elections. FY2009 total aid for this category is not yet determined; about $900 million in democracy and governance aid is to be provided in FY2009, including through a FY2009 supplemental request now under congressional consideration.

Table 1. Afghanistan Political Transition Process

Interim Administration	Formed by Bonn Agreement. Headed by Hamid Karzai, an ethnic Pashtun, but key security positions dominated by mostly minority "Northern Alliance." Karzai reaffirmed as leader by June 2002 "emergency loya jirga." (A jirga is a traditional Afghan assembly).
Constitution	Approved by January 2004 "Constitutional Loya Jirga" (CLJ). Set up strong presidency, a rebuke to Northern Alliance that wanted prime ministership to balance presidential power, but gave parliament significant powers to compensate. Gives men and women equal rights under the law, allows for political parties as long as they are not "un-Islamic"; allows for court rulings according to Hanafi (Sunni) Islam (Chapter 7, Article 15). Set out electoral roadmap for simultaneous (if possible) presidential, provincial, and district elections by June 2004. Named ex-King Zahir Shah to non- hereditary position of "Father of the Nation;" he died July 23, 2007.
Presidential Election	Elections for President and two vice presidents, for 5-year term, held Oct. 9, 2004. Turnout was 80% of 10.5 million registered. Karzai and running mates (Ahmad Zia Masud, a Tajik and brother of legendary mujahedin commander Ahmad Shah Masud, who was assassinated by Al Qaeda two days before the Sept. 11 attacks, and Karim Khalili, a Hazara) elected with 55% against 16 opponents. Second highest vote getter, Northern Alliance figure (and Education Minister) Yunus Qanooni (16%). One female ran, got about 1%. Hazara leader Mohammad Mohaqiq got 11.7%; and Dostam won 10%. Funded with $90 million in international aid, including $40 million from U.S. (FY2004 supplemental, P.L. 108-106).
Parliamentary Elections	Elections held Sept. 18, 2005 on Single Non-Transferable Vote" System; candidates stood as individuals, not part of party list. Parliament consists of a 249 elected lower house (Wolesi Jirga, House of the People) and a selected 102 seat upper house (Meshrano Jirga, House of Elders). Voting was for one candidate only, although number of representatives varied by province, ranging from 2 (Panjshir Province) to 33 (Kabul Province). Herat has 17; Nangahar, 14; Qandahar, Balkh, and Ghazni, 11 seats each. The body is 28% female (68 persons), in line with the legal minimum of 68 women - two per each of the 34 provinces. Upper house appointed by Karzai (34 seats, half of which are to be women), by the provincial councils (34 seats), and district councils (remaining 34 seats). There are 23 women in it, above the 17 required by the constitution. Because district elections (400 district councils) were not held, provincial councils selected 68 on interim basis. 2,815 candidates for Wolesi Jirga, including 347 women. Turnout was 57% (6.8 million voters) of 12.5 million registered. Funded by $160 million in international aid, including $45 million from U.S. (FY2005 supplemental appropriation, P.L. 109-13).
Provincial Elections/	Provincial elections held Sept. 18, 2005, simultaneous with parliamentary elections.
District Elections	Exact powers vague, but now taking lead in deciding local reconstruction Provincial council sizes range from 9 to the 29 seats on the Kabul provincial council. Total seatsare 420, of which 121 held by women. 13,185 candidates, including 279 women. Some criticize the provincial election system as disproportionately weighted toward large districts within each

Table 1. (Continued)

	province. District elections not held due to complexity and potential tensions of drawing district boundaries.
Cabinet	Full-term 27 seat cabinet named by Karzai in December 2004. Heavily weighted toward Pashtuns, and created new Ministry of Counter-Narcotics. Rahim Wardak named Defense Minister, replacing Northern Alliance military leader Mohammad Fahim. Qanooni not in cabinet, subsequently was selected *Wolesi Jirga* Speaker. Northern Alliance figure Dr. Abdullah replaced as Foreign Minister in March 2006. Cabinet reshuffle in October 2008 including appointment of Muhammad Hanif Atmar as Interior Minister.
Next Elections	Presidential and provincial elections to be held Aug. 20, 2009. Parliamentary, district, and municipal elections to follow in 2010. Each election to cost $200 million.

Substantial FY2009 aid is being extended to the IDLG for its operations and to support the Social Outreach Program discussed above. In FY 2009, according to a September 25, 2008 State Department fact sheet, USAID is providing $8.5 million to support the IDLG and to fund the Social Outreach Program and a separate "Governor's Performance Fund" intended to promote good governance. Another $95 million is going to the IDLG to help it construct new district centers and rehabilitate fifty provincial and district offices.

2009 Elections

The next major political milestone in Afghanistan is the 2009 presidential and provincial elections. The provincial elections component has been receiving little attention in international media. On February 3, 2009, Afghanistan's Independent Election Commission (IEC) set August 20, 2009 as the election date—a change from a date mandated by Article 61 of the Constitution as April 21, 2009—in order to allow at least 30 days before Karzai's term expires on May 22, 2009. The IEC decision on the latter date cited Article 33 of the Constitution as mandating universal accessibility to the voting—and saying that the April 21 date was precluded by difficulties in registering voters, printing ballots, training staff, advertising the elections, and the dependence on international donor funding, in addition to the security questions.[7] This decision caused the UF bloc to say it would not "recognize" Karzai's presidency after May 22.

In response to the UF criticism that he seeks to prolong his term and use his incumbency to his advantage, Karzai said in late February 2009 that he would run for re-election no matter the date. To reinforce that assertion, on February 28, 2009, Karzai issued a presidential decree directing the IEC to set the elections in accordance with all provisions of the constitution. However, observers say Karzai's decree was largely political because it is widely recognized that Afghan authorities would not be ready to hold elections by the April 21 date. The IEC reaffirmed on March 4, 2009 that the election must be held on August 20, 2009.

Karzai's maneuvers and the official decision did not stop the UF from insisting that Karzai step down on May 22 in favor of a caretaker government. Karzai argued that the Constitution does not provide for any transfer of power other than in case of election or death of a President. The Afghan Supreme Court backed that decision on March 28, 2009. The Obama Administration publicly backed both the IEC and the Supreme Court rulings even though such backing would be viewed as an Obama Administration endorsement of Karzai. Ambassador Holbrooke has said on several occasions that the United States is strictly neutral, and that Ambassador Timothy Carney would head the U.S. election effort at U.S. Embassy Kabul and ensure that the United States is even-handed in the elections.

Despite the political dispute between Karzai and his opponents, enthusiasm among the public appears to be high. Registration (updating of 2005 voter rolls) began in October 2008 and was completed as of the beginning of March 2009. About 15.6 million total Afghans updated their registration information, according to NATO. However, there were also reports of some registration fraud, with some voters registering on behalf of women who do not, by custom, show up at registration sites. U.S./NATO military operations in some areas, including in Helmand in January 2009, were conducted to secure registration centers.

The elections are expected to cost about $200 million; on March 31, 2009. At a U.N.-led conference in the Netherlands, the United States committed $40 million of that amount, which is part of a planned $175 million U.S. funding for elections in FY2009.

Outlines of the Contest

Politically, Karzai has benefited from the August 2009 date because it gives him more time to restore his popularity and gives more time for the infusion of U.S. troops (about 21,000 additional due by August 2009, plus about 3,000 partner combat troop contributions) to secure the Pashtun areas which will be the source of many Karzai votes. The UF sensed vulnerability on the part of Karzai and the April 2009 date appeared to suit that faction politically. However, as 2009 has progressed, the opposition had largely changed its position on the election date because April was too early to field a candidate that might defeat Karzai. With the August date set, candidates registered their candidacies during April 24 - May 8, 2009.

The conventional wisdom among observers is that the two-round election virtually assures victory by an ethnic Pashtun. In the election-related political jockeying,[8] Karzai obtained an agreement from Muhammad Fahim (a Tajik), formerly his antagonist and a UF member, to run as his first vice presidential running mate. Karzai, Fahim, and incumbent second Vice President Karim Khalili registered their ticket on May 4, 2009, just before Karzai left to visit the United States for the latest round of three way strategic talks (U.S.-Pakistan-Afghanistan). The Fahim choice was criticized by human rights and other groups because of Fahim's long identity as a mujahedin commander/militia faction leader, but the selection, and Fahim's acceptance, was viewed as a major political coup for Karzai by splitting the UF bloc.

Anti-Karzai Pashtuns attempted, unsuccessfully, to coalesce around one challenger. Former Interior Minister Ali Jalali (who resigned in 2005 over Karzai's compromises with faction leaders), and former Finance Minister (2002-2004) and Karzai critic Ashraf Ghani, tried to forge a single ticket, but did not reach agreement. In the end, Ghani registered his candidacy, but without Jalali or strong representation from other ethnicities in his vice presidential slots. He has appeared frequently in U.S. media broadcasts saying Karzai has failed to establish legitimate and successful governance, but he has spent much time in the

United States and Europe and might lose support among some average Afghans who might view him as a global technocrat who is not necessarily in touch with day to day problems in Afghanistan. Ghani may show strength in the east of Afghanistan, the seat of his Ahmedzai clan, but is unlikely to draw substantial support in the south, the base of Pashtun support for Karzai.

As noted above, neither was the UF was not successful in forging a united front to challenge Karzai. Burhanuddin Rabbani (Afghanistan president during 1992-1996), the elder statesman of the UF bloc, reportedly insisted that an ethnic Tajik (the ethnic core of the UF) head the UF ticket. Observers in Kabul say the UF had always leaned toward former Foreign Minister Dr. Abdullah Abdullah to its slate, and Dr. Abdullah did register to run. His running mates are Dr. Cheragh Ali Cheragh, a Hazara who did poorly in the 2004 election, and a little known Pashtun, Homayoun Wasefi. However, Wasefi is not likely to pull many Pashtun votes from Karzai or Ghani's slates. Some reports in May 2009 say that Ghani and Abdullah are still discussing a joint ticket, which would require one of them to drop out of the presidential slot and substitute as a replacement vice presidential running mate, but no agreement has been announced. Another problem for the UF is that Ahmad Zia Massoud (currently one of Karzai's Vice Presidents) did not win support of the bloc to head its ticket. Massoud is the brother of Ahmad Shah Masoud (see above), who was killed purportedly by Al Qaeda two days before the September 11 attacks on the United States, and Ahmad Zia has support among followers of his slain brother.

Other Pashtun contenders Ghul Agha Shirzai, a member of the powerful Barakzai clan, and Anwar al-Haq Ahady, the former Finance Minister and Central Bank governor, did not run. Shirzai reportedly reached an arrangement with Karzai the week of the registration period that headed off his candidacy. Nor did Bush Administration U.S. Ambassador to U.N., Afghan-born Zalmay Khalilzad himself run; he organized a conference of Karzai opponents in Dubai in early March 2009 and was, up until the last minute, said to be trying to build support for a candidacy or to unify anti-Karzai factions. As noted above, he is now discussing with Karzai a position in his post-election cabinet/government if Karzai is re-elected.

Because his ticket appears to unite major ethnic groups and demonstrates splits within the Tajik/UF grouping , Karzai is now viewed as a clear favorite for re-election. Some observers say that Karzai's main potential opponents are basing their election strategy on creating the impression that the Obama Administration prefers that Karzai not be re-elected. It is not certain that, even if this impression took hold, that Afghan voters would cast their ballots on this basis.

On the other hand, as noted, Karzai's popularity has been undermined by perceptions of ineffectiveness and corruption and it is possible he might be defeated at the polls. Karzai has in some measure used some U.S. policy setbacks to bolster his electoral prospects. He has railed against civilian casualties resulting from U.S./NATO operations. Following an August 21, 2008, airstrike that some Afghans said killed 90 civilians (the incident is in dispute) near Herat city, the Afghan cabinet called for bringing foreign forces under Afghan law, replacing an 2001 interim "status of forces agreement" with the coalition. Afghanistan and the United States conducted a joint investigation of the incident. Another major incident occurred in Farah Province in early May 2009, on the eve of Karzai's visit to the United States.

Other significant candidates, of the 45 slates that registered by the May 8 deadline are shown in the box below.

Other Candidates

Abd al-Salam Rocketi ("Mullah Rocketi) - A Pashtun, reconciled Taliban figure, member of the lower house of parliament. May do unexpectedly well if Taliban sympathizers participate, but some believe he might drop out later and endorse Karzai.

Hedayat Amin Arsala – A Pashtun, was a Vice President during 2001-2004. He is a prominent economist and perceived as close to the former royal family.

Abd al Jabbar Sabit - A Pashtun, was fired by Karzai in 2007 for considering run against Karzai in the election.

Shahnawaz Tanai - A Pashtun. Served as Defense Minister in the Communist government of Najibullah (which was left in place after the Soviets withdrew in 1989) but led failed coup against Najibullah in April 1990.

Mirwais Yasini. Another strong Pashtun candidate. 48-year-old deputy speaker of the lower house of parliament but also without well known non-Pashtun running mates.

Haj Nasrullah Baryalai. Pashtun tribal leader from Jalalabad. Some say he is a candidate to watch, although he attracts little attention outside Afghanistan.

Ramazan Bashardost. A Hazara, mentioned above, running on platform of anti-corruption and improving government services.

Conclusion

Some believe that U.S. policy requires a new Afghan president untainted by corruption among associates. Others believe that Karzai's opponents might not necessarily perform better if they are elected, and would similarly favor their clansmen and other inner circle members. Still, U.S. policy is said to increasingly be accommodating the likelihood of a Karzai re-election, in large part because of the apparent disarray among his opponents.

A major fear among experts is that the election will be marred by violence, or by real or perceived fraud. Some believe that if many candidates enter the race, there will be small percentages separating each candidate, magnifying the effect of any fraud. If the election is derailed by unending fraud charges or the grave security situation, it is possible that Afghan leaders could convene a *loya jirga* to select a president. Some believe that this process could lead to the emergence of a Karzai opponent if the Obama Administration exerts influence on behalf of a challenger. Others say any U.S. interference in any Afghan process could produce a backlash against the United States.

Another fear among some experts is that Afghan voters will end up selecting a non-Pashtun as President. While such an outcome could represent a legitimate outcome of a democratic process, some believe that Afghanistan's Pashtuns—who view it as their right to rule Afghanistan—will not accept that outcome and would rise in rebellion.

Table 2. Major Pashtun Tribal Confederations

Clan/Tribal Confederations	Location	Example
Durrani	Qandahar	
Popalzai	Qandahar	Hamid Karzai, President of Afghanistan; Jelani Popal, head of the Independent Directorate of Local Governance
Alikozai	Qandahar	N/A
Barakzai	Qandahar, Helmand	Ghul Agha Shirzai (Governor, Nangarhar Province)
Achakzai	Qandahar, Helmand	
Noorzai	Qandahar	Noorzai brothers, briefly in charge of Qandahar after the fall of the Taliban in November 2001
Ghilzai	Paktia, Paktika and Khost	Mullah Omar
Ahmadzai	Paktia, Paktika, Khost	Mohammed Najibullah (pres.1986-1992)
		Ashraf Ghani, Finance Finance Minister 2002-2004
Taraki		Nur Mohammed Taraki (leader 1978-1979)
Kharoti		Hafizullah Amin (leader, September - December1979)
Zadran	Paktia, Khost	Pacha Khan Zadran (see text) ; Insurgent leader Jalaludin Haqqani
Kodai		
Mangal	Paktia, Khost	Ghulab Mangal (Governor of Helmand Province)
Orkazai		
Shinwari	Nangarhar province	Fasl Ahmed Shinwari, former Supreme Court Chief Justice
Mandezai		
Sangu Khel		
Sipah		
Wardak (Pashtu-speaking Non-Pashtun)	Wardak Province	Abdul Rahim Wardak (Defense Minister)
Afridis	Tirah, Khyber Pass, Kohat	
Zaka khel		
Jawaki		
Adam khel		
Malikdin, etc		
Yusufzais	Khursan, Swat, Kabul	
Akozais		
Malizais		
Loezais		
Khattaks	Kohat, Peshawar, Bangash	
Akorai		
Terai		
Mohmands	Near Khazan, Peshawar	
Baizai		
Alimzai		

Uthmanzais		
Khawazais		
Wazirs	Mainly in Waziristan	
Darwesh khel		
Bannu		

Source: This table was prepared by Hussein Hassan, Information, Research Specialist, CRS. Louis Dupree, and Abdul Rahman Pazhwak, Edited by: Shah Muhammad Rais, Pashtunistan, 2003. S. Iftikhar Hussain, Some Major Pukhtoon Tribes Along The Pak-Afghan Border, Area Studies Center, University of Peshawar, Pakistan, 2000. Brigadier Haroon Rashid, The History of the Pathans, Vol 1: The Sarbani Pathans, Islamabad, Pakistan, 2002. N/A indicates no example is available.

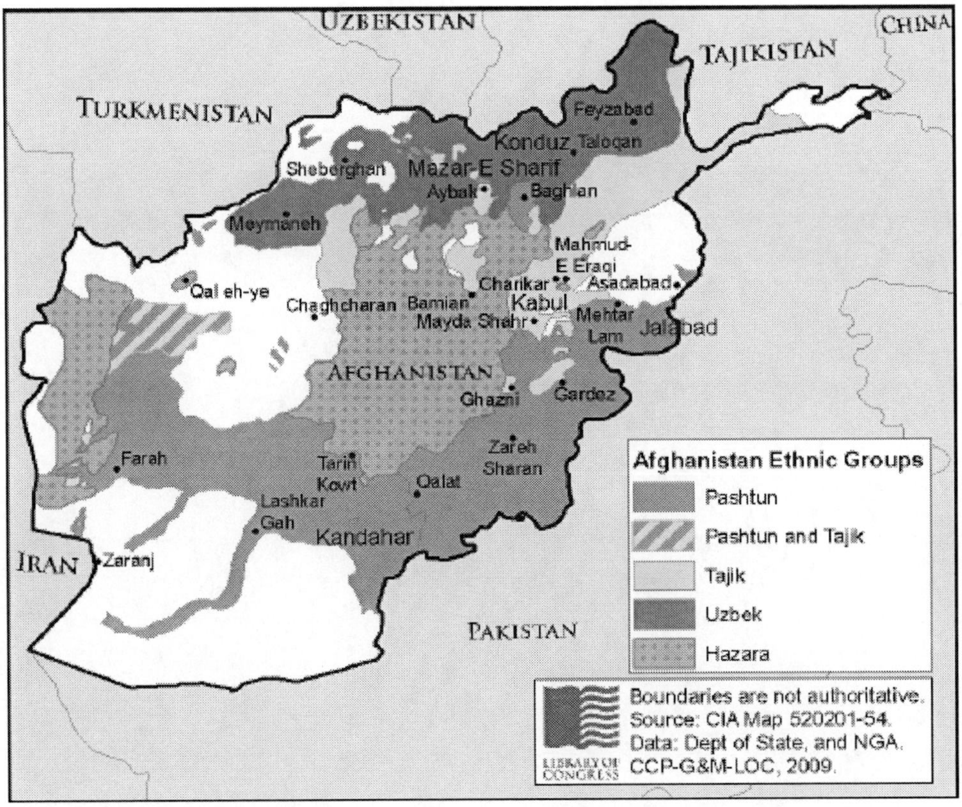

Figure 1. Afghanistan Ethnic Groups

End Notes

[1] For text, see http://www.un.org/News/dh/latest/afghan/afghan-agree.htm.

[2] Sayyaf led the *Ittihad Islami* (Islamic Union) mujahedin party during the war against the Soviet occupation.

[3] The mujahedin party he headed during the anti-Soviet war was the Afghan National Liberation Front.

[4] Some information in this section is from the State Department reports on human rights in Afghanistan for 2007. March 11, 2008 http://www.state.gov/g/drl/rls/ hrrpt/2007/100611.htm; the International Religious Freedom Report, released September 19, 2008. http://www.state.gov/g/drl/irf/2007/90225.htm; and Defense Department "Report on Progress Toward Security and Stability in Afghanistan." June 2008.

[5] CRS e-mail conversation with National Security aide to President Karzai. December 2008.

[6] Filkins, Dexter. "Bribes Corrode Afghan's Trust in Government." *New York Times*, January 2, 2009.

[7] Statement of the Independent Election Commission Secretariat. February 3, 2009, provided to CRS by a Karzai national security aide.

[8] Some of the information in this section obtained in CRS interviews with a Karzai national security aide. December 2008.

In: Asian Economic and Political Issues, Volume 14
Editor: David A. Marek
ISBN: 978-1-61728-019-1

Chapter 7

PAKISTAN'S NUCLEAR WEAPONS: PROLIFERATION AND SECURITY ISSUES*

Paul K. Kerr and Mary Beth Nikitin

SUMMARY

Pakistan's nuclear arsenal consists of approximately 60 nuclear warheads. Pakistan continues fissile material production for weapons, and is adding to its weapons production facilities and delivery vehicles. Pakistan reportedly stores its warheads unassembled with the fissile core separate from non-nuclear explosives, and these are stored separately from their delivery vehicles. Pakistan does not have a stated nuclear policy, but its "minimum credible deterrent" is thought to be primarily a deterrent to Indian military action. Command and control structures have been dramatically overhauled since September 11, 2001 and export controls and personnel security programs have been put in place since the 2004 revelations about Pakistan's top nuclear scientists, A.Q. Khan's international proliferation network.

Pakistani and some U.S. officials argue that Islamabad has taken a number of steps to prevent further proliferation of nuclear-related technologies and materials and improve its nuclear security. A number of important initiatives such as strengthened export control laws, improved personnel security, and international nuclear security cooperation programs have improved the security situation in recent years.

Instability in Pakistan has called the extent and durability of these reforms into question. Some observers fear radical takeover of a government that possesses a nuclear bomb, or proliferation by radical sympathizers within Pakistan's nuclear complex in case of a breakdown of controls. While U.S. and Pakistani officials express confidence in controls over Pakistan's nuclear weapons, continued instability in the country could impact these safeguards. For a broader discussion, see CRS Report RL33498, *Pakistan-U.S. Relations*, by K. Alan Kronstadt.

---

* This is an edited, reformatted and augmented version of a CRS Report for Congress publication, Report #RL34248, dated June 12, 2009.

Background

Chronic political instability in Pakistan and the current offensive against the Taliban in the northwest of the country have called attention to the issue of the security of the country's nuclear weapons. Some observers fear that Pakistan's strategic nuclear assets could be obtained by terrorists, or used by elements in the Pakistani government. Chair of the Joint Chiefs of Staff Admiral Michael Mullen described U.S. concern about the matter during a September 22, 2008 speech:

> To the best of my ability to understand it—and that is with some ability—the weapons there are secure. And that even in the change of government, the controls of those weapons haven't changed. That said, they are their weapons. They're not my weapons. And there are limits to what I know. Certainly at a worst-case scenario with respect to Pakistan, I worry a great deal about those weapons falling into the hands of terrorists and either being proliferated or potentially used. And so, control of those, stability, stable control of those weapons is a key concern. And I think certainly the Pakistani leadership that I've spoken with on both the military and civilian side understand that.

U.S. officials continue to be concerned about the existential threat posed by nuclear weapons in a destabilized Pakistan. General David H. Petraeus, Commander, U.S. Central Command, testified March 31, 2009, that "Pakistani state failure would provide transnational terrorist groups and other extremist organizations an opportunity to acquire nuclear weapons and a safe haven from which to plan and launch attacks."

President Obama addressed this issue in an April 29, 2009, press conference, stating, "I'm confident that we can make sure that Pakistan's nuclear arsenal is secure, primarily, initially, because the Pakistani army, I think, recognizes the hazards of those weapons falling into the wrong hands. We've got strong military-to-military consultation and cooperation." He also recognized the sensitivity of the issue for Pakistan, saying, "We want to respect their sovereignty, but we also recognize that we have huge strategic interests, huge national security interests in making sure that Pakistan is stable and that you don't end up having a nuclear-armed militant state."[1] Declining to engage in "hypotheticals" when asked if the United States is ready to secure the nuclear arsenal if the Pakistani government could not do so, President Obama said he felt "confident that that nuclear arsenal will remain out of militant hands."

General Petraeus reaffirmed this confidence on May 10: "With respect to the—the nuclear weapons and—and sites that are controlled by Pakistan … we have confidence in their security procedures and elements and believe that the security of those sites is adequate."[2] Admiral Mullen echoed this assessment during a May 14, 2009, hearing before the Senate Armed Services Committee, but added that "we're limited in what we actually know" about Islamabad's nuclear arsenal." Leon Panetta, Director of the Central Intelligence Agency, similarly acknowledged in a May 18 speech that the United States does not possess the intelligence to know the locations of all of Pakistan's nuclear weapons-related sites.

Pakistani efforts to improve the security of the country's nuclear weapons have been on-going and include some cooperation with the United States. Since the 1998 Pakistani and Indian nuclear tests, the international community has increased attention to reducing the risk of nuclear war in South Asia. The two countries most recently came to the brink of full-scale war in 1999 and 2002, and, realizing the dangers, have developed some risk reduction measures to prevent accidental nuclear war. Islamabad has also developed its command and control systems and improved security of military and civilian nuclear facilities. Since the 2004 revelations of an extensive international nuclear proliferation network run by Pakistani nuclear official Abdul Qadeer Khan, as well as possible connections between Pakistani nuclear scientists and Al Qaeda, Islamabad has made additional efforts to improve export controls and monitor nuclear personnel. The main security challenges for Pakistan's nuclear arsenal are keeping the integrity of the command structure, ensuring physical security, and preventing illicit proliferation from insiders.

Nuclear Weapons

Pakistan's nuclear energy program dates back to the 1950s, but it was the loss of East Pakistan (now Bangladesh) in a bloody war with India that probably triggered a political decision in January 1972 (just one month later) to begin a secret nuclear weapons program. Deterring India's nuclear weapons and augmenting Pakistan's inferior conventional forces are widely believed to be the primary motivation for Islamabad's nuclear arsenal. Observers point to the peaceful nuclear explosion by India in 1974 as the pivotal moment which gave additional urgency to the program. Pakistan's path to the bomb was through uranium enrichment technology, mastered by the mid-1980s. Highly-enriched uranium (HEU) is one of two types of fissile material used in nuclear weapons; the other is plutonium. The country's main enrichment facility is a gas centrifuge plant located at Kahuta, although Pakistan may have other enrichment sites.[3]

Islamabad gained technology from many sources. This extensive assistance is reported to have included, among other things, uranium enrichment technology from Europe, blueprints for a small nuclear weapon from China, and missile technology from China.

The United States had information during the 1970s that Pakistan was pursuing nuclear weapons designs, but exactly when Pakistan produced a workable nuclear explosive device is unclear.[4] A 1985 National Intelligence Council report stated that Pakistan "probably has a workable design for a nuclear explosive device" and was "probably ... a year or two away from a capacity to produce enough" highly enriched uranium for such a device. A 1993 National Security Council report to Congress stated that Islamabad's nuclear weapons efforts "culminated with the capability to rapidly assemble a nuclear device if necessary by the end of the 1980s."[5] Khan stated in an interview published in May 1998 that Islamabad "attained" the capability to detonate such a device "at the end of 1984."[6] In any case, President Bush's failure to certify in 1990 that Pakistan did not "possess a nuclear explosive device" led to a cut-off in military and financial aid under the Pressler Amendment.[7]

When India conducted nuclear weapon tests on May 12, 1998, Pakistan's government responded two weeks later on May 28 and May 30 with six tests at the Chagai Hills test site in western Pakistan. Test yields were about 10 kilotons and 5 kilotons, according to seismic analysis.[8] The United States imposed additional sanctions after the tests, but these were lifted after the September 11th, 2001 terrorist attacks on the United States.

Most observers estimate that Pakistan has about 60 nuclear weapons.[9] Pakistan's nuclear warheads use an implosion design with a solid core of HEU, approximately 15-20 kilograms per warhead.[10] Islamabad reportedly continues to produce highly-enriched uranium for weapons at a rate of at least 100 kilograms per year.[11]

Pakistan has also pursued plutonium-based warheads and continues to produce plutonium for weapons. Pakistan has received Chinese and European assistance for at least some of its plutonium program. The 40-50 megawatt heavy water Khushab plutonium production reactor has been operating since 1998.[12] It appears that Islamabad is constructing two additional heavy water reactors, which will expand considerably Pakistan's plutonium production capacity, at the same site.[13] Additionally, Pakistan has a reprocessing facility[14] at the Pakistan Institute of Science and Technology (PINSTECH) and is apparently constructing other such facilities. *Nuclear Fuel* reported in 2000 that, according to "senior U.S. government officials," Pakistan had begun operating a "pilot-scale" reprocessing facility at the New Laboratories facility at PINSTECH.[15] Islamabad also appears to be constructing a second reprocessing facility at the site [16] and may be completing a reprocessing facility located at Chasma.[17]

Islamabad's construction of additional nuclear reactors and expansion of its reprocessing capabilities could indicate plans to increase Pakistan's nuclear weapons arsenal in the near future. Indeed, Defense Intelligence Agency Director Michael Maples told the Senate Armed Services Committee on March 10 that "Pakistan continues to develop its nuclear infrastructure, expand nuclear weapon stockpiles and seek more advanced warheads and delivery systems." Similarly, Admiral Mullen confirmed during the May 14 hearing that the United States has "evidence" that Pakistan is expanding its nuclear arsenal.

Delivery Vehicles

Pakistan has two types of delivery vehicles for nuclear weapons: aircraft controlled by the Pakistan Air Force and surface-to-surface missiles controlled by the Pakistan Army. Pakistan could deliver its nuclear weapons using F-16s purchased from the United States, provided modifications are made. It is widely believed that Pakistan has made modifications to the F-16s previously sold to them.[18] Although concerns have been raised about the impact of these sales on the strategic balance in South Asia,[19] the U.S. government maintains that the sale of additional F-16s to Pakistan will not alter the regional balance of power.[20] The contract for provision of an additional 36 aircraft was signed on September 30, 2006, as was the contract for the weapons for those aircraft and a contract to perform the mid-life upgrade on Pakistan's F-16A/B model aircraft. Pakistan's F-16 fleet will therefore be expanded, but it is unclear what portion of the fleet will be capable of a nuclear mission. Mirage III and V aircraft could also be used, although would have limited range. A-5's may have been modified to carry a nuclear payload.[21]

After India's first test of its *Prithvi* ballistic missile in 1988, Pakistan jump-started its own missile program and has three types of ballistic missiles thought to be nuclear-capable: the solid fuel *Hatf-III* (*Ghaznavi*) and *Hatf-IV* (*Shaheen*) with a range of 100-290 and 200-650 km respectively; and the medium-range *Hatf-V* (*Ghauri*) with a 1200 km range. Maples stated on March 10 that Islamabad has made "significant progress" on the *Hatf-VI* (*Shaheen-2*) missile, which, when deployed, "would become Pakistan's longest ranged ballistic missile, capable of reaching targets out to 2000 kilometers."[22] Maples also indicated that Pakistan is developing nuclear-capable cruise missiles; the *Babur* (ground-launched) and the *Ra'ad* (air-launched). Islamabad continues to carry out ballistic missile tests, but notifies India in advance in accordance with an October 2005 bilateral missile pre-notification pact.[23]

Nuclear Doctrine

Pakistan's strategic doctrine is undeclared, and will probably remain so, but prominent officials and analysts have offered insights concerning its basic tenets.[24] Describing the guiding principle as minimum credible nuclear deterrence, high level officials' statements point to four policy objectives for Islamabad's nuclear weapons: deter all forms of external aggression; deter through a combination of conventional and strategic forces; deter counterforce strategies by securing strategic assets and threatening nuclear retaliation; and stabilize strategic deterrence in South Asia.[25] Pakistani officials have also indicated that this nuclear posture is designed to preserve territorial integrity against Indian attack, prevent military escalation, and counter its main rival's conventional superiority.[26]

Pakistani officials have stated that they have already determined the arsenal size needed for a minimum nuclear deterrent and they will not engage in an arms race with India. However, Pakistan's Permanent Representative to the International Atomic Energy Agency (IAEA) wrote in July 2008 that the U.S.-India nuclear cooperation agreement, which entered into force in December 2008, could cause a nuclear arms race between Pakistan and India.[27] Moreover, a Foreign Ministry spokesperson indicated during a May 21, 2009, press briefing that, despite the government's continued opposition to a "nuclear or conventional arms race in South Asia,"

Pakistan may need to increase its nuclear arsenal in response to Indian conventional and nuclear arms expansion. As noted, U.S. officials have acknowledged Islamabad's nuclear expansion.

Pakistan has also pledged no-first-use against non-nuclear-weapon states, but has not ruled out first-use against a nuclear-armed aggressor, such as India, that attacks Pakistan.[28] Some analysts say this ambiguity serves to maintain deterrence against India's conventional superiority. And the Foreign Ministry spokesperson stated May 21 that "there are acquisitions of sophisticated weaponry by our neighbour which will disturb the conventional balance between our two countries and hence, lower the nuclear threshold." Other analysts argue that keeping the first-use option against New Delhi allows Islamabad to conduct sub-conventional operations, such as support for low intensity conflict or proxy war in Kashmir, while effectively deterring India at the strategic level.[29] Pakistan has reportedly addressed issues of survivability through second strike capability, possible hard and deeply buried storage and launch facilities, road-mobile missiles, air defenses around strategic sites, and concealment measures.[30]

Command and Control

Pakistan's command and control over its nuclear weapons is compartmentalized and includes strict operational security. The government's command and control system is based on "C4I2SR" (command, control, communication, computers, intelligence, information, surveillance and reconnaissance). Islamabad's Strategic Command Organization has a three-tiered structure, consisting of the National Command Authority (NCA), the Strategic Plans Division (SPD), and the Strategic Forces Commands.

The NCA supervises the functions and administration of all of Pakistan's organizations involved in nuclear weapons research, development, and employment, as well as the military services that operate the strategic forces.[31] The President is Chairperson of the NCA; the Prime Minister is the Vice-Chairperson. The NCA also includes the chair of the joint chiefs of staff, the Ministers of Defense, Interior, and Finance, the Director- General of the SPD, and the Commanders of the Army, Air Force, and Navy. The final authority to launch a nuclear strike requires consensus within the NCA; the Chairperson must cast the final vote. The NCA is comprised of two committees, the Employment Control Committee (ECC) and the Development Control Committee (DCC), each of which includes a mix of civilian and military officials. The ECC's functions include establishing a command and control system over the use of nuclear weapons. The DCC "exercises technical, financial and administrative control over all strategic organisations, including national laboratories and research and development organisations associated with the development and modernisation of nuclear weapons."[32]

The SPD is headed by a Director General from the Army and acts as the secretariat for the NCA. The SPD's functions include formulating Islamabad's nuclear policy, strategy, and doctrine; developing the nuclear chain of command; and formulating operational plans at the service level for the movement, deployment, and use of nuclear weapons. The Army, Air Force, and Navy each have their own strategic force command, but operational planning and control remains with the NCA. The SPD coordinates operational plans with the strategic forces commands. According to current and former Pakistani officials, Islamabad employs a system which requires that at least two, and perhaps three, people authenticate launch codes for nuclear weapons.[33]

On December 13, 2007, President Musharraf formalized these authorities and structure in the "National Command Authority Ordinance, 2007."[34] The NCA was established by administrative order, but now has a legal basis. Analysts point out that the timing of this ordinance was meant to help the command and control system weather political transitions and potentially preserve the military's strong control over the system. The ordinance also addresses the problems of the proliferation of nuclear expertise and personnel reliability. It outlines punishable offenses related to breach of confidentiality or leakage of "secured information," gives the SPD authority to investigate suspicious conduct, states that punishment for these offenses can be up to 25 years imprisonment, and applies to both serving and retired personnel, including military personnel, notwithstanding any other laws. As a result, Pakistani authorities say that the ordinance should strengthen their control over strategic organizations and their personnel.

Security Concerns

Pakistan's nuclear weapons are reportedly stored unassembled, with the fissile core separated from the non-nuclear explosives. These components are stored separately from delivery vehicles. A 2001 Department of Defense report says that Pakistan can probably assemble the weapons fairly quickly.[35] Nevertheless, separate storage may provide a layer of protection against accidental launch or prevent theft of an assembled weapon. On the other hand, it may be easier for unauthorized people to remove a weapon's fissile material core if it is not assembled. Dispersal of the assets may also create more potential access points for acquisition and may increase the risk of diversion.[36]

As the United States prepared to launch an attack on the Afghan Taliban after September 11, 2001, President Musharraf reportedly ordered that Pakistan's nuclear arsenal be redeployed to "at least six secret new locations."[37] This action came at a time of uncertainly about the future of the region, including the direction of U.S.-Pakistan relations. Islamabad's leadership was uncertain whether the U.S. would decide to conduct military strikes against Pakistan's nuclear assets if Islamabad did not assist the United States against the Taliban. Indeed, President Musharraf cited protection of Pakistan's nuclear and missile assets as one of the reasons for Islamabad's dramatic policy shift.[38]

These events, in combination with the 1999 Kargil crisis, the 2002 conflict with India at the Line of Control, and revelations about the A.Q. Khan proliferation network, inspired a variety of reforms to secure the nuclear complex. Risk of nuclear war in South Asia ran high in the 1999 Kargil crisis, when the Pakistani military is believed to have begun preparing nuclear-tipped missiles.[39] It should be noted that, even at the high alert levels of 2001 and 2002, there were no reports of Pakistan mating the warheads with delivery systems.[40]

In the fall of 2007 and early 2008, Pakistan faced another crucial moment in its history and some observers expressed concern about the security of the country's arsenal if political instability were to persist.[41] Former Prime Minister Benazir Bhutto said in an interview on November 5, 2007, that while President Musharraf says he is firm control of the nuclear arsenal, she is afraid this control could weaken due to instability in the country.[42] Similarly, Michael Krepon of the Henry L. Stimson Center has argued that "a prolonged period of turbulence and infighting among the country's President, Prime Minister, and Army Chief" could jeopardize the army's unity of command, which "is essential for nuclear security."[43] During that time, U.S. military officials also expressed concern about the security of Pakistan's nuclear weapons.[44] Director General of the International Atomic Energy Agency (IAEA), Mohamed ElBaradei, also has expressed fears that a radical regime could take power in Pakistan, and thereby acquire nuclear weapons.[45] Experts also worry that while nuclear weapons are currently under firm control, with warheads disassembled, technology could be sold off by insiders during a worsened crisis.[46]

However, U.S. intelligence officials have expressed greater confidence regarding the security of Islamabad's nuclear weapons. Deputy Secretary of State John D. Negroponte in testimony to Congress on November 7, 2007 said he believed that there is "plenty of succession planning that's going on in the Pakistani military" and that Pakistan's nuclear weapons are under "effective technical control."[47] Similarly, Donald Kerr, Principal Deputy Director of National Intelligence, told a Washington audience May 29, 2008, that the Pakistani military's control of the country's nuclear weapons is "a good thing because that's an institution in Pakistan that has, in fact, withstood many of the political changes over the years." A Department of Defense spokesperson told reporters December 9, 2008, that Washington has "no reason at this point to have any concern with regards to the security" of Islamabad's nuclear arsenal. More recently, Maples stated March 10 that Islamabad "has taken important steps to safeguard its nuclear weapons," but "vulnerabilities exist."

Other governments have also voiced opinions regarding the security of Pakistan's nuclear arsenal. For example, Indian National Security Adviser M. K. Narayanan said that the arsenal is safe and has adequate checks and balances.[48] Similarly, Secretary of State for Foreign and Commonwealth Affairs David Miliband told the *Charlie Rose Show* December 15, 2008, that Islamabad's nuclear weapons "are under pretty close lock and key." Russian Deputy Prime Minister Sergei Ivanov sounded somewhat less optimistic in a March 24, 2009, television interview, stating that Moscow is "very much concerned" about the security of Pakistan's arsenal.[49]

Pakistani officials have consistently expressed confidence in the security of the country's nuclear arsenal. Then-President Musharraf stated in November 2007 that Pakistan's nuclear weapons are under "total custodial controls."[50] More recently, President Asif Ali Zardari told CNN December 2, 2008, that the country's nuclear command and control system "is working well." Additionally, a Pakistani Foreign Ministry spokesperson stated May 21, 2009, that "there is simply no question of our strategic assets falling into the wrong hands. We have full confidence in our procedures, mechanisms and command and control systems."

In addition to the above scenarios, the security of Pakistan's nuclear weapons could also be jeopardized by another conflict between India and Pakistan, Michael Krepon argued, explaining that an "escalating war with nuclear forces in the field would increase the probability of accidents, miscalculations, and the use of nuclear weapons." This is because when tensions rise precipitously with India, the readiness level of Pakistan's nuclear deterrent also rises. Because the geographical coordinates of Pakistan's main nuclear weapon storage sites, missile, and air bases can be readily identified from satellites—and therefore targeted by opposing forces—the dictates of deterrence mandate some movement of launchers and weapons from fixed locations during crises. Nuclear weapons on the move are inherently less secure than nuclear weapons at heavily-guarded storage sites. Weapons and launchers in motion are also more susceptible to "insider" threats and accidents.[51] Such a war would also place stress on the army's unity of command, Krepon added.

U.S. plans to secure Pakistani nuclear weapons in case of a loss of control by the Pakistani government were famously addressed in Secretary of State Condoleezza Rice's confirmation hearing in January 2005. In response to a question from Senator John Kerry asking what would happen to Pakistan's nuclear weapons in the event of a radical Islamic coup in Islamabad, Secretary Rice answered, "We have noted this problem, and we are prepared to try to deal with it."[52] On November 12, 2007, responding to press reports about this contingency, a Pakistan Foreign Office spokesperson said, "Pakistan possesses adequate retaliatory capacity to defend its strategic assets and sovereignty," emphasizing that Islamabad's nuclear weapons have been under "strong multi-layered, institutionalized decision-making, organizational, administrative and command and control structures since 1998."[53] The issue of U.S. contingency plans to take over Pakistani strategic assets was raised again in the press following Benazir Bhutto's assassination, and was met with similar assurances by Pakistan's government.[54]

The United States reportedly offered Pakistan nuclear security assistance soon after September 11th, 2001.[55] U.S. assistance to Islamabad, which must comply with nonproliferation guidelines, has reportedly included the sharing of best practices and technical measures to prevent unauthorized or accidental use of nuclear weapons, as well as contribute to physical security of storage facilities and personnel reliability.[56] Some press reports say that the United States provided Pakistan with Permissive Action Links (PALs) in 2003, although former Pakistani military officials have said Pakistan has developed PALs for their warheads without assistance.[57] PALs require a code to be entered before a weapon can be detonated. As noted above, Islamabad employs a system requiring that at least two, and perhaps three, people authenticate launch codes for nuclear weapons. Security at nuclear sites in Islamabad is the responsibility of a 10,000-member security force, commanded by a two-star general.

Former Deputy Secretary of State Richard Armitage confirmed in a November 2007 interview that there has been U.S. assistance in this area, explaining that the United States was unlikely to intervene militarily in a crisis in Pakistan because "we have spent considerable time with the Pakistani military, talking with them and working with them on the security of their nuclear weapons. I think most observers would say that they are fairly secure. They have pretty sophisticated mechanisms to guard the security of those."[58] Rolf Mowatt-Larssen, former Director of the Office of Intelligence and Counterintelligence at the U.S. Department of Energy, pointed out in May 2009 that "there's not a lot of transparency into" how Islamabad spends the U.S. funds, but he nevertheless characterized them as "money well spent."[59]

The U.S. government has also reportedly offered assistance to secure or destroy radioactive materials that could be used to make a radioactive dispersal device, and to ship highly enriched uranium used in the Pakistani civilian nuclear sector out of the country.[60] It is not clear what Pakistan's response has been to these proposals.

Proliferation Threat

Many observers are concerned that other states or terrorist organizations could obtain material or expertise related to nuclear weapons from Pakistan.[61] Beginning in the 1970s, Pakistan used clandestine procurement networks to develop its nuclear weapons program. Former Pakistani nuclear official A.Q. Khan subsequently used a similar network to supply Libya, North Korea, and Iran with materials related to uranium enrichment.[62]

Al-Qaeda has also sought assistance from the Khan network. According to former Director of Central Intelligence George Tenet, the United States "received fragmentary information from an intelligence service" that in 1998 Osama bin Laden had "sent emissaries to establish contact" with the network.[63] Other Pakistani sources could also provide nuclear material to terrorist organizations. According to a 2005 report by the Commission on the Intelligence Capabilities of the United States Regarding Weapons of Mass Destruction, al-Qaeda "had established contact with Pakistani scientists who discussed development of nuclear devices that would require hard-to-obtain materials like uranium to create a nuclear explosion."[64] Tenet explains that these scientists were affiliated with a different organization than the Khan network.

The current status of Pakistan's nuclear export network is unclear, although most official U.S. reports indicate that, at the least, it has been damaged considerably. Director of National Intelligence John D. Negroponte implied that the network had been dismantled when he asserted in a January 11, 2007, statement to the Senate Select Committee on Intelligence that "Pakistan had been a major source of nuclear proliferation until the disruption of the A.Q. Khan network."[65] More recently, a January 12, 2009, State Department press release said that the network "is no longer operating." For its part, Pakistan's Foreign Office stated February 7, 2009, that Pakistan "has dismantled the nuclear black market network."

However, when asked about the network's current status during a July 25, 2007, Senate Foreign Relations Committee hearing, Undersecretary for Political Affairs Nicholas Burns replied that:

> I cannot assert that no part of that network exists, but it's my understanding based on our conversations with the Pakistanis that the network has been fundamentally dismantled. But to say that there are no elements in Pakistan, I'm not sure I could say that.

Similarly, the London-based International Institute for Strategic Studies found in a May 2007 report that "at least some of Khan's associates appear to have escaped law enforcement attention and could ... resume their black-market business."[66]

Asked about Pakistan's cooperation in investigating the network, Burns acknowledged that the United States has not had "personal, consistent access" to Khan, but added that he did not "have all the details of everything we've done." Similarly, the IAEA has not yet been able to interview Khan directly, according to an agency official. However, Islamabad has responded to written questions from the IAEA and has been cooperative in its investigation of Iran's nuclear program.[67] Khan himself told *Dawn News TV* May 29, 2008, that he would not cooperate with U.S. or IAEA investigators. A Pakistani Foreign Office spokesperson told reporters in May 2006 that the government considered the Khan investigation "closed"—a position an Office spokesperson reiterated February 6, 2009.

The State Department announced January 12, 2009, that it was imposing sanctions on 13 individuals and three companies for their involvement in the Khan network. The sanctions were imposed under the Export-Import Bank Act, the Nuclear Proliferation Prevention Act, and Executive Orders 12938 and 13382.

Pakistan's Response to the Proliferation Threat

Undersecretary Burns testified in July 2007 that the Bush administration has "told the Pakistani government that it is its responsibility ... to make sure" that neither the Khan network nor a "similar organization" resurfaces in the country. Since the revelations about the Khan network, Pakistan appears to have increased its efforts to prevent nuclear proliferation. But whether and to what extent these efforts have been successful is not yet clear. It is worth noting that, because Khan conducted his proliferation activities as a government official, they do not necessarily indicate a failure of Islamabad's export controls.

Pakistani officials argue that Islamabad has taken a number of steps to prevent further proliferation of nuclear-related technologies and materials.[68] For example, Islamabad adopted in September 2004 new national export controls legislation which includes a requirement that the government issue control lists for "goods, technologies, material, and equipment which may contribute to designing, development, stockpiling, [and] use" of nuclear weapons and related delivery systems. According to a February 2008 presentation by Zafar Ali, Director of Pakistan's Strategic Export Controls Division (SECDIV),[69] the lists, which were issued in October 2005 and are to be periodically updated, include items controlled by multilateral export control regimes, such as the Nuclear Suppliers Group, the Australia Group, and the

Missile Technology Control Regime.[70] The export controls legislation also includes a catch-all clause, which requires exporters to notify the government if they are aware or suspect that goods or technology are intended by the end-user for use in nuclear or biological weapons, or missiles capable of delivering such weapons.[71]

The legislation includes several other important elements, such as end-use and end-user certification requirements and new penalties for violators. Since its adoption, Pakistan has established the SECDIV and an associated Oversight Board. The SECDIV is responsible for formulating rules and regulations for implementing the legislation. The board is comprised of officials from multiple agencies and is headed by Pakistan's Foreign Secretary.

Islamabad says that it has also taken several other steps to improve its nuclear security. For example, the government announced in June 2007 that it is "implementing a National Security Action Plan with the [IAEA's] assistance." That same month, Pakistan also joined the U.S.—and Russian-led Global Initiative to Combat Nuclear Terrorism. As noted above, the December 2007 National Command Authority Ordinance also includes measures to prevent the spread of nuclear-related materials and expertise.

Pakistani officials participating in an April 2007 Partnership for Global Security workshop argued that Islamabad has improved the reliability of its nuclear personnel by, for example, making its security clearance procedures more stringent. However, the officials also acknowledged that Islamabad still needs to do more to control its nuclear expertise.[72] Similarly, Admiral Mullen stated May 14, 2009, that the country's personnel reliability system must "continue to improve."

The United States has also provided export control assistance to Pakistan. Burns described several such efforts in his July 2007 testimony.[73] And according to an October 2007 U.S. Government Accountability Office report, Islamabad was during FY2003-FY2006 the second-largest recipient of bilateral U.S. assistance designed to improve target countries' export controls. Pakistan received such assistance from the Departments of State, Energy, and Homeland Security.[74]

ISSUES FOR CONGRESS

Members of Congress have also expressed concerns regarding the security of Pakistan's nuclear weapons and related material. Senator Richard Lugar has spoken out in favor of using the cooperative threat reduction tools in Pakistan to help with the security of nuclear, biological, and chemical materials and weapons in the country.[75]

Additionally, a number of pieces of legislation appear designed to influence Islamabad's policies regarding the Khan network. Section 2 of H.R. 1463, which was introduced March 12, 2009, and referred to the House Foreign Affairs Committee the same day, states that U.S. military assistance may be provided to Pakistan only if the President certifies that Islamabad is both making A.Q. Khan available to the United States for questioning and "providing adequate assurances to the United States Government that it will monitor Khan's movements and activities in such a manner as to prevent his participation in any efforts to disseminate nuclear technology or know-how." This section allows the President to waive restrictions on U.S. assistance imposed pursuant to the proposed legislation if the President "certifies to Congress that it is in the national interests of the United States to do so."

H.R. 2481, the United States-Pakistan Security and Stability Act, which was introduced May 19, 2009, and referred the same day to the House Foreign Affairs Committee, the House Armed Services Committee, and the House Intelligence Committee, would require the President to "develop and transmit to the appropriate congressional committees a comprehensive interagency strategy and implementation plan for long-term security and stability in Pakistan." The strategy is to include a "description of how United States assistance" authorized by the bill "will be used to achieve the objectives of United States policy toward Pakistan," one of which is "to empower and enable" Islamabad to "maintain robust command and control over its nuclear weapons technology." The bill would authorize foreign assistance for Pakistan, including funds for improving the government's counter-insurgency capability.

H.R. 1886, the Pakistan Enduring Assistance and Cooperation Enhancement Act of 2009, authorizes U.S. assistance to Pakistan for a variety of purposes. These include strengthening democratic institutions and law enforcement, as well as supporting economic development, education, human rights, and heath care. The bill would also authorize additional U.S. security assistance for Islamabad. However, Section 206 of the bill places conditions on some of this assistance; it states that no U.S. military assistance shall be provided to Pakistan if the President has not made a series of determinations, one of which is that the government "is continuing to cooperate with the United States in efforts to dismantle supplier networks relating to the acquisition of nuclear weapons related materials, including, as necessary, providing access to Pakistani nationals associated with such networks." The section includes a national security waiver. The bill also requires a report to Congress that includes a "description of Pakistan's efforts to prevent proliferation of nuclear-related material and expertise" and an "assessment of whether assistance provided to Pakistan pursuant to this Act has directly or indirectly aided the expansion of Pakistan's nuclear weapons program." The conference report underlines continuing concerns about getting full information about the activities of the Khan network and development of Pakistan's own nuclear arsenal:

> Pakistan's history of nuclear development and Dr. Abdul Qadeer Khan's establishment of a nuclear proliferation network remain a source for concern to many in the United States, particularly since the Committee understands that representatives of the United States have not interviewed certain individuals involved in the network. The Committee believes the United States should continue to engage the Government of Pakistan on the network, and should, as necessary, obtain direct access to the individuals covered by this subsection, including Dr. Khan. The Committee also maintains strong concerns regarding recent reports of Pakistan expansion of its nuclear arsenal. Given the expanding threat of Pakistan's domestic insurgency, the Government of Pakistan's further development of nuclear materials appears inconsistent with its immediate security threats and is unhelpful in the context of efforts to strengthen U.S.-Pakistani relations.

H.R. 1886 was introduced April 2, 2009, and referred the same day to both the House Foreign Affairs Committee and Rules Committee. The Foreign Affairs Committee reported the bill May 22, and the Rules Committee discharged it the same day. The bill was referred to the House Armed Services Committee May 22 and discharged June 2. The House passed H.R. 1886 on June 11.

The Senate is considering the Enhanced Partnership with Pakistan Act of 2009 (S. 962), which would provide aid to Pakistan but does not include conditions regarding the nuclear nonproliferation or nuclear weapons activities. The Senate Foreign Relations Committee will mark up the bill on June 16.

Senator Webb introduced an amendment (S.Amdt. 1202) to the 2009 Supplemental Appropriations Act (H.R. 2346) that would require the President to certify that appropriate measures are taken to ensure that none of the aid could "support, expand, or in any way assist in the development or deployment of the nuclear weapons program of the Government of Pakistan."

End Notes

[1] President Obama's 100th-Day Press Briefing transcript, April 29, 2009, accessed at http://www.nytimes.com/2009/04/ 29/us/politics/29text-obama.html?_r=1&pagewanted=print.

[2] Interview with General David H. Petraeus, FOX News Sunday, May 10, 2009. http://www.foxnews.com/story/ 0,2933,519696,00.html.

[3] Zia Mian, A.H. Nayyar, R. Rajaraman and M.V. Ramana, "Fissile Materials in South Asia: The Implications of the U.S.-India Nuclear Deal," International Panel on Fissile Materials," September 2006. For a list of Pakistani nuclear facilities, see chart in Pakistan chapter of Joseph Cirincione, Jon B. Wolfsthal, and Miriam Rajkumar, *Deadly Arsenals*, Carnegie Endowment for International Peace, 2005.

[4] See, for example, a 1978 Central Intelligence Agency report, available at http://www.faqs.org/cia/docs/44/ 0000107983/(UNTITLED)-RE.html, as well as a 1983 State Department document, available at http://www.gwu.edu/ ~nsarchiv/NSAEBB/NSAEBB114/chipak-11.pdf.

[5] National Security Council, *Report to Congress on Status of China, India and Pakistan Nuclear and Ballistic Missile Programs*, 1993. Available at http://www.fas.org/irp/threat/930728-wmd.htm.

[6] "Pakistan: Qadeer Khan Interviewed on Pakistan N-Test," *The News*, May 30, 1998.

[7] The Pressler Amendment (August 1985) linked aid and military sales to two certification conditions: (1) that Pakistan not possess a nuclear explosive device; and (2) that new aid 'will reduce significantly the risk' that Pakistan will possess such a device. For background summary of sanctions legislation, see CRS Report 98-486, *Nuclear Sanctions: Section 102(b) of the Arms Export Control Act and Its Application to India and Pakistan*, by Jeanne J. Grimmett, and CRS Report RS22757, *U.S. Arms Sales to Pakistan*, by Richard F. Grimmett.

[8] Seismic data showed yields less than those officially announced by Pakistan and India. See Gregory van der Vink, Jeffrey Park, Richard Allen, Terry Wallace and Christel Hennet, "False Accusations, Undetected Tests and Implications for the CTB Treaty," *Arms Control Today*, May 1998 http://www.armscontrol.org/act/1998_05/ vimy98.asp.

[9] "Nuclear Notebook: Pakistan's nuclear forces, 2007," *Bulletin of the Atomic Scientists*, vol. 63, no.3, May/June 2007; Arms Control Association Fact Sheet, http://www.armscontrol.org/factsheets/ Nuclearweapons whohaswhat.asp; "Global Fissile Material Report 2007," International Panel on Fissile Materials http://www.fissilematerials.org/ipfm/ site_down/gfmr07.pdf; SIPRI Yearbook 2007. The International Panel on Fissile Materials estimates that Pakistan has enough fissile material (highly enriched uranium and plutonium) for 65-80 nuclear weapons. This estimate assumes 25 kilograms of HEU per weapon and 4.5-6 kilograms of plutonium per weapon ("Banning the Production of Fissile Materials for Nuclear Weapons: Country Perspectives on the Challenges to a Fissile Material (Cutoff) Treaty," International Panel on Fissile Materials, 2008. http://www.fissilematerials.org/ipfm/site_down/gfmr08cv.pdf).

[10] "Nuclear Notebook," ibid.

[11] "Global Fissile Material Report 2007," ibid.

[12] A Pakistani newspaper reported in April 1998 that, according to a "top government source," the reactor had begun operating ("Pakistan's Indigenous Nuclear Reactor Starts Up," *The Nation*, April 13, 1998). A June 15, 2000 article cited "U.S. officials" who indicated that the reactor had begun operating two years earlier (Mark Hibbs, "After 30 Years, PAEC Fulfills Munir Khan's Plutonium Ambition," *Nucleonics Week*, June 15, 2000). A 2001 Department of Defense report stated that the reactor "will produce plutonium," but did not say whether it was operating (U.S. Department of Defense, *Proliferation: Threat and Response,* January 2001, p. 27).

[13] David Albright and Paul Brannan, "Update on Khushab Plutonium Production Reactor Construction Projects in Pakistan," Institute for Science and International Security, April 23, 2009; Mark Hibbs and Shahid-ur-Rehman, "Pakistan Civilian Fuel Cycle Plan Linked To NSG Trade Exception," *Nuclear Fuels*, August 27, 2007.

[14] "Reprocessing" refers to the process of separating plutonium from spent nuclear fuel.

[15] Hibbs, June 15, 2000. According to a 1983 State Department document, the New Laboratories facility was "capable of extracting small quantities of plutonium," but large enough to "allow for expansion of reprocessing capacity." Available at http://www.gwu.edu/~nsarchiv/NSAEBB/NSAEBB114/chipak-11.pdf.

[16] David Albright and Paul Brannan, "Pakistan Expanding Plutonium Separation Facility Near Rawalpindi," Institute for Science and International Security, May 19, 2009. The 2001 Defense Department report stated that reprocessing facilities "are under construction," but did not identify any sites (*Proliferation: Threat and Response,* p. 27.)

[17] David Albright and Paul Brannan, "Chashma Nuclear Site in Pakistan with Possible Reprocessing Plant," Institute for Science and International Security, January 18, 2007. Construction on the facility was begun during the 1970s with French assistance, but France cancelled it later that decade.

[18] The 1993 National Security Council report to Congress indicated that Pakistan would use these aircraft to deliver nuclear weapons. See National Security Council, *Report to Congress*.

[19] CRS Report RL33515, *Combat Aircraft Sales to South Asia: Potential Implications*, by Christopher Bolkcom, Richard F. Grimmett, and K. Alan Kronstadt; Zachary Ginsburg, "US Renews Fighter Exports to Pakistan," *Arms Control Today*, September 2007. http://www.armscontrol.org/act/2007_09/USPakistan.asp.

[20] "Release of these systems would not significantly reduce India's quantitative or qualitative military advantage. Release of these modifications to Pakistan will neither affect the regional balance of power nor introduce a new technology as this level of capability or higher already exists in other countries in the region." Defense Security and Cooperation Agency news release, June 28, 2006. http://www.dsca.mil/PressReleases/36-b/2006/Pakistan_06-11.pdf.

[21] CRS Report RL30623, *Nuclear Weapons and Ballistic Missile Proliferation in India and Pakistan: Issues for Congress*, by K. Alan Kronstadt.

[22] See also, Nuclear Notebook, ibid.; "Worldwide Ballistic Missile Inventories," *Arms Control Today Fact Sheet*, http://www.armscontrol.org/factsheets/missiles.asp; and Mahmud Ali Durrani, "Pakistan's Strategic Thinking and the Role of Nuclear Weapons," *Cooperative Monitoring Center Occasional Paper 37*, July 2004. http://www.cmc.sandia.gov/cmc-papers/sand2004-3375p.pdf.

[23] "Agreement Between the Republic of India and the Islamic Republic of Pakistan on Pre-Notification of Flight Testing of Ballistic Missiles." Full text on the Henry L. Stimson Center website: http://www.stimson.org /?SN= SA20060207949.

[24] Peter Lavoy, "Pakistan's Nuclear Posture: Security and Survivability," Paper presented to the Conference on Pakistan's Nuclear Future, Nonproliferation Education Center, Washington, DC, April 28, 2006: http://www.npec-web.org/Frameset.asp?PageType=Single&PDFFile=20070121-Lavoy-PakistanNuclearPosture&PDFFolder=Essays.

[25] Mahmud Ali Durrani, "Pakistan's Strategic Thinking and the Role of Nuclear Weapons," *Cooperative Monitoring Center Occasional Paper 37*, July 2004. http://www.cmc.sandia.gov/cmc-papers/sand2004-3375p.pdf.

[26] For an in-depth discussion of minimum deterrence, see Naeem Salik, "Minimum Deterrence and India Pakistan Nuclear Dialogue: Case Study on Pakistan," Landau Network Centro Volta South Asia Security Project Case Study, January 2006. http://www.centrovolta.it/landau/ South%20Asia%20Security%20Program_file%5C Documenti%5CCase%20Studies%5CSalik%20-%20S.A.%20Case%20Study%202006.pdf.

[27] Available at http://verificationthoughts.blogspot.com/2008/07/indian-separation-plan. html.

[28] It is worth noting that President Zardari stated in late 2008 that Pakistan will not be the first to use nuclear weapons against India. See James Lamont and Farhan Bokhari, "Pakistan In Trade And Arms Offer To India," *Financial Times*, November 23, 2008;"Pakistan Against Use Of Nuclear Weapons: Zardari," *Associated Press of Pakistan*, November 22, 2008; "Interview with President Asif Ali Zardari," CNN Larry King Live, December 2, 2008.

[29] Kanti Bajpai, "No First Use in the India-Pakistan Context," *Pugwash Workshop No. 279*, November 2002. http://www.pugwash.org/reports/nw/bajpai.htm.

[30] Lavoy, ibid.

[31] December 2007 Ordinance To Provide For The Constitution And Establishment Of National Command Authority.

[32] Nuclear Black Markets: Pakistan, A.Q. Khan and the Rise of Proliferation Networks, (London: The International Institute of Strategic Studies), 2007. p. 111; Pakistan Announcement of Nuclear-Weapons Command-and-Control Mechanism, Associated Press of Pakistan, February 3, 2000. Nuclear Black Markets, pp. 110-111, has organization charts of the NCA and SPD.

[33] See P. Cotta-Ramusino and M. Martellini, "Nuclear Safety, Nuclear Stability And Nuclear Strategy In Pakistan: A Concise Report Of A Visit By Landau Network - Centro Volta," January 14, 2002. Available at http://www.pugwash.org/september11/pakistan-nuclear.htm; Kenneth N. Luongo and Brig. Gen. (Ret.) Naeem Salik, "Building Confidence in Pakistan's Nuclear Security," *Arms Control Today*, December 2007; Robin Walker, "Pakistan's Evolution as a Nuclear Weapons State: Lt. Gen. Khalid Kidwai's CCC Address, *Strategic Insights*, November 1, 2006.

[34] "President Promulgated National Command Authority Ordinance," *Associated Press of Pakistan*, December 13, 2007.

[35] *Proliferation: Threat and Response,* p. 28.

[36] See Graham Allison, "What About the Nukes?" *Newsweek Web*, December 28, 2007. http://www.newsweek.com/id/ 82259

[37] Molly Moore and Kamran Khan, "Pakistan Moves Nuclear Weapons - Musharraf Says Arsenal Is Now Secure," *Washington Post*, November 11, 2001.

[38] "Partial transcript of Pakistan President Musharraf's televised speech asking the people of Pakistan to support his course of action," September 19, 2001. http://www.washingtonpost.com/wp-srv/nation/specials/attacked/transcripts/ pakistantext_091901.html.

[39] Bruce Riedel, "American Diplomacy and the 1999 Kargil Summit at Blair House," Center for the Advanced Study of India, Policy Paper Series, 2002. http://www.ccc.nps.navy.mil/research/kargil/reidel.pdf.

[40] Lavoy, ibid.

[41] "Opinions Mixed on Pakistani Nuclear Security," *Global Security Newswire*, November 6, 2007. http://www.nti.org/ d_newswire/issues/recent_stories.asp?category=nuclear#6783E660.

[42] Also see comments by David Albright in the same interview. "Pakistan in Crisis: Interview with Benazir Bhutto," *CNN,* November 5, 2007.

[43] "U.S.-Pakistan Strategic Relations," Statement before the Committee on Senate Homeland Security and Governmental Affairs Subcommittee on Federal Financial Management, Government Information, Federal Services, and International Security June 12, 2008.

[44] "Lieutenant General Carter Ham Holds a Defense Department Briefing," *CQ Transcripts*, November 7, 2007.

[45] "Al Baradei to Al Hayat," *Dar Al Hayat*, English Edition on-line, January 10, 2008, http://english.daralhayat.com/ Spec/01-2008/Article-20080110-639032eb-c0a8-10ed-01ae-81ab2ea588db/story.html.

[46] Also see comments by David Albright in "Pakistan in Crisis: Interview with Benazir Bhutto," *CNN,* November 5, 2007.

[47] House Foreign Affairs Committee Hearing on Democracy, Authoritarianism and Terrorism in Contemporary Pakistan, November 7, 2007.

[48] "Pak Nukes Safely Guarded, Says Narayanan," *The Press Trust of India*, December 16, 2007.

[49] Lyubov Pronina and Ellen Pinchuk, "Russia 'Concerned' About Security of Pakistan's Nuclear Arsenal," *Bloomberg*, March 25, 2009.

[50] "Pakistan Nukes Under Control: Musharraf," *Agence France Presse*, November 13, 2007.

[51] Krepon, June, 12, 2008.

[52] "The Nomination of Dr. Condoleezza Rice to be Secretary of State," Hearings before the Senate Foreign Relations Committee, January 18 and 19, 2005. The concept of a contingency plan to take over Pakistan's nuclear assets was first written about by Seymour Hersh, "Watching the Warheads," *The New Yorker*, November 5, 2001.

[53] "Strategic Assets Are Safe, Says FO," *Dawn*, November 12, 2007.

[54] "Pentagon Readies Plan for Pakistan's Nuclear Arsenal," *The Guardian*, December 28, 2007. For a discussion of the difficulties of such a scenario, see Shaun Gregory, "The Security of Nuclear Weapons in Pakistan," Pakistan Security Research Unit Brief Number 22, University of Bradford, November 18, 2007. Available at http://spaces.brad.ac.uk:8080/download/attachments/748/Brief_22finalised.pdf

[55] Alex Wagner, "U.S. Offers Nuclear Security Assistance to Pakistan," *Arms Control Today*, December 2001. http://www.armscontrol.org/act/2001_12/paknucsecdec01.asp.

[56] Joby Warrick, "U.S. Has Concerns Over Security of Pakistan's Nuclear Weapons," *The Washington Post*, November 11, 2007; David Sanger and William Broad, "U.S. Secretly Aids Pakistan in Guarding Nuclear Arms," *The New York Times*, November 17, 2007.

[57] Kaushik Kapisthalam, "Guarding Pakistan's Nuclear Estate," *Asia Times*, April 6, 2005. http://www.atimes.com/atimes/South_Asia/GD06Df04.html; Robert Windrem, "Pakistan's Nuclear History Worries Insiders," *NBC News*, November 6, 2007. http://www.msnbc.msn.com/id/21660667/.

[58] "A Conversation With Former Deputy Secretary of State Richard Armitage," *PBS: The Charlie Rose Show*, November 6, 2007.

[59] Ben Arnoldy, "Could Taliban Get Keys To Pakistan's A-Bomb? Experts See The Islamic Fighters As Less Of A Risk Than Radical Insiders Gaining Access To Nuclear Materials," *The Christian Science Monitor*, May 15, 2009.

[60] Bryan Bender, "Pakistan, US In Talks On Nuclear Security," *The Boston Globe*, May 5, 2009.

[61] For more information on Pakistani proliferation, see CRS Report RL32745, *Pakistan's Nuclear Proliferation Activities and the Recommendations of the 9/11 Commission: U.S. Policy Constraints and Options*, by Richard P. Cronin, K. Alan Kronstadt, and Sharon Squassoni. Also see CRS Report RL33498, *Pakistan-U.S. Relations*, by K. Alan Kronstadt.

[62] Libya obtained uranium enrichment technology and nuclear weapons designs that could support a nuclear weapons program. North Korea currently has a plutonium-based nuclear weapons program, but it is unclear

whether it also has a uranium-based onc. Iran is suspected of pursuing both plutonium- and uranium-based nuclear weapons programs.

[63] Tenet, George and Harlow, Bill, *At the Center of the Storm: My Years at the CIA*, HarperCollins: New York, 2007. p. 261.

[64] The report can be found at http://www.wmd.gov/report/index.html.

[65] Unclassified Statement for the Record Annual Threat Assessment, Senate Select Committee on Intelligence, January 11, 2007.

[66] See http://www.iiss.org/publications/strategic-dossiers/nbm.

[67] Personal communication, November 9, 2007.

[68] Details of Pakistan's nuclear-related legislation can be found in the country's reports to the UN 1540 Committee. Both can be found at http://daccessdds.un.org/doc/UNDOC/ GEN/N04/597/46/PDF/ N0459746 .pdf?OpenElement.

[69] Presentation given to Partnership for Global Security Workshop, "Meeting the Nuclear Security Challenge in Pakistan," February 21-22, 2008. http://www.partnershipforglobalsecurity.org/documents/zafar_export.pdf.

[70] The Nuclear Suppliers Group is a multilateral, voluntary group of nuclear supplier states which have agreed to coordinate their exports of civilian nuclear technology and materials in order to prevent importers from using them to produce nuclear weapons. The Australia Group is a voluntary, informal, export-control arrangement through which participating countries coordinate their national export controls to limit the supply of chemicals and biological agents, as well as related equipment, technologies, and knowledge, to countries and nonstate entities suspected of pursuing chemical or biological weapons capabilities. The Missile Technology Control Regime is an informal, voluntary arrangement in which participants agree to adhere to common export policy guidelines applied to an "annex" that lists items related to the proliferation of ballistic and cruise missiles, rockets, and unmanned air vehicles capable of delivering weapons of mass destruction.

[71] The Chemical Weapons Convention Implementation Ordinance of 2000 regulates the import and export of chemicals in accordance with the convention.

[72] Building Confidence in Pakistan's Nuclear Security: Workshop Synopsis. April 30, 2007.

[73] Burns mentioned Pakistan's participation in the Container Security Initiative and the Secure Freight Initiative. Under these programs, "the United States and Pakistan worked together to install screening and radiation detection equipment to scan U.S.-bound cargo." He also stated that the Department of Energy "is working with Pakistan on radiation source security and is in the process of finalizing an agreement to install radiation detection equipment at Pakistani ports and border crossings."

[74] GAO Report, *Nonproliferation: U.S. Efforts to Combat Nuclear Networks Need Better Data on Proliferation Risks and Program Results,* October 31, 2007.

[75] "Statement by Sen. Lugar on Nunn-Lugar and Pakistan," May 6, 2009, http://lugar.senate.gov/record.cfm?id=312588&

In: Asian Economic and Political Issues, Volume 14
Editor: David A. Marek
ISBN: 978-1-61728-019-1

Chapter 8

HUMAN RIGHTS IN CHINA: TRENDS AND POLICY IMPLICATIONS*

Thomas Lum and Hannah Fischer

SUMMARY

Human rights has been a principal area of U.S. concern in its relations with the People's Republic of China (PRC), particularly since the violent government crackdown on the Tiananmen democracy movement in 1989. Some policy makers contend that the U.S. policy of engagement with China, particularly since granting the PRC permanent normal trade relations status in 2000, has failed to produce meaningful political reform. Others argue that U.S. engagement has helped to accelerate economic and social change and build social and legal foundations for democracy and human rights in the PRC. This chapter analyzes China's mixed record on human rights – major human rights problems, new human rights legislation, and the development of civil society, legal awareness, and social and political activism. This chapter discusses major areas of interest but does not provide an exhaustive account of all human rights abuses or related incidents.

Fear of social unrest, particularly during times of economic uncertainty, appears to motivate the PRC government's resistance toward major political reform. The PRC government has attempted to respond to public grievances and popular calls for redress while subduing activists who attempt to organize mass protests and dissidents who openly call for fundamental change. This approach has both produced incremental improvements in human rights conditions and allowed for continued, serious abuses. Major, ongoing problems include excessive use of violence by security forces, unlawful detention, torture, arbitrary use of state security laws against political dissidents, coercive family planning policies, state control of information, and religious and ethnic persecution. Tibetans, ethnic Uighur Muslims, and Falun Gong adherents have been singled out for especially harsh treatment.

---

* This is an edited, reformatted and augmented version of a CRS Report for Congress publication, Report #RL34629, dated June 12, 2009.

China's leadership has addressed rising public expectations through a combination of economic growth policies and carrot-and-stick political tactics. In so doing, it has planted seeds of potential change. China's developing legal system, while plagued by corruption and political interference, has provided activists with new ways of defending rights. Although generally supportive of the status quo, the urban middle class has begun to engage in narrowly targeted protests against local government policies, following over a decade of social unrest among wage laborers and farmers. Despite a massive censorship effort, the Internet and other communications technologies have made it impossible for the government to clamp down on information as fully as before.

In December 2008, over 300 PRC citizens signed and posted online a document entitled "Charter '08" calling for fundamental changes in China's political system. An additional 8,000 people signed the manifesto before the PRC government shut down the Charter's website. One of its drafters, democratic activist Liu Xiaobo, remained in detention at the time of this writing.

The U.S. government's multifaceted efforts to promote human rights in China have included open or formal criticisms and assessments of the PRC government's human rights policies, official bilateral dialogue, sanctions, and congressionally sponsored legislation, hearings, and investigations. Some Members of the 111th Congress have called for the release of political prisoners and introduced resolutions supporting human rights in China. In March 2009, the House passed H.Res. 226, a resolution recognizing the plight of the Tibetan people. In June 2009, the House and Senate passed H.Res. 489 and S.Res. 171, respectively, commemorating those who demonstrated for democracy or died in the military crackdown in 1989 in Beijing and expressing continued support for human rights and democracy activists in China. The U.S. government also provides funding for rule of law, civil society development, participatory government, labor rights, Tibetan culture, Internet access, and other programs in the PRC.

OVERVIEW

Human rights conditions in the People's Republic of China (PRC) remain a central issue in U.S.- China relations. For many U.S. policy-makers, progress in this area represents a test of the success of U.S. engagement with the PRC, particularly since permanent normal relations status (PNTR) was granted to China in 2000. Many observers argue that legal restrictions on freedoms and cases of political and religious persecution have increased, the leadership remains a dictatorship, and that economic development has strengthened rather than weakened the Communist government.[1] Some policy-makers have pointed to the U.S. Department of State's annual reports on human rights practices in China, which have not noted major improvements in human rights conditions since the democracy movement of 1989.[2] Other analysts and many Chinese citizens contend that economic and social freedoms as well as limitations on governmental controls over most aspects of people's lives have grown considerably during the past two decades. This trend has even allowed for the emergence of occasional, fragile outbursts of "people power." Disagreements over whether progress in human rights has been made often stem from differences over which variables are focused on, such as central government policies, local government actions, civil society, social activism, or short-term versus long-term trends. In many cases, both growing government restrictions and greater assertion of civil rights have occurred simultaneously.

Successive U.S. administrations since 1989 have employed broadly similar strategies for promoting human rights in China. Nonetheless, experts and policy makers have sharply disagreed over what level of emphasis to place on human rights in relation to other concerns in the bilateral relationship, whether open criticism and sanctions or quiet diplomacy and dialogue are more effective, and whether the U.S. objective should be fundamental political change in China or incremental progress in such areas as the rule of law, civil society, and local elections. Some human rights advocates have charged that the Obama Administration in its first months has emphasized economic, environmental, and security concerns at the expense of human rights in its policy towards China. Other analysts have suggested that Sino-U.S. cooperation in these areas creates greater and more favorable opportunities for promoting human rights.

Under the leadership of President Hu Jintao and Premier Wen Jiabao, both in office since 2003, the PRC government has developed along the lines of what some analysts call "responsive authoritarianism." Beijing has striven to become more populist, accountable, and law-based. However, the government has rejected far-reaching political reforms. In response to public calls for democracy in late 2008, PRC leaders reaffirmed the Communist Party's leading role and rejected multi-party democracy and separation of powers.[3] On the one hand, the government has sympathized with segments of the population who have been left out of the economic boom. The central leadership also has formally acknowledged human rights as a concern of the state, continued to develop legal institutions, and implemented limited institutional restraints on the exercise of state power. On the other hand, in practice, Communist Party and government officials have retained a large degree of arbitrary authority, particularly over political dissent.

The PRC government faces a quandary – how to improve governance and reduce sources of social and political instability through anti-corruption campaigns and the implementation of incremental political reforms without unleashing mass pressures for greater change, particularly in times of economic difficulty. PRC leaders have expressed the fear that China's fledgling civil society, combined with foreign "democracy assistance" and the involvement of international nongovernmental organizations, could bring about a "color revolution." "Color revolutions" refer to peaceful democratic movements involving mass demonstrations that have toppled several post- communist authoritarian governments in former Soviet States such as Georgia, Ukraine, and Kyrgyzstan. The Chinese government has enacted legislation aimed at preventing human rights abuses, but without protecting the rights of human rights activists or "defenders." It has tolerated protests against official policies, particularly at the local level, but has arrested protest leaders. Public and semi-public discourse on a wide variety of topics have become routine, but politically sensitive issues remain off-limits. Meanwhile, economic and social tensions have combined with growing rights consciousness and social activism. Many efforts by citizens to express grievances and demand redress, having been met by government inaction, have erupted into large-scale public protests.

A Mixed Picture

The past few years have witnessed a mixed picture on progress in human rights conditions in China. On the one hand, the U.S. State Department's annual human rights reports have stated that China's record has "remained poor." None of the groups suffering the greatest persecution have experienced notable improvement in overall treatment, according to the reports. These include Tibetan Buddhist monks and ethnic Uighur Muslims, leaders of unsanctioned Christian churches, Falun Gong practitioners, political dissidents, and "human rights defenders." On the other hand, the PRC government has enacted laws aimed at reducing some of the most egregious human rights abuses, protecting property rights, and promoting government transparency, and continued to develop mechanisms for consulting with non-state policy experts. The Chinese Communist Party (CCP) and local governments reportedly also have considered or taken minor steps toward abolishing the re-education through labor system or *laojiao*, making elections more competitive, and enabling rural migrants to gain official residency status in some large cities.

Two events in 2008, the Beijing Olympics and the Sichuan earthquake, helped to demonstrate both the power of the state and the potential of China's young civil society. In 2007, many Chinese political activists took advantage of the Olympics' promise of increased openness to make public appeals for political reforms.[4] However, the PRC leadership, rather than act upon President Hu's repeated references to "democracy" at the 17th Party Congress in October 2007, stifled most dissenting voices during the several months leading up to the games. In the immediate aftermath of the May 2008 earthquake, China experienced an unprecedented outburst of unfiltered press coverage and volunteer activity and organization. But in June 2008, the PRC government began suppressing protests regarding shoddy construction of school buildings that collapsed during the disaster and killed an estimated 10,000 children.[5]

Selected Highlights from the State Department's Human Rights Report for 2008

The State Department's annual *Country Reports on Human Rights Practices* stated that China's human rights record remained poor in 2008 and worsened in some areas.[6] According to the report, the PRC remains an authoritarian state in which the permanent leadership role of the Chinese Communist Party is inscribed in the Constitution, while the legislative and judicial branches lack the power to check the CCP and the state. Many political rights remain severely curtailed. In 2008, tighter restrictions on rights were imposed in Tibet and Xinjiang, upon the mass media, toward dissidents and petitioners seeking redress, and on non-governmental organizations (NGOs). According to the State Department, major human rights abuses committed by the state in 2008 included the following:

- **Unlawful or Politically-Motivated Killings:** There were reports of unlawful killings by security forces or their agents during the year.[7]

- **Torture:** Despite government efforts to reduce the practice, reports indicated widespread physical abuse and the use of torture against criminal suspects and political activists under detention.

- **Re-education through Labor (RETL):** The RETL system, or *laogai*, in which individuals are held in administrative detention for "anti-social activity," without formal charges or trial, for a period of up to four years, remained a central feature of social and political control in China.

- **Unlawful Detention:** Unlawful detention and house arrest remained widespread, particularly against scores of human rights activists, lawyers, journalists, and leaders of unofficial Christian churches. According to a government survey, between 2003 and 2007, 33,643 persons were detained for periods longer than that allowed by law.

- **Political Prisoners:** Several thousand persons were serving jail time for either "endangering state security" or the former political crime of "counter-revolution."

- **Coercive Family Planning:** China's "one child policy" continued with sporadic reports of coercive abortions, forced sterilizations, and other unlawful government actions against individuals, some of which triggered protests.[8]

- **Censorship:** Public discussion, speech, or reporting of sensitive or controversial political topics were forbidden. Such topics included the Tiananmen events of 1989, Taiwan, Tibet, Falun Gong, and criticism of the CCP leadership. The government continued to control political content of print media, jam some foreign radio broadcasts, and censor Internet sites, Web logs (blogs), and e-mail.
  Many journalists, editors, and freelance writers, including Internet authors, who broached dissenting views on sensitive political issues, faced harassment, physical assault, detention, or imprisonment.

- **Religious Persecution:** The extent of religious freedom continued to vary widely within the country. Crackdowns against unregistered Protestants and Catholics as well as Tibetans and Uighur Muslims were reported in some areas, and repression and persecution of Falun Gong continued. Freedom to participate in officially sanctioned religious activity continued to increase in most areas, however.

The Birth of Civil Society

Although the PRC leadership remains the final, undisputed authority, non-state actors play a tiny but growing role in policy-making, political discourse, and social activity.[9] In some cases, the state has encouraged social participation, either as a way to improve governance or to allow people to "let off steam." In other cases, social actors have pushed the boundaries of permissible political activity at great personal risk.

Some academics and intellectuals have reported greater involvement in policy-making through the government's consultation of expert opinion and think tanks. They also collaborate with non- state elites and actors, such as NGOs and private entrepreneurs, who often sponsor research projects. Although nearly all of China's think tanks are linked to government institutions, their funding sources and clientele, academic backgrounds, and areas of expertise have become increasingly diverse. They also have become more autonomous, although many budgetary and political constraints upon their activities remain.[10]

In other areas, the range of sensitive topics, such as social unrest, government corruption, and the abuse of power, particularly at the local level, that can be reported or discussed publicly has grown. Religious activity overall, in both sanctioned and unsanctioned places of worship, has increased. Freedom of movement, both within the country and abroad, also has expanded. Lawyers, journalists, and activists have been at the forefront in helping to protect and promote human rights and the public interest. They may form the beginnings of a small, loosely organized, and still largely latent human rights movement, in which "civil elites" work with grass roots groups to safeguard human rights.[11]

Non-Governmental Organizations

Beijing has expressed both an appreciation for the social contributions of NGOs and a wariness toward their potential autonomy and intentions. According to various estimates, there are over 300,000 registered NGOs in China, and over one million in total, including over 200 international organizations.[12] Environmental groups have been at the forefront of NGO development in China. Other areas of non-governmental activity include poverty alleviation, rural development, public health, education, and legal aid. According to many experts, most of the registered NGOs are sponsored by a government body, while those that truly advocate social causes or policy changes account for a very small percentage of all non-profit groups.

After nearly a decade of steady proliferation, in 2005, Beijing began to tighten restrictions on Chinese non-governmental organizations while expressing suspicions toward foreign involvement. The government was especially fearful of the potential of foreign NGOs in China to help foment a "color revolution," and reportedly established an office to monitor foreign NGOs and their Chinese partners. Although the investigations did not result in a broad crackdown on non-governmental organizations, they reportedly have discouraged Chinese NGOs from taking on more politically daring projects.[13]

Human Rights Legislation

While the Hu-Wen government has proven to be politically conservative – placing more emphasis upon maintaining social stability than either major economic or political reforms – it has enacted several major laws that may reduce some of the most egregious patterns of human rights abuse. In 2004, for example, the phrase, "the State respects and protects human rights" was added to the PRC Constitution. Laws and regulations designed to protect human rights include those related to the use of torture, the death penalty, labor conditions, private property, and government transparency:

- **Rights of the Accused:** In July 2006, the state enacted prohibitions on specific acts of torture and requirements that interrogations of suspects of major crimes be video-recorded. These regulations followed a 2004 law forbidding the use of torture to obtain confessions. In March 2007, the Standing Committee of the National People's Congress (NPC) debated a law that would grant suspects the right to remain silent. [14]

- **The Death Penalty:** In March 2007, the Supreme People's Court was granted sole power to review and ratify all death sentences, following four years of discussion among the CCP leadership. Xiao Yang, president of the Supreme People's Court, stated that the death penalty would be exercised "more cautiously for only a small number of extremely serious offenders with hard evidence."[15] An effort to reduce the death penalty may have been responsible for a reduction in the use of capital punishment (from roughly 15,000 annually a decade ago to 6,000, according to some estimates).[16]

Labor Rights: In 2006, the NPC issued a report that highlighted China's labor rights abuses. In March 2007, China's legislature passed a Labor Contract Law. The law, which went into effect in January 2008, reportedly spurred a dramatic rise in labor dispute arbitration cases and lawsuits as well as strikes for higher wages and benefits. However, workers still do not have the right to strike or form their own unions.[17]

- **Property Rights:** In March 2007, the NPC passed a constitutional amendment designed to protect property rights that had been debated since 2002. Although the new Property Law would preserve the state's ownership of all land, backers of the law argued that it would help to protect not only private entrepreneurs but also urban families who own apartments and farmers whose crop lands risk seizure by government-backed real-estate developers.[18] In October 2008, the government issued new measures allowing farmers to lease and transfer or sell rights to use the property allocated to them by the state.[19]

- **Government Transparency:** In April 2007, the PRC government announced new rules, to take effect in 2008, requiring greater disclosure of official information.[20] In addition, institutional and legal mechanisms were set up to provide for greater government responsiveness and accountability. In part, these measures represented attempts to compel local governments to reveal financial accounts related to land takings in rural areas.[21]

- **Organ Transplants:** In 2006 and 2007, PRC regulations banning trade in human organs went into effect. They also stipulated that the donation of organs for transplant be free and voluntary. These restrictions followed growing evidence and international criticism of a booming and unregulated international trade in organs of executed Chinese prisoners, including what one report said were "large numbers" of Falun Gong practitioners.[22] The PRC government denied that organs were taken without the prisoners' permission and rejected allegations that organs were removed from Falun Gong detainees while they were still alive.[23] In 2006, U.S. officials visited a site alleged to be a concentration camp and organ harvesting center for

Falun Gong prisoners, the Sujiatun Thrombosis Hospital in Shenyang city. While expressing ongoing concern about human rights abuses against Falun Gong, they "found no evidence that the site is being used for any function other than as a normal public hospital."[24]

Other Policy Developments

Re-education through Labor

Re-education through labor (RTL), an administrative measure, empowers the police to sentence persons guilty of minor or non-criminal offenses such as petty theft, prostitution, unlawful religious activity, and "disrupting social order" to a maximum of three to four years in detention. Approximately 300 RTL (*laojiao*) centers in China, which can hold roughly 300,000 persons in total, have absorbed large numbers of individuals deemed by the state to undermine social or political stability, such as thousands of Falun Gong adherents earlier this decade.[25] According to some estimates, between 2% and 10% of those in the penal system were detained for political reasons.[26]

Many policy reformers and citizens in China have argued for an overhaul of the *laojiao* system. In March 2007, the Standing Committee of the National People's Congress resumed deliberation on legislation, which had been tabled for two years, that would restrict the use of re-education through labor sentencing, shorten terms, improve conditions at such centers, and provide better protections of the legal rights of "minor offenders."[27] At the end of 2008, the CCP reportedly indicated that it would fundamentally reform the *laojiao* system to possibly involve shorter sentences and incorporate judicial oversight.[28]

In the Provinces: Renewed Talk of Reform

Policy proposals aimed at more responsive, accountable, and limited government have been broached on and off for two decades, particularly in the provinces. Although such ideas have not produced major political reforms, they continue to reappear. For example, in June 2008, Communist Party leaders in Shenzhen, the pioneering Special Economic Zone bordering Hong Kong, drafted a reform plan that would expand the powers of the municipal people's congress and make elections to the legislative body more competitive. The two-year plan also would provide for greater judicial independence and intra-party democracy. However, some local government officials and political commentators expressed concern that there was insufficient support from the central government, and too much resistance from local power holders, to carry out such a proposal.[29]

On August 31, 2008, Communist Party Secretary of Hunan province, Zhang Chunxian, stated in a televised conference that the focus of China's reforms should turn from economic to political empowerment. Some observers interpreted his remarks as referring to political rights (*quan*). While the CCP is not contemplating relinquishing its monopoly on power, such discussion may refer to greater public supervision of government.[30]

China Human Rights Action Plan

In April 2009, the PRC State Council released a two-year "action plan" to address human rights abuses such as torture, unlawful detention, and the lack of due process and to promise greater civil rights. The government declared that its policy was designed to help bring China up to international standards of human rights as prescribed in the PRC Constitution, the Universal Declaration of Human Rights, and the International Covenant on Civil and Political Rights.[31] Some observers remained skeptical or noted the government's continued emphasis on living standards rather than political rights. Some tied the initiation of the plan to the United Nations Human Rights Council's review of China's human rights record in February 2009. Other analysts, however, suggested that the plan represented a step forward from previous efforts because it appeared to involve the input of academics and other civil society actors and also included benchmarks. Furthermore, they argued, reformers in the government may use the plan as a platform for promoting democratic change.[32]

Olympic Hopes and Disappointments

17th Party Congress

President Hu Jintao's calls for more "people's democracy" and intra-party democracy at the 17th Party Congress in October 2007 caused a hopeful stir among reform-minded officials and many Chinese intellectuals. In February 2008, a Communist Party think tank reportedly launched a book proposing democratic reforms as a means of curbing corruption.[33] However, the government's open tone took a hard line turn following the March 2008 protests in Lhasa, Tibet. During the Olympic torch relay and the aftermath of the Sichuan earthquake, nationalistic fervor filled the mass media while talk of reform was pushed to the sidelines.[34]

Pre-Olympics Crackdown

Many Chinese activists used the spirit of the Beijing Olympics to attempt to pressure the government to adopt reforms more quickly. Some Chinese journalists expressed optimism that the Olympics would, at least temporarily, provide them with greater freedom to report, which they hoped would in turn help to further "chip away" at the government's ability to censor news. In August 2007, a group of prominent Chinese dissidents sent an open letter to Party leaders, calling upon the government to honor its human rights commitments as the Olympics host.[35] In 2007, land rights activist Yang Chunlin penned a letter, signed by over 10,000 citizens, mostly farmers, entitled "We Want Human Rights, Not the Olympics." During the year leading up to the games, however, many activists spoke of a crackdown and sweep of potential "trouble makers," including Falun Gong practitioners, Tibetan and Uighur "separatists," activists, and others. From August to October 2007, when the CCP held its 17th Party Congress, PRC authorities reportedly carried out dozens of arrests, beatings, and abductions of petitioners, activists for human, housing, and land rights, lawyers, and Christian leaders in what some observers called the "worst crackdown in five years."[36] Prior to the Olympics, the PRC government also detained 44 dissident writers and launched what one NGO leader referred to as a "systematic crackdown on the voices of civil society," including some prominent Chinese NGOs.[37] Yang Chunlin was arrested in August 2007 and in March 2008 sentenced to five years in prison for "inciting subversion of state power."

The Sichuan Earthquake and the Response of Civil Society

In the weeks following the 7.9 magnitude earthquake that occurred on May 12, 2008 in Sichuan province, China witnessed an unprecedented burst of volunteer organization and activity, including the involvement of official and unofficial churches and students, and a level of unfettered press coverage that was rare for a natural disaster. One Chinese expert on NGO development stated that the government was "more open and more friendly to NGOs than before."[38] Although PRC authorities reportedly first tried to control news from the epicenter, they could not stop the flow of information, aided by cell phone communications and the Internet. For a few weeks, authorities did not interfere with the coverage of the disaster. Some observers surmised that improved access to information reflected the recent enactment of new "Open Government Information" regulations.

This relatively free atmosphere was soon replaced by government surveillance of NGOs, censorship, travel restrictions, and prohibitions on demonstrations and petitioning by parents of children killed in school buildings. Huang Qi, founder of a human rights website, was detained while investigating allegations of shoddy construction that had contributed to the collapse of schools. Huang was formally charged with "possessing state secrets" in July 2008.[39]

The Twentieth Anniversary of the Tiananmen Square Crackdown

In the months leading up to the twentieth anniversary of the military suppression of the 1989 democracy movement, human rights groups reported an intensified level of surveillance, harassment, intimidation, and arbitrary detentions of social activists, rights defenders, and others. Those affected included people asserting housing, land, and labor rights, lawyers, petitioners, political dissidents, signers of the Charter '08 call for democracy, participants in the 1989 demonstrations, and victims' families. Ding Zilin, the mother of a 17-year-old boy who was killed on June 4, 1989, in Beijing, reportedly was told to leave the capital until the 20th anniversary had passed, although she refused to do so. [40] Ding is a driving force behind Tiananmen Mothers, a network of about 150 family members of Chinese citizens killed in the crackdown that seeks a truthful, public accounting and an official reassessment of the event as well as government compensation for the deaths and assistance for those injured or maimed. Former protest leaders living abroad have been denied entry into China. Zhou Yongjun, a Beijing student leader in 1989 who later became a U.S. permanent resident, was arrested on charges of fraud as he tried to enter China through Hong Kong in October 2008. According to other reports, the PRC government also has clamped down on Internet traffic, including blocking Google's blog service and YouTube in May 2009.[41]

SELECTED HUMAN RIGHTS ISSUE AREAS

Persecution of Political Dissent

China's state security law is used liberally and often arbitrarily against political dissidents. According to PRC government data, in 2007, 742 people were arrested for "endangering state security," the highest number since 1999.[42] In 2008, this number more than doubled, to 1,600.[43] According to the Congressional-Executive Commission on China, in 2008, more than 900 persons were serving prison terms for activities related to expression, assembly, spiritual practice, and religious worship.[44] About 30 people are believed to remain in jail in connection with their involvement in the 1989 Tiananmen demonstrations.[45] Furthermore, during the past year, there were numerous reports indicating that some dissidents and human rights activists were tortured in government custody while others were harassed by police or assaulted by unidentified assailants believed to be linked to the government or business interests. Sentences or harassment of prominent dissidents in 2008 included the following:

- Human rights activist Hu Jia was sentenced to 3½ years in prison for "inciting subversion of state power."
- Zheng Enchong, a lawyer and housing rights activist, has faced harassment from local security personnel since his release from prison in 2006, particularly after he gave an interview for Voice of America in April 2009 discussing Shanghai housing policies.
- Gao Zhisheng, a rights lawyer who has defended Falun Gong practitioners since 2004, has been repeatedly detained by PRC authorities. In February 2009, PRC police took Gao from his home.
- Liu Xiaobo, a critic of the PRC government who was active in the 1989 Tiananmen Square democracy movement, was detained on December 8, 2008, in connection with his role in the drafting of Charter '08, a written call for democracy signed by 300 Chinese intellectuals and disseminated online.

State Control of the Press

The state still directly controls the largest mass media outlets, pressures other media regarding major or sensitive stories, and imposes severe measures against its critics. However, overall, the PRC government exercises less control over news and information than it did a decade ago. One scholar characterizes state control of the media as evolving from one of "omnipresence to selective enforcement."[46] The greater volume of news reporting has not translated into significant advances in freedom of expression, but nor has an increase in regulations affecting journalists and other critical voices significantly curbed the flow of information, thanks in large part to the Internet. In some cases, the government has supported journalistic efforts to expose official corruption and incompetence, particularly at the local level. According to some observers, a recent tactic of the central government appears to be to allow relatively open reporting on social crises, such as the scandal over tainted baby formula and milk, as long as it assigns blame to economic enterprises or lower level officials.[47]

Increasingly commercialized media outlets negotiate a delicate balance between responding to growing public demands for information and remaining within the bounds of what authorities will allow and advertisers will support. Under the economic reform policies of the past two decades, a burgeoning private media industry has developed, compelling many newspapers and television stations as well as Internet service providers to push the limits of cultural, social and, to a small extent, political content. State media also have had to provide more probing and provocative fare in order to attract readers, stay competitive, and respond to news and public opinion appearing on the Internet. Nearly all media organizations in China rely upon subscriptions and ad sales to help sustain themselves financially. One study suggests that, on the one hand, media commercialization has propelled an unprecedented flow of information and helped to bolster the media's role as a government watchdog. On the other hand, many profitable media enterprises may be reluctant to take risks, fearing government sanctions and the loss of advertising revenue.[48]

Beijing has remained vigilant toward media activities that challenge CCP authority. At the end of 2007, 29 journalists and 51 cyber-dissidents reportedly remained in detention for political reasons.[49] In 2008, the Committee to Protect Journalists documented the cases of 28 imprisoned journalists while the PEN American Center reported that 19 persons remained in prison for politically sensitive postings and other activities online.[50]

In October 2008, the central government permanently adopted the Olympics-related temporary regulations that had expanded press freedoms for foreign journalists. These include permitting foreign journalists to travel within the country and to interview Chinese subjects without official permission.[51] Although the Foreign Correspondent's Club of China noted improvements in government access and transparency, the new regulations did little to prevent state interference and harassment in many circumstances.[52] Furthermore, in February 2009, the PRC government issued a code of conduct for Chinese news assistants of foreign news agencies (Chinese journalists are forbidden from working for foreign media). According to human rights groups, the code represents a setback in press freedom in China. For example, it prohibits news assistants from engaging in independent reporting.[53]

The tug-of-war between society's demand for news and information and the state's attempts to maintain social and political control is likely to continue. The central government has employed a two-pronged approach, relying on traditional coercive tactics such as intimidation and incarceration of critics as well as adapting to both society's growing expectations and innovations in communications technologies. Meanwhile, China's media and online political voices have pushed back with increasing frequency, though such movements remain fleeting. In addition, growing numbers of young Internet users reportedly are chafing against information controls and expressing such frustrations online.[54]

The government closure in January 2006 of the politically provocative supplement "Freezing Point" in the relatively progressive *China Youth Daily* provoked an angry response by Chinese writers, academics, lawyers, and other citizens, particularly via the Internet.[55] In April 2004, the senior editor and other executives of Guangzhou-based *Southern Weekend*, a weekly known for investigative journalism, were sentenced to prison terms on charges of embezzlement, reportedly provoking an anti-government petition by dozens of prominent journalists and academics. The real reason for the crackdown, many believed, was the newspaper's reporting of a suspected reemergence of the Severe Acute Respiratory Syndrome (SARS) virus. However, the weekly eventually resumed its muckraking efforts.

In June 2008, *Southern Weekend* published an extensive article on the Sichuan earthquake and one school's substandard construction. In September 2008, a *Southern Weekend* editor reportedly wrote in his blog that prior to the Beijing Olympics, the newspaper had received information about tainted milk supplies, and implied that the state had forbade it from investigating the story further.[56] Another leading investigative publication related to business, *Caijing*, has reported upon the government handling of the SARS outbreak in 2002-2003, corporate fraud, and corruption scandals. The magazine was temporarily shut down in late 2008 by the government, which claimed that it had violated media regulations, after *Caijing* exposed suspicious cash transfers at the Agricultural Bank of China.[57]

Religious and Ethnic Issues

According to many sources, the extent of religious freedom varies widely within the country. Participation in *officially sanctioned* religious activity has increased in most areas. The PRC Constitution protects "normal" religious activities and those that do not "disrupt public order, impair the health of citizens or interfere with the educational system of the state." New regulations, enacted in March 2005, protect the rights of registered religious groups to publish literature, collect donations, possess property, and train and approve clergy. In the past year, the State Administration for Religious Affairs (SARA) set up a new unit to supervise folk religions as well as religions outside the five officially-recognized major religions (Buddhism, Protestantism, Roman Catholicism, Daoism, and Islam), including the Eastern Orthodox Church and the Church of Jesus Christ of Latter-day Saints.[58] Many experts assert that these laws grant the government broad latitude to determine what religious groups are lawful and to deny civil liberties to others.

The religious and religious-ethnic groups that have clashed the most with the state in the past decade have been unregistered Protestant and Catholic congregations, Tibetan Buddhists, and Uighur-minority Muslims in the Xinjiang Uighur Autonomous Region (XUAR). The International Religious Freedom Act of 1998 (P.L. 105-292) established the United States Commission on International Religious Freedom (USCIRF) to monitor religious freedom around the world and make policy recommendations to the President and Congress. Based largely upon the Commission's reports, the Department of State has identified China as a "country of particular concern" (CPC) for "particularly severe violations of religious freedom" for ten consecutive years (1999-2008). This designation has subjected the PRC to U.S. sanctions pursuant to P.L. 105-292 (a ban on the U.S. export of crime control and detection instruments and equipment to China). In August 2005, the USCIRF traveled to China for the first time. The Commission made what may be described as informative but superficial or controlled visits to significant religious places, and lamented the lack of access allowed in their investigation.[59]

Christians in China

Overall, Christians in China find increasing acceptance in society and, within limits, from the government. The PRC leadership has begun to acknowledge the positive role that Christianity can play in promoting social development, yet remains deeply suspicious and fearful of its potential power as a source of autonomous organization. A meeting on religion convened by top Party leaders in December 2007 that seemed to welcome the role of religion in China's development was seen by some observers as grounds for hope regarding a more tolerant religious policy.

By some estimates, the number of Christians in China ranges from 40 million to over 60 million, with nearly two-thirds gathering in unofficial churches.[60] Membership in official Christian churches alone has grown by 50% in the past decade, according to the government. Some studies have suggested that Christianity's rise in China, as well as the growth of other religions, reflects greater freedom and affluence among some Chinese, and the need to cope with dramatic social and economic changes among others.[61]

Many government abuses of Christian worshippers involve ambiguities over which groups are required to register – small home gatherings are officially tolerated – or disputes over which side – the church or the government – has failed to abide by registration guidelines. Many Chinese Protestants have rejected the official church, also known as the Three Self Patriotic Movement, for political or theological reasons, while some congregations have claimed that their applications have been rejected by the local religious affairs bureau.[62] Government officials have argued that some foreign Christian groups have discouraged unofficial churches, often referred to as "house churches," from registering with the state.[63] House churches lack legal protections, and remain highly vulnerable to the often-unchecked authority of local officials. In some regions and cities, particularly in the more affluent southeast, unofficial congregations generally meet with little or no state interference, while in other areas, particularly in Henan and Shandong provinces and in many rural areas, such independent gatherings reportedly have experienced regular harassment by local authorities and their leaders have been beaten, detained, and imprisoned.[64]

The China Aid Association (CAA), a U.S.-based non-profit organization that monitors religious freedom in China, reported over 2,000 incidents in which house churches were persecuted by the government in 2008, compared to 788 in 2007. CAA also reported 764 cases of Chinese Christians detained or arrested in 2008, up 10% compared to 2007, and 35 cases of Christians sentenced to prison terms, more than double that of the previous year.[65] Police released most detainees after sessions said to involve interrogation, intimidation, and sometimes torture. In the year leading up to the Olympics, according to some reports, the government tightened restrictions, arresting leaders of house churches, harassing members of congregations, shutting down places of worship, and denying visas to foreign missionaries.[66]

Beijing and the Vatican, which broke diplomatic ties in 1951, have engaged in a dialogue in the past few years toward improving relations. One of the key obstacles to normalizing ties is China's rejection of the Holy See's authority to appoint bishops. In a May 2007 "Letter to Chinese Catholics," Pope Benedict conveyed greater flexibility toward Catholic churches that are registered with the government.[67] According to the State Department, as of 2008, an estimated 90% of bishops in the official Catholic Church in China (the Chinese Catholic Patriotic Association) have reconciled with the Vatican and a large majority of them have been approved by the Holy See.[68] However, government harassment and detentions of unregistered Catholic bishops, priests, and laypersons have continued and progress in talks between the two sides reportedly have stalled.[69] In May 2008, the Shanghai government imposed new restrictions on Chinese Catholics making the annual pilgrimage to the Marian shrine of Sheshan, and set up a heavy security presence at the Sheshan cathedral, thereby reducing the number of religious travelers to 5,000 compared to 11,000 in 2007. According to some analysts, the PRC government feared possible social unrest or political implications from such a large gathering of Chinese Catholics from the official and unofficial Churches as well as Catholics from Hong Kong.[70]

Tibetan Protests

During the past year, policies restricting Tibetan religious practices continued, while local resentment simmered regarding the influx of Han Chinese, the majority ethnic group in China, to Lhasa, capital of the Tibet Autonomous Region (TAR). According to official Chinese statistics, Tibet's resident population is 2.84 million (2007). Han Chinese form a small minority in the TAR (4%), but constitute half of Lhasa's population. Many Han Chinese believe that the PRC government has brought positive economic and social development to the region. By contrast, many Tibetans claim that such development has not benefited them economically and has accelerated the erosion of their traditional culture. In September 2007, the State Administration for Religious Affairs issued a set of regulations that required all Tibetan lamas wishing to reincarnate to obtain prior government approval through the submission of a "reincarnation application." The Dalai Lama's Special Envoy to the United States, Lodi Gyaltsen Gyari, described the new regulations as a blow against "the heart of Tibetan religious identity."[71]

On March 11, 2008, the 49th anniversary of the Tibetan uprising against Chinese rule, 300 Buddhist monks demonstrated peacefully to demand the release of Tibetan prisoners of conscience. These demonstrations sparked others by monks and ordinary Tibetans demanding independence from China or greater autonomy, one of the most sensitive political issues for Beijing. On March 15, demonstrations in Lhasa turned violent as Tibetan protesters confronted PRC police and burned shops and property owned by Han Chinese. From exile in India, the Dalai Lama, the Tibetan spiritual leader, denied involvement and appealed to both the Chinese government and his followers to refrain from violence. The PRC government blamed the Dalai Lama for instigating the riots and labeled his followers "separatists."[72]

Official PRC news sources reported that 19 persons died in the riots and emphasized Chinese casualties, while Tibetan groups suggested that roughly 200 persons were killed by paramilitary troops in several Tibetan areas in western China, where approximately 100 protests broke out during the following weeks. A PRC court sentenced 30 Tibetans, including six Buddhist monks, to jail terms ranging from three years to life in prison for their alleged roles in the Lhasa riots, according to state media. Estimates of the number of monks and nuns detained during the aftermath of the unrest range from several hundred to over one thousand. In addition, the Municipal Intermediate People's Court in Lhasa reportedly sentenced two Tibetans to death for committing arson resulting in deaths during the unrest and handed down two suspended death sentences.[73] The government also expanded and intensified the already widespread "patriotic education" campaigns in monasteries and nunneries.

PRC leaders and representatives of the Dalai Lama met in May 2008 to help defuse the crisis while the PRC government continued to publicly demonize the exiled Tibetan leader.[74] Some Chinese lawyers were disbarred for offering to defend Tibetans arrested for taking part in the demonstrations.[75] The eighth round of talks between Beijing and envoys of the Dalai Lama, which took place in October 2008, failed to bring about any fundamental progress on the issue of greater autonomy for Tibet. In March 2009, the PRC government tightened security in the TAR and Tibetan areas in neighboring provinces in order to prevent possible demonstrations commemorating the 50th anniversary of the Tibetan uprising.

Uighur Muslims

Estimates of China's Muslim population range from 20 million to 30 million people. Most Muslim communities in the western provinces of Ningxia, Gansu, Qinhai, and Yunnan reportedly coexist peacefully with non-Muslims and experience little conflict with local authorities.[76] However, social and political tensions and harsh religious policies have long plagued China's far northwestern Xinjiang Uighur Autonomous Region (XUAR). The XUAR is home to 8.5 million ethnic Uighur Muslims (45% of the population), one of several Turkic ethnic groups in the region. The PRC government fears not only Uighur demands for greater religious and cultural freedom but also their linkages to Central Asian countries and foreign Islamic organizations, including terrorist groups. The East Turkestan Islamic Movement, a Uighur organization that the PRC alleges to have ties to Al Qaeda and that advocates the creation of an independent Uighur Islamic state, is on the United States' and United Nations' lists of terrorist organizations.[77]

Because of perceived national security-related concerns, the PRC government monitors and imposes restrictions upon Uighur society more stringently than it does most other religious and ethnic groups, focusing on Uighur religious leaders and practices. Such restrictions include those related to the training and duties of imams, Uighur and Arabic language, literature, and education, public access to mosques, the celebration of Ramadan, contacts with foreigners, travel abroad, and the *hajj*. Uighur children and youth (under 18) are forbidden from entering mosques and government workers are not allowed to practice Islam. According to Amnesty International, in 2007, Uighurs were the only known group in China to be sentenced to death for political crimes such as "separatist activities."[78]

In March 2008 in northwestern Xinjiang, PRC authorities suppressed demonstrations involving an estimated 600 ethnic Uighurs who were calling upon the government to scrap a proposed ban on headscarves, grant greater autonomy to Uighur-populated regions, and release political prisoners. The protests reportedly were triggered by the death in custody of a prominent Uighur businessman. The government showed little sign of relenting, and in April 2008 claimed to have broken up two terrorist cells that allegedly had plotted to bomb hotels during the Beijing Olympics.[79]

Falun Gong

Falun Gong combines an exercise and meditation regimen derived from *qigong* with spiritual beliefs. It reportedly gained millions of adherents across China in the late 1990s. On April 25, 1999, thousands of practitioners gathered in Beijing to protest the government's growing restrictions on their activities. Following a crackdown that began in the summer of 1999 and deepened in intensity over a period of about two years, the group, which the government labeled a dangerous or "evil" cult, has largely diminished as a social or political problem in China. Nonetheless, the continuation of government vigilance against Falun Gong indicates that some followers continue to practice or refuse to recant. Since the crackdown, estimates and claims of the number of Falun Gong adherents who have died in state custody have ranged from several hundred to a few thousand, including 100 deaths in 2008.[80] U.S.-based Falun Gong organizations have reported many cases of torture and abuse of adherents under detention or serving jail sentences. The PRC government has acknowledged that deaths in custody have occurred but denied that they were caused by mistreatment.[81]

VARIABLES OF CHANGE

The PRC government has been adept at employing a seemingly ad hoc combination of coercive and non-coercive approaches toward human rights issues. In addition, since the early 1990s, the CCP leadership has displayed an unprecedented level of unity on major policy issues while two decades of rapid economic growth have helped to legitimate the party's authority. Some potential, incremental improvements in human rights conditions in China are likely to stem from government policy. Chinese leaders have displayed a willingness and eagerness to improve government performance and accountability and to solicit some non-state input on policy issues, while economic reforms, new communications technologies, and related social changes have created new spaces for free expression and social activism. However, the state also has used other means to reduce or squelch public discourse and activity that have political relevance. Such methods range from manipulating the mass media and co-opting members of the intellectual, professional, and entrepreneurial classes to selectively harassing, intimidating, arresting, and punishing dissidents, activists, and ethnic and religious leaders. The re-education through labor system remains a key component of the state's capacity for removing large numbers of disaffected people from society. Whether the PRC government can continue on its present course may depend upon the outcomes of several ongoing developments in Chinese politics and society.

Central vs. Local Governments

Many analysts assign partial blame for human rights abuses in China to local officials. On the one hand, local and provincial level misconduct often has complicated or undermined central government efforts at reducing human rights abuses. On the other hand, much of the problem has arisen from the Chinese leadership's unwillingness to institute far-reaching reforms. Although the central government has made some progress in enacting laws aimed at curbing the most egregious human rights abuses, it has not created institutions that would help enforce these laws, such as checks and balances and direct or competitive elections beyond the lowest administrative levels. Nor has it allowed for the press, human rights lawyers, and activists to act as true watchdogs or advocates. Meanwhile, many local governments have experienced revenue shortfalls under the economic reforms of the past two decades, thereby reducing their ability to provide public services and driving them into collusive relationships with private developers. These conditions have been the source of many human rights abuses and mass protests of the past several years.

The PRC leadership thus far has been able to avoid much of the blame in many conflicts related to land seizures, public health threats, environmental pollution, and other sources of public anger and protest. Rather than focusing their attention on larger, systemic problems, aggrieved citizens generally have demonstrated against corrupt local officials for not acting in accordance with the law, while viewing central leaders as well-intentioned. Beijing often has openly criticized or punished local officials and expressed sympathy for aggrieved residents while allowing police to detain or arrest protest leaders.[82] The central government has applied a relatively flexible approach toward mass demonstrations especially in cases in which the press, Internet, or local television stations have generated widespread publicity in favor of the protesters.[83] Some analysts argue that mass pressures for greater human rights protections by way of fundamental political reform may gather strength only as more of the public perceives local problems and activism in national political terms.

Rights Awareness and Legal Activism

China's legal system has made significant strides since the Cultural Revolution (1966-1976), when the court system was severely weakened and heavily politicized. According to some analysts, PRC legal reforms could ultimately provide foundations for far reaching social and political changes, by nurturing public consciousness of rights and the rule of law and providing institutions for exercising political rights and holding the government accountable.[84] The state still wields disproportionate power against citizens and legal activists and continues to interpret the law arbitrarily in many cases. However, unlike overt and large scale political movements of the past, such as the democracy movement of 1989, which the PRC leadership ultimately viewed as hostile toward the state, many of today's legal activists have managed to survive in a gray area in which the state grudgingly acknowledges the legitimacy of their claims.[85]

Although some experts suggest that most Chinese still do not place much faith in the nation's courts, other analysts contend that PRC citizens have rising expectations that the state will honor basic legal rights. According to many reports, rising legal awareness and the development of laws have resulted in the growth of legal activity, especially since 2004, when the Chinese government enshrined the protection of human rights in the PRC constitution. Chinese citizens increasingly are turning to the courts to assert claims and even to sue public officials.[86] More than 150,000 cases are filed annually against the government, although the rate of success remains low. Some reports point to a trend of modest growth in cases and a more dramatic growth in the number of appeals. PRC lawyers also have begun to file "public interest" cases in growing numbers. Though rarely successful, these cases often draw temporary publicity through the mass media and help to further spread legal consciousness, according to some experts.[87]

China's legal profession has grown quickly, albeit from a small base. The country reportedly has 122,000-130,000 full-time lawyers, a third of them practicing in Beijing. This number translates to one attorney for every 10,000 citizens, compared to about one for every 300 in the United States.[88] In 2008, the PRC Law on Lawyers was amended to provide limited protections for lawyers and their clients, although potential state interference in the legal process remains a serious problem. These reforms include allowing defense lawyers to meet with clients without first seeking permission from judicial authorities, although only after defendants have been interrogated alone; banning police from observing conversations between lawyers and clients; and exempting statements made by lawyers in the courtroom from prosecution, except those that "harm national security, intentionally slander others, or seriously disrupt courtroom order." The PRC court system also has implemented programs to strengthen the competence and professionalism of judges and the effectiveness of the judicial system.[89]

Despite reforms around the edges, the legal and judicial systems in China remain flawed in basic ways. Although there appears to be an increasing number of cases that are dismissed by PRC courts due to insufficient evidence, the government continues to place a heavy emphasis on establishing the guilt of defendants. There is no adversary system, no presumption of innocence, no protection against double jeopardy, and no law governing the type of evidence that may be introduced. In many cases, police, prosecutors and judges disregard the protections that Chinese law does offer.[90] In criminal and political cases, sentences are decided not by judges but by a court committee named by the Party.

China's changing legal environment has provided an opening for human rights attorneys, albeit one that is fraught with risks for both citizens and lawyers. Since 2000, several dozen lawyers in China have made names for themselves by taking on sensitive rights cases against government entities or economic enterprises with government connections.[91] In January 2006, a group of prominent Chinese attorneys and legal scholars established the Association of Human Rights Attorneys for Chinese Christians in order to educate and defend house church leaders.

Chinese law firms and lawyers who have pursued politically sensitive cases have faced a range of troubles, including closure of offices, intimidation, beatings, disbarment, house arrest, kidnappings, and prison sentences. The State Department lists several prominent Chinese attorneys who were disbarred in 2008 because of their political activities.[92] Many human rights and defense lawyers have been harassed by officials or beaten by agents of local governments or economic interests. Others have been falsely accused of committing slander, perjury, fabrication of evidence, or the graver crimes of subversion or revealing state secrets.

Social Unrest

Economic changes have created new social classes and widening disparities of income and power. Because legal, judicial, and enforcement mechanisms have largely failed to protect the economic and political rights of many disadvantaged Chinese, social protest has become a common form of expression and means of resolving grievances. In the past several years, major types of social unrest have included state-owned enterprise workers demonstrating against layoffs; migrant factory and construction laborers protesting lack of pay; farmers objecting to unfair taxation and usurious fees, confiscation of land for development projects, and loss of agricultural land due to environmental degradation; and homeowners opposing forcible evictions related to urban development. In cases of land confiscation and home evictions, much popular anger has been directed at collusive deals between local officials and private investors and the lack of fair compensation. Relatively new sources of social unrest have included farmers movements to claim ownership of land; the closing of thousands of factories due to climbing labor and energy costs, the rising value of the Chinese currency, and the global economic crisis; unemployment among recent college graduates (an estimated 15%-50% cannot find work); consumer price inflation; and coercive enforcement of the one-child policy.[93] So far, however, protests largely have targeted local officials, policies, or companies but have not joined forces to form broad-based movements or challenged the PRC political system.

PRC data on social unrest provide glimpses into the government's preoccupation with social stability but often are conflicting or incomplete. In 2006, the Ministry of Public Security announced that 87,000 "public order disturbances" had occurred in 2005, an increase of 6.6% compared to the previous year. Many of these cases involved criminal or individual acts rather than social protests, according to some analysts. The government also has reported significant, but declining, numbers of "mass incidents" or large protests, which peaked at 74,000 in 2004.[94] Central government policies designed to decrease tax burdens on farmers and labor abuses in factories reportedly have reduced some forms of social grievance. However, many analysts argue that mass incidents have been on the rise rather than on the decline as official data suggest.[95]

Many observers have noted an alarming rise in mass protests since the end of 2008. The global recession's impact on China reportedly has pushed unemployment rates up to 9% in the cities and nearly 20% in rural areas, with disproportionate impacts on the poor. Labor disputes reportedly doubled in 2008, according to an official source.[96] The loss of an estimated 20 million urban jobs for rural migrants has compelled millions of them to return to their home villages where economic opportunities are already limited.[97] Compounding the problem, the enforcement of new laws designed to protect labor rights and the environment has slackened in order to reduce costs on struggling companies.[98]

According to some analysts, social unrest has stemmed from not only economic hardship and anger over abuses of power by and collusion among government officials and private developers, but also the growing popular awareness and understanding of legal rights. The PRC government has applied a carrot-and-stick approach toward disgruntled social groups, often sympathizing with them and pressuring local authorities to give in to some demands while arresting protest leaders and intimidating social activists. The developing legal consciousness of many Chinese citizens, combined with small but vital networks of lawyers, journalists, and activists attracted to human rights causes, has assured that social pressures for advancing human rights are likely to continue.

Mainstream Protests

While the PRC has experienced over a decade of social unrest among socially and politically marginalized groups such as wage laborers and farmers, in the past two years, protest activities have begun to sprout among more affluent, urban Chinese. These incidences may signal new trends in protest activity: They have been less isolated and displayed greater organizational capacity; the government's responses have been relatively restrained; grievances have been less about participants' livelihoods and more about quality of life issues and the lack of government consultation. [99] According to many analysts, the state in China has remained strong in relation to society largely because social groups have been divided or co-opted by the state. The CCP leadership deeply fears disparate groups – wage laborers, farmers, entrepreneurs, urban homeowners, intellectuals, and others – linking up to form a broad-based movement. The following are examples of recent middle class protest activities:

- In May 2007, students and professors at Xiamen University in Fujian Province reportedly sent out a million text messages calling on city residents to assemble to protest the planned construction of a Taiwan-financed petro-chemical plant. Estimates of the number protesters, whose march was video-recorded, range from 7,000 to 20,000 people. Construction of the plant was temporarily halted.
- In January 2008, thousands of suburban homeowners in Shanghai gathered at People's Square and embarked on a raucous protest walk through some of the city's

main thoroughfares to publicly oppose plans to construct a maglev (magnetic levitation) high-speed train line through their neighborhoods. These protests can be viewed on YouTube.[100] The city government delayed the line's construction and in March 2009 it was reported that the project was suspended indefinitely. Many analysts attribute the city's decision largely to the demonstrations.[101]

- In June 2008, tens of thousands of people—estimates range from 10,000 to 30,000—rioted and torched government buildings in Weng'an County in Guizhou province. The protest was sparked by the drowning of a 17-year old girl, which local police declared was a suicide. Her parents and many residents suspected that she had been raped and killed, and that local officials were protecting the true perpetrators. The protest was remarkable because it was reported in the official media, citizen commentary online was widespread, and central and local officials acknowledged "legitimate" grievances that may have contributed to the people's distrust of government, including the demolition of homes and forced relocations to make way for development. Local police officials were replaced following the riots.
- At the end of August 2008, one week after the closing ceremonies of the Olympic games, hundreds of Beijing residents living near a newly built waste-fueled thermal power plant protested against the fumes emanating from the facility. No arrests were reported.[102]
- In November 2008 in Sichuan province, 9,000 taxi drivers in Chongqing went on strike to protest the proliferation of illegal taxis, excessive fees, difficulties of obtaining gasoline, and other issues after the municipal government and taxi companies failed to address their complaints. That same week, 1,000 teachers in the province walked off their jobs to protest lack of pay.[103]
- In May 2009, university students in Nanjing demonstrated after security personnel enforcing regulations toward street vendors allegedly attacked stalls run by students. Thousands of students reportedly clashed with police.

New Agents of Change?

Some political theorists and policy makers have argued that the growth of the middle and entrepreneurial classes in developing market economies creates pressures for democracy. According to these hypotheses, demands for rights and democracy stem from emerging class desires to protect economic interests and political influence, a growing sense of entitlement, and confidence in their capacity to affect or participate in government decision-making. However, many studies of China's changing society show how some social groups who have benefitted greatly from economic reforms value incremental over dramatic political change.

One study concludes that the Chinese middle class, which constitutes about 15% of the total population according to some calculations, "do think and act in accordance with democratic principles."[104] Other observations suggest, however, that many members of China's rising middle class, a product of economic reforms, have displayed either a lack of interest in politics or a preference for political stability rather than rapid reform. They have been careful not to jeopardize their hard-won economic gains, and have expressed some fear of grassroots democracy.[105]

Rather than asserting its independence from the state, China's business sector has remained heavily dependent upon it, and often seeks close relations with, relevant government agencies. The CCP, in turn, has welcomed business persons into the Party. The PRC government wields influence over the private sector not only through its jurisdiction over business transactions, but also through its control over many other areas of the economy, such as finance and property. Furthermore, the weakness of China's legal system means that many business persons must seek relations with government officials in order to protect their assets or enforce contracts. According to several studies, private entrepreneurs favor strengthening the rule of law and support long-term political reform, but also value social stability and are satisfied with the current, slow pace of change, which has largely served their interests.[106]

China's critical intellectuals, another potential agent of change, have been relatively quiescent during the past decade. The crackdown upon the China Democracy Party in 1998-99 crushed nearly all hope of fundamental change for a decade, while growing opportunities for making money, travel, academic career development, and even policy input have helped to dampen the urgency of reform. The PRC government has co-opted many intellectuals, tying the success of their careers to the continuity of CCP policy.[107] Furthermore, many educated and politically- aware Chinese are not as enamored of Western political models as they were during the late 1980s, for various reasons, including the suspicion that Western efforts to promote democracy in China may be part of an effort to weaken the PRC; fears that radical political change would undermine economic development or bring about difficulties similar to those facing other post- communist countries, such as Russia; and the decline of U.S. standing as a global leader since the beginning of the Iraq war.[108] Among the younger generations of Chinese, many reportedly are liberal in outlook and assertive regarding their rights, but also are career-oriented, politically pragmatic, and fiercely patriotic. Although Chinese youth often are critical of their own government, many are quick to reject Western criticism of their country.[109]

Charter '08

On December 10, 2008, over 300 Chinese citizens signed and posted online a document entitled "Charter '08," inspired by "Charter 77," the Czechoslovakian democratic movement that began in 1977, and commemorating the 60th anniversary of the United Nations' adoption of the Universal Declaration of Human Rights. The manifesto upheld human rights and called for fundamental changes in China's political system, including a new constitution, separation of powers, an independent judiciary, direct elections, and freedoms of assembly, expression, and religion. It also recommended that a commission be established to investigate past government abuses of human rights.

The Charter represented a bold departure from the incremental approach to reform subscribed to by many liberal-minded intellectuals and officials during the past decade. Furthermore, the document was especially provocative regarding the central government's dealings with Taiwan, Tibet, Hong Kong, and other special jurisdictions, proposing to negotiate with Taiwan "as equals," a "federation of democratic communities," and flexibility toward national minority areas. Finally, in what may instill the greatest fears within the PRC leadership of political unrest, the Charter was eventually signed by over 8,000 citizens representing a cross-section of Chinese society, including not only dissidents and public intellectuals but also workers, farmers, entrepreneurs, professionals, local officials, and others.[110] However, according to some analysts, despite its symbolic appeal, the PRC leadership and some liberal intellectuals have calculated that the Charter will not have a short-term impact as a catalyst for a broad-based, democratic movement.[111]

The PRC government arrested one of the document's drafters, prominent democratic activist Liu Xiaobo, and shut down the Charter's website. Over 1,000 intellectuals reportedly signed an online petition calling for Liu's release. In February 2009, 16 members of the Communist Party old guard reportedly signed an open letter addressed to President Hu Jintao and the CCP Standing Committee calling for political reform, freedom of assembly and press.[112] The government has been careful not to arouse further public anger and international condemnation, and has limited its crackdown. Roughly 100 signatories to the Charter reportedly have been harassed or interrogated and some reportedly have lost career-related privileges, but as of June 8, 2009, six months after his arrest, only Liu has remained in detention.[113]

New Communications Technologies

The PRC government's efforts at censoring the Internet have been strenuous and effective, but not fully successful. In 2008, China overtook the United States in terms of the number of Internet users, with nearly 300 million people online, about one in every four Chinese, including 70 million bloggers. Despite its revolutionary qualities as a communications medium, the Internet has not opened the floodgates of political discourse in China as some had hoped or envisioned, and some analysts argue that the Internet has enhanced government propaganda and surveillance capabilities.[114] Nonetheless, the Internet has made it impossible for the government to restrict information as fully as before. Furthermore, Internet and cell phone technologies have enhanced the abilities of groups to assemble and to record large protests. A reported increase in arrests for political crimes since 2006 reflects both a government clampdown on dissent and growing political activism, including the rise of "a new generation of dissenters who are increasingly well informed about their scant legal rights and more inclined to spread their views using the Internet."[115]

Beijing has employed a variety of "hard" and "soft" techniques and approaches to control online content and behavior, including electronic filtering, regulation of Internet Service Providers, monitoring of Internet cafes, and intimidation through the arrests of high profile "cyber dissidents."[116] According to some analysts, the government cannot control all Internet content and use, but its selective targeting creates an undercurrent of fear and promotes self censorship. The government also has attempted to sway online debates by entering the chat room fray. An estimated 280,000 "Web commentators" – many of them university students – reportedly are employed by state entities to "guide public opinion" or steer discussion online.[117]

To some extent, the Internet has proven to be less of a political tool than many observers had expected or hoped, although vast areas for cultural and social expression have opened up online. Those who mine the Internet for political information reportedly make up a small minority of all users. Greater political information is available for Chinese who use "proxy servers," which help circumvent government filtering, or who frequent English language sites. However, according to one study, less than 8% of Internet users in China access proxy servers "sometimes" to "frequently."[118] Chinese online chat rooms and blogs also have been hotbeds of ultra-nationalist sentiment.

Many major U.S. online (English) news sites, such as the *Washington Post*, *New York Times*, and *CNN*, are frequently available. Since the end of the Beijing Olympics, Voice of America's website generally has been allowed, although it is still subject to selective blocking. However, for many of China's educated elites who are proficient in English as well as government officials concerned about political control, it is not the availability of foreign news to a minority of interested Chinese citizens that is significant, but rather the ability to foment political change on the basis of such information. Such ability remains substantially curtailed. Furthermore, some analysts suggest that the limited amount of Internet freedom in China defuses political activism by allowing people to vent their opinions online.[119] Finally, many Chinese Internet users support the idea of censorship, particularly the government's efforts to ban online pornography, gambling, illegal commerce, phishing, and spam.[120]

In the middle of the decade, bulletin board systems (BBS) and blogs burst onto the online scene, providing forums for Chinese to express opinions publicly and often anonymously. BBS and blogs became the principal medium for political discourse in China. One study found that 61% of blogs carried "critical" opinions, including those related to society, government, corporations, and public figures, while 36% of blogs demonstrated "pluralism" or two or more different perspectives.[121] After the government required BBS participants to register their real names with forum hosts, BBS activity fell dramatically, while blogs surged in popularity.[122] In the Xiamen University protests of 2007, local residents sent text messages about the demonstrations to bloggers in other cities, who posted reports on the Web, thus keeping "one step ahead of the censors."[123]

Some experts on the Internet in China have acknowledged government repression while remaining optimistic about the medium's power. One political blogger stated that although media controls had multiplied under President Hu Jintao, they had not translated into less freedom overall, thanks to the Internet.[124] A university professor described the constant struggle with government censors this way:

> I have noted the life span of new forms on the Internet here has been about one or two years. Bulletin boards were very free, and after one or two years, they were restricted. Then we saw the emergence of personal Web sites, and after one or two years they were restricted. Then we had blogs. After a year or two, they moved to restrict them, too. I think the Internet in China will always find a way forward, because of technology and other factors. I am actually very optimistic.[125]

U.S. Efforts to Advance Human Rights in China

In the past two decades, successive U.S. administrations cumulatively have developed a comprehensive array of tactics and programs aimed toward promoting democracy, human rights, and the rule of law in China, but their effects have been felt primarily along the margins of the PRC political system. The U.S. government has pressured China from without through openly criticizing the country's human rights record and calling upon the PRC leadership to honor the rights guaranteed in its own constitution, bring its policies in line with international standards, release prisoners of conscience, and undertake major political reforms. The U.S. government also has provided funding for programs within China that help strengthen the rule of law, civil society, government accountability, and labor rights. It has supported U.S.-based non-profit organizations and Internet companies that monitor human rights conditions in China and help enable Chinese Web users to access Voice of America (VOA), Radio Free Asia, and other websites that are frequently blocked by the PRC government.

Some experts argue that economic and diplomatic engagement with China have failed to set any real political change in motion. In this context, some contend, U.S. efforts to promote democracy and human rights have been largely ineffectual. Many policy makers argue that tangible improvements in PRC human rights policies should be a condition for full economic and diplomatic relations with China as well as cooperation on other issues. Others counter that U.S. engagement policies have helped to set conditions in place that are conducive for progress.[126]

A number of policy makers have accused the Obama Administration of de-emphasizing human rights in its early overtures to China. In February 2009, Secretary of State Hillary Clinton stated in Beijing that disagreements on human rights "cannot block the possibility of significant cooperation" on bilateral issues such as the global economic crisis, climate change, and international security threats. In May 2009, House Speaker Nancy Pelosi, a staunch critic of China's human rights policies since 1989, and a bi-partisan congressional delegation traveled to the PRC and met with governmental and non-governmental groups in a visit primarily focused on forging bilateral cooperation on climate change. The delegation also raised human rights issues in meetings with the PRC government, delivered a letter to President Hu Jintao requesting the release of prominent political prisoners, and met with Catholic Bishop Aloysius Jin Luxian in Shanghai. Some analysts suggested that Clinton's and Pelosi's visits reflected a pragmatic approach to both advancing U.S. interests and promoting human rights in China. This method would include developing a stable bilateral relationship through which to quietly discuss human rights issues, and creating more opportunities to raise concerns privately rather than criticizing the PRC government openly.[127]

Openly Criticizing China

Some analysts argue that the U.S. government should take principled stands against China's human rights abuses more frequently, openly, and forcefully, while others believe that such methods can undermine human rights efforts. Many prominent dissidents or former prisoners of conscience have claimed that international pressure or attention protected them from harsher treatment by PRC authorities. While some members of civil society groups have welcomed a more assertive U.S. human rights policy, others have cautioned that the Chinese government often has restricted their activities when they were viewed as tied to foreign governments. In some cases, the PRC government has made small concessions in order to help reduce or avoid open U.S. or global criticism. Some analysts suggested that Beijing's decision to restart the U.S.-PRC human rights dialogue in 2008 was linked to the U.S. government's decision not to include China in a list of "worst human rights violators," although the State Department continued to harshly criticize China's record in its annual report. In other cases, the Chinese leadership has reacted angrily or responded in a "tit for tat" manner when the U.S. government has publicly denounced its human rights.[128] Beijing suspended the dialogue in 2004 after the Bush Administration sponsored an unsuccessful U.N. resolution criticizing China's human rights record.

Some Members of Congress have sponsored numerous non-binding resolutions condemning or calling upon the PRC government to improve various human rights policies. These include the imprisonment and detention of prominent political, religious, and ethnic figures; persecution of Tibetans and Uighurs; control over the Internet and other mass media; the one-child policy; and treatment of North Korean refugees. Related bills include those that would restrict U.S.-China trade on the basis of PRC human rights abuses or prohibit U.S. funding to American officials attending the opening ceremonies of the Beijing Olympics. Some Members of the 111th Congress have introduced resolutions supporting Charter '08 and calling for the release of dissident Liu Xiaobo (H.Res. 156 and S.Res. 24) and urging the PRC government to cease committing human rights violations against the Uighur people (S.Res. 155). In March 2009, the House passed H.Res. 226, recognizing the plight of the Tibetan people. In June 2009, the House and Senate passed H.Res. 489 and S.Res. 171, respectively, commemorating those who demonstrated for democracy or died in the military crackdown in 1989 in Beijing and expressing continued support for human rights and democracy activists in China.

Human Rights Dialogue

The human rights dialogue between the United States and China was established by President Clinton and President Jiang Zemin in 1998. Thirteen rounds have been held beginning in 2001. Beijing suspended the dialogue in 2004 after the Bush Administration sponsored an unsuccessful U.N. resolution criticizing China's human rights record. In February 2008, while Secretary of State Condoleezza Rice was in Beijing and prior to the release of the State Department's annual human rights report, the PRC government announced that it would resume human rights talks with the United States. In May 2008, the two sides held "constructive and productive" discussions on a wide range of issues. Assistant Secretary of State for Democracy, Human Rights, and Labor David Kramer told reporters that the talks included the following topics: prisoners of conscience, freedom of religion, the situation in Tibet, the Muslim majority in Xinjiang, and media and Internet freedom.[129]

Some human rights experts suggest that the PRC government has been able to deflect international criticism on human rights by holding dialogues without having made real improvements in its policies and practices.[130] For example, in July 2008, as Secretary of State Condoleezza Rice met with PRC Foreign Minister Yang Jiechi in Beijing and hailed the resumption of talks on human rights, a group of Chinese human rights attorneys reportedly were detained as they attempted to meet with two visiting Members of Congress.[131] Others suggest that while the dialogue may produce limited short-term results, the absence of such dialogue reduces the overall effectiveness of U.S. human rights policies toward China.[132]

Rule of Law and Civil Society Programs

United States foreign operations appropriations for China chiefly have supported democracy- related programs, particularly rule of law development. Some experts argue that foreign-funded rule of law and civil society efforts in China have produced limited gains due to PRC political constraints. Others contend that such programs have helped to build social foundations for political change and have bolstered reform-minded officials in the PRC government.

Between 2000 and 2008, the United States government authorized or made available roughly $182 million for programs in China, of which $159 million was devoted to human rights and democracy activities and to Tibetan communities. The U.S. Congress has played a leading role in supporting these and related programs, appropriations for which have grown from an annual average of $11.1 million during the 2000-2004 period to $31.5 million during the 200 5-08 period.[133] Major program areas include legal training, legal aid, criminal defense, labor rights, civil society development, media reform, participatory government, and preserving Tibetan culture.

Congress also has provided financial support to U.S. educational institutions for exchange programs with Chinese universities. Several American law schools now offer exchange programs or law degree programs in China. Temple University's Beasley School of Law, which has received USAID assistance, offers a Masters of Laws program in conjunction with Tsinghua University in Beijing. The program reportedly has graduated 800 Chinese legal professionals, including officials and prosecutors, law professors, and legal staff.[134] According to some experts, U.S. law programs in China provide relatively secure settings for the discussion of sensitive legal and related political topics.[135]

The National Endowment for Democracy (NED) is a private, non-profit organization created in 1983 and funded by the United States government to promote democracy around the world. NED programs constituted over one-third of all U.S. democracy funding in China during the 1999- 2003 period, and continue to play a significant role. [136] The Endowment's programs in China, administered through its "core institutes," have included legal aid, labor rights, investigative reporting, HIV/AIDS awareness, and "activist training."[137] NED also funds several U.S.-based organizations that monitor human rights conditions in China, including Tibet and Xinjiang, research and publish newsletters and journals on democracy-related topics, and disseminate political works from China. NED's non-governmental status affords it greater ease and flexibility with which to support relatively overt democratic groups.

Public Diplomacy

The U.S. government aims to influence the hearts and minds of progressive-minded Chinese educated elites through its public diplomacy programs. According to the Department of State, nearly half of all PRC citizens participating in U.S. educational and cultural exchange programs are engaged in activities related to democracy, human rights, and religious freedom. Both the Fulbright Scholarship and Humphrey Fellowship exchange programs devote significant resources for rule of law studies. The U.S. International Visitor

Leadership Program sponsors U.S. speakers to travel to China to discuss rule of law issues and brings PRC counterparts to the United States. In 2007, 409 U.S. citizens and 696 PRC citizens participated in U.S. educational and cultural and exchange programs.[138]

In the two decades since the Tiananmen military crackdown in 1989, many Chinese have come to equate democracy with political instability or view it as harmful to economic growth. One analyst suggests that, rather than touting the virtues of freedom and democracy as abstract ideas, the U.S. government should bolster public diplomacy efforts as a means toward addressing Chinese doubts about democracy. In particular, U.S. public diplomacy efforts should help to persuade the emerging PRC middle class that democracy, stability, social development, and economic growth are mutually reinforcing.[139]

Internet Freedom

The U.S. government has funded programs to help circumvent PRC Internet censorship and called upon U.S. Internet providers that have entered the Chinese market to promote or protect human rights. The International Broadcasting Bureau supports counter-censorship technologies (approximately $2 million per year) that help enable Internet users in China, Iran, and other restricted countries to access Voice of America and other censored U.S. governmental and nongovernmental websites and to receive VOA e-mail newsletters. The Consolidated Appropriations Act for FY2008 (P.L. 110-161) allocated $15 million out of the Human Rights and Democracy Fund for an Internet freedom initiative to expand access and information in Asia, the Middle East, and elsewhere. [140] The Global Online Freedom Act of 2009 (H.R. 2271), introduced in May 2009, would establish an Office of Global Internet Freedom (OGIF) in the Department of State. The act would prohibit U.S. companies that provide Internet services in countries that restrict the free flow of information from providing personal user information to the governments of such countries and assisting such governments in the censorship of information.

In May 2008, the Senate Committee on the Judiciary, Subcommittee on Human Rights and the Law held a hearing entitled "Global Internet Freedom: Corporate Responsibility and the Rule of Law." Representatives from Google, Yahoo, and Cisco Systems testified before the subcommittee regarding their operations in China. Many U.S. observers accused U.S. information technology corporations of either cooperating with PRC censorship systems or supplying China with censorship technology. However, some Chinese "cyber dissidents" argued that on balance, U.S. Internet companies in China helped to accelerate information flow and provide more opportunities for free expression, despite their operating within the PRC's censorship regime.[141]

Yahoo's China operations have been especially singled out for criticism by human rights groups. In 2004, Yahoo's Hong Kong office provided information to PRC authorities about the identity of a Chinese Yahoo e-mail account holder, Shi Tao. Shi, a journalist, reportedly had forwarded information about a state directive regarding the 15th anniversary of the Tiananmen demonstrations to an overseas democracy organization. In March 2005, a PRC court sentenced Shi to 10 years in prison for "leaking state secrets." In August 2008, Google, Yahoo, and Microsoft reached an agreement in principle on a voluntary code of conduct for their activities in China as well as other countries that restrict Internet use. In December 2008, the three companies established the Global Network Initiative, a set of guidelines for Internet companies confronted with issues related to privacy and censorship in countries such as China.

Sanctions

Many U.S. sanctions on the PRC in response to the Tiananmen military crackdown in 1989 remain in effect, including some foreign aid-related restrictions, such as required "no" votes or abstentions by U.S. representatives to international financial institutions regarding loans to China (except those that meet basic human needs).[142] Congress also has required that U.S. representatives to international financial institutions support projects in Tibet only if they do not encourage the migration and settlement of non-Tibetans (majority Han Chinese) into Tibet or the transfer of Tibetan-owned properties to non-Tibetans, which some fear may erode Tibetan culture and identity.

The U.S. government suspended funding for the United Nations Population Fund (UNFPA) from 2002 through 2008 because of the UNFPA's programs in China, where the State Department determined that coercive family planning practices had occurred. In February 2009, the Obama Administration announced that it would restore U.S. funding for the UNFPA. The Omnibus Appropriations Act, FY2009 (P.L. 111-8), allocated $50 million for the Population Fund. However, none of these funds may be used for a country program in China.[143]

Labor Rights

The U.S. government has promoted PRC adherence to international labor standards. U.S. officials monitor PRC compliance with the 1992 U.S.-China Memorandum of Understanding and 1994 Statement of Cooperation on the issue of prison labor. In 2000, the measure granting permanent normal trade relations (PNTR) status to China (P.L. 106-286) authorized the Department of Labor to establish a program to promote worker rights and related rule of law training. The United States and China have conducted exchanges on coalmine safety, dispute resolution, occupational safety and health, wage and hour (payroll) administration, and pension programs.[144]

Congressional-Executive Commission on China

Between 1989 and 1999, the U.S. Congress attempted to monitor and hold the PRC government accountable for human rights violations through the annual renewal of "most favored nation" (MFN) trading status. P.L. 106-28 6, the measure granting permanent normal trade relations (PNTR) treatment to China, ended this mechanism, but included provisions on human rights. The PNTR act established the Congressional-Executive Commission on China (CECC) to monitor human rights and the rule of law in China and to submit an annual report with recommendations to the President and Congress.[145] The body consists of nine Senators, nine Members of the House of Representatives, five senior Administration officials appointed by the President, and a staff of ten. On its website, the Commission provides human rights-related news and analysis, keeps track of pertinent PRC laws and regulations, and maintains a database of political prisoners.[146] Since its inception, the CECC has held roughly 80 public hearings and roundtables on rights-related topics, including the following: the Beijing Olympics, rule of law development, social unrest, religious freedom, ethnic minorities, political reform, labor conditions, mass media, property rights, and the Internet in China. It has an annual operating budget of approximately $2 million.

FURTHER READING

U.S. Department of State, *2008 Country Reports on Human Rights Practices*—China (February 25, 2009).

U.S. Department of State, *International Religious Freedom Report 2008*—China (September 2008).

Congressional-Executive Commission on China, *Annual Report 2008* (October 31, 2008).

Annual Report of the United States Commission on International Religious Freedom (May 1, 2009).

China Aid Association, *Annual Report of Persecution by the Government on Christian House Churches within Mainland China* (January 2009).

Reporters without Borders, China—*Annual Report 2008* (February 2008).

China Human Rights Defenders, http://crd-net.org

Dui Hua Foundation, http://www.duihua.org

Human Rights in China, http://www.hrichina.org

Laogai Research Foundation, http://www.laogai.org

Ying Ma, "China's Stubborn Anti-Democracy," *Policy Review*, February/March 2007.

U.N. Human Rights Council

The United Nations Human Rights Council was formed in 2006 to replace the U.N. Commission on Human Rights (UNCHR), which had been criticized for being held sway by non-democratic countries. The United States sponsored several resolutions at the Commission criticizing China's human rights record, but none were successful; China was able to thwart voting on most resolutions through "no-action motions."[147] The United Nations established the Universal Periodic Review (UPR) mechanism by which the Human Rights Council assesses the human rights records of all U.N. members once every four years.[148]

The UPR Working Group conducted a periodic review of China in February 2009. Representatives of some countries, including Australia, Canada, the Czech Republic, Germany, the Netherlands, the United Kingdom, and New Zealand, voiced serious concerns about China's human rights conditions, while other representatives, including those from many developing or non-democratic countries, expressed support of China's practices.[149] Some human rights advocates criticized the United States government for not voicing concerns or suggestions at the review.[150] State Department officials responded that the Obama Administration did not want to participate in the review until it had formulated a policy on the Council, which the U.S. government under the Bush Administration had refused to join. In May 2009, the Obama Administration sought and was granted a seat on the 47-member Council.

APPENDIX

A number of jailed or detained rights defenders have gained national and international attention for their efforts on behalf of causes involving aggrieved citizens. Some of them have been harassed or denied civil liberties by Chinese authorities off and on over a period of several years. Many of these activists are experts on PRC law and have targeted specific violations by local officials, rather than challenging the PRC leadership or broad policy. The government has charged these individuals with various crimes, including "subversion of state power," "supplying state secrets to foreigners," and illegal business practices. In most cases, their punishments have been less severe that those of past dissidents who had attempted to organize or represent political or religious groups on a national scale and those of many Tibetan and Uighur activists.

The following list is not exhaustive and is intended to provide examples of prominent rights defenders, government critics, journalists, and religious figures who are reported to have been imprisoned or detained by the PRC government or denied civil rights. The names are drawn from the Congressional-Executive Commission on China's Political Prisoner Database and other sources.

Table A-1. Profiles of Selected Imprisoned Dissidents and Activists[151]

Chen Guangcheng	Chen Guangcheng, a legal rights advocate, is best known for his efforts in 2005 challenging illegal family planning practices in Linyi county, Shandong province. PRC authorities arrested Chen in June 2006. A local court sentenced him to four years and three months in prison for "intentional destruction of property" and "gathering people to disturb traffic order."
Gao Zhisheng	Gao Zhisheng, a human rights attorney, has represented numerous individuals, activists, writers, and religious leaders. On October 18, 2005, Gao wrote an open letter to President Hu Jintao and Premier Wen Jiabao, urging an end to persecution of Falun Gong practitioners. He was convicted on December 22, 2006, of "inciting subversion of state power" and handed a suspended sentence. In February 2009, Gao was presumed to be taken by government authorities to an undisclosed location.
Guo Feixiong	Guo Feixiong, a rights activist, assisted residents of Taishi village, Guangdong province, who had been involved in an effort to recall their village chief because of his alleged graft. On November 14, 2007, PRC authorities sentenced Guo to five years in prison for "illegal operation of a business."
Guo Quan	Guo Quan, a former Nanjing University professor and prominent political blogger, was arrested in December 2008 on charges of "subversion of state power." In December 2007, Guo founded the New People's Party to represent "dispossessed ordinary people," including petitioners and former military personnel.

Table A-1 (Continued)

Hu Jia	Hu Jia has advocated on behalf of HIV/AIDS patients, other rights defenders, and environmental issues. Hu was placed under surveillance in 2006 for his support of legal advocate Chen Guangcheng. On April 3, 2008, Hu was sentenced to three years, six months' imprisonment for "inciting subversion of state power." In October 2008, the European Parliament awarded Hu the Sakharov Prize for Freedom of Thought.
Huang Qi	Huang Qi, an Internet activist, maintained a website, http://www.64tianwang.com, devoted to finding missing persons, including trafficked girls. In 2008, Huang visited the Sichuan earthquake zone and published articles online criticizing the government's response to the disaster. Huang was imprisoned from 2003 to 2005 for "inciting subversion of state power." In 2008, he was arrested and charged with "possessing state secrets."
Liu Xiaobo	Liu Xiaobo, a critic of the PRC government who was active in the 1989 Tiananmen Square democracy movement, was arrested on December 8, 2008, and placed under "residential surveillance" pending an investigation. Liu had played a leading role in the drafting of Charter '08, a written call for democracy signed by 300 Chinese intellectuals and disseminated online in December 2008.
Shi Tao	Shi Tao, an editor, was sentenced to 10 years' imprisonment on April 27, 2005, for "disclosing state secrets to foreigners." Shi reportedly had e-mailed information about a government order regarding the 15th anniversary of the Tiananmen student demonstrations to an overseas democracy organization.
Su Zhimin	Su Zhimin, the underground bishop of Baoding city, Hebei province (whose position is not recognized by the PRC government), was detained briefly in 1996. He was again arrested in October 1997, after he reportedly wrote an open letter to the National People's Congress urging religious freedom. Since then, with the exception of a reported sighting in 2003 at a hospital in Baoding, his whereabouts have remained unknown.
Tenzin Delek	Tenzin Delek, a Tibetan Buddhist leader and monk, was sentenced to death with a two-year reprieve in 2003 on charges of separatism and on alleged involvement in a bombing. Due to international pressure, in 2005, Tenzin's sentence was commuted to life in prison.
Wang Bingzhang	Wang Bingzhang, a Chinese dissident and permanent U.S. resident, established the pro-democracy *China Spring* magazine in 1982 in Canada. In 1998, while in China, Wang helped found the China Democracy Party, for which he was deported by PRC authorities. In 2002, Wang reportedly was apprehended in while meeting with Chinese labor leaders in Hanoi. He was repatriated to China where he faced charges of espionage and "organizing and leading a terrorist group." In February 2003, a Shenzhen court sentenced Wang to life in prison.
Yang Chunlin	Yang Chunlin, a land rights activist, was arrested in August 2007 and sentenced to five years in prison for "inciting subversion of state power." Yang was accused of writing essays critical of the Communist Party and accepting money from a "hostile" foreign group. In 2007, he wrote an open letter to the government entitled "We Want Human Rights, Not the Olympics." It was signed by over 10,000 citizens, mostly farmers.

End Notes

[1] For a variation of this view, see James Mann, *The China Fantasy: How Our Leaders Explain Away Chinese Repression*, New York: Viking, 2006.

[2] Hon. Thaddeus McCotter and John J. Tkacik, Jr. "The China Delusion," *The Heritage Foundation*, August 28, 2008.

[3] Christopher Bodeen, "China Drives Home Rejection of 'Western' Democracy," *Associated Press*, March 9, 2009.

[4] Edward Cody, "Chinese Dissidents to Appeal to Government on Human Rights," *Washington Post*, August 7, 2007; Maureen Fan, "In China, Rights Activists Use Olympics to Push for Reforms," *Washington Post*, March 24, 2008.

[5] Edward Wong, "Grieving Chinese Parents Protest School Collapse," *International Herald Tribune*, July 16, 2008.

[6] U.S. Department of State, 2007 Country Reports on Human Rights Practices – China (March 11, 2008) and 2008 Country Reports on Human Rights Practices – China (February 25, 2009).

[7] In the first three months of 2009, 15 cases of "suspicious deaths" in Chinese jails were reported. In April 2009, the PRC government announced a plan to educate police on proper jail procedures. Austin Ramzy, "In China, Suspicious Jail Deaths on the Rise," *Time.com*, April 30, 2009.

[8] Exceptions to the one-child rule are made for ethnic minorities, couples whose first child was a girl (in rural areas) or one with a disability, and couples who agreed to pay a "social compensation fee" or fine.

[9] "Non-state" actors in China, such as academics, NGOs, and private entrepreneurs, while they do not perform political or bureaucratic functions, are tied to the state in myriad significant ways, unlike their American counterparts.

[10] He Li, "The Role of Think Tanks in Chinese Foreign Policy," *Problems of Post-Communism*, Vol. 49, no. 2 (March/April 2002).

[11] Paul Mooney, "Beijing Silences 'One-Man Rights Organization'," *South China Morning Post*, January 27, 2008; Edward Cody, "In Chinese Uprisings, Peasants Find New Allies," *Washington Post*, November 26, 2005.

[12] http://www.chinadevelopmentbrief.com; Ying Ma, "China's Stubborn Anti-Democracy," *Policy Review*, February/March 2007.

[13] Paul Mooney, "How to Deal with NGOs—Part 1, China, *YaleGlobal Online*, August 1, 2006.

[14] Zhu He, "'Right to be Silent' May Be Granted," *China Daily*, May 18, 2007.

[15] Zhao Yuanxin and Xie Chuanjiao, "No Turning Back on Death Rule," *China Daily*, March 15, 2007.

[16] Peter Ford, "Amid Human Rights Protests, A Look at China's Record," *Christian Science Monitor*, April 10, 2008.

[17] "China Rocked by Labor Disputes Due to Legal Reforms, Inflation Fears," *Nikkei Weekly*, July 14, 2008.

[18] Edward Cody, "Lawmakers Approve Measure to Protect Private Property," *Washington Post*, March 16, 2007.

[19] While the state owns all land in China, farmers are granted rights of use via long term (30-year) contracts with the state. Maureen Fan, "China to Allow Land Leasing, Transfer," *Washington Post*, October 20, 2008.

[20] Edward Cody, "China Announces Rules to Require Government Disclosures," *Washington Post*, April 24, 2007.

[21] Suisheng Zhao, "Political Reform in China: Toward Democracy or a Rule of Law Regime," *Asia Program Special Report No. 131*, Woodrow Wilson International Center for Scholars, June 2006; Richard Baum, "The Limits of Consultative Leninism," *Asia Program Special Report No. 131*, Woodrow Wilson International Center for Scholars, June 2006.

[22] David Matas and David Kilgour, "Bloody Harvest: Revised Report into Allegations of Organ Harvesting of Falun Gong Practitioners in China," January 2007.

[23] Gregory M. Lamb, "China Faces Suspicions about Organ Harvesting," *Christian Science Monitor*, August 3, 2006; Glen McGregor, "China Buffs Image with Transplant Rules," *Ottawa Citizen*, November 27, 2007; Ethan Gutmann, "China's Gruesome Organ Harvest," *The Weekly Standard*, November 20, 2008.

[24] U.S. Department of State Daily Press Briefing, April 14, 2006.

[25] The State Department's 2007 Report on Human Rights Practices states that, according to some observers, more than half of re-education through labor detainees were first time or returning Falun Gong practitioners.

[26] Minnie Chan, "Kinder Face for Notorious Re-education Camps," *South China Morning Post*, February 21, 2007; Jim Yardley, "Issue in China: Many Jails Without Trial," *New York Times*, May 9, 2005.

[27] Debate on reform of the laojiao system was suspended from 1999 to 2003, during the crackdown on the Falun Gong group, and then tabled again in 2005. Wu Jiao, "New Law to Abolish Laojiao System," *China Daily*, March 1, 2007.

[28] Jerome Cohen, "Legal Reform Can Promote Harmony," *South China Morning Post*, December 25, 2008.

[29] Edward Cody, "Pioneering City Offers Peek at Political Ferment," *Washington Post*, June 30, 2008.

[30] Wu Zhong, "Party Time for China," *Asia Times* http://www.atimes.com, September 10, 2008.

[31] The PRC has signed, but not ratified, the International Covenant on Civil and Political Rights.

[32] "China Releases First Human Rights Action Plan," *Associated Press*, April 13, 2009.

[33] Geoff Dyer, "Beijing Promises Human Rights Initiative," *Financial Times.com*, November 4, 2008.

[34] Willy Lam, "China's Reforms Buried under Rubble," *Far Eastern Economic Review*, vol. 171, no. 5 (June 2008).

[35] Edward Cody, "Chinese Dissidents to Appeal to Government on Human Rights," op. cit.
[36] Chinese Activists Arrested, Beaten in 'Worst Crackdown in Five Years,'" *BBC Monitoring Asia Pacific*, October 12, 2007.
[37] Jill Drew, "China's Silencing Season," *Washington Post*, July 10, 2008; Peter Ford, "China Cracks Down on NGOs," *The Christian Science Monitor*," December 6, 2007.
[38] Peter Ford, "China Quake: Controls Cautiously Lifted on Flood of Volunteers," *The Christian Science Monitor*, May 29, 2008.
[39] Klaudia Lee, "Lawyers Finally Allowed to See Arrested Dissident Campaigner Denied Access to Legal Counsel for Two Months," *South China Morning Post*, September 24, 2008.
[40] "China Targets Activists Ahead of Tiananmen Anniversary," *States News Service*, April 30, 2009; Jane Macartney, "Mother Told Not To Honour Son," *The Times*, May 20, 2009.
[41] "Hong Kong Paper Says China Blocking Google, YouTube," *BBC Monitoring Asia Pacific*, May 20, 2009.
[42] Ford, "Amid Human Rights Protests, A Look at China's Record," op. cit.
[43] Dui Hua Foundation, March 25, 2008.
[44] http://www.cecc.gov.
[45] "Tensions Rise in China ahead of Tiananmen Massacre Anniversary," *Kyodo News*, May 14, 2009.
[46] Hongying Wang and Xueyi Chen, "Globalization and the Changing State-Media Relations in China," Paper Prepared for Presentation at the 2008 Annual Conference of the American Political Science Association, August 38-31, 2008.
[47] Ariana Eunjung Cha, "Public Anger over Milk Scandal Forces China's Hand," *Washington Post*, September 19, 2008.
[48] Hongying Wang and Xueyi Chen, "Globalization and the Changing State-Media Relations in China," op. cit.; Christopher Walker and Sarah Cook, "China's Commercialization of Censorship," *Far Eastern Economic Review*, May 2, 2009.
[49] 2007 Country Reports on Human Rights Practices – China, op. cit.
[50] 2008 Country Reports on Human Rights Practices – China, op. cit.
[51] Human Rights Watch, "China: Extend New Media Rules to Chinese Reporters," October 21, 2008.
[52] 2008 Country Reports on Human Rights Practices – China, op. cit.
[53] Human Rights Watch, "China: New Restrictions Target Media," March 18, 2009.
[54] Howard W. French, "Great Firewall of China Faces Online Rebels," *New York Times*, February 4, 2008.
[55] Edward Cody, "Chinese Media Lash Out at Government's Censure," *Washington Post*, January 8, 2008; Chris Buckley, "Chinese Outcry Against Censorship Will Grow," *Reuters News*, January 26, 2006.
[56] Howard W. French, "China Tries Again to Curb Independent Press in South," *New York Times*, April 15, 2004; Iain Marlow, "The Disaster that Finally Shook Up China's Media," *The Independent*, June 16, 2008; Frank Ching, "China Must Open Up to Restore its Reputation," *New Straits Times*, October 9, 2008.
[57] Christopher Walker and Sarah Cook, "China's Commercialization of Censorship," op. cit.
[58] The religion with the largest number of followers in the PRC, at roughly 100 million, is Buddhism.
[59] United States Commission on International Religious Freedom, *Annual Report 2006*, May 2006.
[60] Because many Chinese worship in unsanctioned churches, it is difficult to determine the number. "Survey Finds 300M China Believers," *BBC News*, February 7, 2007; Central Intelligence Agency, *The World Factbook—China*, August 2008.
[61] Associated Press, "Poll Shows 300M in China 'Religious'," *South China Morning Post*, February 7, 2007.
[62] "Three Self" refers to independence from foreign missionary or other religious influence—self-governance, self-support (i.e., financial independence from foreigners) and self-propagation.
[63] Brookings Institution, "Religion in China: Perspectives from Chinese Religious Leaders," September 11, 2008.
[64] 2008 Country Reports on Human Rights Practices – China, op. cit.
[65] China Aid Association USA, Annual Report of Persecution by the Government on Christian House Churches within Mainland China, January 2009.
[66] Maureen Fan, "Beijing Curbs Rights it Says Citizens Have to Worship," *Washington Post*, August 10, 2008.
[67] U.S. Department of State, *International Religious Freedom Report, 2008* – China (September 2008).
[68] 2008 Country Reports on Human Rights Practices – China, op. cit.
[69] Marianne Barriaux, "China's Catholics Celebrate Easter amid Familiar Tensions," *Agence France Presse*, April 11, 2009.
[70] The Hong Kong diocese canceled its pilgrimage due to the restrictions. "Government Attack against Sheshan Bears Fruit, Number of Pilgrims Cut by Half," *AsiaNews.it*, May 8, 2008.
[71] "The Question of Tibet," International Debates (Congressional Digest), May 2008.
[72] See CRS Report RL34445, *Tibet: Problems, Prospects, and U.S. Policy*, by Kerry Dumbaugh.
[73] Vaclav Havel, El Hassan Bin Talal, and Desmond Tutu, et al. "Death in Lhasa," *Cyprus Mail*, April 23, 2009.
[74] John Ruwitch, "China Condemns Dalai Lama Ahead of Planned Talks, *Reuters*, May 3, 2008.
[75] Edward Cody, "China Sanctions Lawyers Offering to Help Tibetans," *Washington Post*, June 3, 2008.
[76] Ben Blanchard, "Religion, Politics Mix Awkwardly for China's Muslims," *Washington Post*, May 26, 2006.
[77] See CRS Report RL33001, *U.S.-China Counterterrorism Cooperation: Issues for U.S. Policy*, by Shirley A. Kan.

[78] Amnesty International Report 2008, May 5, 2008.

[79] Edward Cody, "During Crackdown in Tibet, Uighurs Pursued Own Protest," *Washington Post*, April 3, 2008; Michael Bristow, "China Confirms Xinjiang Protests," *BBC News*, April 2, 2008; Martin I. Wayne, "Al Qaeda's China Problem," PacNet Newsletter [pacnet@hawaiibiz.rr.com], February 3, 2007; Annual Report of the United States Commission on International Religious Freedom (May 2007); Edward Wong, "Wary of Islam, China Tightens Vice," *New York Times*, October 19, 2008.

[80] http://faluninfo.net/]; *2008 Country Reports on Human Rights Practices – China*, op. cit.; Andrew Jacobs, "China Still Presses Crusade Against Falun Gong," *New York Times*, April 28, 2009. For further information, seeCRS Report RL33437, *China and Falun Gong*, by Thomas Lum.

[81] M2 Presswire, "Amnesty International: China—Falun Gong Deaths in Custody Continue to Rise as Crackdown Worsens," December 20, 2000.

[82] Edward Cody, "China Announces Rules to Require Government Disclosures," op. cit.

[83] Edward Cody, "China's Local Leaders Hold Absolute Power," *Washington Post*, June 10, 2008.

[84] Jamie P. Horsley, "The Rule of Law in China: Incremental Progress," *The China Balance Sheet in 2007 and Beyond (Phase II Papers)*, Center for Strategic and International Studies, May 2007.

[85] Paul Mooney, "Beijing Silences 'One-Man Rights Organization'," *South China Morning Post*, January 27, 2008.

[86] Tim Johnson, "A Legal Revolution," *Knight Ridder Foreign Service,"* November 9, 2003; "Constitutional Change Giving New Momentum to China Protests," *Kyodo News*, April 24, 2004.

[87] Joseph Kahn, "When Chinese Sue the State, Cases Are Often Smothered," *New York Times*, December 28, 2005; John L. Thornton, "Long Time Coming," *Foreign Affairs*, Vol. 87, no. 1 (January/February 2008).

[88] Geoffrey A. Fowler, Sky Canaves, and Juliet Ye, "Chinese Seek A Day in Court—With New Faith in Rule of Law, More Citizens File Suits," *Wall Street Journal*, July 1, 2008.

[89] Benjamin L. Liebman, "China's Courts: Restricted Reform," *The China Quarterly*, no. 191 (September 2007).

[90] Jim Yardley, "Desperate Search for Justice: One Man vs. China," *New York Times*, November 12, 2005.

[91] Edward Cody, "China Uses Heavy Hand Even with Gadflies," *Washington Post*, April 9, 2008.

[92] 2008 Country Reports on Human Rights Practices – China, op. cit.

[93] Bill Powell, "China's At-Risk Factories," *Time*, April 28, 2008; Edward Cody, "Farmers Rise in Challenge to Chinese Land Policy," *Washington Post*, January 14, 2008.

[94] "China Looks for Solution to a Few Problems in Rural Areas," *People's Daily Online*, March 1, 2006; "China's Security Officials Urge Stability for Upcoming CPC Congress, Olympics," *People's Daily Online*, April 18, 2007.

[95] Luis Ramirez, "Mass Disturbances Increasing in China," *VOAnews.com*, January 19, 2006; Willy Lam, "Hu Jintao's Great Leap Backward," *Far Eastern Economic Review*, vol. 172, no. 1 (Jan-Feb 2009).

[96] Saibal Dasgupta, "Labour Disputes Double in China," *The Times of India*, May 11, 2009.

[97] Ariana Eunjung Cha, "As China's Jobless Numbers Mount, Protests Grow Bolder," *Washington Post*, January 13, 2009; Ariana Eunjung Cha, "In China, Despair Mounting among Migrant Workers," *Washington Post*, March 4, 2009.

[98] Lauren Keane, "Protest-Hit China Says Job Stability Top Priority," *Washington Post*, November 20, 2008; "A Great Migration into the Unknown," *Economist.com*, January 29, 2009.

[99] Edward Wong, "In China March, Hints of a Movement: Protest of Pollution Is Latest in a Series," *International Herald Tribune*, May 6, 2008.

[100] http://www.youtube.com/watch?v=-7iikjHOOsA

[101] Rowan Callick, "China's Middle-Class Protesters Derail New Train Link," *The Australian*, March 13, 2009.

[102] "Post-Olympic Stress Disorder," *Economist.Com*, September 11, 2008.

[103] Ariana Eunjung Cha, "With Strikes, China's New Middle Class Vents Anger," *Washington Post*, December 17, 2008.

[104] Jie Chen and ChunLong Lu, "Does China's Middle Class Think and Act Democratically?" *Journal of Chinese Political Science*, Vol. 11, no. 2 (Fall 1996).

[105] See Willy Wo-Lap Lam, *Chinese Politics in the Hu Jintao Era*, M.E. Sharpe: Armonk, NY, 2006.

[106] Bruce J. Dickson, "Integrating Wealth and Power in China: The Communist Party's Embrace of the Private Sector," *The China Quarterly*, no. 192, December 2007; Kellee S. Tsai, "China's Complicit Capitalists," *Far Eastern Economic Review*, January/February 2008; Bruce J. Dickson and Jie Chen, "Engaging the State: Political Activities of Private Entrepreneurs in China," Paper Prepared for Presentation at the 2008 Annual Conference of the American Political Science Association, August 38-31, 2008.

[107] Lam, Chinese Politics in the Hu Jintao Era, op. cit.

[108] For examples, see Pew Global Attitudes Project, "Global Unease With Major World Powers," June 27, 2007.

[109] Teresa Wright, "Disincentives for Democratic Change in China," *East-West Center Asia Pacific Issues*, No. 82, February 2007; Brookings Institution, "Understanding China's 'Angry Youth': What Does the Future Hold," April 29, 2009.

[110] Merle Goldman, "Clinton's Missed Opportunity in China," *Boston Globe*, February 26, 2009.

[111] Rebecca MacKinnon, "What Does the '08 Charter Mean? Too Soon to Tell…" [rconversation.blogs.com], January 20, 2009; "Party Leaders 'Split' over Democracy Campaign," *South China Morning Post*, February 24, 2009.

[112] "Reformist Party Elders Urge Beijing to Take Steps Towards Political Reform," *BBC Monitoring Asia Pacific*, February 21, 2009.

[113] "Beijing Blinks at 'Charter '08'," *Christian Science Monitor*, December 26, 2008; Michael Wines, "A Manifesto on Freedom Sets China's Persecution Machinery in Motion," *New York Times*, May 1, 2009; "'Charter' Democrats in China," *Wall Street Journal*, March 31, 2009.

[114] John J. Tkacik, Jr., "China's Orwellian Internet," *Heritage Foundation Backgrounder #1806*, October 8, 2004.

[115] Maureen Fan, "'State Security' Arrests in China Doubled in '06, Group Reports," *Washington Post*, November 29, 2007.

[116] Some experts estimate that the PRC government has employed 30,000 "Internet police." "On the Wrong Side of Great Firewall of China," *New Zealand Herald*, November 27, 2007.

[117] David Bandurski, "China's Guerrilla War for the Web," *Far Eastern Economic Review*, Vol. 171, no. 5 (July/August 2008).

[118] Rebecca MacKinnon, "Bloggers and Censors: Chinese Media in the Internet Age," *China Studies Center*, May 18, 2007.

[119] Andrew Jabocs, "China's Web Wild Card: Economic Downturn Crisis a Threat to Censors' Tight Control," *International Herald Tribune*, February 6, 2009.

[120] Rebecca MacKinnon, "Is Web 2.0 a Wash for Free Speech in China," *RConversation* http://rconversation.blogs.com.

[121] "Chinese Bloggers Are Really Edgy," *Wall Street Journal*, June 14, 2008.

[122] See also Rebecca MacKinnon, "Flatter World and Thicker Walls? Blogs, Censorship and Civic Discourse in China," *Public Choice*, Vol. 134 (January 2008).

[123] Edward Cody, "Text Messages Giving Voice to Chinese," *Washington Post*, June 28, 2007.

[124] "Isaac Mao and Michael Anti at Hong Kong U.," April 17, 2007. http://rconversation.blogs.com/rconversation/2007/04/isaac_mao_and_m.html.

[125] Howard W. French, "Chinese Discuss Plan to Tighten Restrictions on Cyberspace," *New York Times*, July 4, 2006.

[126] For recent debate on the topic, see David M. Lampton, "'The China Fantasy,' Fantasy," *The China Quarterly*, No. 191 (September 2007); James Mann, "Rejoinder to David M. Lampton," *The China Quarterly*, No. 191 (September 2007).

[127] Glenn Kessler, "In China, Clinton Says Human Rights 'Can't Interfere' with Talks," *Washington Post*, February 20, 2009; Elise Labott, "Clinton Defends Stance on Human Rights," *CNN*.com, March 11, 2009; Ariana Eunjung Cha and Glenn Kessler, "Pelosi Mum on Rights before Trip to China," *Washington Post*, May 24, 2009; "Pelosi, Bipartisan Congressional Delegation Holds Press Conference in Beijing," *PR Newswire*, May 29, 2009.

[128] Melinda Lu, "Saying No to Bush," *Newsweek*, November 22, 2005.

[129] "U.S. Says Human Rights Talks with China 'Constructive'" *AFP*, May 27, 2008.

[130] See Brookings Institution (past event), "Ten Years after Tiananmen: U.S., China and Human Rights," June 1, 1999.

[131] Jill Drew and Edward Cody, "Chinese Lawyers Arrested before Meeting with Congressmen," *Washington Post*, July 1, 2008.

[132] Kristine Kwok, "Resume Rights Talk, China and U.S. Urged," *South China Morning Post*, April 17, 2008.

[133] For further information, see CRS Report RS22663, *U.S.-Funded Assistance Programs in China*, by Thomas Lum.

[134] Temple University School of Law, Rule of Law Projects in China: 2007-08 Annual Report.

[135] Jen Lin-Liu, "The Paper Chase Comes to China," *The Chronicle of Higher Education*, May 14, 2004.

[136] General Accounting Office, "Foreign Assistance: U.S. Funding for Democracy-Related Programs," February 2004.

[137] NED's core institutes or grantees are the International Republican Institute (IRI); the American Center for International Labor Solidarity (ACILS); the Center for International Private Enterprise (CIPE); and the National Democratic Institute for International Affairs (NDI).

[138] U.S. Department of State, Bureau of Democracy, Human Rights, and Labor, Advancing Freedom and Democracy Reports—2008: China, May 23, 2008; Interagency Working Group, FY 2007 U.S. Government-Sponsored International Exchanges & Training.

[139] Ying Ma, "China's Stubborn Anti-Democracy," op. cit.

[140] "State Department Gets Funds to Fight Internet Censorship," *Federal Times*, January 14, 2008.

[141] Human Rights Watch, "'Race to the Bottom:' Corporate Complicity in Chinese Internet Censorship," August 2006.

[142] See CRS Report RL31910, *China: Economic Sanctions*, by Dianne E. Rennack.

[143] The "Kemp-Kasten" amendment to the FY1985 Supplemental Appropriations Act (P.L. 99-88) bans U.S. assistance to organizations that support or participate in the management of coercive family planning programs. For further information, see CRS Report RL32703, *The U.N. Population Fund: Background and the U.S. Funding Debate*, by Luisa Blanchfield.

[144] Bureau of Democracy, Human Rights, and Labor, *Advancing Freedom and Democracy Reports—2008*, op. cit.

[145] P.L. 106-286, Title III, Section 301.

[146] http://www.cecc.gov.

[147] Since the U.S. government began sponsoring resolutions criticizing China's human rights record in 1991, they have been blocked by "no action" motions nearly every time. Only one, in 1995, was considered by the UNCHR, but lost by one vote. The last such U.S. resolution was introduced in 2004.

[148] See CRS Report RL33608, *The United Nations Human Rights Council: Issues for Congress*, by Luisa Blanchfield.

[149] Human Rights in China (HRIC), "China's UN Human Rights Review: New Process, Old Politics, Weak Implementation Prospects," February 9, 2009.

[150] "U.S. Concerned about Chinese Blogger," *CNN.com*, February 10, 2009.

[151] Compiled by Hannah Fischer, Information Research Specialist. All profiles were developed using the Political Prisoner Database of the Congressional-Executive Commission on China, http://www.cecc.gov, along with other media sources.

In: Asian Economic and Political Issues, Volume 14
Editor: David A. Marek
ISBN: 978-1-61728-019-1

Chapter 9

NORTH KOREAN COUNTERFEITING OF U.S. CURRENCY*

Dick K. Nanto

SUMMARY

The United States has accused the Democratic People's Republic of Korea (DPRK or North Korea) of counterfeiting U.S. $100 Federal Reserve notes (Supernotes) and passing them off in various countries, although there is some doubt by observers and other governments that the DPRK is capable of creating Supernotes of the quality found. What has been confirmed is that the DPRK has passed off such bills in various countries and that the counterfeit bills circulate both within North Korea and around its border with China. Defectors from North Korea also have provided information on Pyongyang's counterfeiting operation, although those statements have not been corroborated. Whether the DPRK is responsible for the actual production or not, trafficking in counterfeit has been one of several illicit activities by North Korea apparently done to generate foreign exchange that is used to purchase imports or finance government activities abroad.

Although Pyongyang denies complicity in any counterfeiting operation, at least $45 million in such Supernotes thought to be of North Korean origin have been detected in circulation, and estimates are that the country has earned from $15 to $25 million per year over several years from counterfeiting. The illegal nature of any counterfeiting activity makes open-source information on the scope and scale of DPRK counterfeiting and distribution operations incomplete. South Korean intelligence has corroborated information on North Korean production of forged currency prior to 1998, and certain individuals have been indicted in U.S. courts for distributing such forged currency. Media reports in January 2006 state that Chinese investigators had independently confirmed allegations of DPRK

* This is an edited, reformatted and augmented version of a CRS Report for Congress publication, Report #RL33324, dated June 12, 2009.

counterfeiting. In June 2009, press reports claimed that the DPRK produced counterfeit U.S. bills even after 2007.

For the United States, the alleged North Korean counterfeiting represents a direct attack on a protected U.S. national asset and may provide a rationale to impose financial sanctions on the DPRK. The earnings from counterfeiting and related activities also could be important to Pyongyang's finances. Profits from any counterfeiting also may be laundered through banks or other financial institutions.

U.S. policy toward the alleged counterfeiting is split between law enforcement efforts and political and diplomatic pressures. On the law enforcement side, individuals have been indicted and the Banco Delta Asia (BDA) bank in Macao (a territory of China) was named as a primary money laundering concern under the Patriot Act. In June 2007, the BDA issue was resolved and the Six-Party Talks resumed. At the time, Pyongyang promised that it would punish the counterfeiters and destroy their equipment. The law enforcement effort has become entwined with diplomatic efforts and pressures to resolve the North Korean nuclear and missile issues. Following North Korea's second nuclear test and several missile launches in May 2009, the United States reportedly has been considering further financial sanctions on the DPRK based partly on its alleged counterfeiting.

The United States has accused the Democratic People's Republic of Korea (DPRK or North Korea) of counterfeiting U.S. $100 Federal Reserve notes (Supernotes) and passing them Toff in various countries. There is considerable doubt, however, that the DPRK is capable of creating Supernotes of the quality found. The existing evidence is considered to be "intelligence" and not disclosed. However, considerable overt links have been uncovered tying Pyongyang to the counterfeiting operation. It is thought that the alleged counterfeiting activity in the DPRK is government sponsored (not criminal activity).[1] What has been confirmed is that the DPRK has passed off such bills in various countries and that the counterfeit bills circulate both within North Korea and around its border with China. In June 2009, press reports claimed that the DPRK produced counterfeit U.S. bills even after 2007.[2] Even if counterfeit bill production has been halted, genuine Supernotes are expected to remain in circulation for the foreseeable future making it possible for the DPRK to continue to use any existing stocks of counterfeit Supernotes.

The purpose of this chapter is to provide a summary of what is known from open sources on the DPRK's alleged counterfeiting of U.S. currency, examine North Korean motives and methods, and discuss U.S. interests and policy options.

Although Pyongyang denies complicity in any counterfeiting operation, estimates are that at least $45 million in such Supernotes of North Korean origin are in circulation and that the country has earned from $15 to $25 million per year over several years from counterfeiting.[3] South Korean intelligence has corroborated information on past production of forged currency—at least until 1998—and several U.S. court indictments indicate that certain individuals have been accused of distributing such forged currency. In 2009, the State Department reported that counterfeit $100 U.S. notes (Supernotes) continue to turn up in various countries, including in the United States, although it is not clear whether these notes are new or from existing stocks[4] Counterfeiting is considered to be one of several illicit activities by the DPRK apparently done to generate foreign exchange that is used to support the ruling regime, purchase imports, and finance government activities abroad.[5]

For the United States the allegedly large-scale counterfeiting of U.S. currency by the DPRK is a direct challenge to U.S. interests. Any counterfeiting, whether done by North

Korea or not, could undermine confidence in the U.S. dollar and, if done extensively enough, potentially damage the U.S. economy. It also is a direct attack on a protected asset of the United States and a violation of U.S. and other laws. If being done by the DPRK government, it violates accepted international norms and is a direct affront to the United States. It also could affect the willingness of financial institutions in certain areas to accept legitimate U.S. currency. Currency dealers in Asia already impose surcharges on suspected types of U.S. bank notes when exchanging them for other currencies.

U.S. policy toward the alleged counterfeiting is split between law enforcement efforts and political and diplomatic pressures. On the law enforcement side, individuals have been indicted, and in September 2005, the U.S. Treasury named Banco Delta Asia (BDA), bank in the Chinese territory of Macao, as a primary money laundering concern under the Patriot Act, Section 311.[6] This financial sanction was designed to curb the suspected counterfeiting by preventing the DPRK from laundering proceeds from its illicit activities through BDA. This triggered a financial chain reaction under which banks, not only from the United States but from other nations, declined to deal with even some legitimate North Korea traders. The BDA action froze $25 million in North Korean accounts and caused financial institutions in other countries also to close many of their North Korean accounts, even those for legitimate business. For the year following the financial restrictions, they were Pyongyang's main complaint and the reason it gave for boycotting the Six-Party Talks on denuclearization. Even after returning to the talks in December 2006, Pyongyang refused to discuss denuclearization officially until the Banco Delta financial sanctions were lifted.[7] On February 13, 2007, as a sideline to a new Six-Party agreement, the United States assured North Korea that it would settle the BDA issue. It took until June, however, for the $25 million to be transferred through the New York Federal Reserve Bank to a bank in Russia. North Korea confirmed its receipt on June 25, 2007. At the time, Pyongyang promised that it would punish the counterfeiters and destroy their equipment.

Following the BDA case, law enforcement efforts at the national level have become entwined with diplomatic efforts and pressures to resolve the issue of the North Korean nuclear weapons and potential ballistic missiles. After the DPRK's second nuclear test on May 25, 2009, and several firings of potential ballistic missiles, the United States reportedly has been considering using DPRK counterfeiting of U.S. currency as the basis for additional financial sanctions.[8]

The counterfeiting, to the extent that the DPRK government is involved, affects U.S. national security in a broader sense. North Korea is a Stalinist regime with serious human rights and other problems. It is led by a communist dictator with a taste for luxury imports and need to subsidize his inner circle of supporters and broader ranks of party cadres. Yet the North Korean economy scarcely produces enough to feed its population and incurs a billion-dollar trade deficit each year. Proceeds from counterfeiting could be used to maintain the regime's power or contribute to instability in East Asia.

Limits on Information

Because counterfeiting is a form of clandestine criminal activity, those involved attempt to keep it out of the public eye and undetected to the maximum extent possible. Hence, open source information on the scope and scale of DPRK counterfeiting and distribution operations is largely incomplete. Also, since the DPRK is a relatively closed society, information on any production of counterfeit U.S. currency there—other than that received from defectors—is likely to be the product of intelligence sources and methods. Hence, it is unlikely that such information would be made public for fear of compromising ongoing intelligence gathering operations.

On the other hand, involvement of DPRK citizens and officials in the distribution of so called "Supernotes" is more readily demonstrated once criminal investigations have been completed, arrests have been made, indictments issued, and convictions and/or confessions obtained. Indeed, a number of such indictments have been issued, and presumably a number of ongoing investigations remain in the pipeline. U.S. officials appear to be increasingly sensitive to a need to support public allegations with the weight of *de facto* legal evidence.

A Criminal State?

The DPRK government appears to have two major goals: to maintain the ruling regime and to be recognized as belonging to the club of nuclear, space, and newly industrializing economic countries. Both of these goals require funds. North Korea also needs to raise approximately $1 billion per year to finance its merchandise trade deficit.[9] The DPRK imports more than it exports and must generate enough foreign exchange to cover the difference through some means—either legal or illegal. Legal means include borrowing, foreign investments, foreign aid, remittances from overseas Koreans, selling military equipment not reflected in trade data, and by selling services abroad. Illegal methods include the counterfeiting of hard currency, illegal sales of military equipment or technology, sales of illegal drugs or counterfeit cigarettes and pharmaceuticals, or by shipping illegal cargo between third countries. The country also can dip into its meager foreign exchange reserves.

Allegations of counterfeiting by North Korea fits into a pattern of illicit activities linked to Pyongyang. These include production and trafficking in counterfeit cigarettes and counterfeit pharmaceuticals (for example "USA" manufactured Viagra).[10] However, according to a 2009 report by the State Department, drug trafficking by the DPRK appears to be down considerably with no instances of drug trafficking suggestive of state-directed trafficking for six years, but there still is insufficient evidence to say for certain that state-sponsored trafficking has stopped. However, reports of non-narcotics-related acts of criminality suggest that DPRK tolerance of criminal behavior may exist on a larger, organized scale, even if no large-scale narcotics trafficking incidents involving the state itself have come to light. Reports continue from the press, industry, and law enforcement agencies of DPRK links to large-scale counterfeit cigarette trafficking in the North Korean Export Processing Zone at Rajiin. According to the State Department, however, it is unclear the extent to which DPRK authorities are complicit in this illegal activity, although it is all but certain that they are aware of it. The State Department also reported that counterfeit $100 U.S. notes (Supernotes) continue to turn up in various countries, including in the United States. There are reports, for example, of supernote seizures in San Francisco, and a very large supernote seizure in Pusan, South Korea.[11] Supernotes are uniquely associated with the DPRK, but it is not clear if recent seizures are of notes which have been circulating for some time, or if they are recently issued new notes.[12]

According to the State Department, there also has been substantial evidence that North Korean governmental entities and officials have been involved in the laundering of the proceeds of narcotics trafficking and other illicit activities and that they have been engaged in other illegal activities, including activities related to counterfeiting, through a number of front companies.[13]

Supernote Counterfeiting

DPRK production and trafficking of "Supernotes" have been addressed in 2006 by National Intelligence Director John Negroponte in testimony before Congress. He stated that North Korea "produces and smuggles abroad counterfeit U.S. currency as well as narcotics and other contraband."[14]

In a Senate Committee on Government Affairs hearing in 2003, William Bach, the Director of the Office of African, Asian and European Affairs in the Bureau for International Narcotics and Law Enforcement Affairs of the U.S. Department of State, stated:

> The U.S. Secret Service Counterfeit Division is aware of numerous cases of counterfeiting with North Korean connections. Typical of such cases was one reported in Macao in 1994, when North Korean trading company executives, who carried diplomatic passports, were arrested for depositing $250,000 in counterfeit notes in a Macao bank. There are numerous other counterfeiting incidents with links to Macao banks, North Korea, and North Korean diplomats.[15]

Counterfeiting of foreign currency is apparently a phenomenon that is not new to the government of North Korea. Seoul's War Memorial Museum reportedly contains DPRK-manufactured South Korean currency from the 1950's, the production of which reportedly continued into the 1960s.[16]

South Korean media reports cite a 1998 South Korean National Intelligence Service (NIS) Report to the effect that North Korea forges and circulates U.S. $100 banknotes worth $15 million a year. Subsequent reports to the South Korean National Assembly in the same year and in 1999 are cited in the media as stating that North Korea operates three banknote forging agencies and that more than $4.6 million in bogus dollar bills had been uncovered on thirteen occasions since 1994.[17]

Press reports of February 2, 2006 cite the account by a Uri Party Member of South Korea's Parliament of a closed briefing by South Korea's National Intelligence Service to members of Korea's National Assembly to the effect that North Koreans were arrested abroad for counterfeiting offenses in the 1990s but that the Service had no evidence of the North making bogus currency after 1998.[18] Informed South Korean sources have confirmed the above stated content of the briefing, but insist that the NIS lack of hard evidence of DPRK Supernote production after 1998 should not necessarily be construed to mean that such activity has ceased. Post-1998 South Korean media reports note that South Korean authorities have continued to seize bogus U.S. currency—including 1,400 counterfeit U.S. $100 bills in April 2005, but that they have not traced the source.[19] Subsequent press reports state that the

United States has provided South Korea with examples of DPRK source counterfeit 2001 & 2003 series $100 notes. Moreover, the U.S. has reportedly determined that at least $140,000 worth of counterfeit notes seized by South Korean police in April 2005 was manufactured in the DPRK as part of a batch produced in 2001, and distributed by Pyongyang.[20]

On June 13, 2003, South Korea, the United States and Japan held a North Korea policy coordination group meeting and announced an agreement that reportedly stated, "The three countries' delegations express concern about the illegal activities of organizations in North Korea, including drug smuggling and money counterfeiting."[21] Moreover, media reports on January 20, 2006, stated that Chinese investigators have independently confirmed allegations of DPRK counterfeiting.[22]

Arrests and indictments point to DPRK trafficking in bogus U.S. currency. In August 2005, federal law enforcement authorities completed two undercover operations in New Jersey and in California which focused on the activities of members of China's Triad criminal syndicates. The operations, named Royal Charm and Smoking Dragon, reportedly netted some $4 million in Supernotes believed to be of North Korean origin. Illicit narcotics, and counterfeit brand cigarettes and pharmaceuticals were seized as well.[23]

One of the indictments issued in the above cited cases identifies Chao Tung Wu, a Taiwanese in custody for dealing in counterfeit bills, and alleges that he told undercover agents that the government of a nation—identified in the indictment as "country 2"—was producing counterfeit notes.[24] Country two has been widely cited in the media as being North Korea. Another law enforcement operation led to the arrest in Northern Ireland of Sean Garland, a leading member of an Irish Republican Army faction on charges of circulating more than $1 million of Supernotes (believed to be DPRK government produced) in Britain and Eastern Europe.[25] A request for his extradition to the United States ensued in mid-October 2005.

As recently as March 2006, counterfeit Supernotes were reportedly seized by police in Hong Kong from a Chinese-American man in transit from Macau.[26] In April 2006, a Korean reporter claimed in an article in a South Korean newspaper that obtaining fake $100 bills that likely were manufactured in North Korea was a "piece of cake" in the Chinese town of Dandong just across the DPRK's northern border. According to the reporter, counterfeit bills similar to real currency fetch about 40% of their face value. Carefully manufactured $100 Supernotes go for $60 to $70 each. North Koreans refer to the counterfeit dollars as "kattalio" and the business of dealing in them as "the kattalio game." After the Banco Delta financial sanctions, the article stated that Pyongyang proclaimed that anyone involved in illegal drugs or fake notes would be severely punished. In March 2006, two men convicted of such activities were publicly executed. Since the Banco Delta sanctions, the number of counterfeit notes circulated through North Korea reportedly has dropped.[27] However, it may be that the number of counterfeit notes circulating within North Korea has increased since imposition of the Banco Delta sanctions.[28]

In July 2007, a South Korean newspaper reported that $100 Supernotes were circulating among North Korean merchants at a value of $70 each. The reason for using the counterfeits given by the merchants was that the largest denomination of the DPRK won was 5,000 which implied that it took about 600 bills for a $1,000 transaction. So they used counterfeit bills as a medium of exchange. At the time, inflation also was causing the purchasing power of the won to depreciate rapidly.[29]

Denial of Counterfeiting by North Korea

The DPRK has consistently denied allegations of state involvement in criminal activity, specifically in any counterfeiting activity, and it has vowed to resist U.S. Pressure over the matter.[30] A January 24, 2006 commentaries carried by the state-run Korean Central News Agency reported that Pyongyang "does not allow such things as bad treatment of the people, counterfeiting, and drug trafficking."[31] In what may be an indication of DPRK willingness to curb any illicit counterfeiting activity, the DPRK Foreign Ministry announced on February 9, 2006, that "there is no evidence proving (North Korea's) issue of counterfeit notes or money laundering" but that the country "will as ever actively join the international actions against money laundering.... It is the consistent policy of the (North Korean) government to oppose all sorts of illegal acts in the financial field." The Foreign Ministry spokesman went on to say that the DPRK has "perfect legal and institutional mechanisms to combat such illegal acts as counterfeiting notes and money laundering, and any illegal acts are liable to severe punishment."[32]

Some observers also doubt that the DPRK has the technology or resources needed to produce the high-quality bills. They have pointed to the successive versions of the Supernotes found and the high cost of equipment and supplies. One has concluded that the Supernotes are an illegal printing of the genuine note.[33]

Assuming that production of bogus U.S. currency is actually taking place in North Korea, some suggest that this does not necessarily mean that such activity is being done under government sponsorship, direction, or supervision. They argue that counterfeiting is a criminal phenomenon that is widespread throughout the world, and it is rarely, if ever, state-sponsored. Others say that there may be merit to such arguments, but North Korea could be an exception to any such norms. North Korean defectors have pointed to government sponsorship of counterfeiting, but their testimonies have not been corroborated.

It can be said that it is widely acknowledged that the Pyongyang regime engages—or has engaged—in a broad range of *other* crime for profit activity. Hence, inhibitions against counterfeiting may not be strong. The sophisticated type of equipment reportedly required for the production of Supernotes is generally tightly controlled and generally restricted for sale to governments. Finally, North Korea is a closed authoritarian regime, and, as such, it is unlikely that any counterfeiting activity—which requires centralized production—would not be government sponsored, or at some point, come under government control.

Policy Implications

For the United States the North Korean counterfeiting of U.S. currency combined with secondary effects has a direct bearing on U.S. interests. Counterfeiting of one nation's currency by another generally is considered to be an act of economic warfare—a direct attack on the U.S. financial system.[34] There is a large difference between criminal counterfeiting by private parties and that done or sanctioned by a nation. The counterfeiting, itself, might undermine confidence in the U.S. dollar and, if done extensively enough, potentially damage the U.S. economy. If the extent of counterfeiting were in the range of $15 million to $25 million per year, however, this would represent a relatively small amount compared with the total U.S. supply of currency or the amount circulating abroad. As of February 2006, currency in circulation—that is, U.S. coins and paper currency in the hands of the public—totaled about $780 billion. Since 1994, the value of currency in circulation has risen at the rate of 6.5% per year, mostly stemming from foreign demand. The U.S. Federal Reserve estimates that between one-half and two-thirds of the value of currency in circulation is held outside the United States.[35] In the United States, most domestic transactions (by value) are done either electronically or by checks, not cash. As of December 2008, 73% of the value of currency in circulation consisted of $100 notes ($625 billion), the denomination allegedly counterfeited by the DPRK.[36]

Counterfeiting also can reduce the confidence by foreigners in the dollar. The dollar has become the predominant medium of exchange in international transactions. Such degraded confidence in the dollar usually can be manifested either by a surcharge on certain denominations when converting dollars to foreign exchange or in certain denominations of the dollar not being accepted at all. Currently, this affects Americans and other holders of dollar currency who rely on cash for transactions rather than credit cards, checks, or bank transfers. If the counterfeiting were to become extensive enough, however, it might depress the overall exchange value of the dollar.

Even though the suspected amount of counterfeiting by the DPRK is relatively small when compared with all U.S. currency in circulation, its importance to Pyongyang and the ruling communist party could be significant. It apparently helps fund travel abroad, meet "slush fund" purchases of foreign goods, and subsidize the lifestyles of the privileged class in Pyongyang.

Even though the macroeconomic effect of a counterfeiting operation generating around $15 million to $25 million per year is minor, counterfeiting, itself, is a violation of U.S. law. The Treasury, including the Secret Service, and the Federal Reserve have primary responsibilities for addressing the counterfeiting of U.S. currency. The Federal Reserve's role is to distribute and ensure the physical integrity, including the authenticity, of U.S. currency. The Secretary of the Treasury is responsible for issuing and protecting U.S. currency. The Bureau of Engraving and Printing produces the currency. It has announced that one of its priorities for FY2007 is to redesign the $100 note.[37] The Secret Service conducts investigations of counterfeiting activities, provides counterfeit-detection training, and is responsible for anticounterfeiting efforts abroad.[38]

So far, the United States had taken a two-pronged (but overlapping) approach toward North Korea's alleged counterfeiting activities: law enforcement and political/security pressures. The law-enforcement prong involves prosecuting or sanctioning individuals and/or institutions involved in the distribution of the bogus currency.

Law Enforcement and the Banco Delta Asia Action

There have been several criminal prosecutions of persons in which counterfeit currency thought to have come from North Korea has been involved. This includes seeking extradition for Sean Garland, former President of the Workers' Party of Ireland, who is accused of conspiring with others, including elements of the government of North Korea, to establish a counterfeiting operation involving production of almost perfect copies of U.S. dollars[39] and large U.S. sting operations, named Royal Charm and Smoking Dragon, that reportedly netted some $4 million in Supernotes believed to be of North Korean origin. Illicit narcotics, and counterfeit brand cigarettes and pharmaceuticals were seized as well.[40]

On September 15, 2005, the U.S. Treasury imposed USA PATRIOT Act Section 311 designations against Banco Delta Asia (BDA) in Macau. In the action, Treasury stated that the bank was a "primary money laundering concern" because, among other findings, sources indicated that "senior officials in Banco Delta Asia are working with DPRK officials to accept large deposits of cash, including counterfeit U.S. currency, and agreeing to place that currency into circulation."[41]

On September 20, 2005, the Financial Crimes Enforcement Network of Treasury imposed special measures against Banco Delta Asia that prohibited U.S. institutions or agencies from opening or maintaining correspondent accounts on behalf of BDA and required covered financial institutions to exercise due diligence to ensure that no correspondent account is being used indirectly to provide services to BDA.[42]

The U.S. action against Banco Delta Asia caused an avalanche of responses both in financial and political circles. It caused such a run on accounts at the bank that the government of Macau had to take over BDA's operations and place a temporary halt on withdrawals. According to press reports, the Macau government shut down all North Korea-related accounts including those belonging to 9 DPRK banks and 23 DPRK trading companies. These reportedly included accounts from the core organs of the North Korean Regime.[43] When details of the accounts reached Kim Jong-Il, he reportedly was surprised to find that some accounts had been kept secret from him and some account-holders either did not exist or had already died.[44]

The financial effects of the BDA action were larger than expected. The crackdown also spread around the region, with Chinese, Japanese, Vietnamese, Thai, and Singaporean banks making life much tougher for North Korean account holders. In Macau, the North Korean trading firm used by Pyongyang as a de facto consulate rolled up its operations as the Macau government placed Banco Delta Asia into receivership. Not only did the action deprive major DPRK companies of an international financial base and cut into the secret personal accounts of the Pyongyang leadership, but it appears to have obstructed some legitimate North Korean trade. DPRK banks and traders reportedly are having difficulty finding other lenders to conduct their overseas business. Banks from other nations (such as the United Overseas Bank of Singapore and the Korea Exchange Bank of South Korea) have moved to sever contacts with North Korea, fearing that they, too, could face U.S. legal action.[45]

On March 7, 2006, North Korea's Li Gun (head of the North America division of North Korea's Foreign Ministry) met with Assistant U.S. Treasury Secretary Daniel Glaser at the United Nations in New York as part of a back channel for communicating with each other.[46] The U.S. side spent about 20 minutes explaining its actions against Banco Delta Asia and what it expected from the DPRK. The DPRK reportedly suggested several actions to resolve the issue and for it to return to the six-party talks (including the lifting of the financial sanctions on Banco Delta Asia, forming a joint U.S.-North Korean task force to examine the counterfeiting concerns, giving North Korea access to the U.S. banking system, and providing North Korea with technical help on identifying counterfeit bills).[47] Separately, the U.S. ambassador in Seoul indicated that Washington wanted Pyongyang to prove that tools used to counterfeit U.S. currency had been destroyed as evidence that North Korea had abandoned such illegal activities.[48]

In December 2006, North Korea agreed to return to the six-party talks, but during the talks Pyongyang refused to discuss denuclearization officially until the Banco Delta financial sanctions were lifted.[49] Pyongyang, however, did send the president of the Foreign Trade Bank of North Korea (Oh Gwang-chul) along with other financial experts to meet with Deputy Assistant Treasury Secretary Daniel Glaser in the first meeting of a working group on U.S. financial sanctions that met alongside six-party talks. A second meeting was held in January 2007. In these talks, the U.S. side reportedly stated that the BDA issue could be resolved early if North Korea punished the counterfeiters and destroyed their equipment.[50] This was viewed by some as an easing of the U.S. position as it linked the BDA action to the six-party talks and opened the possibility for resolving the BDA issue in order for the talks to go forward. The Bush Administration had held that the U.S. financial sanctions against Banco Delta for collaboration with North Korean criminal activities were a separate issue from the nuclear negotiations.

On February 13, 2007, a new six-party agreement on North Korea's nuclear program and energy needs was concluded.[51] In announcing this Agreement, Assistant Secretary of State Hill pledged to settle with North Korea within 30 days the issue of U.S. financial sanctions against the Banco Delta bank and the freezing of North Korean accounts of $25 million in Banco Delta. After several failed attempts to transfer the $25 million, the DPRK recovered its funds in June 2007 when the New York Federal Reserve Bank agreed to transfer them through its facilities to a bank in Russia. (The transfer through the Federal Reserve Bank arguably made the funds no longer illicit.) This allowed the DPRK to proceed with its commitments under the February 13 agreement.

Since Portugal has returned Macao to China, Beijing had supervisory responsibility over Banco Delta Asia. China has been attempting to modernize its banking system, and for one of its banks to be accused of money laundering clearly did Beijing no good. This has placed pressure on China to ensure that Banco Delta Asia and other banks are clean. Immediately after the Banco Delta action, major Chinese banks dealing with foreign exchange reportedly refrained from transactions with North Korean-related firms.[52] China conducted a three-month investigation of the accusations against Banco Delta Asia that, according to South Korean diplomatic sources, confirmed the suspicions. However, a confidential audit of the BDA by Ernst & Young ordered by Macanese banking regulators reportedly found no evidence that the bank knowingly laundered counterfeit U.S. currency on behalf of North Korea.[53] China reportedly tried to convince North Korea, however, that it needed to take steps in the matter.[54] Traditionally, North Koreans have used Chinese banks for many of their international transactions, and some surmise that Kim Jong-il's trip to southern China in January 2006 may have included an attempt to move some North Korean accounts to a financial institution there. The U.S. Treasury has said that some reports suggest that North Korean agencies had transferred assets to banks in China.[55] Others note that Austrian banks had not refrained from making transactions with North Korea.[56]

Political/Security Measures

The political/security prong attempts to stop the alleged counterfeiting activity by changing the cost-benefit calculus of decision makers in Pyongyang. The strategy is to increase costs and reduce benefits in order to induce decision makers to halt the activity. The inducements used are aimed primarily at raising costs and include the Illicit Activities Initiative, the Proliferation Security Initiative, diplomatic pressures, as well as possible military threats and other policy related measures.

The Illicit Activities Initiative, coordinated by the U.S. Department of State, is aimed precisely at North Korea's alleged counterfeiting and other illicit activities. It was developed in cooperation with other nations,[57] but was downplayed as a diplomatic solution to the North Korean nuclear issue was pursued during the waning years of the G.W. Bush administration. The initiative reportedly now is located in the Korea Desk at the State Department.

The Proliferation Security Initiative (PSI) is part of the larger counter proliferation effort worldwide and aimed at more countries and groups than just North Korea—but the DPRK does receive a particular focus. The PSI activity has received support from more than 60 countries and more formal participation from 11 countries, particularly Japan, Australia, the United Kingdom, France, Germany, Italy, and Spain. Under the PSI, participating countries cooperate to prevent transfers of weapons of mass destruction-related items to or from nation states and non state actors of proliferation concern. It does this through intelligence sharing, diplomatic efforts, law enforcement, and interdiction.[58] Following the DPRK's second nuclear test, South Korea announced that it was joining the PSI. Pyongyang considered this to be equivalent to a "declaration of war" and indicated that it no longer is bound to the Korean War armistice and will militarily respond to any foreign attempt to inspect its ships.[59]

The U.N. resolution being considered in June 2009 reportedly contains provisions for tightening provisions for searching ships (under specific conditions) suspected of carrying banned nuclear or missile cargo.[60]

Policymakers reportedly are divided on the ultimate goal of squeezing North Korea on its alleged illicit activities. A group of policymakers (sometimes referred to as the "hawks") favoring regime change seeks ultimately to induce a crisis within the DPRK that would lead to the downfall of Kim Jong-il. One way to achieve this is to cut off the money the DPRK generates from counterfeiting, selling illicit drugs, and exporting missiles. A second group of policymakers more in favor of engagement, seeks to resolve the North Korean problem mainly by negotiations. Its goal is to change the "bad behavior" of the DPRK by bringing the country into the circle of peaceful nations and inducing it to act in accord with international standards.[61] Each group backs initiatives to curb Pyongyang's alleged counterfeiting, but each sees the measures in a different light.

The position of the United States is that counterfeiting is an illegal activity that cannot be allowed to continue. The South Korean government also has taken a firm position on the counterfeiting issue. It has clearly communicated to North Korea that such illicit activities are not acceptable and that Pyongyang should unequivocally turn away from such illicit behavior once and for all.[62] Seoul reportedly has tried in vain to reach a compromise with the United States to consider Pyongyang's counterfeiting activities illegal conduct by individual North Korean firms and not by the government of the DPRK.[63] One observer stated that the bigger question being asked by China and South Korea is why is the United States has been chasing after North Korea's "loose change" when the country is making plutonium, the real currency of state power?[64]

The response by other nations to the alleged counterfeiting by the DPRK is intertwined with other strategic and political interests. In the case of South Korea, President Lee Myung-bak has taken a much harder line toward the DPRK in contrast to the previous administration that was seeking some compromise with the United States on the degree of financial and other pressure to exert on Pyongyang.

The basic interests of the United States lie in stopping the proliferation of weapons of mass destruction and in denuclearization, but financial sanctions can be pursued independently of those by the United Nations or by other countries. As was seen in the Banco Delta Asia case, financial sanctions can have far reaching affects and can reach into the heart of Pyongyang.

Japan also seeks to defuse tensions with the DPRK, but Japan has cooperated with the United States in both the Proliferation Security and Illicit Activities Initiatives. In talks in February 2006 on normalization of relations with Pyongyang, Japan announced that it intended to take up North Korea's illicit activities, including counterfeiting, in order to strengthen policy coordination with the United States and the European Union.[65]

The current strategy of the Obama Administration is to protect U.S. interests, to coordinate policy and sanctions toward the DPRK with Japan, South Korea, China, and Russia, to work through the United Nations, and to proceed with unilateral action if necessary. The United States is prepared to engage North Korea in bilateral talks under the Six-Party Talk[66] umbrella if the DPRK is willing to engage in serious negotiations over its denuclearization.[67]

If the Obama Administration imposes new financial sanctions on the DPRK, they are likely to use counterfeiting of currency as one rationale for the sanctions. The role of Congress in the counterfeiting issue is intertwined with the larger nuclear and proliferation issues. Congress plays a role in oversight of Obama Administration actions, in holding hearings to clarify U.S. policy, or using the congressional pulpit to send messages to North Korea.[68] The United States has suggested to the DPRK that it join the Asia-Pacific Group on Money Laundering (APG), a 30-member group (including the United States, Japan, and South Korea) launched in 1997 as a sub-organization of the Organization of Economic Cooperation and Development. It is aimed at preventing illegal financial activities in the Asia-Pacific region and would subsequently require the disclosure of all of the DPRK's illicit financial activities.[69] North Korea experts believe, however, that it will not be easy for the North to join the 30-member group.

The BDA action (combined with UN sanctions prohibiting exports of luxury goods to the DPRK) seemed to generate results because they harmed the North Korean elites, including Kim Jon-Il, directly. Policies aimed at an economic collapse in North Korea, however, appear to be off the table at this time—partly because China seems willing to provide just enough food and fuel to prevent one from occurring because it does not want to deal with the flood of immigrants and economic and political effects that would follow should such a collapse occur.

How the broader strategic considerations will govern future responses to the problem of North Korean counterfeiting of U.S. currency and other crime-for-profit-activity is now unclear. What is clear is that the BDA sanctions made Pyongyang more willing to meet and talk seriously with the United States and other of the six-party countries and they provided real evidence to Pyongyang that flaunting international laws and norms can cause serious negative consequences for its inner circle of elites. In U.S. discussions with the DPRK on the normalization of relations, ceasing any counterfeiting of U.S. currency would seem to be *sine qua non*.

The implications for U.S. policy of the BDA action go beyond the problems with the DPRK. The Patriot Act has provided the United States with a powerful tool to disrupt the financial underpinnings of unsavory regimes or hostile groups. The use of this tool is still under development, and it is not clear whether it should be employed as an end in itself or as a tactical weapon that is part of a larger strategic plan with ample coordination between the Departments of the Treasury, State, and Defense.

U.S. law enforcement actions against foreign banks and their operations, moreover, have far reaching consequences for an industry that often prefers to be secretive and has operational interests that often compete with each other. Banks must provide service to customers of all kinds and take a loss on counterfeit currency found that is surrendered to government authorities. At the same time they may be asked to cooperate in enforcing laws that may hurt their customers or reduce their earnings. BDA-type actions (which can be seen as sending mixed signals or which are followed by about-face changes in policy) also give rise to the question of what effect they might have on U.S. leverage with the banking community and on cooperation from banks on other international problems. At issue here is whether in the future, foreign banks will be as willing to take measures that will be unpopular with their customers given the risk that the United States may at some point reverse course because national security interests or diplomatic exigencies hold sway?

End Notes

[1] A news report alaimed that O Kuk Ryol, Vice Chairman of the DPRK's National Defense Commission and his family are taking the lead in the production and circulation of Supernotes. O Kuk ryol reportedly is leading the preparation for the power transfer from current leader Kim Jong-il to his son Kim Jong-un. "Fake N. Korean Supernotes Smuggled into SK," Dong-A Ilbo Online (Seoul), June 4, 2009.

[2] "Fake N. Korean Supernotes Smuggled into SK," Dong-A Ilbo Online (Seoul), June 4, 2009.

[3] See section "Supernote Counterfeiting," below.

[4] U.S. Department of State, Bureau of International Narcotics and Law Enforcement Affairs, *2009 International Narcotics Control Strategy Report , Volume I: Drug and Chemical Control*, Washington, DC, February 27, 2009, Country Reports: North Korea.

[5] For details, see Staff of U.S. Representative Ed Royce, *Gangster Regime: How North Korea Counterfeits United States Currency*, Staff Report, Washington, DC, March 12, 2007.

[6] Section 311 of the Patriot Act authorizes the Treasury to use financial force against foreign jurisdictions, banks, or classes of transactions that are of "primary money laundering concern," to isolate the designated entity and protect the U.S. financial system from tainted capital running through the entity. Section 311 authorizes the Secretary of the Treasury to require U.S. financial institutions to take certain "special measures" against identified targets.

[7] Kyodo World Service. 6-way Talks' Delegates Leave Beijing After 5-Day Discussions. December 23, 2006. Note: The United States does not consider the actions to be sanctions, but North Korea has characterized them as such.

[8] Jon Herskovitz, "U.S. Might Impose Counterfeiting Sanctions on North Korea," Global Security Initiative by National Journal Group, June 4, 2009. Online edition.

[9] Note that such estimates of scale of the DPRK's foreign exchange deficit may be exaggerated as the amount may be offset by undetermined amounts of aid from the Peoples Republic of China.

[10] In July 2004, for example, the U.S. Secret Service reportedly uncovered a network selling counterfeit North Korean made cigarettes, pharmaceuticals, and $100 bills. See Frederik Balfour et. al., "Fakes," *Business Week*, February 7, 2005. Criminal indictments subsequently ensued. See generally: BBC News, "What is a superdollar?", June 20, 2004.

[11] Kim Rahn, "9,900 Supernotes Smuggled Into S. Korea," *Korea Times*, June 4, 2009.

[12] U.S. Department of State, Bureau of International Narcotics and Law Enforcement Affairs, *2009 International Narcotics Control Strategy Report , Volume I: Drug and Chemical Control*, Washington, DC, February 27, 2009, Country Reports: North Korea.

[13] United States Department of State, Bureau for International Narcotics and Law Enforcement Affairs, 2009 *2009 International Narcotics Control Strategy Report , Volume I: Money Laundering and Financial Crimes*, Washington, DC, February 27, 2009. p. 316.

[14] See testimony of John Negroponte before the Senate Intelligence Committee on the issue of Worldwide Threats to the United States, February 2, 2005. Note that Negroponte's remarks came at a time when the six-party talks on North Korea's nuclear ambitions remained stalled over North Korea's insistence that the United States remove proposed Treasury Department sanctions against Banco Delta Asia for its alleged role in laundering proceeds of DRPK criminal activity and distributing of DPRK produced counterfeit U.S. currency. See "North Korean Counterfeiting Complicates Nuclear Crisis," by Martin Fackler, *New York Times*, January 29, 2006, p. 3.

[15] Bach, William. Hearing Testimony. Drugs, Counterfeiting, and Weapons Proliferation: The North Korean Connection. Hearing Before the Financial Management, the Budget, and International Security Subcommittee of the Committee on Governmental Affairs, United States Senate 108th Congress, First Session, S.Hrg. 108-157, May 20, 2003. p. 6.

[16] See "The 'Soprano State?' North Korean Involvement in Criminal Activity and Implications for International Security," by Sheena E. Chestnut (hereinafter cited as *Chestnut*), Stanford University Honors Thesis, May 20, 2005, p.81 citing Cumings, Bruce, *Korea's Place in the Sun: A Modern History* (Norton, New York) 1997, and Michishita, Narushigwe, "Calculated Adventurism: North Korea's Military-Diplomatic Campaigns," *Korean Journal of Defense Analysis*, Vol. XVI, No.2, Fall 2004. Note that the term "Soprano State" was originally coined by *U.S. News and World Report* investigative journalist David Kaplan in 2003; see "The Far East Sopranos," by David E. Kaplan, *U.S. News and World Report*, January 27, 2003.

[17] See "Seoul's U-Turn on N. Korean Counterfeiting Could be Fatal," *Chosun Ilbo* (English Edition), December 25, 2005. The title of the 1988 report is cited as "A New Threat in the 21st Century: Realities and Responses to International Crimes."

[18] See "Korea Exchange Bank cuts ties with Macau bank accused of laundering money for North Korea," *Associated Press Report* (Seoul) February 3, 2006. See also "No sign of North Korea making fake bills since 1998: spy agency," *Yonhap*, February 3, 2006. Note that media reports contain at least a handful of reports by defectors that lend credence to the notion that the DPRK produced counterfeit greenbacks under government direction prior to 1996. For a consolidated overview of such reports see Sheena Chestnut, *Soprano State*, pp. 86-89.

[19] See "Seeking international cooperation to stop manufacturing of North Korea's money," *Chosun Ilbo* (Internet Version), December 27, 2005. Media report suggestions that the DPRK may have ceased production of counterfeit greenbacks prior to the end of 1998, however, may be contradicted by at least one defector who fled the North in 2000. According to one press report, the defector, a chemist connected to the Sean Garland case, was reportedly part of a team of North Korean experts ordered to produce fake U.S. $100 bills. However, what is publically known about him, his activities, and their connection to the DPRK regime appears at this point to be anecdotal and sketchy at best. See "Counterfeiting cases point to North Korea," by Josh Meyer and Barbara Demick, *L. A. Times*, December 12, 2005. Note that often statements by individuals termed "North Korean defectors," have been considered unreliable when it comes to intimate knowledge of highly secretive, closed, DPRK programs.

[20] See "U.S. says S. Korea fake notes made in North," by Jon Herskovitz and Jack Kim, Reuters, February 27, 2006. Accounts in subsidiaries of the Bank of China, Hong Kong have been frozen as a result of reported links to the DPRK's trade in Supernotes, and other criminal activities. See "HK link to Pyongyang 'Supernotes' N Koreans have cut counterfeit deals in the city, with payments made via Bank of China subsidiary," by Greg Torode, *South China Morning Post*, February 26, 2006.

[21] See "Seeking international cooperation to stop manufacturing of North Korea's money," *Chosun Ilbo* (Internet Version), December 27, 2005.

[22] See "North Korean Counterfeiting Complicates Nuclear Crisis," by Martin Fackler, *New York Times*, January 29, 2006, p. 3.

[23] See generally, remarks of Acting Assistant Attorney General, John C. Richter of August 22, 2005 http://www.usdoj.gov/criminal/pr/speeches/2005/08/2005_4193_rmrksOprSmokngDrgnNroylChrm082405O.pdf.

[24] See "Arrest ties Pyongyang to counterfeit $100 bills," by Bill Gertz, *Washington Times*, September 20, 2005, p. A1.

[25] See "North Korean Counterfeiting Complicates Nuclear Crisis" by Martin Fackler, *New York Times*, January 29, 2006, p. 3. See "Garland stands accused by US over counterfeit made in North Korea," *Irish Times*, October 17, 2005. Garland was arrested October 7, 2005, as a result of pending U.S. proceedings against him. See also Department of Justice Press Release of October 8, 2005, on Arrest of Leader of Irish Workers Party.

[26] Torode, Greg. "Fake US Supernotes Find Their Way to HK. Pyongyang's Counterfeit Bills Are Seized from American in Transit." *South China Morning Post*, March 5, 2006, p. 3. Supernotes have reportedly shown up on 2005-2006 in Peru, Paraguay, Mongolia, Hong Kong, and Ethiopia.

[27] Kwak Tae-chung. Getting North Korean-made Counterfeit Notes is a "Piece of Cake"—Supernotes Identical to Real Ones Circulated Through the North Korea-China Border—The Powerful Economic Sanctions by the United States Has Reduced the Quantity. *Seoul Weekly Dong-A*, April 25, 2006, pp. 30-31. Original article in Korean, translated by the Open Source Center as ROK Weekly on Decreases in Circulation of DPRK-made Illegal Products in China.

[28] See Interview with Kansai University's Professor (Young Hwa?) Lee carried by Japan's TBS-TV, in an interview during a program on "Narcotics Economy in the Making of North Korea," January 16, 2007, 17:30-18:30 local time.

[29] "Fake dollars curculated as 'official currency' in North Korea," *The Daily NK (Reported by BBC Monitoring Asia Pacific, March 26, 2008,* July 31, 2007, Internet edition.

[30] A Swiss report on North Korean counterfeiting is reported to have expressed serious doubt that North Korea is capable of manufacturing the fake bills, which it said were superior to the real ones. See Hall, Kevin G., Swiss Authorities Question U.S. Counterfeiting Charges against North Korea, McClatchy Newspapers, May. 22, 2007 http://www.mcclatchydc.com/staff/kevin_hall/v-print/story/16472.html

[31] This is but one of a string of DPRK denials. David L. Asher, former Coordinator of the State Department's North Korea Working Group, in his February 1, 2006 remarks to the American Enterprise Institute cited another DPRK denial: "We had neither counterfeited currency nor gotten involved in any illegal trafficking."

[32] See KCNA (official North Korean News Agency) broadcast of 1006 GMT, February 9, 2006. Reported in "North Korea vows to join international anti-money laundering drive," *MSN News*, February 9, 2006, and untitled AP report from Seoul of February 9, 2006. Statements by a DPRK Foreign Ministry spokesperson are typically reserved for high level communications with the outside world. Reuters and Agence France Presse (AFP) reported on the broadcast as well.

[33] Kevin G. Hall, "Mysterious $100 "supernote" counterfeit bills appear across world," *McClatchy Newspapers*, January 12, 2008, carried in the *Kansas City Star.*

[34] Asher, David L. "The North Korean Criminal State, its Ties to Organized Crime, and the Possibility of WMD Proliferation." The Nautilus Institute. Policy Forum Online 05-92A: November 15th, 2005.

[35] The Federal Reserve Board. Currency and Coin Services. On Internet at http://www.federalreserve.gov/paymentsystems/coin/default.htm.

[36] The Federal Reserve Board. Currency in Circulation: Value. On Internet at http://www.federalreserve.gov/paymentsystems/coin/currcircvalue.htm.

[37] The Department of the Treasury. *Budget in Brief FY2007*. p. 87.

[38] U.S. General Accountability Office. Testimony. Counterfeit U.S. Currency Abroad: Observations on Counterfeiting and U.S. Deterrence Efforts. February 27, 1996 (GAO/T-GGD-96-82).

[39] "US Pursues 'Sick Old Republican' in Counterfeit Scam," *The Sunday Independent (Ireland)*, February 1, 2009.

[40] See generally, remarks of Acting Assistant Attorney General, John C. Richter of August 22, 2005, http://www.usdoj.gov/criminal/pr/speeches/2005/08/2005_4193_rmrksOprSmokngDrgnNroylChrm082405O.pdf.

[41] The Department of the Treasury. Treasury Designates Banco Delta Asia as Primary Money Laundering Concern under USA Patriot Act. Press Release JS-2720. September 15, 2005. See *Federal Register*, Vol. 70 No. 181, September 20, 2005 (Notices), p. 55214. The finding asserts that at least one regular North-Korean-front client of BDA was widely reported to be conducting "numerous illegal activities, including distributing counterfeit currency and smuggling counterfeit tobacco products" for over a decade. See also Department of Treasury Press Release of September 15, 2005 (JS-2720), on Treasury Designation of Banco Delta Asia as a Primary Money Laundering Concern and Treasury Dept. FINCEN Advisory of December 13, 2005, on Guidelines to Financial Institutions on the Provision of Banking Services to North Korean Government Agencies and Associated Front Companies Engaged in Illicit Activities which encourages financial institutions worldwide to take precautions that they are not used as a conduit for the laundering of proceeds of DPRK illicit activities.

[42] See *Federal Register*, Vol. 70 No. 181, September 20, 2005 (Notice of Proposed Rulemaking) p. 55217ff.

[43] See *Wall Street Journal Asia*, "North Korea's economy feels fallout of U.S. move-Lenders sever ties after sanction threat against Macau bank," by Gordon Fairclough, February 14, 2006. Note that as generally private North Korean individuals do not hold accounts outside the country, widespread speculation exists that the nine individual accounts seized belong to the upper echelons of the DPRK elite. The U.S. has accused Banco Delta Asia of accepting and circulating DPRK origin Supernotes.

[44] General Secretary Kim Did Not Know the Existence of Some North Korean Accounts Frozen in Macau. *Sentaku*, July 1, 2007, p. 21. (Original in Japanese, translated by Open Source Center, article No. JPP20070728032001)

[45] Fairclough, Gordon. "Politics & Economics: Banks Cut Ties to North Korea—U.S. Threat Toward One Lender Has Surprisingly Big Ripple Effect." *The Wall Street Journal*, February 14, 2006. P. A6.

[46] U.S. Department of the Treasury. Treasury Officials Brief North Koreans on Actions to Stem DPRK Illicit Financial Activity. Press Release JS-4099, March 7, 2006. "N. Korea Agrees to Discuss Counterfeit Issue with U.S." *The Chosun Ilbo*. (Digital edition) February 24, 2006.

[47] Kessler, Glenn. N. Korea Sets Terms for Return to Nuclear Talks . *The Washington Post*, March 9, 2006. P. A16. DPRK Reportedly Proposed 'Method' to Resolve Financial Dispute, Waits for US Response. Open Source

Center report of Yonhap news article: N. Korea Vows Not To Join Nuclear Talks Unless U.S. Sanctions Are Lifted, March 8, 2006. Center-Left ROK Daily Carries Exclusive Interview With DPRK Delegate to New York Meeting. Open Source Center report of article in *Seoul Hankyoreh* (Internet version) in Korean. March 8, 2006.

[48] Herskovitz, Jon and Jack Kim. U.S. Says S. Korea Fake Notes Made in North. Reuters News, February 22, 2006.

[49] Kyodo World Service. 6-way Talks' Delegates Leave Beijing After 5-Day Discussions. December 23, 2006. Note: The United States does not consider the actions to be sanctions, but North Korea has characterized them as such.

[50] U.S. Offers Compromise Over N. Korea's Dollar Forgeries. *Chosun Ilbo* (Digital Chosun), December 20, 2006.

[51] For details, see CRS Report RL33567, *Korea-U.S. Relations: Issues for Congress*, by Larry A. Niksch.

[52] Chinese Banks Cut Transactions with North Korea-related Firms (From Kyodo News Service). BBC Monitoring Asia Pacific. March 13, 2006.

[53] Hall, Kevin G. *Macau Bank Audit Comes Up Clean*, *News & Observer*, Raleigh, N.C., April 17, 2007. pg. A.3. (The audit was obtained by the McClatchy Newspapers.)

[54] ROK Daily Cites Diplomatic Source: PRC Confirms DPRK Money-Laundering in Macau. Open Source Center report of article by *Chosun Ilbo* (WWW-Text in English), January 11, 2006. [*Chosun Ilbo* headline: "China Finds N.Korea Guilty of Money Laundering"]

[55] Treasury Issues Advisory on North Korean Banking. Bulletin News Network, the White House Bulletin, March 16, 2006.

[56] Major Chinese Banks Refrain From Dealing with N. Korean Firms. Kyodo News. March 13, 2006.

[57] James A. Kelly. An Overview of U.S.-East Asia Policy, Testimony before the House International Relations Committee, Washington, DC. June 2, 2004.

[58] U.S. Department of State. Bureau of Nonproliferation. The Proliferation Security Initiative (PSI) (Fact Sheet). May 26, 2005. Congressional Research Service CRS Report RS21881, *Proliferation Security Initiative (PSI)*, by Sharon Squassoni.

[59] "S. Korea joins PSI, North irate," *UPI.com*, May 27, 2009.

[60] Colum Lynch and Blaine Harden, "Major Powers Approve Draft U.N. Resolution on North Korea," *Washington Post*, June 11, 2009, Internet edition.

[61] Sanger, David. Questions Without Answers: the Korean Conundrum [Review]. *The New York Times*, January 19, 2006. Pg. E.9.

[62] Ambassador Lee Tae-sik's Speech Given at the St. Regis Hotel (Washington, DC). The Korea-US Alliance - A Partnership for the Future, February 7, 2006. Korea Economic Institute. http://www.keia.com/2-Publications/2-6-Other/ LeeTSspeech.pdf.

[63] ROK Editorial Says ROK-US 'Discord' Over DPRK Counterfeiting 'Worrisome." *Dong-A Ilbo*, in Korean, January 25, 2006, p. 31. Translation by the U.S. Embassy in Seoul. Provided by Open Source Center.

[64] Hayes Says Counterfeiting Issue Sidetracks Nuclear Negotiations. *Nautilus Weekly*, February 27 - March 3, 2006. Quote by Nautilus Institute Executive Director Peter Hayes speaking on Chicago Public Radio's Worldview Program.

[65] Japan to raise North Korea's alleged laundering, drug trafficking in talks (From Kyodo News Service), BBC Monitoring Asia Pacific, February 1, 2006. p. 1.

[66] CRS Report RL33567, *Korea-U.S. Relations: Issues for Congress*, by Larry A. Niksch.

[67] Stephen Bosworth, Testimony before the Senate Foreign Relations Committee, U.S. Congress, *North Korea, Back at the Brink?*, 112th Cong., 1st sess., June 11, 2009.

[68] For legislation, see; CRS Report RL33567, *Korea-U.S. Relations: Issues for Congress*, by Larry A. Niksch.

[69] U.S. asks NK to Join Int'l Group on Money Laundering. Yonhap English News. March 12, 2006.

In: Asian Economic and Political Issues, Volume 14
Editor: David A. Marek
ISBN: 978-1-61728-019-1

Chapter 10

INDONESIA: DOMESTIC POLITICS, STRATEGIC DYNAMICS, AND AMERICAN INTERESTS*

Bruce Vaughn

SUMMARY

Indonesia is the world's fourth most populous country and the most populous Muslim nation. It is also a moderate Muslim state that is strategically positioned astride key sea lanes that link East Asia with the energy resources of the Middle East. Indonesia is seen by many as a valuable partner in the struggle against radical Islamist militants in Southeast Asia. Indonesia is continuing to democratize and develop its civil society and rule of law under the leadership of President Susilo Bambang Yudhoyono (SBY), who many view as reform-minded. However, a legacy of abuse of human rights by the military that stems from the three-decade reign of former President Suharto, who stepped down in 1998, remains unresolved.

The parliamentary elections of 2009 further consolidated Indonesian democracy and marked a continued preference by Indonesian voters for secular-nationalist parties rather than Islamic or Islamist political parties. President Yudhoyono's Democrat party made significant gains due to the voters' approval of the president. Observers predict that President Yudhoyono will win the presidential election scheduled for July 2009.

U.S. foreign policy concerns have focused on building relations with Indonesia to more effectively counter the rise of militant Islamist extremists, as well as to develop relations with a geopolitically important state. The United States has sought to promote democracy, the rule of law, and human rights in Indonesia in addition to American trade and investment interests there.

The election of President Barack Obama, who spent part of his childhood in Indonesia, and his subsequent outreach to the Muslim world has done much to spur expectations in

* This is an edited, reformatted and augmented version of a CRS Report for Congress publication, Report #RL32394, dated June 17, 2009.

Indonesia and the United States that the bilateral relationship will be enhanced during his administration. Expectations for development of the bilateral relationship were also lifted by the November 2008 proposal by President Yudhoyono to develop a strategic partnership between Indonesia and the United States. This initiative was followed by Secretary of State Hillary Clinton's decision to travel to Indonesia during her first trip abroad as Secretary of State in February 2009.

This chapter surveys key aspects of Indonesia's domestic politics and strategic dynamics in addition to provide general background information on Indonesia. It also provides an overview of the bilateral relationship between the United States and Indonesia. The report examines issues of ongoing congressional interest, including Indonesia's role in the struggle against violent Islamist extremists, security assistance, human rights, religious freedom, promotion of democracy and good governance, trade, foreign assistance, and regional geopolitical and strategic interests. The report seeks to provide a broader context for understanding the complex interrelated nature of many of these issues.

Recent Events: Indonesia's Parliamentary and Presidential Elections

Parliamentary Elections

On April 9, 2009, Indonesians went to the polls in the third parliamentary election held since Indonesia's transition from the authoritarian New Order era of former President Suharto. The 2009 parliamentary elections followed elections held in 1999 and 2004 and mark a further consolidation of Indonesian democracy as well as a robust endorsement of President Susilo Bambang Yudhoyono (SBY) and his Democrat Party, and a strong and increasing preference for secular-nationalist parties over Islamic or Islamist parties.[1] The President's Democratic Party, Partai Demokrat (PD), is now the single largest political party in Indonesia. The Indonesian Parliament is elected separately from the executive. In 2004, 84% of the 148 million registered voters cast votes. This was a lower percentage turn out from the 93% of the 118 million voters that cast ballots in the 1999 parliamentary elections.[2]

Several factors appear to have contributed to the Democrat Party's victory in the April 2009 parliamentary elections. Declining food and fuel prices as well as programs for the poor improved Yudhoyono's and his Party's standing.[3] According to Marcus Mietzner of the Lowy Institute in Sydney, Australia: "... it was the introduction of massive cash programs for the poor that triggered Yudhoyono's meteoric rise from electoral underdog to almost unassailable front runner ... the government spent approximately $2 billion on compensation payments ..."[4]

A related factor in the election appears to have been shifting Indonesian perceptions of the economy from 2005 to 2009. More Indonesians generally felt that the national economic condition was worsening, but by early 2009, this negative perception changed as more Indonesians came to believe that the national economic condition was now better than the previous year. In February 2009, 37% believed that the economy was better while 31% believed it was worse.[5]

Another key factor appears to be the general popularity of President SBY as well as positive perceptions of his anti-corruption drive. Some 80% of Indonesians polled believed that SBY was good, or very good, in fighting corruption. Indonesian voters also believed that the Democrat Party was the least corrupt of the political parties by an increasing margin in the lead up to the April 2009 parliamentary election. That said, Indonesians believe that the parliament and the judiciary are the two most corrupt institutions in Indonesia.[6] Indonesians have a consistently negative perception of the legislative branch.[7]

The apparent lack of resonance of Islamist messages with Indonesian voters appears to have been a key factor in the parliamentary election results.[8] It appears that the Indonesian voter is less ideological and more pragmatic than some assumed.[9] The Islamic vote declined from 38.1% of the vote in the 2004 election to 27.8% of the vote in 2009. Indonesian Islamic parties received 44% of the vote in the 1955 election and 37.59% in 1999.[10] Some have cautioned that the fortunes of the Prosperous Justice Party (PKS), the United Development Party (PPP), the National Mandate Party (PAN), the National Awakening Party (PKB), and other Islamic or Islamist parties that did not make the representative threshold of 2.5% had stable or declining performance more because of internal divisions and political stagnation than as a result of a major shift in voter attitudes.[11] Others also point to the inability of Islamic parties to "translate ideological identity into concrete programs."[12]

A politically significant outcome of the parliamentary election is that the Democrat Party attained sufficient votes and seats to be allowed to nominate its own presidential candidate. Indonesian election law requires parties to attain 20% of the seats in the 560 Member House of People's Representatives (DPR) or 25% of the national vote to be able to nominate a presidential candidate. The Democrats' strong performance in the parliamentary election, by nearly tripling their vote from their 2004 electoral performance and crossing the 20% nomination threshold with 20.9% of the vote, meant that President Yudhoyono was in a stronger position on the issue of coalition partners and the selection of his vice presidential running mate.

Another observation of the Indonesian electorate in 2009 leads some to conclude that conventional wisdom on Indonesia appears to have overestimated the importance of religion, and civil-military relations. It now appears to some analysts that religion and civil-military issues are not as salient as they once were in Indonesian politics.[13] Although political stability is enhanced by the decline of divisive issues in the political milieu, the apparent move toward personality politics may not be stabilizing in the long run. In the view of many, the Democrat Party lacks structure and is driven by its members' support for Yudhoyono as an individual.

Presidential Elections

The Indonesian president is directly elected in a separate presidential election that is held after the parliamentary elections. Under Indonesian law the president and his or her vice president run for election together. The current presidential election is scheduled for July 8, 2009. If one candidate for president receives over 50% of the vote in the first round, they become president. If no single candidate receives over 50% then a subsequent run off round will be held in September between the two leading candidates for president. In May 2009 SBY was leading with 67% of Indonesians polled favoring him.[14] This margin narrowed to 52.5% by mid-June 2009.[15]

Analysts are currently focused on the three pairs of presidential and vice presidential candidates. President Yudhoyono, who has been described as a moderate, cautious, and intelligent man of common sense, has picked Boediono as his vice presidential running mate.[16] Some have observed that Yudhoyono chose Boediono for his abilities rather than for his political standing. Boediono was Central Bank Governor and was a relative unknown who does not bring with him a vote block in parliament. That said, he has a doctorate from the Wharton School at the University of Pennsylvania and was Coordinating Minister for Economic Affairs before taking his post at the Central Bank. He is credited with devising the government initiative to disperse cash to Indonesia's poorest 19 million families and is thought to be a key architect of Yudhoyono's economic policies.[17]

Yudhoyono's current vice president from Golkar, Jusuf Kalla, is running against Yudhoyono with former General Wiranto of the Hanura Party. Wiranto was accused of human rights abuses in East Timor by a U.N.-backed Special Tribunal.[18] Former President Megawati Sukarnoputri of PDI-P will also be running for president with vice presidential running mate Probowo Subianto. Probowo is leader of Gerindra, a former Kopassus [Special Forces] Commander, and the former son-in-law to former President Suharto. Probowo's critics believe he was responsible for violence towards anti-Suharto intellectuals and students, as well as against the ethnic Chinese community in Jakarta, during Indonesia's transition from Suhato's authoritarian New Order to *reformasi* and more open government in 1998.[19]

The outcome of the parliamentary and presidential elections in Indonesia are important to the United States for several reasons. First, American security interests could potentially be threatened by the rise of Islamist political forces in Indonesia. The strong performance by the Democrat party and other national secular parties in the 2009 parliamentary election indicates that Islamist political fortunes are declining and not rising as had been feared in the wake of the 2004 elections. Second, Indonesia is a strategically located state and a leader in Association of Southeast Asian Nations (ASEAN) and other regional organizations in Asia. As such, American geopolitical interests can be furthered by the election of a government that would seek to work with the United States to further mutual geopolitical and security interests in the region. A third factor concerns the expansion of democracy and the rule of law in Indonesia and the region. U.S. foreign policy also would hope that the elections produce a government in Indonesia that would strengthen human rights, religious freedom and bilateral trade ties.

Table 1. Recent Indonesian Parliamentary Election Results

Party	% votes 2009	Seats 2009	% votes 2004	Seats 2004	% votes 1999	Seats 1999
Democrat Party	20.9	148	7.45	57		
Golkar	14.5	108	21.58	128	22.44	120
PDI-P	14.0	93	18.53	109	33.74	154
PKS	7.9	59	7.34	45	1.4	14
PAN	6.0	42	6.44	52	7.12	35
PPP	5.3	39	8.15	58	10.71	39
PKB	4.9	26	10.57	52	12.61	51
Gerindra	4.5	30				
Hanura	3.8	15				

Source: IFES, httpi/www.electionguide.org. The Economist Intelligence Unit, May 2009. Syafiq Hasyim, "Blending Dakwa and Politics: The Case of PKS Justice Prosperous Party," in *The Rise of Religion-Based Political movements*.

Notes: Data gaps are explained by the parties in question not running in the election year indicated.

INDONESIA AT A GLANCE

Population: 240.3 million with a growth rate of 1.1%

Life expectancy: 70.76

Area: 1,826,440 sq. km (about three times the size of Texas)

Geography: An archipelagic state of 17,000 islands, including some 6,000 occupied islands

Capital: Jakarta, 8.8 million

Ethnic Groups: 490 ethnic groups, Javanese 45%, Sundanese 14%, Madurese 7.5%, coastal Malay 7.5%, others 26%

Languages: Bhasa Indonesia, official modified form of Malay, and local dialects including many Austronesian and Papuan languages. 13 languages have over one million speakers

Literacy Rate: 90.4%

Religion: Muslim 86.1%, Protestant 5.7%, Catholic 3%, Hindu 1.8%

GDP growth: 6.1% 2008, 3.5% 2009 est.

GDP by Sector: Agriculture 13.5%, industry 45.6%, services 40.8%

Labor force by sector: Agriculture 42.1%, industry 18.6%, services 39.3%

Per capita GDP purchasing power parity: $3,900 Unemployment rate: 8.4%

Main exports: Appliances, textiles

Destination of Exports: Japan 21.6%, Singapore 11.7%, United States 11.,1%, China 10.1%.

Natural resources: petroleum, tin, natural gas, nickel, timber, copper, soils, coal, gold, silver

Sources: U.S. Department of State; CIA, The World Fact Book; Economist Intelligence Unit; BBC News

OVERVIEW

With an estimated population of 240.3 million, Indonesia is the world's most populous Muslim nation and is the world's fourth most populated nation overall after China, India and the United States. Its population is growing by approximately three million people a year.[20] It has extensive natural resources. A large percentage of world trade transits the strategically important straits of Malacca that link the Indian Ocean littoral to the South China Sea and the larger Pacific Ocean basin. Indonesia is also perceived by many as the geopolitical center of the Association of Southeast Asian Nations (ASEAN), which is a key actor in the geopolitical dynamics of the larger Asia-Pacific region. Indonesia continues to emerge from a period of authoritarian rule and is consolidating its status as one of the world's largest democracies. Indonesia also represents a moderate form of Islam that has the potential to act as a counterbalance to more extreme expressions of Islam. Despite this, radical Islamists and terrorist cells have operated in the country. Internal strife and social dislocation stemming from intercommunal discord, autonomous and secessionist movements, political machinations among elites, Islamist extremism, government corruption, and economic uncertainty have all undermined stability in Indonesia in the past. More recently Indonesia has been consolidating democratic gains, building a more robust civil society, and strengthening its economy, which suffered major setbacks during the Asian financial crisis of 1997/98.

Potential Issues for Congress

The key challenge for the United States and Indonesia is how to build on recent progress in the relationship and the good will felt towards President Obama and President Yudhoyono and deliver demonstrable results in developing a strategic and comprehensive partnership between the two countries. High expectations will likely require tangible progress to be made in the near to midterm to maintain positive momentum in the relationship. It appears that both the Obama and Yudhoyono administrations are committed to taking the relationship forward. A conference sponsored by the U.S.-Indonesia Society in April 2009 suggested a number of areas for enhanced bilateral cooperation. Specifically, the USINDO report focused on bilateral cooperation in the areas of education, democracy and reform, multilateral and bilateral trade relations, food security cooperation, global climate change, bilateral security relations, and investment and business cooperation.[21]

The Bush Administration's lifting of restrictions on International Military Education and Training (IMET), Foreign Military Financing (FMF), and Foreign Military Sales (FMS) in 2005 helped deepen the bilateral relationship and provided a basis for further improved relations. Indonesia also moved forward on the following issues of concern to the United States.[22]

- The expansion and consolidation of Indonesia's democracy through the 2004, and subsequent 2009 parliamentary and presidential elections.
- The election of President Yudhoyono, who is generally seen as reform-oriented.
- The goodwill towards, and increased understanding of, Indonesia in the United States in the wake of the December 26, 2004 tsunami.
- The U.S. perception of Indonesia as an increasingly valuable partner in the war against militant Islamist extremists, and valuable U.S. assistance to Indonesian counterterrorism security organizations.
- Timor-Leste's desire to develop positive relations with Indonesia.
- The arrest of Anthonius Wamang, a suspect in the shooting of two Americans near Timika, in the Indonesian province of Papua.
- Peace in Aceh.
- Increasing appreciation among American policy makers of the strategic and geopolitical importance of Indonesia.
- Indonesia's position on the East Asian Summit.[23]

Much non-governmental organization and Congressional interest has focused on past abuses in Timor-Leste. This focus has abated somewhat as Timor-Leste has sought to move beyond the past and build good relations with Indonesia. Ongoing interest remains over the human rights situation in Papua and West Papua Indonesia, which could slow current forward momentum in the bilateral relationship should new human rights issues come to light.

Military-to-Military Ties and Human Rights

In 2005, the Administration of President George Bush moved to open International Military and Education and Training (IMET), Foreign Military Financing (FMF), and Foreign Military Sales (FMS) programs for Indonesia. This was viewed by many as a first step toward normalizing the military-to-military relationship. Indonesia has been a key player in the war against terror in Southeast Asia and an increasingly important geopolitical actor in the Asia-Pacific region. Despite these developments, many continue to have concern over human rights abuses in Indonesia. Senator Patrick Leahy has stated that "a key gap remains regarding justice for the victims of atrocities." Other Members, however, have emphasized the progress Indonesia has made in several areas. Senator Christopher Bond, for instance, has stated that President Yudhoyono has made "a strong commitment to reform, to a recognition of human rights and to fighting corruption."[24] An example of military cooperation with Indonesia is the Tri-border initiative that involves radar and maritime operations in the Makassar Strait to monitor possible terrorist or pirate activity.[25] Other examples of U.S.-Indonesian military cooperation include U.S. assistance to Indonesia's new defense university and U.S. assistance with the procurement of C130 Hercules transport aircraft, which, according to Defense Minister Juwono Sudarsono, will take advantage of U.S. discount pricing and foreign military financing.[26]

During the Cold War, the United States was primarily concerned about communist influence in Indonesia. After the Cold War, congressional views on Indonesia were more influenced by ongoing concerns over human rights abuses by the Indonesian National Defense Forces (TNI). The events of 9/11 added the concern of how best to pursue the war against terror in Southeast Asia. Some Members of Congress remain dissatisfied with progress on bringing to justice Indonesian military personnel and police responsible for human rights abuses in East Timor and Papua. The January 2006 arrest of Anthonius Wamang, who is thought to have led an attack near the town of Timika in Papua that killed two Americans, did much to resolve what had been an obstacle to developing the relationship. As the United States moved from the post-Cold War world to fight the war against terror, human rights concerns have increasingly been weighed against American security interests, and particularly the need to develop effective counterterror cooperation with Indonesia to combat radical Islamic groups. There is also increasing appreciation of Indonesia's geopolitical position within Southeast Asia and the larger East Asia region among American decision-makers.

Some analysts have argued that the need to obtain effective counterterror cooperation and to secure American strategic interests in the region necessitates a working relationship with Indonesia and its key institutions, such as the military. Other observers take the view that the promotion of American values, such as human rights and religious freedom, should guide

U.S. relations with Indonesia while others would put trade and investment first. Some have viewed military cooperation between the U.S. military and the Indonesian military during relief operations following the December 2004 tsunami in Sumatra as having focused attention on the issue of the need for military to military cooperation.

HISTORICAL BACKGROUND

Modern Indonesia has been shaped by the dynamic interaction of indigenous cultures with external influences—especially the succession of influences of Hinduism, Buddhism, Islam, Dutch colonial rule, and a powerful and nationalistic independence movement. The geographic definition of modern Indonesia began to take shape under Dutch direct colonial rule, which began in 1799. The Dutch East Indies were occupied by Japan during World War II. Following the Japanese surrender in 1945, independence was declared by nationalist leader Sukarno. After a four-year anti-colonial insurrection, the Republic of Indonesia gained its independence from the Dutch in 1949. The Dutch retained control of the present day territory of Papua and West Papua until the transition period 1963-1969.[27]

Indonesian independence was followed by a period of parliamentary democracy, which was replaced in 1959 by President Sukarno's "Guided Democracy" that lasted until 1965.[28] In the late 1950s the United States provided clandestine assistance to military rebellions in outlying provinces of Indonesia out of fear that the communist PKI was gaining control of the country.[29] On September 30, 1965, the military, under General Suharto, neutralized Sukarno. One interpretation of events is that the military stepped in to avert a communist coup. In the aftermath, an estimated 500,000 Indonesians lost their lives in riots and purges that were characterized as "anti-communist." President Suharto ruled Indonesia until 1998. During this 32-year period, his authoritarian "New Order" provided the political stability thought necessary by his supporters for fast paced economic growth. Indonesia's economy grew at an average annual rate of almost 7% from 1987 to 1997.[30] Suharto's death in January 2008 served as a point of reflection on his rule during which economic development and political stability came at the price of corruption and repression.[31]

A period of reform, or "*reformasi,*" followed Suharto's fall. Suharto was succeeded by B.J. Habibie (1998-99), Abdurrahman Wahid (1999-200 1), and the daughter of former President Sukarno, Megawati Sukarnoputri (200 1-2004). Despite the political instability during this period, a number of key reforms designed to enhance good governance and expand democracy were implemented. Particularly important was a 1999 law that transferred enormous authority from the central government to provincial and district-level government. However, by 2003, the momentum for reform appeared to be faltering.[32] President Yudhoyono is thought to have moved the reform agenda forward but only to a limited extent.

The source of legitimacy, or lack thereof, for government has changed for the Indonesian people over time. The Dutch colonial administration was viewed as illegitimate. The Sukarno Presidency sought to base its rule on moral concepts but it did not provide sufficient economic development.

This was subsequently provided by President Suharto until 1997, when the Asian financial crisis undermined his ability to do so. At that point, with economic growth declining, Indonesians were no longer prepared to accept what was increasingly viewed as a corrupt and authoritarian regime. This brought on the era of democratic reform whose energy, prior to 2004, had appeared to be dissipating before fully completing its goal of instituting responsive and representative government.

POLITICAL TRANSITION

Indonesia has done much to consolidate its democratic reform process following the Suharto era, which ended abruptly amid chaotic mass protests in 1998. Since his departure, civil society has expanded, and a vigorous and open media has emerged. In addition to the first direct election of the president, the military no longer has seats in parliament and the police have been separated from the military. Indonesia has made significant progress toward institutionalizing its democracy and more firmly establishing civil society.[33] Indonesia's parliamentary elections in April 2004, and the Presidential elections of July and September 2004, were deemed by international observers to be free and fair, and they did much to instill confidence in Indonesia's democratic process. The parliamentary elections of 2009 further consolidated the democratic process in Indonesia.[34] Political polls in Indonesia are generally viewed as being well-run.

Indonesia's national legislative structure consists of three separate bodies. First is a House of Representatives (DPR) of 550 members elected from party lists in multi-seat districts. The DPR has the primary role in passing laws. Second is a 132-seat Regional Representative Council (DPD) whose members are elected directly. Third is the People's Consultative Assembly (MPR), which is composed of members of both the DPR and the DPD. It is responsible for passing constitutional amendments and conducting presidential impeachments. Decentralization in recent years has placed increased importance on government at the local level.

THE ROLE OF THE MILITARY

The Indonesian National Defense Force (TNI) is generally regarded as the strongest institution in Indonesia. Its origins date to the struggle for independence. The TNI traditionally has been internally focused, playing a key role in Indonesian politics and preserving the territorial integrity of the nation—largely from internal threats—rather than focusing on external security concerns. Its strong tradition of secular nationalism has acted to help integrate the nation. The key elements of the military in Indonesia are the Army Strategic Reserve Command, the Army Special Forces Command, other special forces, and the Military Regional Commands. There are also Air Force and Naval commands. While the military now has a less formal role in the politics of the nation than it had in the Suharto era, it remains a key actor behind the scenes.[35] Some observers are concerned about its indirect influence over politics. The Indonesian military has attracted negative attention through its past involvement with human rights abuses in East Timor, Aceh, Papua, and Maluku, although current problems appear largely limited to Papua and West Papua.

During the initial period of reform, the TNI officially abandoned the doctrine of *dwifungsi*, or dual function, which gave it an official role in the politics of the nation.[36]

Appointed members to the legislative bodies from the military were removed, while the police were separated from the TNI. Efforts were also begun to more firmly establish civilian control of the armed forces. Supporters of the reform agenda in Indonesia would like to see additional measures taken, including reform of the army's territorial structure, a full withdrawal of the military from business activities, and improving the military's sensitivity to human rights.[37]

The TNI budget is thought to be to a large extent self-generated. This part of the TNI budget is largely outside governmental control.[38] The TNI will likely continue to play a key role in the evolution of the Indonesian polity in the years ahead. It could continue to play a largely constructive role supporting democratic change, or at least not obstructing it, or it could act to slow change. It will also likely seek to preserve its prominent place in Indonesian society.[39]

While slowed, there are still signs that the reform process continues in Indonesia. A policy document to guide the government in its efforts to take over TNI controlled businesses was commissioned in 2008. As of June 2008, it was reported that the TNI controlled some 1,520 business units, 1,071 cooperatives, and 25 foundations in Indonesia. A 2004 law requires the TNI to get out of business by 2009.[40]

One proposal for how Indonesia could address some of its military budget shortfall involves a continuation of the reform process. Some have put forward the idea that by dismantling the territorial command structure, which is a legacy of the former *dwifungsi* role of the New Order military, Indonesia could save money that could be redirected to the air force or navy which are focused on more conventional military roles and are arguably underfunded given the vast sea and air space encompassed by the Indonesian archipelago.[41] State Minister for Administrative Reform Taufiq Effendi has stated that significant funds will be allocated to reform the military, police, and Attorney General's office. Under his plan the take home pay of the lowest ranks of police and military personnel will double.[42]

AUTONOMOUS AND SECESSIONIST MOVEMENTS

Center-periphery tensions between the dominant Javanese culture and minority groups in outlying regions have been sources of political instability and strife for the Indonesian state. Indonesia has in recent years adapted its approach to such strife and done much to alleviate autonomous or secessionist tensions. This relatively more moderate approach has reached accommodation where other efforts to quell Indonesia's centrifugal tendencies have failed.

The primary security threats to Indonesia are generally thought to come from within. The political center of the Indonesian archipelago is located in Jakarta on Java, the densely populated island where 60% of Indonesia's population lives. Traditionally, power has extended from Java out to the outlying areas of Indonesia. This has been true both under Dutch rule, when Jakarta was known as Batavia, and the modern Indonesian state. Throughout its history there has been resistance in peripheral areas to this centralized control. This manifested itself in the predominantly Catholic former Indonesian province of East Timor, which is now an independent state, as well as in the far west of Indonesia, in Aceh, and in the far eastern part of the nation, in Papua and West Papua. Each of these regions has strong ethnic, cultural, and/or religious identities very different from those of Java.

Such diversity has led to debate about whether Indonesia is an organic state or an artificial creation of Dutch colonial rule. Analysis of early Indonesian history reveals a level of integration in terms of economics and trade, if not extensive political unity. While early indigenous empires were precursors of the Indonesian state, political unity is generally considered to have been a product of Dutch colonial rule, including a series of lengthy wars to subdue outlying islands and independent political units. It has been suggested that a key lesson of Indonesian history is that "unifying the archipelago administratively can only be done by the use of force."[43] Forces of economic integration, or the creation of a national identity stemming from the nationalist movement which started in Java in 1908,[44] could be viewed as other integrative forces.

Timor-Leste[45]

The Portuguese, whose influence in Timor-Leste dates to the 1 600s, gave up control of the island in 1975. With the Portuguese departure, three main parties emerged. Of these, Frente Revolucionaria do Timor Leste Independente (Fretelin), a leftist leaning group, soon emerged as the dominant party. On December 7, 1975, Indonesia invaded East Timor with the then tacit compliance of the United States and Australia.[46] Indonesia, Australia, and the United States are thought to have been concerned that East Timor would turn into another Soviet satellite state similar to Cuba. A third of the population of East Timor is thought to have died as a result of fighting or war-induced famine during the subsequent guerilla war fought by Fretelin against Indonesia's occupation.[47]

On August 30, 1999, East Timorese voted overwhelmingly to become an independent nation. 98.6% of those registered to vote in the referendum voted, with 78.5% rejecting integration with Indonesia. In the wake of the vote, pro-integrationist militias attacked pro-independence East Timorese and destroyed much of East Timor's infrastructure. More than 7,000 East Timorese were killed and another 300,000, out of a total population of 850,000, were displaced, many to West Timor. Hardline elements of TNI formed pro-integrationist militias in East Timor. These groups sought to intimidate the East Timorese into voting to remain integrated with Indonesia under an autonomy package being offered by then President Habibie.[48]

It is thought that the TNI had two key reasons for trying to forestall an independent East Timor. First, there was an attachment to the territory after having fought to keep it as a part of Indonesia. Second was the fear that East Timorese independence would act as a catalyst for further secession in Aceh and Papua. The subsequent devastation of East Timor may have been meant as a warning to others who might seek to follow its secessionist example. Some believe that TNI involvement in the violence stemmed largely from local "rogue" elements. Others believe that it was orchestrated higher up in the military command structure.[49]

East Timor gained independence in 2002. Since that time, Indonesia and East Timor have worked to develop good relations. The joint Commission of Truth and Friendship was established to deal with past crimes.[50] A 2,500 page report issued in early 2006 by the East Timorese Commission for Reception, Truth and Reconciliation (CAVR), which was given to United Nations General Secretary Kofi Annan, found Indonesia responsible for abuses of East Timorese during its period of rule over East Timor. The report reportedly found that up to

180,000 East Timorese died as a result of Indonesian rule.[51] This created tension in the bilateral relationship between Indonesia and East Timor. Nevertheless, then East Timorese President Xanana Gusmao and President Yudhoyono reaffirmed their commitment to continue to work to resolve differences between the two countries.[52] More recently, the new President Ramos Horta called on the people of TimorLeste to accept that Indonesians that committed human rights abuses in East Timor would never be brought to justice so that East Timor could move forward.[53]

The United Nations tribunal, which included the Serious Crimes Investigation Unit, shut down in May 2005. During its six-year operation, the tribunal convicted some East Timorese militia members for their role in the atrocities of 1999, but was unable to extradite any indictees from Indonesia. A parallel Indonesian investigation ended in acquittals for all Indonesians. A 2005 U.N. Commission of Experts found the Jakarta trials for crimes committed in 1999 to be "manifestly inadequate."[54]

Aceh

Aceh is located at the extreme northwestern tip of the Indonesian archipelago on the island of Sumatra. The 4.4 million Acehenese have strong Muslim beliefs as well as an independent ethnic identity. Many Acehenese have in the past viewed Indonesia as an artificial construct that is no more than "a Javanese colonial empire enslaving the different peoples of the archipelago whose only common denominator was that they all had been colonized by the Dutch."[55]

The Acehenese fought the Portuguese in the 1 520s as well as the Dutch in later years.[56] The Dutch Aceh War lasted from 1873 to 1913; making it possibly the longest continuous colonial war in history. As a result of their resistance and independence, Aceh was one of the last areas to come under Dutch control. Its struggle for independence from Indonesia was once again taken up by the group Gerakan Aceh Merdeka (GAM) until a peace agreement was reached in the wake of the December 2004 tsunami which killed over 130,000 people and devastated much of Aceh. The peace agreement signed by GAM and the government of Indonesia in Helsinki in August of 2005 brought an end to a conflict that claimed an estimated 15,000 lives. Under the agreement, partial autonomy was granted to Aceh as was the right to retain 70% of the provinces considerable oil and gas revenue.

The recently resolved struggle dates to 1976. In the late 1980s, many of GAM's fighters received training in Libya. GAM then began to reemerge in Aceh. This triggered suppression by the TNI from which GAM eventually rebounded. Former President Megawati then called on the military to once again suppress the Free Aceh Movement. This was the largest military operation for the TNI since East Timor. The decision to take a hard-line, nationalist stance on Aceh was popular at the time among Indonesian voters outside of Aceh.[57]

Under the leadership of President Yudhoyono, Indonesia leveraged the opportunity presented by the 2004 tsunami and achieved a peace settlement where previous peace efforts have come unraveled. Under the agreement, the Free Aceh Movement (GAM) disarmed in December 2005 as the Indonesian Military TNI dramatically reduced its presence in Aceh.

The election of December 2006 selected a radical ex-rebel candidate to be governor of Aceh over other candidates more closely aligned with Jakarta. Former independence fighter

Irwandi Yusuf received approximately 40% of the vote in a field of eight candidates. The Islamic PKS party candidate received 10% of the vote.[58] As governor, Irwandi has emphasized improving Aceh's economy, including efforts to attract foreign investment. An October 2007 International Crisis Group report pointed to post conflict complications and stated "The behaviour of many elected Free Aceh Movement (GAM) officials and ex-combatants is part of the reason for gloom: Acehenese voters seem to have substituted one venal elite for another. Extortion, robbery and illegal logging involving ex-combatants ... are cause for concern."[59] It was reported in May 2008 that the central government would allow local Aceh parties to contest elections in 2009 in accordance with the 2006 Aceh Administration Law.[60] GAM renamed its local party Partai Aceh and indicated that this marked the end of its armed struggle for independence.[61]

West Papua and Papua

The region, formerly known as West Irian or Irian Jaya, refers to the western half of the island of New Guinea and encompasses the two Indonesian provinces of West Papua and Papua. West Papua and Papua have a population of approximately two million and an area of approximately 422,000 square kilometers, which represents about 21% of the land mass, and less than 1% of the population of Indonesia. Papua has a long land border with Papua New Guinea to the east. About 1.2 million of the inhabitants of West Papua and Papua are indigenous peoples from about 250 different tribes, the rest have transmigrated to the region from elsewhere in Indonesia. There are about 250 language groups in the region. Papuans are mostly Christians and animists. The province is rich in mineral resources and timber. [62]

Papuans are a Melanesian people and are distinct from the Malay people of the rest of the Indonesian archipelago. Like Indonesia, Papua and West Papua were part of the Dutch East Indies. Many Papuans have a sense of identity that is different from the main Malay, and predominately Muslim, identity of the rest of the Indonesian archipelago, and many favor autonomy or independence from Indonesia.[63]

Papua did not become a part of Indonesia at the time of Indonesia's independence in 1949. The Dutch argued that its ethnic and cultural difference justified Dutch control until a later date. Under President Sukarno, Indonesia began mounting military pressure on Dutch West Papua in 1961. The United States sponsored talks between Indonesia and the Dutch and proposed a transfer of authority over Papua to the United Nations. Under the agreement the United Nations was to conduct an "Act of Free Choice" to determine the political status of Papua. The "Act of Free Choice" was carried out in 1969, after Indonesia had assumed control over Papua in 1963. The "Act of Free Choice," which led Papua to become part of Indonesia, is generally not considered to have been representative of the will of Papuans. A referendum on Indonesian control over Papua was not held. Instead, a group of 1,025 selected local officials voted in favor of merging with Indonesia.

Papuan groups continue to oppose Indonesian control over Papua and West Papua. The Free Papua Movement, or Organisasi Papua Merdeka (OPM), emerged in opposition to Indonesian control. By some estimates, as many as 100,000 Papuans are thought to have died as the result of military operations during the course of this conflict.[64] Others assert that this figure is an overestimation. Coordinator of the Institute for Human Rights and Advocacy

John Rumbiak has reportedly stated that "The Government in Jakarta has allowed the military to prevail in Papua, to take the security approach which has denied ordinary people their rights and enriched military officers who are making big money for themselves through dealings with mining, logging and oil and gas interests."[65]

The arrest and trial of Anthonius Wamang, who was sentenced to life in prison in November 2006 for carrying out an attack in 2002 that killed two Americans working for the Freeport mine near Timika, Papua, has done much to resolve an issue that had been an impediment to closer relations between the United States and Indonesia. The mine is operated by a subsidiary of Freeport McMoRan of New Orleans. Some have wondered why Wamang and his co-defendants did not use the trial to reassert earlier statements that the Indonesian military was involved.[66]

The Human Rights Watch report, *Endemic Abuse and Impunity in Papua's Central Highlands,* of July 2007 made the following statement.

> Among our key findings are that while civilian complaints of brutal treatment by soldiers continue to emerge, police officers rather than soldiers are responsible for most serious rights violations in the region today. We found that both army troops and police units, particularly mobile paramilitary police units (Brigade mobil or Brimob), continue to engage in largely indiscriminate village "sweeping" operations in pursuit of suspected militants, using excessive, often brutal, and at times lethal force against civilians.[67]

A June 2008 report by the International Crisis Group warned of the potential for inter-communal conflict in Papua. It pointed out that tensions were most acute along the west coast of Papua and that "continuing Muslim migration from elsewhere in Indonesia" was a key factor that is increasing strain between Christians and Muslims in Papua.[68]

INTER-COMMUNAL STRIFE AND PAN ISLAMIC MOVEMENTS

While the vast majority of Indonesians practice a moderate form of Islam, a very small radical minority have sought to establish an Islamic state. Some extremists are hostile to the Christian minority and an even smaller group would use violence to establish an Islamic Khalifate throughout the Muslim areas of Southeast Asia. While they represent an extremely small percentage of the population, such groups have created much internal turmoil in Indonesia. A distinction can be drawn between groups such as the now disbanded Lashkar Jihad that focused on Indonesian inter-communal conflict between Muslims and Christians in Maluku, and factions of Jemaah Islamiya (JI), which have used terrorist methods to promote an extreme Islamist agenda with linkages to al Qaeda. There have also been allegations that Lashkar Jihad was a tool of hardliners within the military that opposed the reform movement and who allowed, or possibly even assisted, Lashkar Jihad activities that destabilized the nation, thereby highlighting the need for a strong military that could impose order.[69] There has also been inter-group conflict elsewhere in Indonesia such as between Muslims and Christians in Sulawesi and the Maluku, and between local Dayaks and internal Madurese migrants in Kalimantan.[70]

Much attention has been focused on the potential rise of Islamic sentiment in Indonesia in recent years. This was most notable in a political context with the rise of the PKS Justice

Party in the 2004 election. In that election, the PKS increased its seats to 45 from 7 (out of 550) following the 1999 parliamentary election. Many attributed the success of the PKS in parliamentary elections in 2004 to its campaign platform of good governance and its party organization rather than to its Islamist character. The PKS is not the largest Muslim party and does not represent the large Muslim mainstream groups. Some 90.4% of Indonesians believe religious affairs should be within the framework of the state ideology of Pancasila and the constitution. Some 91.6% of Indonesians believe that Indonesia's state ideology is correctly based on Pancasila.[71] The lack of further success by Islamic political parties in the 2009 election allayed concerns that political Islam would radicalize Indonesia.

Despite the success of the national-secular political parties there have been challenges to the secular nature of the Indonesian state over cultural and moral issues. Not only the strictly fundamentalist Muslims but also more traditional Muslims protest the influence of Western cultural and moral values in Indonesian society. The challenge has four components.

One is the direct action by radical Muslim groups against businesses and institutions which they accuse of representing Western cultural and moral values. The most widely publicized group is the Islamic Defenders Front (FPI). The FPI targets such businesses for direct, violent action. Squads of FPI cadre have forcibly shut down gambling dens, discos, nightclubs and bars that serve alcoholic beverages, and brothels. The FPI also has targeted Christian churches. Attacks by the FPI and like-minded Muslim groups have forced the closure of upwards of 100 Christian churches since September 2004, including more than 30 in West Java alone.[72] The FPI is estimated to have supporters in the tens of thousands at most. It and similar groups receive financial backing from Saudi Arabia. Its influence is felt widely partly because police and law enforcement authorities have adopted a permissive attitude toward its activities. Arrests of FPI members are few and infrequent despite the government's revisions of public assembly laws to make it easier to disband violence-prone groups.[73] Despite some ongoing activity it appears that this type of militant action is less intense than in years past.

The second component is pressure by Muslim groups on authorities to establish Islamic Sharia law. This is felt primarily on the provincial and local levels. The State Department's human rights report for 2006 cited an estimate that more than 56 Sharia-based local laws have been issued throughout Indonesia. These laws often require that women wear head scarves, require that officials read the Koran in Arabic, segregate men and women in public places, and prohibit alcohol and gambling. So far, the central government have not challenged the constitutionality of such laws.[74]

The third is judicial action against non-Muslims or Indonesians who are accused of insulting Muslim beliefs. For instance, the fact that the Indonesian government prosecuted the editor of Playboy Indonesia for breaching the country's indecency laws after mounting protest against the magazine by fundamentalist Muslim groups is one example.[75]

The fourth component is in education, particularly in the thousands of "pesantren" Islamic boarding schools in Indonesia. Observers warn that the instruction in these schools increasingly is of a fundamentalist nature that emphasizes intolerance of other religions and non-Muslim, secular practices. Former Indonesian President Abdurrahman Wahid warned in April 2007 that the teaching of fundamentalist Islam in the pesantren schools is an acute problem and that the problem is spreading into Indonesian universities.[76]

Indonesian GDP, % Real change

1996	7.8%
1997	4.7%
1998	-13.1%
1999	0.8%
2000	4.9%
2001	3.5%
2002	3.7%
2003	4.1%
2004	5.1%
2005	5.3%
2006	5.5%
2007	6.3%
2008	6.1%
2009	3.5% est.

Source: Economist Intelligence Unit Database

THE ECONOMY

Indonesia continues to struggle to lift masses out of poverty and to reduce unemployment while developing its infrastructure and attracting foreign investment. The World Bank *Country Partnership Strategy (2009-12): Investing in Indonesia's Institutions* stated that in 2007 nearly half of Indonesia's population was living below or just above the poverty line, that job creation was growing at a slower rate than the rate of population growth, that parts of eastern Indonesia remained underdeveloped, and that Indonesia received low marks in certain health and infrastructure indicators.[77] Corruption remains a problem and there is a complex regulatory environment and unequal resource distribution between regions. As global demand has fallen, prices for Indonesian commodities have dropped. Some 13.5% of GDP comes from agriculture while it employs 42.1% of the workforce. Industry and services account for 45.6% and 40.8% percent of GDP and 18.6% and 3 9.3% of employment respectively. [78] Per capita income stands at $3,900 in 2009. Export destinations in 2008 include Japan (21.6%), Singapore (11.7%), the United States (11.1%), and China (10.1%). Indonesia is considered to have a balanced economy with all major sectors contributing though it is experiencing pressure from the international economic downturn. Foreign businesses have in the past been reluctant to invest in Indonesia in part because of concerns about the legal and judicial framework.

Indonesian economic growth is expected to slow to 2.4%-3.5% in 2009 from 6.1% in 2008.[79] The government has sought to address the collapse of merchandise exports in 2009 in part with a plan that would require government employees to buy Indonesian produced products. The 2009 budget estimates a deficit of 2.6% of GDP, up from a previous 1% of GDP. The government has also embarked on new spending initiatives including infrastructure projects. A large part of the deficit arises from reduced revenue. Food and fuel prices contributed to an inflation rate of 10.1% in 2008. The rupiah exchange rate against the dollar was volatile in the closing months of 2008 before government intervention. Unemployment is anticipated to increase from 8.4% in 2008 to 10.6% in 2009 and may reach 11.3% in 2010. According to the Economist Intelligence Unit, "although Indonesia's exports continued to contract sharply in March (2009), there are signs that the country may be over the worst of the current downturn in trade."[80]

Despite having been a key oil exporter, Indonesia has in recent years become a net oil importer. Indonesia's oil production peaked at 1.6 million barrels per day (bpd) in 1995. Observers note that Indonesia will need foreign investment to help it boost production in its aging oil fields.[81] Indonesia is thought to have an estimated 8.6 billion barrels of oil and 182 trillion cubic feet of natural gas in reserves.[82]

THE ENVIRONMENT

President Yudhoyono has raised Indonesia's profile on environmental issues in recent years and the United States and Indonesia have begun to cooperate in the area. Indonesia hosted the 13th Conference of the Parties of the United Nations Framework Convention on Climate Change in December 2007 and the World Ocean Conference in May 2009. Deforestation is the main contributor to Indonesia's carbon emissions which are the third highest in the world after the United States and China when deforestation effects are taken into account. Indonesia has immense biological diversity in its tropical rainforests and in its archipelagic marine environment. This is under threat from various pressures including, logging, climate change, and pollution.[83]

The logging of Indonesia's forests, both legal and illegal, is an issue of increasing concern to many. Indonesia has the world's third largest tropical forests and the world's largest timber trade. Rain forests are thought to be an important sink for global atmospheric carbon and play a vital role in climate. Rain forests contain an estimated two-thirds of the planet's plant and animal species. It is estimated that logging and other clearing of rain forests has reduced their extent from 14% of the earth's surface to 6%. A special report by *The Economist* estimated that about 2 million hectares of Indonesian forest, an area the size of Massachusetts, are logged each year.

In the 15 years leading up to 2006, Indonesia lost one quarter of its forests. One 2006 estimate projected that at current rates of logging Indonesia's forests would be logged out in 10 years.[84] The destruction of Indonesia's forests would likely lead to widespread species extinction. It is estimated that illegal logging deprives Indonesia of some $3 billion annually. Burning of logged land to clear it for palm plantations and other uses in Southeast Asia led to widespread haze over the region in 1997, which accounted for an estimated 8% of greenhouse gasses emitted worldwide in that year.[85]

The United States and Indonesia moved to begin to address the problem of illegal logging in April 2006. Bilateral talks were initiated to reach an agreement to deal with the problem of illegal logging in Indonesia which is estimated to account for 80% of all logging in Indonesia.[86] The United States and Indonesia signed a bilateral agreement to combat illegal logging and associated trade in November 2006. The United States initially committed $1 million to fund remote sensing of illegal logging and to develop partnerships with non-governmental organizations and the private sector. The agreement established a working group under the U.S.-Indonesia Trade and Investment Framework Agreement.[87]

Indonesia has the most threatened species of mammals in the world. Poaching, deforestation, and illegal logging continue to threaten the existence of orangutans, the Sumatran Tiger, and the Javan Rhino. Ninety percent of the orangutan's habitat has been destroyed as land is cleared with fire by illegal logging, plantation companies, and farmers. It is thought that orangutans will disappear if present deforestation trends continue.[88] The Javanese Tiger and the Balinese Tiger became extinct in the 1970s. Only about 400 Sumatran Tigers are thought to remain alive. This is a dramatic decrease from an estimated 1,000 Sumatran Tigers in the 1970s. Their decrease is similarly attributed to a combination of deforestation, illegal logging, and poaching. Effective control of the illegal trade in wild animal parts is thought to be essential for the species survival.[89] The Javanese Rhino is similarly threatened with only 60 thought to remain in the wild.[90]

Indonesia hosted the World Ocean Conference in May 2009 where Indonesia, Timor-Leste, Papua New Guinea, the Solomon Islands, and the Philippines met and adopted a 10-year action plan to address threats to the maritime environment, particularly with coral reefs, fish, and mangroves. The agreement, the Coral Triangle Initiative on Coral Reefs, Fisheries and Food Security, is not legally binding but covers some six million square-kilometers of ocean.[91] Climate change is particularly threatening to Indonesia as sea level rise would adversely affect many of Indonesia's low-lying coastal areas.

RELIGIOUS FREEDOM

Though Indonesia is overwhelmingly Muslim, its constitution protects religious minority groups. Non-Muslims generally enjoy a general level of freedom in their beliefs within Indonesian society. That said, inter-communal strife can boil over into violence in places such as Poso and Ambon. A government panel recommended in April 2008 that the Ahmadiyya group be banned. This decision followed a January 2008 fatwa by Indonesia's highest religious authority, the Indonesian Ulama Council, to ban the sect for its deviance. The Ulama Council shortly thereafter submitted its fatwa to the Indonesian Attorney General's Office and asked the government to ban the group.

The Ahmadiyya of Indonesia, like other Ahmadiyya around the world, believe that their founder Mirza Ghulam Ahmad, who founded the religion in 1889 in the Punjab in British India, was a prophet. The Ahmadiyya belief was first brought to Indonesia from India in 1925. Their views place them at odds with more mainstream Muslims who believe that The Prophet Mohammad was the last prophet. Ahmadiyya do accept Mohammad as a prophet and one of God's messengers. As a result of their differences, many in Muslim society, including in Indonesia, do not view Ahmadiyya as true Muslims. It is reported that they have no open supporters among Indonesia's elite.[92] Some Indonesians have been calling for the Ahmadiyya to be banned and driven out of Indonesia. It is estimated that there are some 200,000 to 500,000 Ahmadiyya in Indonesia.[93]

Attacks against Ahmadiyya and their Mosques have grown in recent years. The extremist Komando Laskar Islam, thought to be affiliated with the Islamic Defenders Front (FPI), attacked an alliance of moderate groups, known as the National Alliance for Freedom of

Religion and Faith, that was demonstrating peacefully in support of religious freedom on June 1, 2008, at the Indonesian National Monument Square (Monas) in Jakarta. The FPI has in the past been involved with demonstrations against the U.S. Embassy and the offices of Playboy magazine.

According to one report, the government of Indonesia through the Attorney General's Office has banned the group from practicing in Indonesia due to its view that the Ahmadiyya are a deviant sect and because they are causing restlessness in the Muslim community in Indonesia.[94] On April 18, 2008, the day following reports that the group had been banned, Indonesian Vice President Jusuf Kalla stated that there would be no detention of Ahmadis.[95]

The Ulama Council subsequently felt that the government did not go far enough in its actions. On April 20th thousands of Muslim hardliners protested to demand the active disbanding of the Ahmadiyya. It is thought that Muslim extremists would go beyond banning of the practicing of the Ahmadiyya belief and would favor adopting further measures that would actively seek to disband and/or drive the group out of Indonesia.[96] Some outside commentators view the decision to crackdown on the Ahmadiyya as pandering to Islamic extremism. This placed the government of Susilo Bambang Yudhoyono in a difficult position in the lead up to elections scheduled for April 2009.[97]

The government's response in 2008 appeared to seek to avoid alienating both religious extremists and moderates in the period leading up to elections in 2009. On the one hand, the government issued a decree banning the sect from spreading its message. On the other hand, it pledged not to persecute Ahmadiyya. Its move to arrest those extremists that used violence against moderates demonstrating in support of religious tolerance in 2008 also demonstrates the government's desire to place limits on how far the extremists can go.

The FPI has also been responsible for past actions against Jakarta nightclubs and pool halls.[98] The moderates' rally on June 1, 2008, was seeking to "reclaim political space for groups adhering to the secular state ideology Pancasila."[99] The Monas incident points to ongoing tension within the Indonesian polity between pluralism and religious extremism. It is unclear just how widespread this is. Human Rights Watch has called on President Yudhoyono to reverse the government decree that allows persecution of Ahmadiyya for "spreading interpretations and activities which deviate from the principal teachings of Islam."[100]

The State Department International Religious Freedom Report 2008 stated that "... recommendations by government appointed bodies and a subsequent government decree restricting the ability of the Ahmediya to practice freely were significant exceptions" to the general practice of respecting religious freedom in Indonesia. The report also noted the use by some groups of "violence and intimidation to force at least 12 churches and 21 Ahmadiya mosques to close."

HUMAN RIGHTS

Much attention in the United States has been focused on human rights in Indonesia. The State Department's annual human rights report of 2008 states that the Indonesian government "generally respected the human rights of its citizens and upheld civil liberties." The report noted that "basic freedoms have expanded since 1999" but also stated that problems remain, including "killings by security forces; vigilantism; harsh prison conditions; impunity for prison authorities and some officials; corruption in the judicial system; limitations on free speech; societal abuse and discrimination against religious groups ..." among other concerns. The report noted that civilian control of the military was weakened by the partially self-financed nature of the TNI.

Human Rights Watch observed in its 2009 World Report that Indonesia "saw little human rights progress." The report was critical of Indonesia for a general lack of effort to "pursue accountability" for past abuses and observed that "endemic police torture also routinely goes unpunished." The report also criticized the government for bowing to pressure from Islamic hardline groups on the Ahmadiyya issue and stated that "deeply rooted distrust of Jakarta [in Papua] is still a time bomb; failure to address human rights—including security force abuse—is one important reason the distrust has not been dispelled."[101] Others have pointed to the candidacy of former General Wiranto and General Prabowo Subianto, both of whom are suspected of Suharto era human rights abuses, as vice presidential candidates in the July 2009 presidential election as evidence of a lack of forward progress on human rights in Indonesia.[102]

One investigation and trial that may be viewed as a test case is that against Pollycarpus Budihardi Priyanto, who was convicted of killing human rights activist and critic of Indonesia's military Munir Thalib with arsenic poisoning while on a Garuda flight bound for Amsterdam on September 7, 2004. Pollycarpus' sentence to 14 years in prison for the crime was overturned by the Supreme Court in October 2006 though he did receive two years in prison for falsifying documents. He was released from prison on December 25, 2006.[103] Priyanto was found guilty of the crime a second time in 2008 and was sentenced to 20 years in prison. He has since sought another judicial review to overturn his case.[104]

During the investigation it became known that Pollycarpus had numerous telephone conversations with State Intelligence Agency (BIN) official Major General Muhdi Purwo Prandjono.[105] Many have hoped a successful investigation and trial of those responsible for Munir's death may signal an end to a culture of impunity in Indonesia for such crimes.[106]

The Struggle against Radical Islamist Extremists

In recent years, Indonesia has successfully hunted down radical Islamist extremists who broke Indonesian law.[107] The U.S. Department of State's 2008 country report on terrorism in Indonesia observed that Indonesia had experienced its third year without serious terrorist incident and that the government of Indonesia "continued to build a legal and law enforcement environment conducive to fighting terrorism" and that Indonesia's counterterrorism efforts "drastically reduced the ability of terrorist groups" to operate.[108] That said, "the problem has not [entirely] gone away." A report by the International Crisis Group described how a jihadi group in Palembang, South Sumatra, developed to the point where it killed a Christian teacher and planned further attacks.[109] The State Department 2008 report states that Indonesian terrorist groups "remained a security threat, but with reduced ability to carry out attacks."[110]

The United States lifted its travel warning on Indonesia in the Spring of 2008 as a result of the improved security situation in Indonesia.[111] It appears that the terrorist organization Jemaah Islamiya (JI) was subject to internal division. Many JI members reportedly were displeased with the October 2002 Bali bombing which killed and injured more Indonesians than foreigners. The large-scale attack killed approximately 200 people. President Yudhoyono has made it a priority to capture or neutralize key JI members. Since the 2002 Bali bombing, Indonesian police and counterterrorism organizations have arrested nearly 500 JI cadre.[112] Key JI bombmaker Azahari bin Husin was killed in a shootout in East Java in November 2005. Since that time, counterterrorism authorities have focused on capturing his associate, Noordin Top, and have arrested a number of militants linked to Top.[113] In June 2007, authorities made a major breakthrough, arresting the head of the overall JI organization, Zarkasih, and JI's military commander, Abu Dujana. It was reported in March 2006 that Al Qaeda helped fund suicide attacks in Indonesia in the previous four years with money brought to Indonesia through Thailand and Malaysia.[114]

Divisions within JI have apparently revolved around the extent to which JI should focus on western targets as opposed to focusing on instituting Islamist rule in Indonesia. Some are also focused on imposing an Islamic Chaliphate not only in Indonesia but also in Malaysia and Brunei and Muslim areas of the Philippines and Thailand. A majority are thought to favor a focus on Indonesia.[115] The JI also is reportedly split over whether to continue major terrorist attacks or shift tactics toward political action and attacks against smaller targets. Violent efforts to rekindle inter-communal violence between Christians and Muslims in Sulawesi and the Muluccas have largely been contained. JI has not conducted a major terrorist attack since 2005, and experts believe that the arrests of Zarkasih and Abu Dujana have weakened the organization substantially.[116]

Many Indonesians view the war against terror in a fundamentally different way than the United States. This was particularly so prior to the Bali bombing. The Bali bombing, and the Marriott bombing of August 2003, changed the government's perception of the threat and evoked a rigorous response from the police. Prior to these bombings, Indonesia viewed JI as foreign and focused on anti-western activities. Since the Bali bombing, U.S. and Indonesian leaders have worked together to address the threat.

Health Issues: Avian and Swine Flu

Concern continues that Indonesia remains poorly prepared to deal with a large-scale pandemic. Most cases of the H5N1 virus in Indonesia are thought to have been transmitted through contact with birds. There is continuing concern however, that the virus could mutate and become readily communicable between people. In May 2008, a sudden die off of thousands of domestic birds in the area of Rimbo Bujang District, Tebo regency, Jambi Province led officials to act to stem the transmission of the bird flu to humans.[117] Indonesian inspectors have sought to disinfect areas where birds are kept and promote improved hygiene but face a daunting challenge as many people in Indonesia keep small numbers of birds. It is estimated that some 500,000 birds are kept in Jakarta alone. Indonesia lacks resources to implement adequate anti-Avian Flu measures.[118]

U.S. efforts to work with Indonesia to address the problem have encountered difficulty causing a problem in the bilateral relationship. NAMRU-2 is a biomedical research laboratory established in 1970 to study diseases such as malaria, dengue fever, enteric infections, and other emerging infectious diseases such as avian influenza.[119] Indonesian critics of the facility have called on the Indonesian government to reject the extension of cooperation with the United States on NAMRU2. DPR Commission IX Chairman Dr. Ribka Tjiptaning stated that there is no reason to extend cooperation and breach national sovereignty.[120]

Health Minister Siti Fadilah Supari raised Indonesia's health alert status in response to the World Health Organization's decision to raise the alert level to the highest level in June 2009. At that time there were no reported cases of the H1N1 swine flu in Indonesia. Indonesia reportedly had no vaccine to treat the new flu in June 2009.[121]

EXTERNAL RELATIONS

Indonesian foreign policy has been shaped largely by two men, Presidents Sukarno and Suharto, although more recent presidents, particularly Yudhoyono, have sought to increase the nation's presence on the world stage. Once a leading force in the Non-Aligned Movement (NAM) of the early Cold War era, Indonesia has traditionally sought to remain largely independent from great power conflict and entangling alliances. Sukarno's world view divided the world into new emerging forces and old established forces. Sukarno sought to fight the forces of neo-colonialism, colonialism, and imperialism, which brought his government closer to China in 1964-65. Suharto's New Order lessened Sukarno's anti-western rhetoric and focused on better relations with other Southeast Asian nations. Under Suharto, Indonesia was one of the founding members of the Association of Southeast Asian States (ASEAN) in 1967 and played a key leadership role in the organization. Indonesia's internal problems since 1998 have kept it largely internally focused. As a result, it has not played as active a role in the organization as in past years. Indonesia exerts a moderate voice in the Organization of Islamic Conference (OIC) and is a member of Asia-Pacific Economic Cooperation (APEC). In recent years, Indonesia has done more to project itself as a moderating force in the Muslim world, positioning itself as a potential bridge between Islam and the West.[122]

Indonesia's strategic interests are largely regional. Indonesia signed the Timor Gap Treaty with Australia in 1991. The treaty provided for a mutual sharing of resources located in the seabed between Australia and the then-Indonesian province of East Timor. This lapsed with the independence of East Timor. Australia and Indonesia also signed a security agreement in 1995 that fell short of an alliance but called for mutual consultations on security matters. Indonesian displeasure with Australia's support of East Timor independence in 1999 led Indonesia to renounce the agreement. Indonesian ties with the West have at times been strained over alleged human rights abuses by the TNI. Indonesia and Australia have cooperated in the area of counterterrorism in recent years. Indonesia and Australia signed a new security pact in 2006, known as the Lombok Treaty, which came into force in 2008.[123]

In 1990 Indonesia and China normalized ties, which had been strained since the alleged abortive coup by the Indonesian Communist Party (PKI) in 1965. China and Indonesia have an unresolved territorial dispute related to the South China Sea, particularly near the Natuna Islands at the southern end of the South China Sea. In recent years ties have warmed between Indonesia and China. President Yudhoyono traveled to Beijing in 2005 and signed a strategic agreement with Chinese President Hu Jintao.[124] In June 2008, Zhou Yongkang, a Member of the Standing Committee of the of the Political Bureau of the Communist Party of China

Central Committee stated that China wanted to push forward the strategic partnership with Indonesia and further promote the growth of bilateral relations between Indonesia and China while he was visiting Jakarta.[125] Chinese investments in Indonesia, particularly in the energy realm, have grown markedly in recent years.

Tensions between Indonesia and Malaysia flared in May 2009 over conflicting maritime claims to the oil-rich waters near their border between Kalimantan and Sabah in the Celebes Sea. A Naval confrontation occurred in May 2009 with Indonesian ships reportedly minutes away from firing on Malaysian vessels. The two nations had a similar naval confrontation in March 2005 over the area. Both Indonesia and Malaysia have granted concessions to Shell, Unocal, and the Italian oil and gas firm ENI SPA in the disputed region.[126]

Democracy is increasingly a component of Indonesia's engagement with its external environment. Indonesia launched the Bali Democracy Forum in November 2008 with the aim of "promoting regional and international cooperation in the field of democracy." The Bali Forum is taking an inclusive approach that brings together democracies as well as those "aspiring to be more democratic." The forum is to act as a platform for countries to "exchange ideas and knowledge and share experience and best practices."[127] Indonesia also established the Institute for Peace and Democracy at the University of Udayana on Bali to support the initiative. Indonesia has also supported the new ASEAN Charter, which is supportive of democratic development and human rights.

UNITED STATES-INDONESIAN RELATIONS

The election of President Barack Obama, who spent part of his childhood in Indonesia, as well as his outreach to the Muslim world, as demonstrated by his June 4, 2009 speech in Cairo, has done much to spur expectations in Indonesia and the United States that the bilateral relationship will be significantly enhanced during his administration.[128] As one example of Indonesian attitudes, Member of the Indonesian House of Representatives (DPR) Abdillah Toha reacted to Obama's speech and outreach to the Muslim world by stating "we should not waste this opportunity. A president like Obama, who has stated that positive engagement with the Islamic nations is one of his administration's foreign policy priorities, may not come around in another 50 years."[129]

Expectations for further development of the bilateral relationship were also lifted as a result of the November 2008 proposal by President Susilo Bambang Yudhoyon to develop a strategic partnership between Indonesia and the United States.

> Indonesia and America ... must begin to think hard about our 21st century partnership.... A U.S.-Indonesia strategic partnership would have to be based on equal partnership and common interests. It has to bring about mutual and real benefits for our peoples. It has to be for the long term, and have strong people-to-people content.... [130]

This initiative was followed by Secretary of State Clinton's travel to Indonesia during her first trip abroad as Secretary of State in February 2009. Clinton reportedly stated, "If you want to know if Islam, democracy, modernity and women's rights can coexist, go to Indonesia."[131] In her remarks with Indonesian Foreign Minister Wirajuda in Jakarta in February 2009, Clinton noted:

> ... the desire on the part of both of our presidents and our countries to form a comprehensive partnership, one that provides a framework for advancing our common interests on a range of regional and global issues, from environmental protection and climate change to trade and investment, from democracy promotion to health and education, from regional security, to counter terrorism.

Wirajuda echoed this sentiment and stated "we agreed to expand and deepen our bilateral cooperation within a comprehensive partnership."[132]

Clinton and Wirajuda renewed their commitment to build a comprehensive partnership during Wirajuda's visit to Washington in June 2009. At that time Secretary Clinton announced a $10 million initiative to promote bilateral educational linkages. [133] Wirajuda was reportedly pleased with President Obama's speech in Cairo and pointed out that Indonesia could be a good partner for the United States in its efforts to improve relations with Muslim countries.[134]

Such a partnership would likely be advanced by a visit by President Obama to Indonesia. Wirajuda stated that it is likely that President Obama will travel to Indonesia in November 2009 around the time of the Asia Pacific Economic Cooperation (APEC) summit in Singapore.[135] A draft partnership document by the Indonesian Department of Foreign Affairs reportedly proposed four sectors for the partnership: (1) political and security, (2) economic and development cooperation, (3) social cultural and education, and (4) follow-up mechanisms.[136]

Bilateral government to government relations between Indonesia and the United States improved significantly beginning in 2005. Bilateral cooperation on counterterrorism increased at the same time that U.S. appreciation of Indonesia's strategic importance and increasingly democratic government improved. There has been improvement in Indonesians' perceptions of the United States.

While bilateral government-to-government relations have improved, there have been a number of areas of friction, including with American companies operating in Indonesia. Louisiana-based Freeport McMoRan's subsidiary PT Freeport Indonesia came under scrutiny by environmental interests and was subject to demonstrations.[137] A blockade of the mine near Timika was carried out by disgruntled small-scale local miners who had been prevented from mining the waste from the mine.[138] In April 2007, thousands of Freeport workers protested over wages and benefits and demanded that Freeport hire more native Papuans.[139]

In another case, Denver-based Newmont Mining Corporation paid a $30 million out of court settlement for the Indonesian government to drop efforts to pursue a civil lawsuit against the company for alleged dumping of mercury and arsenic into a bay as part of its Buyat Bay gold mining operations in Sulawesi.[140] Newmont has denied it has dumped such toxic waste into the bay through its submarine tailing disposal system. Environmentalists have been critical of the deal.[141]

The 2006 arrest and trial of individuals involved with the 2002 murder of two Americans near Timika in Papua did much to take a key area of friction between the two nations off the table. In June 2008 it was reported that the United States had offered assistance to Indonesia to establish a National Defense University.[142]

The U.S. Naval Medical Research Unit (NAMRU-2) provides a "forward presence that combines virology, microbiology, epidemiology, immunology, parasitology, and entomology into a comprehensive capability to study tropical diseases where they occur."[143] The

Indonesian public, and a growing number of politicians, government officials, and some experts, are coming to view the NAMRU-2 lab as not in the interest of Indonesia. Some Indonesian experts have deemed current cooperation on NAMRU-2 as not having clear goals for Indonesia and not concerned with the health priorities of Indonesia.[144]

Geopolitical and Strategic Interests

The Malacca, Sunda, and Lombok straits are some of the world's most important strategic sea lanes. Close to half of the total global merchant fleet capacity transits the straits around Indonesia.[145] A significant proportion of Northeast Asia's energy resources transit these straits. The United States continues to have both economic and military interest in keeping the sea lanes of communication open.[146] The waters around Indonesia have had some of the highest incidents of piracy in the world. Further energy deposits may also be found in the waters of Southeast Asia.

Some strategic analysts are concerned about growing Chinese influence in the region. China was perceived as being more assertive in the 1990s, for example, by fortifying a disputed shoal in the South China Sea known as Mischief Reef. China is now seen as being more cooperative. It agreed to a regional code of conduct in the South China Sea in 2002. China signed a Joint Declaration on Strategic Partnership with ASEAN in October 2003 and is developing a China-ASEAN Free Trade Agreement to augment its existing bilateral trade agreements with many ASEAN members. This has been viewed as a possible foundation for a strategic partnership.[147] China and Indonesia also announced a series of agreements amounting to what some have described as a "strategic partnership" in April 2005. At the same time, China is expanding its naval capability.

U.S. Assistance to Indonesia

The bilateral comprehensive partnership between the United States and Indonesia provides a framework for the U.S. assistance program for Indonesia. U.S. assistance is focused on several key areas including "higher quality basic education; universities that resolve tough development problems; sustainable management of forests, marine fisheries and energy; enhanced regional security and stability; effective government that delivers services; effective health and family planning services; and increased employment."[148] Other priorities of U.S. assistance include support for the further development of democracy in Indonesia, support for the rule of law and human rights, maternal and child health, and support for economic growth through the development of trade, investment, and infrastructure.

Security Assistance

The State Department FY2010 Budget Justification for Foreign Operations discusses Indonesia's "notable success in combating terrorism" and points out that U.S. assistance will "support Indonesia's emerging role as a leader in regional security." Indonesia has participated in the Regional Defense Counter Terrorism Fellowship Program, which includes intelligence cooperation, civil-military cooperation in combating terrorism and maritime security. Indonesia has also participated in the Theater Security Cooperation Program with the U.S. Pacific Command. This has involved Indonesia in counterterrorism seminars promoting cooperation on security as well as subject matter expert exchanges.[149] Indonesian Marines and U.S. Navy Seals have held joint counterteror exercises.[150]

Table 2. U.S. Foreign Assistance to Indonesia

Account	FY2007	FY2008	FY2009	FY2010 request
CSH[a]	$27,507	$25,737	$30,500	30,730
CSH-State		250	250	250
DA	29,524	70,953	71,000	132,930
ESF	69,300	64,474	65,000	300
FMF	6,175	12,872	15,700	20,000
HIV/AIDS	250	-	-	-
IMET	1,398	1,037	1,500	1,800
INCLE	4,700	6,150	6.150	11,570
NADR	8,881	5,117	6,450	6,750
P.L. 480 Title II	10,951	-	-	
Total	**158,686**	**186,590**	**196,550**	**204,330**

Source: "FY2010 Congressional Budget Justification for Foreign Operations," U.S. Department of State, released May 2009.

a. Child Survival and Health (CSH), Development Assistance (DA), Economic Support Funds (ESF), Foreign Military Financing (FMF), International Military Education and Training (IMET), International Narcotics Control and Law Enforcement (INCLE), Non-proliferation Anti-terrorism Demining and Related Programs Export Control and Border Security Assistance NADR-EXBS, Non-proliferation Anti-terrorism Demining and Related Programs Antiterrorism Assistance (NADR-ATA).

Military-to-military ties between the United States and Indonesia have ebbed and flowed since the 1950s. This has been conditioned by both the disposition of the regime in Jakarta to the United States and by U.S. perceptions of the TNI's record on human rights. A significant relationship was established by the 1960s. This was expanded in the wake of Sukarno's demise.

The Administration's policy on assistance to Indonesia is informed by the role that Indonesia plays in the war against terror in Southeast Asia. U.S.-Indonesian counterterror capacity building programs have included funds for the establishment of a national police counterterrorism unit and for counterterrorism training for police and security officials. Such assistance has also included financial intelligence unit training to strengthen anti-money laundering, counterterror intelligence analysts training, an analyst exchange program with the Treasury Department, and training and assistance to establish a border security system as part of the Terrorist Interdiction Program.[151] A major accomplishment of these programs is the increasing capabilities of Detachment 88, an elite counterterrorism unit that has received assistance from the United States and Australia. Detachment 88 has been responsible for tracking down scores of JI cadre, including Azahari bin Husin, Zarkasih, and Abu Dujana.[152]

The United States is promoting counterterrorism in Southeast Asia on a regional and multilateral basis as well as on a bilateral basis with Indonesia. Such an approach is viewed as complementing and promoting bilateral assistance and focuses on diplomatic, financial, law enforcement, intelligence and military tools. Two key objectives of the U.S. government are to build the capacity and will of regional states to fight terror. These objectives are pursued through a number of programs. The United States-ASEAN Work Plan for Counter-Terrorism has identified information sharing, enhancing liaison relationships, capacity building through training and education, transportation, maritime security, border and immigration controls, and compliance with United Nations and international conventions, as goals for enhanced regional anti-terrorism cooperation.

The Anti-Terrorism Assistance Program, directed at law enforcement training and associated hardware, has aided Indonesia, among others. In addition, Financial Systems Assessment Teams and the Terrorist Interdiction Program (which focuses on border controls) have also assisted Indonesia. The United States has also supported the Southeast Asian Regional Center for Counterterrorism in Kuala Lumpur. Foreign Emergency Support Teams are designed for rapid deployment in response to a terrorist related event while Technical Support Working Groups work with regional partners to find technical solutions to problems such as bio-terrorism warning sensors.[153]

Tsunami Relief

On December 26, 2004, an undersea earthquake off the coast of Sumatra triggered a tsunami wave that killed an estimated 122,000 Indonesians (with an additional 114,000 missing) and left over 406,000 displaced persons in Indonesia. Most of the devastation was in Aceh in northwest Sumatra, which was the closest landfall to the epicenter of the Indian Ocean earthquake. This disaster led to a massive international relief effort in which the United States played a leading role. In Indonesia, this included helicopter-borne assistance from the aircraft carrier *USS Abraham Lincoln*, which was accompanied by the *USS Bonhomme Richard*, and the *USS Fort McHenry*. Before their departure from the area 2,800 relief missions were flown, some 2,200 patients were treated, and 4,000 tons of relief supplies were delivered.[154] In the wake of the tsunami, the U.S. government pledged a total of $397.3 million in humanitarian and recovery assistance for Indonesia.[155]

Options and Implications for the United States

The present offers a unique moment for a significant expansion and deepening of bilateral relations with Indonesia that could have broader implications for U.S. engagement with ASEAN and with Muslim nations. Past debate concerning U.S. policy towards Indonesia has been framed by human rights and security interests. Based on past debate in Congress, individual decision- makers' approaches to this question will likely involve a consideration of a mix of U.S. foreign and strategic policy interests with Indonesia. These will likely include a consideration of possible tradeoffs between a foreign policy approach that stresses the promotion of human rights and one that seeks to strengthen bilateral ties in order to assist in the struggle against violent Islamist extremists and to promote U.S. geopolitical interests.

As part of its oversight role, Congress may opt to focus on a range of policy options for relations with Indonesia. A non-zero sum approach might seek to blend American foreign policy interests by developing a comprehensive partnership to promote democracy, good governance, civil society, and the rule of law as well as human rights and security interests. Supporters of this approach believe that it could have an indirect positive impact on Indonesia's human rights record as well as reinforce ties between the two states.

- **Develop a significant expansion of bilateral ties with Indonesia to further interests of mutual benefit including a constructive dialogue between the United States and the Muslim world.** Indonesia's status as a moderate, democratic nation is of particular interest to the United States as the Obama Administration reaches out to the Muslim world. U.S. credibility in the Muslim world has been hurt by perception that the U.S. is waging war against Islam. By reaching out to Indonesia the United States could begin to address these misperceptions and develop more constructive relations not only with Indonesia but also with other moderate Muslim countries. Expanding bilateral educational exchanges, research grants, and language training could educate Indonesia's present and future elites while giving them an enhanced understanding of the United States and its values. Such educational exchanges could also provide Americans the opportunity to better understand Indonesia and the role that it plays in its region and in the Islamic world.

- **Continue to focus on Indonesia's pivotal role in the struggle against radical violent Islamists in Southeast Asia.** Indonesia likely will remain an indispensable partner in the struggle against violent Islamists in Southeast Asia for years to come. Many view it as prudent that the United States maintain a good working relationship with Indonesia. Such an approach could build on momentum in developing bilateral military-to-military ties built in 2005 and 2006, and develop enhanced exchanges, training, and military-to-military relationships in order to bring the full capabilities of the TNI into the struggle against radical Islamists while continuing to work with the Indonesian police.

- **Continue to focus on human rights concerns over past abuses by the Indonesian military.** Many feel that there remains a serious lack of accountability for past human rights abuses by the Indonesian military, particularly the human rights abuses perpetrated by pro-integrationist militias in East Timor in 1999, and continued abuse in Papua and West Papua, and that more could be done on either a bilateral or multilateral basis, or both, to increase accountability for abuses past and present. Such an approach could involve a closer working relationship with the United Nations.[156]

- **Place continued emphasis on the promotion of democracy and the rule of law in Indonesia.** Such an approach in Indonesia could include additional funding and other support to continue consolidating democratic reforms, political party development, member-constituent relations, and strengthening of national legislative bodies.[157] The promotion of democratic values could also have a positive impact on other issue areas such as the promotion of human rights.

- **Give the geopolitical importance of Indonesia more weight when considering bilateral ties.** Indonesia's position on the Straits of Malacca, as a moderate Muslim country, as the largest member of ASEAN, and as a state that does not seek to exclude the U.S. from regional multilateral fora or from the region gives it geopolitical importance to the United States. In light of expanding Chinese influence in the region, it is prudent that relations with Indonesia be developed so that Indonesia does not seek to move away from the United States in international fora or develop alternative strategic relationships. Indonesia remains one of the least well understood geopolitically important nations to America.

- **Support Indonesian participation in prominent multilateral fora.** Indonesia has demonstrated a desire to engage the international community on a range of topics including regional economic and strategic architectures and the environment. Working with Indonesia in such fora could be mutually beneficial.

- **Place enhanced emphasis on environmental issues, including rainforest destruction, preservation of bio-diversity, and climate change.** Indonesia is the world's third largest emitter of carbon behind the United States and China. U.S. assistance to Indonesia to help it protect its rainforests from illegal logging would help protect the environment upon which Indonesia's bio-diversity is dependent and also preserve an important sink for carbon.

- **Do more to advance American trade and investment interests in Indonesia.** Continued emphasis on further developing trade and investment ties may help move the two states towards a closer economic relations and potentially an FTA. American companies have also encountered difficulties in Indonesia in recent years and may benefit from enhanced support or guidance from the U.S. government.

Elements of all of the options discussed here can be found in current American foreign policy towards Indonesia, though the mix in emphasis has shifted over time.

Source: Map Resources. Adapted by CRS.

Figure 1. Map of Indonesia

End Notes

[1] Islamic parties are viewed here as those inspired by Islamic values but that would not seek to use the state to explicitly codify these values into law that would apply to all Indonesians while Islamists would be more likely to do so. Militant Islamists are those that would use violence to pursue their agenda.

[2] "Election Guide Indonesia," IFES, http://www.electionguide.org/country.php?ID=102.

[3] Country Report Indonesia, *Economist Intelligence Unit,* May 2009.

[4] Marcus Mietzner, "Indonesia's 2009 Elections: Populism, Dynasties and the Consolidation of the Party System," *Lowy Institute for International Affairs*, May 2009.

[5] Lembaga Survei Indonesia, (Saiful Mujani/William Liddle) as referenced in presentation viewgraphs by Marcus Mietzner, Lowy Institute, Australia. Marcus Mietzner, "Indonesia's 2009 Elections: Populism, Dynasties and the Consolidation of the Party System," *Lowy Institute for International Affairs*, May 2009.

[6] "Parliament and the Judiciary the Most Corrupt Institutions," *Media Indonesia*, June 4, 2009.

[7] "Indonesia," National Democratic Institute, http://www.ndi.org/content/indonesia.

[8] Lembaga Survei Indonesia, (Saiful Mujani/William Liddle) as referenced in presentation viewgraphs by Marcus Mietzner, Lowy Institute, Australia.

[9] N. Karmini, "Muslims reject Hardline," *The Advertiser*, May 12, 2009.

[10] "Indonesian Islamic Parties in Decline," *States News Service*, May 12, 2009. Bahtiar Effendi, "Islamic Parties Have Long Been at an Impasse," *The Jakarta Post*, April 17, 2009.

[11] Marcus Mietzner, "Indonesia's 2009 Elections: Populism, Dynasties and the Consolidation of the Party System," *Lowy Institute for International Affairs*, May 2009.

[12] Bahtiar Effendy, "Insight: Islamic parties Have Long Been at an Impasse," *Jakarta Post*, April 17, 2009.

[13] William Liddle, "Indonesia's July 9 Presidential Elections," USINDO Presentation, June 3, 2009.

[14] "Opinion Polls-Indonesia's Presidential Elections," *Reuters,* May 14, 2009.

[15] "Opinion Polls: Indonesia's Presidential Election," *Reuters,* June 15, 2009.

[16] Richard Lloyd Parry, "Dictator's Former Henchmen Offers Winning Smile to Voters," *The Times*, April 9, 2009.

[17] "Indonesia's Yudhoyono Confirms Boediono as YP Candidate," *Channel News Asia*, May 15, 2009.

[18] Philip Bowring, "Indonesia's Prospects," *International Herald Tribune*, May 20, 2009.

[19] Adam Gartrell, "Poll fury hits Riot Generals," *The Courier-Mail,* May 13, 2009.

[20] "Indonesia's Population Increasing by 3 Million Yearly," *Xinhua News Agency,* June 3, 2008.

[21] "The 2009 U.S.-Indonesia Comprehensive Partnership: Engaging the Non-Government Sector," *The United States-Indonesia Society*, Conference Findings and Recommendations, April 16-17, 2009.

[22] This is an expanded version of a list developed by CRS Specialist Larry Niksch.

[23] Indonesia reportedly worked to have a more expansive membership in the recently formed East Asian Summit to include Australia, New Zealand and India in addition to the ASEAN states, China, Japan, and Korea. Other countries, led by China, reportedly favored a more exclusive grouping that left out India, Australia, and New Zealand. This move was viewed by some observers as favorable to American interests. Sunny Tanuwidjaja, "The East Asian Summit and Indonesia," *The Jakarta Post,* February 1, 2006.

[24] Ken Guggenheim, "Fight Looms in Congress Over Easing Indonesia Military Restrictions," *Associated Press*, February 2, 2005.

[25] John Haseman and Edward Lachica, "The U.S.-Indonesia Security Relationship: The Next Steps," U.S.-Indonesia Society, January, 2009.

[26] "U.S. to Help RI in Procurement of Six Hercules," *Jurnal Nasional,* June 1, 2009. "RI's First Defense University," *The Jakarta Post*, March 12, 2009.

[27] Much of the background information is drawn from a comprehensive chapter by Harvey Demaine, "Indonesia: Physical and Social Geography," in *The Far East and Australasia* (Surrey: Europa Publications, 2002).

[28] Michael Vatikiotis, *Indonesian Politics Under Suharto: The Rise and Fall of the New Order* (London: Routledge Publishers, 1998). p. 1.

[29] John Bresnan, ed. *Indonesia: The Great Transition*. (Lanham: Rowman and Littlefield, 2005) pp. 245-7.

[30] "Background Note: Indonesia," Department of State, Bureau of East Asian and Pacific Affairs, October 2003. Michael Vatikiotis, *Indonesian Politics Under Suharto: The Rise and Fall of the New Order* (London: Routledge Publishers, 1998). p. xviii.

[31] "The Death of Suharto: Epitaph of a Crook and a Tyrant," *The Economist,* January 31, 2008.

[32] "Survey of Indonesian Electorate," *Asia Foundation*, December 9, 2003.

[33] John McBeth, "The Betrayal of Indonesia," *Far Eastern Economic Review*, June 26, 2003.

[34] Damien Kingsbury, "Indonesia: 2007," *Asian Survey,* February 2008.

[35] Rizal Sukma, "The Military and Politics in Post-Suharto Indonesia," in Thang Nguyen and Frank Jurgen Richter, eds., *Indonesia Matters: Diversity, Unity, and Stability in Fragile Times* (Singapore: Times Media Private Ltd. 2003).

[36] For a detailed analysis of earlier role of the military in politics, see Harold Crouch, *The Army and Politics in Indonesia* (Ithaca: Cornell University Press, 1978).

[37] Angel Rabasa and John Haseman, *The Military and Democracy in Indonesia: Challenges, Politics, and Power* (Santa Monica: RAND Corp. 2002).
[38] Col. John Haseman, William Liddle and Salim Said, "The Evolving Role of the TNI," USINDO Security Workshop, October 16, 2003.
[39] Angel Rabasa and John Haseman, *The Military and Democracy in Indonesia: Challenges, Politics, and Power* (Santa Monica: RAND Corp. 2002).
[40] Adianto Simamora, "Policy to Put TNI Out of Business On the Way," *The Jakarta Post,* May 29, 2008.
[41] Endy Bayuni, "Not Enough Money for the Military? Try Sending them 'Back to Barracks,'" *The Jakarta Post,* May 27, 2009.
[42] "Indonesia Aims to Tackle Corruption in Police, Military," *BBC News,* April 28, 2009.
[43] Merle Ricklefs, "The Future of Indonesia," *History Today*, December 1, 2003.
[44] Jusuf Wanandi, "Indonesia: A Failed State?" *The Washington Quarterly*, Summer, 2002, p. 135.
[45] Timor-Leste is also commonly known as East Timor.
[46] "Ford and Kissinger Gave Green Light to Indonesia's Invasion of East Timor, 1975," *The National Security Archives*, December 6, 2001.
[47] Michael Mally, "Regions: Centralization and Resistance," in Donald Emmerson ed. *Indonesia Beyond Suharto: Polity, Economy, Society, Transition* (Armonk: M.E. Sharp, 1999). p. 98.
[48] John Haseman, "Indonesia," in David Wiencek, ed. *Asian Security Handbook 2000* (Armonk: M.E. Sharpe Publishers, 2000).
[49] Emerson, p. 356.
[50] "Indonesia: International Relations," *The Economist Intelligence Unit,* May 17, 2005.
[51] Sian Powell, "Xanana and SBY Let Shame File Slide," *The Australian*, February 18, 2006.
[52] Rob Taylor and Olivia Rondonuwu, "Gusmao, Yudhoyono Meet in Bali," *AAP Bulletins,* February 17, 2006.
[53] "East Timor President Sees Bright Future if Country Forgets Past," *Agence France Presse*, July 19, 2008.
[54] Human Rights Watch, "East Timor," at http://www.hrw.org.
[55] Kirsten Schulze, *The Free Aceh Movement (GAM): Anatomy of a Separatist Movement* (Washington: East West Center, 2004).
[56] S. Wiuryono, "The Aceh Conflict: The Long Road to Peace," *Indonesian Quarterly*, 3rd Quarter, 2003.
[57] John Haseman, "Indonesia: A Difficult Transition to Democracy," in David Wiencek and Ted Carpenter eds. *Asian Security Handbook*, 3rd ed. *Terrorism and the New Security Environment* (Armonk: M.E. Sharpe, Inc., 2004).
[58] Mark Forbes, "Aceh Rebel's Big Election Win a Snub to Jakarta," *The Sydney Morning Herald,* December 13, 2006.
[59] "Aceh: Post-Conflict Complications," *International Crisis Group,* October 4, 2007.
[60] "Govt to Approve 12 Aceh Parties," *The Jakarta Post,* May 26, 2008.
[61] Hoti Simanjuntak, "GAM Evolves Into New Political Party," *The Jakarta Post,* May 23, 2008.
[62] "A People Under the Jackboot," *The West Australian*, September 18, 2004.
[63] "When Jacob Rumbiak was 11," *Port Philip Leader,* April 4, 2005.
[64] "Indonesian Police, Demonstrators Clash in Papua Province," *Oster Dow Jones,* May 10, 2005.
[65] "A People Under the Jackboot," *The West Australian*, September 18, 2004.
[66] John McBeth, "The Murder Muddle," *The Straits Times,* November 11, 2006.
[67] "Out of Sight: Endemic Abuse and Impunity in Papua's Central Highlands," *Human Rights Watch,* July, 2007.
[68] "Indonesia: Communal Tensions in Papua," *International Crisis Group Report,* June 16, 2008.
[69] See Sydney Jones' work for the *International Crisis Group,* http://www.crisisgroup.org.
[70] Amit Chanda, "Seven Killed in Indonesia, as Violence Flares up Again in Restive Maluku Province," *Global Insight Daily,* May 17, 2005.
[71] Robin Bush, "The Future of Islamic Parties and Islamic Politics in Indonesia," *The Asia Foundation*, 2008.
[72] Yuli Tri Suwarni, "Another Christian Church Attacked in Bandung, *Jakarta Post* (internet version), June 4, 2007.
[73] Tom McCawley, "Once Free, Indonesian Cleric Could 'Revitalize' Radicals," *Christian Science Monitor*, June 14, 2006. Bret Stephens, "The Arab Invasion," *The Wall Street Journal Asia*, April 18, 2007.
[74] Blake Respini, and Herdi Sahrasad, "The Rise of Sharia Seems not a Threat to Civil Society," *Jakarta Post* (internet version), May 19, 2007. Jane Perlez, " Spread of Islamic Law in Indonesia Takes Toll on Women," *New York Times*, June 27, 2006.
[75] Sadanand Dhume, " Playboy in Indonesia," *The Wall Street Journal Asia*, March 30, 2007. "Playboy Exposes Indonesian Tensions," *The Wall Street Journal Asia*, April 11, 2007.
[76] Bret Stephens, "The Journal Interview with Abdurrahman Wahid: the Last King of Java," *The Wall Street Journal Asia*, April 10, 2007. Alpha Amirrachman, "Pesantren Communities unable to Accept Pluralism, Tolerance," *Jakarta Post* (internet version), January 27, 2006.
[77] "Country Partnership Strategy (2009-2012): Investing in Indonesia's Institutions," The World Bank, http://www.worldbank.org/mitrindonesia.
[78] "Indonesia," *The CIA World Factbook*, May 14, 2009.
[79] "Country Report Indonesia," *The Economist Intelligence Unit*, May 2009.

[80] "Country Report Indonesia," *The Economist Intelligence Unit*, May 2009.
[81] Andi Abdussalam, "Indonesian Oil Output Showing Upward Trend," *Antara News,* May 14, 2008.
[82] "Pertamina, Talisman to Cooperate on Indonesia Oil," *Reuters*, June 23, 2008.
[83] "Background Note: Indonesia," U.S. Department of State, March 2009.
[84] Tanja Vestergaard, "Indonesia Launches Talks with U.S. on Fight Against Illegal Logging," *Global Insight Daily Analysis*, April 5, 2006.
[85] "Special Report: The Logging Trade," *The Economist,* March 25, 2006.
[86] Tanja Vestergaard, "Indonesia Launches Talks with U.S. on Fight Against Illegal Logging," *Global Insight Daily Analysis*, April 5, 2006.
[87] Office of the U.S. Trade Representative, "Agreement on Illegal Logging as Part of Effort to Deepen Trade and Investment Relations," November 16, 2008.
[88] Niniek Karmini, "Orangutans Flee Indonesian Forest Fires," *The Associated Press,* November 6, 2006.
[89] Oyos Saroso, "Poachers Moving into Northern Sumatra," *The Jakarta Post,* May 31, 2008.
[90] "World's Rarest Rhinos Captured on Video," *Reuters,* May 29, 2008.
[91] Jonathan Wootliff, "Historic Agreement in Manado Throws Coral Habitats a Lifeline," *Jakarta Post*, May 19, 2009.
[92] Bramantyo Prijosusilo, "Comparing the Ahmadiyah and the Hizbut Tahrir," *The Jakarta Post,* April 16, 2008.
[93] Salim Osman, "Ban Minority Sect, Islamic Holy Body Urges Jakarta Govt," *The Straits Times,* January 2, 2008.
[94] Salim Osman, "Jakarta Cracks Down on Deviant Islamic Sect," *The Straits Times,* April 17, 2008.
[95] "Indonesian Vice President Says No Arrest on Followers of Banned-Sect," *Xinhua News Agency,* April 18, 2008.
[96] Salim Osman, "Ban Minority Sect, Islamic Holy Body Urges Jakarta Govt," *The Straits Times,* January 2, 2008.
[97] "Indonesians Demand Ban on Sect," *BBC News,* April 20, 2008.
[98] "Indonesia Detains 59 Muslim Radicals," *The Age,* Melbourne, June 4, 2008.
[99] Fatima Astuti, "Fallout From Jakarta's Monas Incident: What is to Be Done with Fringe Groups?" *RSIS Commentaries,* Singapore, June 11, 2008. Pancasila, or the five principles, refers to the official political ideology of Indonesia. The five principles are: belief in one God, humanitarianism, the unity of Indonesia, consultative and representative Democracy, and social justice.
[100] "Reverse Ban on Ahmadiyyah Sect," *Human Rights Watch,* June 10, 2008.
[101] "World Report 2009: Indonesia," *Human Rights Watch*, 2009 http://www.hrw.org .
[102] Sunanda Creah, "Indonesian Election Setback for Human Rights," *Reuters,* May 19, 2009.
[103] "President Summons Top Security Officials Over Munir Case," *LKBN Antara,* December 26, 2006.
[104] "Killer of Indonesian Activist Files for Review," *Agence France Presse,* June 4, 2008.
[105] "Indonesia Sentences Killer of Rights Activist to 14 years in Prison," *Thai News Service*, January 12, 2006.
[106] M. Taufiqurrahman, "Two Years on, Munir Murder Case is Cast in Shadows," *The Jakarta Post,* January 4, 2007.
[107] For further information, see CRS Report RL31672, *Terrorism in Southeast Asia*, by Bruce Vaughn et al.
[108] U.S. Department of State, "Country Reports: East Asia and Pacific Overview," *Country Reports on Terrorism 2008*, April 30, 2009.
[109] "Indonesia: Radicalisation of the Palembang Group," *International Crisis Group*, May 20, 2009.
[110] U.S. Department of State, "Country Reports: East Asia and Pacific Overview," *Country Reports on Terrorism 2008*, April 30, 2009.
[111] Lilian Budianto, "Washington Lifts Travel Warning," *The Jakarta Post,* May 26, 2008.
[112] McCawley, Tom. "Indonesia's terrorist hunt bears fruit." *Christian Science Monitor*, June 15, 2007. p. 6.
[113] Tewily Nathalia, "Indonesia Looks for New Group's Links to al Qaeda," *Reuters,* January 31, 2006.
[114] Zakki Hakim, "Al Qaeda Aid in Indonesia Attacks Cited," *Philadelphia Inquirer,* March 1, 2006.
[115] See Sydney Jones' definitive work for the *International Crisis Group,* http://www.crisisgroup.org.
[116] Seth Mydans, "Indonesian terror group limits attacks," *New York Times*, June 18, 2007.
[117] "Bird Flu Alert in Tebo," *The Jakarta Post*, May 21, 2008.
[118] "Asia Remains Key in Battle Against Bird Flu," *US Fed News,* January 3, 2007.
[119] Public Affairs Section, "The Truth About NAMRU-2," U.S. Embassy Fact Sheet, April 23, 2008.
[120] "DPR Want Government to Reject NAMRU-2," Sinar Harapan, as reprinted in U.S. Embassy Jakarta Public Affairs Section, *Indonesian News Roundup,* June 5, 2008.
[121] "Indonesia on Alert Against Pandemic," *Kompas,* June 6, 2009.
[122] Rizal Sukma, "Indonesia's Foreign Policy Since Reformasi: Change and Continuity," *CSIS Southeast Asia Bulletin,* June 2008.
[123] "Australia-Indonesia Security Pact Comes Into Force," *Agence France Presse,* February 6, 2008.
[124] "Indonesia: International Relations and Defense," *The Economist Intelligence Unit,* May 27, 2008.
[125] "Senior CPC Leader Vows to Enhance Cooperation with Indonesia," *Xinhua News Agency,* June 18, 2008.
[126] "Indonesia, Malaysia Face Off at Sea," *Asia Sentinel*, May 29, 2009.
[127] "The Bali Democracy Forum Inauguration," Institute for Peace and Democracy, November 9-11, 2008.
[128] "Remarks by the President on a New Beginning," Cairo University, Cairo The White House, June 4, 2009.
[129] "Responding to Obama's Speech," *Republika*, June 13. 2009.

[130] President Yudhoyono as quoted in "The 2009 U.S.-Indonesia Comprehensive Partnership:" Engaging the Non-Government Sector," USINDO Conference, April 16-17, 2009.

[131] Mark Landler, "Clinton Praises Indonesian Democracy," *New York Times*, February 18, 2009.

[132] Hillary Rodham Clinton, Secretary of State, "Developing a Comprehensive Partnership with Indonesia," Department of State, February 18, 2009.

[133] "Secretary of State Clinton Meets with Foreign Minister Wirajuda," *U.S. Embassy Press Release,* June 9, 2009.

[134] "US Praises Elections in Indonesia," *Seputar Indonesia*, June 10, 2009.

[135] "Obama to Visit in November," *Seputar Indonesia*, June 11, 2009.

[136] Rizal Sukma and Bunyan Saptomo, "Toward a U.S.-Indonesia Comprehensive Partnership," Jakarta, May 20, 2009.

[137] Mark Forbes, "Investment Fears Over Mine protest," *Sydney Morning Herald*, March 4, 2006.

[138] "Papuans Protesting Daily over Freeport Mine in Indonesia," *Agence France Presse,* March 7, 2006.

[139] "Protest, talks continue over pay with US gold, cooper firm in Indonesia." *Agence France Presse*, April 20, 2007.

[140] P. Kyne and I. Sentana, "Newmont, Indonesia Settle Civil Suit," *The Wall Street Journal,* February 17, 2006.

[141] "Indonesia, USA's Newmont Reach 30m-dollar Settlement," *BBC News,* February 17, 2006.

[142] "US Offers to Assist Indonesia with Setting Up Defense University," *BBC News,* June 3, 2008.

[143] Naval Medical Research Unit 2, Jakarta, Indonesia.

[144] "NAMRU-2 Disadvantageous Indonesia," *Septutar*, June 3, 2008, as reprinted in U.S. Embassy Indonesian News Roundup, June 3, 2008.

[145] Ed Masters, *Report of the National Commission on U.S. Indonesian Relations* (Seattle: National Bureau of Asian Research, 2003).

[146] John Noer with David Gregory, *Chokepoint: Maritime Economic Concerns in Southeast Asia* (Washington: National Defense University Press, 1996).

[147] Edward Masters, House Committee on International Relations, Subcommittee on Asia and the Pacific, Testimony for a Hearing on the United States and Asia: Continuity, Instability, and Transition, March 17, 2004.

[148] "FY2010 Congressional Budget Justification for Foreign Operations," U.S. Department of State, released May 2009.

[149] "United States-Indonesia Military Relations," *Congressional Record*, Senate, Page S734, February 1, 2005.

[150] "US, Indonesian Navies Hold Joint Anti-Terror Exercises," *Oster Dow Jones*, May 10, 2005.

[151] Information drawn from State Department Fact Sheet, "Summary of Counter Terrorism Assistance for Indonesia," October 2003 update.

[152] Tom McCawley, "Indonesia's terrorist hunt bears fruit," *Christian Science Monitor*, June 15, 2007.

[153] Drawn from State Department budget justification material.

[154] "Indonesia: Tsunami Reconstruction," USAID, May 11, 2005, http://www.usaid.gov.

[155] "USAID Rebuilds Lives After the Tsunami," *USAID Tsunami Reconstruction,* March 24, 2006.

[156] Human Rights Watch, "East Timor," http://hrw.org.

[157] For an example of some existing activities see National Democratic Institute, "Asia: Indonesia," http://www.ndi.org.

INDEX

9

9/11, 165, 227
9/11 Commission, 165

A

academics, 15, 172, 175, 178, 199
accountability, 106, 173, 183, 191, 240, 248
accounting, 3, 9, 23, 45, 85, 107, 176
activism, xi, 167, 169, 183, 184, 189, 190
Activists, 199, 200
adjustment, 29, 57, 100
advertising, 144, 178
Afghanistan, v, viii, x, 11, 16, 21, 110, 133, 134, 135, 136, 137, 138, 139, 140, 141, 142, 143, 144, 145, 146, 147, 148, 149
Africa, 90
age, 31, 58, 87
ageing population, 31
aggression, 18, 19, 155
agricultural market, 27
agricultural sector, 57
agriculture, 40, 50, 56, 58, 89, 236
Air Force, 154, 156, 229
airports, 6
Al Qaeda, 16, 143, 146, 153, 182, 201, 241, 252
alcohol, 235
ambiguity, 127, 155
anger, 17, 21, 183, 185, 186, 189
antidumping, 26, 27
apparel, 61, 76, 81, 82
armed conflict, 113
armed forces, 30, 40, 138, 230
arrest, 60, 138, 171, 183, 185, 189, 210, 226, 227, 234, 239, 244
arsenic, 240, 244
ASEAN, 224, 225, 242, 243, 245, 247, 249, 250
Asia Pacific Economic Cooperation, 21, 244
Asian countries, 58
assassination, 102, 115, 158
assault, 37, 135, 140, 171
assessment, 152, 162
assets, vii, 1, 3, 7, 9, 47, 50, 74, 75, 103, 139, 152, 157, 158, 165, 188, 214
Association of Southeast Asian Nations, 224, 225
attacks, viii, 11, 16, 102, 105, 111, 115, 116, 117, 143, 146, 152, 153, 155, 240, 241, 252
Attorney General, 142, 218, 219, 230, 238, 239
Australasia, 250
Australia, 15, 16, 21, 27, 68, 69, 70, 74, 88, 160, 166, 196, 215, 222, 231, 242, 246, 250, 252
authority, 125, 134, 141, 156, 169, 171, 178, 180, 183, 228, 233, 238
autonomy, 58, 100, 112, 113, 114, 172, 181, 182, 231, 232, 233
avian influenza, 241
awareness, xi, 108, 167, 184, 186, 193
Azerbaijan, 105

B

background, vii, ix, xii, 94, 123, 163, 222, 250
background information, xii, 222, 250
ballistic missiles, 22, 50, 60, 73, 154, 207
Bangladesh, 52, 110, 153
banking, 7, 80, 213, 214, 217
banks, 3, 4, 6, 7, 9, 68, 81, 83, 206, 207, 209, 213, 214, 217
bargaining, 45, 85
basic needs, 110
behavior, viii, 35, 36, 42, 43, 50, 106, 189, 215
Beijing, xi, 18, 19, 37, 41, 60, 62, 78, 79, 80, 124, 129, 131, 132, 168, 169, 170, 172, 175, 176, 178, 179, 180, 181, 182, 183, 184, 187, 189, 190, 191, 192, 193, 196, 199, 200, 201, 202, 214, 217, 220, 242
Belgium, 80

beliefs, 182, 232, 235, 238
benchmarks, 32, 33, 91, 175
binding, 37, 113, 192, 238
biological weapons, 161, 166
BIS, 68, 90
black market, 47, 52, 160
blame, 55, 111, 178, 183
blogger, 190, 197
blogs, 171, 190, 202
bonds, 7, 9, 68
border control, 247
border crossing, 138, 166
border security, 246
Brazil, 17, 65, 67, 68
breakdown, x, 6, 151
bribes, 59, 139
Britain, 96, 102, 139, 210
brothers, 148
Buddhism, 111, 179, 200, 228
budget deficit, 107
bureaucracy, 53
Burma, 102, 110

C

Cambodia, 102
campaigns, 102, 169, 181
Canada, 24, 26, 70, 75, 89, 102, 119, 140, 196, 198
candidates, 143, 145, 146, 147, 223, 224, 232, 240
capacity building, 246, 247
capital flows, 3, 67
capital markets, 68
capital outflow, 3
capital punishment, 173
carbon, 237, 249
career development, 188
carrier, 20, 247
cast, 98, 114, 146, 156, 222
catalyst, 189, 231
category a, 3
cell, 176, 189
censorship, xi, 168, 176, 189, 190, 194, 195
Central Asia, 106, 120, 182
central bank, 8
central planning, 55
certification, 161, 163
chain of command, 156
channels, 43, 52, 72, 77, 137
chemical industry, 62
Chief Justice, 148
childhood, xii, 221, 243
children, 31, 40, 51, 95, 111, 170, 176, 182
Christianity, 179, 180
CIA, 15, 40, 41, 52, 97, 166, 225, 251
circulation, 205, 206, 212, 213, 217
City, 126, 199, 219
civil liberties, 179, 197, 239
civil rights, 169, 175, 197
civil service, 97
civil society, xi, xii, 167, 168, 169, 170, 175, 191, 193, 221, 226, 229, 248
civil war, ix, 93, 94, 95, 104, 105, 110, 111, 112, 116
Civil War, 100, 112, 115, 119, 120, 121
climate change, 191, 237, 244, 249
closure, 91, 178, 185, 235
CNN, 142, 158, 164, 165, 190, 202, 203
coal, 40, 57, 67, 72, 81, 225
codes, 68, 156, 159
coercion, 32, 126
Cold War, 77, 82, 83, 227, 242
collaboration, 214
collusion, 186
colonial rule, 228, 231
colonization, 15
command economy, 55
commerce, 51, 190
commercial bank, 3
common sense, 224
communication, 61, 62, 137, 156, 166, 245
communist countries, 188
Communist Party, 42, 123, 169, 170, 174, 175, 189, 201, 242
community, ix, 6, 17, 30, 93, 94, 95, 99, 103, 104, 106, 110, 114, 140, 152, 217, 224, 239, 249
compensation, 31, 32, 85, 176, 185, 199, 222
competence, 184
competition, x, 133, 134
competitive advantage, 26
competitive conditions, 26
competitiveness, 6, 8
compliance, 49, 195, 231, 247
complications, ix, 123, 128, 233
components, 61, 66, 67, 141, 156, 235
confessions, 173, 208
confidence, x, 20, 98, 103, 105, 112, 113, 133, 151, 152, 157, 158, 187, 207, 211, 212, 229
conflict, ix, 93, 94, 95, 96, 99, 102, 103, 104, 105, 106, 107, 108, 109, 110, 111, 113, 114, 116, 117, 126, 129, 140, 142, 155, 157, 158, 182, 232, 233, 234, 242
conflict resolution, 99, 106
confrontation, 16, 39, 84, 243
Confucianism, 54
congressional interests, 94
consciousness, 12, 169, 184, 186
consensus, 17, 99, 106, 116, 134, 156
consent, 114

consolidation, 135, 222, 226
Constitution, 30, 143, 144, 164, 170, 172, 175, 179
construction, 4, 37, 56, 57, 61, 62, 69, 71, 78, 80, 91, 102, 154, 164, 170, 176, 179, 185, 186, 187
consulting, 52, 170
consumer goods, 6, 9
consumers, 6, 58
consumption, 7
Container Security Initiative, 166
contingency, 158, 165
control, viii, x, 11, 50, 56, 58, 59, 100, 106, 116, 117, 137, 142, 151, 152, 153, 155, 156, 157, 158, 160, 161, 162, 166, 171, 176, 177, 178, 179, 188, 189, 190, 192, 211, 228, 230, 231, 232, 233, 238, 240
corn, 58, 77
corporate fraud, 179
corporations, 31, 32, 77, 190, 194
corruption, x, xi, 110, 133, 136, 137, 138, 139, 140, 141, 146, 147, 168, 169, 172, 175, 177, 179, 222, 226, 227, 228, 240
cosmetics, 61
costs, 22, 44, 60, 77, 78, 104, 105, 109, 117, 130, 185, 186, 214
counterterrorism, 21, 226, 240, 241, 242, 244, 246, 247
Court of Appeals, 125
CPC, 179, 201, 252
credibility, 110, 248
credit, 12, 13, 24, 68, 72, 83, 127, 212
credit rating, 68
crime, 171, 179, 211, 216, 240
criminal activity, 206, 207, 211, 218
criminal behavior, 208
criminality, 208
criminals, 14, 18, 142
criticism, viii, 12, 18, 35, 36, 37, 39, 112, 136, 139, 142, 144, 169, 171, 173, 188, 191, 192, 194
crops, 104, 140
cruise missiles, 155, 166
Cuba, 85, 231
culture, xi, 168, 181, 193, 195, 230, 240
currency, 3, 7, 8, 9, 38, 44, 47, 56, 58, 60, 62, 73, 74, 91, 185, 205, 206, 207, 208, 209, 210, 211, 212, 213, 214, 215, 216, 217, 218, 219
Czech Republic, 68, 196

D

Daewoo, 77
data gathering, 64, 86
database, 60, 70, 88, 90, 196
death, ix, 31, 40, 46, 51, 74, 93, 115, 117, 142, 144, 172, 173, 181, 182, 198, 228, 240
death penalty, 142, 172, 173
deaths, 102, 103, 176, 181, 182, 199
debt, vii, 1, 3, 4, 7, 8, 9, 16, 84, 104, 118
debt service, 104
decentralization, 96
decision makers, 214
decision making, 44, 45, 55
decisions, 20, 55, 57, 125, 129, 134
defendants, 184, 185, 234
defense, viii, 11, 12, 20, 21, 30, 47, 54, 55, 78, 83, 88, 89, 101, 105, 106, 108, 109, 110, 116, 124, 126, 127, 131, 134, 135, 184, 185, 193, 227
deficit, ix, 3, 12, 24, 36, 41, 50, 51, 64, 73, 217, 236
deforestation, 237, 238
delivery, x, 37, 74, 151, 154, 157, 160
democracy, ix, x, xi, xii, 93, 108, 133, 134, 142, 167, 168, 169, 170, 174, 175, 176, 177, 184, 187, 188, 190, 191, 192, 193, 194, 198, 221, 222, 224, 226, 228, 229, 243, 244, 245, 248
Democrat, xii, 221, 222, 223, 224
democratic elections, 134
Democratic Party, 13, 28, 29, 222
democratization, 129
dengue, 241
dengue fever, 241
Denmark, 18, 68
Department of Commerce, 27, 65, 76
Department of Defense, 157, 163
Department of Energy, 48, 159, 166
Department of Justice, 218
deposits, 68, 213, 245
deprivation, 54
destruction, 75, 103, 197, 237, 249
detainees, 141, 173, 180, 199
detection, 166, 179, 212
detention, xi, 103, 167, 168, 171, 174, 178, 182, 189, 192, 239
deterrence, 155, 158, 164
developing countries, 2, 75
developing nations, 73
development assistance, 48, 69, 76
development banks, 69
devolution, 96, 100, 106, 113
direct action, 235
direct investment, 2, 24, 69, 76
disaster, ix, 21, 93, 103, 104, 108, 170, 176, 198, 247
disaster relief, 21, 108
disclosure, 49, 173, 216
discourse, 169, 171, 183, 189, 190
discrimination, 72, 96, 141, 240
displaced persons, 102, 110, 116, 247
displacement, 110, 111
distribution, 57, 74, 114, 134, 205, 208, 212, 236

District of Columbia, 125
diversity, 231, 237, 249
division, 16, 77, 213, 240
Doha, 27
domestic economy, vii, 1, 7, 9, 64
donations, 109, 179
donors, 69, 88, 105, 114, 118, 138, 140
draft, 30, 105, 138, 244
drought, 51, 57, 105
drug smuggling, 210
drug trafficking, 74, 83, 208, 211, 220
drugs, 44, 47, 50, 64, 67, 74, 208, 210, 215
due process, 174
dumping, 27, 244
durability, x, 151
duration, 32, 136
duties, 138, 140, 182
duty free, 61, 75

E

earnings, 73, 104, 206, 217
East Asia, vii, xii, 11, 14, 25, 41, 46, 47, 51, 89, 130, 132, 207, 220, 221, 226, 227, 250, 252
East Timor, 224, 227, 229, 230, 231, 232, 242, 248, 251, 253
Eastern Europe, 210
economic activity, viii, 13, 36
economic assistance, 42, 43, 45, 46, 51, 77, 79, 82
economic boom, 169
economic change, 180
economic competitiveness, 108
economic cooperation, 43, 46, 78, 84
economic crisis, 185, 191
economic development, ix, x, 19, 41, 93, 133, 140, 162, 168, 188, 228
economic downturn, 6, 7, 105, 236
economic growth, vii, xi, 1, 2, 4, 6, 7, 9, 12, 25, 50, 108, 168, 183, 194, 228, 236, 245
economic integration, 62, 231
economic leverage, vii, 77
economic migrants, 79
economic performance, viii, 36, 43
economic policy, 6
economic problem, 12, 24
economic reform, viii, 35, 36, 43, 53, 57, 59, 62, 178, 183, 187
economic reforms, 53, 57, 59, 183, 187
economic systems, 78
economics, vii, 40, 54, 231
Education, 107, 109, 139, 143, 164, 202, 226, 227, 246
educational exchanges, 248
educational system, 179
Egypt, 59, 80
election, x, xii, 19, 29, 98, 99, 115, 119, 129, 133, 137, 143, 144, 145, 146, 147, 221, 222, 223, 224, 225, 226, 229, 232, 235, 240, 243
electoral coalition, x, 133
electricity, 6, 43, 44, 53, 58, 63
e-mail, 149, 171, 194, 198
embargo, 12, 50, 81
employees, 22, 31, 32, 111, 126, 236
employment, 8, 9, 13, 57, 156, 236, 245
energy, xii, 10, 18, 38, 41, 43, 44, 46, 48, 56, 63, 65, 76, 81, 153, 185, 214, 221, 229, 243, 245
energy efficiency, 18
engagement, xi, 16, 19, 47, 61, 113, 130, 167, 168, 191, 215, 243, 247
enthusiasm, 145
entrepreneurs, 172, 173, 186, 188, 199
environment, 185, 186, 236, 238, 240, 249
environmental degradation, 185
environmental issues, 18, 198, 237, 249
environmental protection, 244
environmental technology, 19
EPA, 25
epidemiology, 244
espionage, 85, 198
ethnic groups, ix, 93, 146, 179, 182, 225
ethnic minority, 135
ethnicity, x, 133
EU, 2, 26, 98
Europe, 67, 86, 102, 146, 153
European Community, 69, 70
European Union, 2, 9, 27, 85, 95, 102, 216
evil, 46, 182
evolution, vii, 132, 230
exchange rate, 8, 9, 25, 40, 52, 58, 236
exclusion, 113, 128
execution, 87
Executive Order, 74, 160
exercise, 21, 22, 46, 169, 182, 213
expanded trade, 82
expenditures, 55, 71, 105
expertise, 38, 156, 159, 161, 162, 172
explosives, x, 151, 156
exporter, 2, 45, 73, 237
exports, 2, 4, 7, 9, 12, 24, 38, 43, 44, 47, 50, 57, 64, 67, 73, 75, 76, 77, 78, 81, 82, 84, 85, 87, 104, 107, 166, 208, 216, 225, 236
expulsion, 128, 136
external environment, 105, 243
external influences, 228
external relations, 90
extradition, 210, 212

F

failure, 27, 79, 101, 111, 116, 152, 153, 160, 240
faith, 138, 142, 184
family, xi, 18, 31, 58, 59, 71, 74, 77, 97, 142, 147, 167, 176, 195, 197, 203, 217, 245
family members, 74, 176
family planning, xi, 167, 195, 197, 203, 245
famine, 51, 231
farmers, xi, 5, 6, 29, 54, 55, 58, 115, 140, 168, 173, 175, 185, 186, 188, 198, 199, 238
FBIS, 89
FDI, 2, 4, 5, 7, 9, 59, 60, 69, 90, 105
fear, x, 41, 46, 138, 147, 151, 152, 169, 187, 189, 195, 208, 228, 231
fears, 12, 41, 58, 157, 182, 186, 188
federal law, 210
Federal Reserve Board, 219
finance, vii, xii, 1, 3, 6, 12, 64, 73, 76, 188, 205, 206, 208
Financial Crimes Enforcement Network, 213
financial crisis, vii, 1, 3, 4, 6, 7, 8, 9, 13, 42, 52, 226, 228
financial institutions, 4, 83, 195, 206, 207, 213, 217, 219
financial markets, 68
financial resources, 116
financial sector, 8
financial support, 9, 140, 193
financial system, 75, 77, 88, 211, 217
financing, 6, 49, 69, 227
firms, 3, 6, 8, 9, 12, 26, 56, 59, 61, 67, 78, 81, 185, 214, 215
fiscal deficit, 104
fish, 67, 81, 238
fishing, 57, 102
flexibility, 130, 180, 188, 193
flood, 41, 216
flooding, 51, 52
focusing, 111, 182, 183, 229, 241
food, 9, 38, 41, 42, 43, 44, 46, 47, 48, 49, 50, 51, 53, 54, 56, 57, 58, 62, 64, 65, 69, 71, 73, 75, 76, 77, 79, 81, 82, 86, 87, 89, 94, 95, 108, 115, 216, 222, 226
food production, 41, 51
Ford, 199, 200, 251
foreign aid, ix, 38, 56, 64, 67, 69, 81, 93, 112, 114, 118, 195, 208
foreign assistance, ix, xii, 36, 41, 48, 162, 222
foreign banks, 217
foreign direct investment, 4, 12, 24, 54, 59, 69
foreign exchange, vii, xii, 1, 3, 7, 9, 57, 58, 64, 67, 86, 104, 205, 206, 208, 212, 214, 217
foreign intelligence, 74
foreign investment, ix, 23, 36, 58, 59, 67, 78, 81, 208, 233, 236, 237
foreign person, 48
foreign policy, xii, 13, 28, 83, 136, 221, 224, 242, 243, 247, 248, 249
forests, 237, 245
France, 69, 70, 89, 119, 120, 121, 122, 131, 164, 165, 200, 215, 219, 251, 252, 253
fraud, 60, 145, 147, 176
free trade, 25, 59, 60, 69, 75
freedom, xii, 51, 111, 141, 171, 175, 177, 178, 179, 180, 182, 189, 190, 192, 193, 194, 196, 198, 222, 224, 227, 238, 239
freezing, 41, 44, 214
friction, 12, 24, 67, 79, 103, 244
friendship, 19
fuel, 16, 21, 38, 39, 41, 42, 49, 69, 73, 75, 81, 83, 84, 86, 117, 139, 154, 163, 216, 222, 236
fund transfers, 83
funding, xi, 6, 21, 22, 47, 69, 77, 108, 109, 118, 125, 131, 144, 145, 168, 172, 191, 192, 193, 195, 248
funds, ix, x, 3, 6, 36, 48, 49, 50, 61, 68, 69, 75, 83, 84, 88, 94, 102, 133, 139, 141, 159, 162, 193, 195, 208, 214, 230, 246

G

Gabon, 80
gambling, 190, 235
GDP, 2, 4, 5, 6, 8, 9, 12, 15, 23, 24, 28, 40, 51, 52, 53, 55, 56, 97, 104, 105, 225, 236
General Accounting Office, 202
Generalized System of Preferences, 91
Georgia, 169
Germany, 17, 42, 65, 67, 68, 70, 77, 84, 88, 97, 134, 196, 215
global climate change, 226
global demand, 236
global economy, vii, 1
global markets, 78
global trade, 2, 8
globalization, 57, 62
goals, 9, 17, 36, 38, 41, 42, 44, 45, 47, 81, 108, 129, 208, 245, 247
God, 238, 252
gold, 63, 225, 244, 253
goods and services, 2
governance, xii, 96, 104, 106, 108, 134, 137, 139, 140, 142, 144, 145, 169, 171, 200, 222, 228, 235, 248
government intervention, 237
government policy, 183
government procurement, 6

government repression, 190
government securities, 7
grants, 20, 108, 109, 248
greenhouse gases, 18
gross domestic product, 12, 23, 24, 52
gross national product, 52
grouping, 29, 30, 146, 250
groups, 17, 19, 47, 60, 74, 83, 88, 91, 96, 100, 101, 102, 108, 110, 111, 112, 115, 118, 135, 142, 145, 152, 170, 172, 176, 178, 179, 180, 181, 182, 186, 189, 191, 193, 194, 197, 215, 217, 227, 231, 233, 234, 235, 238, 239, 240
growth, vii, 1, 2, 4, 9, 50, 51, 52, 97, 104, 105, 180, 184, 187, 194, 225, 243
growth rate, 4, 52, 97, 105, 225
Guangdong, 197
Guangzhou, 178
Guatemala, 68
guidelines, 124, 131, 158, 166, 180, 195
guilty, 174, 240
Guinea, 233, 238

H

hands, 101, 152, 158, 212
harassment, 171, 176, 177, 178, 180
hard currency, 53, 56, 61, 62, 67, 73, 78, 208
harm, 31, 134, 138, 184
harmony, 134, 138
Hawaii, 22
health, 6, 7, 87, 105, 108, 135, 179, 195, 236, 242, 244, 245
health care, 6
health care system, 6
heroin, 73, 74
high school, 2
higher quality, 245
HIV, 193, 198, 246
HIV/AIDS, 193, 198, 246
homeowners, 185, 186
Honda, 32
Hong Kong, 50, 65, 80, 174, 176, 181, 188, 194, 200, 202, 210, 218
hopes, 31, 39, 104, 105
host, 20, 21, 22, 41, 175
hostilities, 47, 77, 95, 115
hostility, 39, 43, 116
House, viii, xi, 11, 13, 14, 15, 16, 17, 20, 21, 22, 27, 28, 29, 30, 31, 32, 48, 73, 91, 106, 131, 135, 136, 143, 161, 162, 165, 168, 180, 191, 192, 196, 200, 220, 223, 229, 243, 253
housing, 5, 6, 53, 104, 175, 176, 177
human development, 105
human development index, 105
human resource development, 16
humanitarian aid, 16, 41, 42, 50, 69, 75, 80, 81, 110
humanitarianism, 252
Hungary, 80
hybrid, 18
hydroelectric power, 57, 105
hygiene, 19, 108, 241
Hyundai, 59, 60, 77, 78

I

identity, 103, 145, 181, 194, 195, 223, 232, 233
ideology, 54, 77, 235, 239, 252
image, 7, 29
IMF, 2, 8, 64, 86, 90, 92, 104, 120
immigration, 31, 126, 247
imperialism, 57, 242
implementation, 20, 22, 85, 113, 162, 169
imports, vii, xii, 1, 2, 4, 9, 12, 14, 17, 24, 25, 26, 27, 38, 41, 42, 47, 50, 51, 57, 64, 65, 67, 69, 74, 76, 77, 80, 81, 82, 84, 104, 205, 206, 207, 208
imprisonment, 52, 156, 171, 192, 198
incentives, ix, 6, 31, 36, 37, 45, 57, 58
incidence, 105, 106
inclusion, 17, 46
income, 29, 72, 88, 185, 236
income support, 29
indecency, 235
independence, 38, 54, 94, 96, 97, 100, 101, 112, 116, 141, 174, 181, 188, 200, 228, 229, 231, 232, 233, 242
India, 17, 21, 46, 65, 94, 96, 97, 110, 119, 120, 121, 122, 140, 153, 154, 155, 157, 158, 163, 164, 165, 181, 201, 225, 238, 250
indication, 12, 211
indigenous, 102, 228, 231, 233
indigenous peoples, 233
Indonesia, v, xii, 52, 68, 103, 221, 222, 223, 224, 225, 226, 227, 228, 229, 230, 231, 232, 233, 234, 235, 236, 237, 238, 239, 240, 241, 242, 243, 244, 245, 246, 247, 248, 249, 250, 251, 252, 253
industrial sectors, 55
industry, 6, 9, 18, 26, 40, 54, 56, 62, 178, 208, 217, 225
ineffectiveness, 146
inefficiencies, 44, 51
infectious disease, 241
inflation, 9, 52, 58, 185, 210, 236
information sharing, 247
information technology, 56, 194
infrastructure, 5, 6, 7, 59, 105, 112, 117, 154, 231, 236, 245
inspections, 16, 41, 73, 80
inspectors, 25, 37, 49, 241

instability, viii, x, 36, 41, 43, 100, 114, 151, 157, 207
institutions, vii, x, 3, 54, 114, 133, 137, 162, 169, 172, 183, 184, 193, 212, 213, 223, 227, 235
instruction, 235
instruments, 179
insurance, 26, 46, 62
integration, 77, 95, 231
integrity, 128, 153, 155, 212, 229
intellectual property, 8
intelligence, 20, 36, 37, 59, 81, 117, 152, 156, 157, 159, 205, 206, 208, 215, 246, 247
intelligence gathering, 59, 208
intentions, 12, 103, 172
interaction, 85, 87, 89, 130, 228
interactions, 125, 130
interest rates, 4, 12
interference, xi, 84, 99, 147, 168, 178, 180, 184
International Covenant on Civil and Political Rights, 175, 199
international financial institutions, 47, 75, 195
international investment, 50
international law, 43, 216
International Monetary Fund, 2, 8, 48, 63, 64, 75, 84, 86, 90, 92, 95
international relations, ix, 36
international standards, 134, 175, 190, 215
international terrorism, 15, 91
international trade, ix, 36, 40, 54, 78, 173
interview, 153, 157, 158, 159, 160, 165, 177, 178, 219
intimidation, 99, 141, 176, 178, 180, 185, 189, 239
investment, xii, 2, 3, 5, 7, 8, 9, 13, 43, 46, 55, 59, 62, 63, 69, 85, 105, 107, 120, 221, 226, 228, 244, 245, 249
investment bank, 9
investors, 3, 9, 12, 53, 62, 67, 68, 185
Iran, 41, 43, 48, 73, 136, 142, 159, 160, 166, 194
Iraq, viii, 11, 16, 22, 46, 73, 110, 188
Ireland, 212, 219
Irish Republican Army, 210
Islam, 135, 142, 143, 179, 182, 201, 225, 228, 234, 235, 238, 239, 242, 243, 248
Islamic law, 136
Islamic world, 248
isolation, 40, 45, 47, 54, 63
Israel, 75
Italy, 97, 215

J

Jamaica, 84, 131
Japanese women, 31
Java, 230, 231, 235, 241, 251
Jirga, 135, 136, 143, 144
job creation, 236
jobs, 2, 4, 9, 53, 61, 78, 97, 186, 187
Jordan, 40
journalism, 178
journalists, 91, 95, 103, 111, 141, 171, 172, 175, 177, 178, 186, 197
judges, 141, 184, 185
judgment, 141, 142
judicial branch, 170
judiciary, 141, 188, 223
jurisdiction, 32, 74, 188
justice, 96, 134, 136, 137, 138, 227, 232
justification, 253

K

keiretsu, 26
kidnapping, 49
killing, 95, 113, 115, 117, 240
Kyrgyzstan, 169

L

labor, xi, 31, 32, 45, 46, 56, 60, 61, 77, 78, 137, 168, 170, 172, 173, 174, 176, 183, 185, 186, 191, 193, 195, 196, 198, 199
labor force, 31
land, 22, 30, 53, 60, 94, 96, 125, 173, 175, 176, 183, 185, 198, 199, 233, 237, 238
land use, 60
Landscape, 134
language, 61, 86, 97, 113, 129, 182, 189, 233, 248
Laos, 42
Latin America, 67
law enforcement, 108, 160, 162, 206, 207, 208, 210, 212, 215, 217, 235, 240, 247
laws, x, xi, 13, 26, 27, 29, 111, 125, 126, 151, 156, 167, 170, 172, 179, 183, 184, 186, 196, 207, 217, 229, 235
lawyers, 171, 175, 176, 178, 181, 183, 184, 185, 186
layoffs, 185
leadership, xi, xii, 18, 20, 29, 40, 57, 83, 87, 96, 138, 152, 157, 168, 169, 170, 171, 173, 179, 183, 184, 186, 188, 190, 191, 197, 213, 221, 232, 242
leakage, 156
legal protection, 180
legislation, xi, 30, 48, 125, 142, 160, 161, 163, 166, 167, 168, 169, 174, 220
lifestyle, viii, 36, 43
likelihood, 147
line, 37, 40, 61, 91, 94, 100, 113, 114, 117, 143, 165, 175, 187, 190, 215, 232
links, 54, 83, 110, 206, 208, 209, 218
living standards, 6, 52, 105, 175

loans, 7, 16, 68, 195
local authorities, 180, 182, 186
local government, xi, 7, 9, 168, 170, 173, 174, 183, 185
local television stations, 183
logging, 233, 234, 237, 238, 249
logistics, 6, 108, 125, 130
Louisiana, 244

M

machinery, 6, 38, 40, 44, 61, 62, 65, 67, 77, 81, 82, 84
mad cow disease, 25
Mainland China, 196, 200
maintenance, 47, 126
Malaysia, 50, 241, 243, 252
males, 58, 142
management, 60, 203, 245
manufacturing, 54, 55, 56, 57, 61, 64, 67, 77, 78, 218, 219
marine environment, 237
mark up, 163
market, 3, 4, 7, 12, 24, 26, 27, 43, 44, 47, 50, 51, 52, 53, 55, 57, 58, 59, 67, 76, 77, 80, 82, 85, 97, 104, 115, 160, 187, 194
market economics, 97
market economy, 43, 47, 51, 55, 59
market incentives, 44
marketing, 41, 51
markets, 2, 8, 9, 38, 45, 46, 50, 51, 52, 53, 54, 58, 67, 77, 78, 80, 84, 86, 102
mass media, 170, 175, 177, 183, 184, 192, 196
maturation, 129
measurement, 23, 33
measures, 16, 29, 38, 48, 51, 57, 74, 80, 103, 112, 130, 137, 153, 155, 158, 161, 163, 173, 177, 213, 215, 217, 230, 239, 241
meat, 19, 81
media, 17, 29, 43, 74, 105, 136, 141, 144, 145, 171, 177, 178, 179, 181, 187, 190, 192, 193, 203, 209, 210, 218, 229
medium of exchange, 210, 212
membership, 17, 40, 75, 86, 128, 130, 131, 250
men, 143, 210, 235, 242
merchandise, 2, 23, 24, 64, 67, 76, 77, 80, 208, 236
mercury, 244
messages, 186, 190, 216, 223
metals, 6, 61, 67
Mexico, 24, 68, 75
Miami, 126
Microsoft, 194
middle class, xi, 54, 168, 186, 187, 194
Middle East, xii, 67, 73, 90, 194, 221
migrants, 170, 186, 234
migration, 96, 195, 234
military aid, 131
military pressure, 233
military spending, 51
militias, 141, 231, 248
mineral resources, 63, 233
minimum wage, 62
mining, 18, 56, 57, 62, 63, 64, 234, 244
minorities, 111, 117, 135, 196, 199
minority, ix, 93, 94, 95, 96, 99, 102, 103, 104, 113, 141, 142, 143, 179, 181, 188, 189, 190, 230, 234, 238
minority groups, 230, 238
missions, 22, 108, 247
model, 57, 97, 154
models, 188
molybdenum, 57, 63
momentum, viii, 12, 13, 29, 226, 227, 228, 248
money, 3, 7, 54, 72, 74, 75, 83, 88, 159, 188, 198, 206, 207, 210, 211, 213, 214, 215, 217, 218, 219, 230, 234, 241, 246
money laundering, 74, 88, 206, 207, 211, 213, 214, 217, 219, 246
Mongolia, 42, 218
monopoly, 174
Moon, 87
morale, 117
moratorium, 142
mortgage-backed securities, 3, 9
mothers, 51
motives, 19, 206
movement, x, 51, 54, 156, 158, 167, 168, 172, 176, 177, 184, 186, 188, 189, 198, 228, 231, 234
murder, 111, 244
Muslim extremists, 239
Muslims, xi, 96, 110, 167, 170, 171, 179, 182, 200, 234, 235, 238, 241, 250

N

narcotics, 54, 73, 138, 139, 208, 209, 210, 213
nation, ix, xii, 21, 39, 40, 45, 75, 78, 85, 93, 95, 96, 102, 165, 184, 195, 210, 211, 215, 221, 225, 229, 230, 231, 234, 242, 248
nation states, 215
national identity, 231
national income, 52, 54
national interests, 23, 44, 50, 161
National Party, 93, 97, 99
national security, vii, 10, 11, 40, 48, 75, 150, 152, 162, 182, 184, 207, 217
National Security Council, 87, 130, 153, 163, 164
nationalism, 36, 40, 42, 100, 229

NATO, 134, 140, 145, 146
natural gas, 225, 237
NCA, 156, 164
negative consequences, 216
negotiating, 45, 86, 112, 113, 116, 137
negotiation, 17, 113, 116, 117
net exports, 2
Netherlands, 69, 70, 145, 196
network, x, 59, 83, 151, 153, 157, 159, 160, 161, 162, 176, 217
New Zealand, 196, 202, 250
newspapers, 76, 141, 178
NGOs, 71, 170, 172, 175, 176, 199, 200
North America, 12, 126, 213
North Korean refugees, 47, 78, 192
Northeast Asia, 41, 89, 90, 92, 245
Northern Ireland, 210
Norway, 69, 70, 95, 113, 116, 121
nuclear arms race, 155
nuclear program, viii, 17, 35, 37, 38, 42, 43, 46, 49, 55, 65, 69, 73, 77, 87, 160, 214
nuclear weapons, vii, x, 17, 19, 38, 39, 41, 42, 43, 44, 45, 46, 48, 49, 55, 79, 80, 83, 151, 152, 153, 154, 155, 156, 157, 158, 159, 160, 161, 162, 163, 164, 165, 166, 207

O

Obama Administration, x, 15, 16, 17, 18, 37, 43, 49, 133, 134, 136, 137, 138, 141, 145, 146, 147, 169, 191, 195, 197, 216, 248
objectives, 127, 155, 162, 247
observations, 187
OECD, 69, 70, 90
offenders, 74, 173, 174
Official Development Assistance, 70
oil, 10, 16, 39, 41, 51, 58, 69, 75, 81, 232, 234, 237, 243
oil production, 237
Omnibus Appropriations Act,, 195
open markets, 58
openness, 117, 170
Operation Enduring Freedom, 21
operator, 59
opinion polls, 29
opposition parties, 21
order, 3, 7, 8, 17, 40, 42, 44, 46, 51, 58, 61, 78, 98, 114, 126, 138, 144, 156, 166, 178, 179, 181, 184, 185, 186, 188, 191, 197, 198, 214, 216, 234, 247, 248
ores, 57, 63, 67, 81
organic chemicals, 76
orientation, 37, 53
oversight, 13, 137, 174, 216, 248
ownership, 8, 19, 50, 55, 126, 173, 185

P

Pacific, vii, 11, 15, 21, 32, 78, 83, 87, 88, 90, 91, 109, 124, 129, 132, 200, 201, 202, 216, 219, 220, 225, 227, 242, 246, 250, 252, 253
Pakistan, v, vii, x, 46, 73, 110, 134, 138, 139, 141, 145, 149, 151, 152, 153, 154, 155, 156, 157, 158, 159, 160, 161, 162, 163, 164, 165, 166
PAN, 223, 224
Paraguay, 218
Parliament, 27, 98, 99, 115, 136, 143, 198, 209, 222, 250
partnership, xii, 25, 222, 226, 243, 244, 245, 248
Pashtun, 134, 135, 137, 138, 139, 143, 145, 146, 147, 148
peace process, 94, 98, 99, 104, 106, 108, 113, 114, 116
peacekeeping, 22, 29, 108
penalties, 161
Pentagon, 20, 22, 131, 165
per capita income, 78
perceptions, 146, 222, 244, 246
personal accounts, 213
Peru, 80, 218
pessimism, x, 133
pharmaceuticals, 208, 210, 213, 217
Philippines, 238, 241
planned economies, 50
planning, 7, 44, 50, 62, 156, 157
pluralism, 190, 239
plutonium, 41, 49, 153, 154, 163, 164, 165, 215
Poland, 70
police, 81, 101, 112, 138, 139, 174, 177, 181, 183, 184, 185, 187, 199, 202, 210, 227, 229, 230, 234, 235, 240, 241, 246, 248
policy choice, ix, 123, 129
policy makers, x, 167, 169, 187, 191, 226
policy reform, 174
political crisis, 98
political instability, 105, 106, 152, 157, 169, 194, 228, 230
political leaders, 100, 102, 106
political opposition, 16
political participation, 94, 106
political parties, xii, 135, 143, 221, 223, 235
political power, 55
politics, vii, xii, 29, 55, 87, 100, 104, 129, 163, 183, 187, 222, 223, 229, 250
pollution, 183, 237
poor, viii, 5, 36, 42, 43, 50, 101, 104, 141, 170, 186, 222

population, viii, ix, 6, 12, 31, 36, 38, 41, 43, 51, 52, 58, 81, 95, 96, 105, 112, 134, 169, 181, 182, 187, 207, 225, 230, 231, 233, 234, 236
population growth, 236
population size, 31
portfolio, 3
ports, 6, 17, 50, 81, 108, 110, 166
Portugal, 214
positive relation, 226
posture, 20, 155
poverty, 96, 105, 114, 172, 236
poverty alleviation, 172
poverty line, 236
poverty reduction, 105, 114
power, vii, viii, 1, 11, 13, 21, 24, 28, 35, 36, 39, 40,
power plants, 84
preference, xii, 100, 187, 221, 222
preferential treatment, 61, 86
presidency, 94, 143, 144
president, xii, 13, 19, 29, 97, 117, 118, 132, 135, 146, 147, 173, 214, 221, 223, 224, 229, 243
President Clinton, 192
pressure, viii, 4, 7, 8, 12, 25, 35, 43, 45, 47, 52, 84, 94, 95, 96, 110, 131, 175, 191, 198, 214, 216, 235, 236, 240
prestige, 46
presumption of innocence, 185
prevention, 39
prices, 4, 8, 27, 42, 52, 58, 65, 81, 83, 222, 236
primary products, 67
prisoners, xi, 18, 31, 32, 168, 173, 181, 182, 190, 191, 192, 196
prisoners of war, 31, 32
privacy, 30, 195
private firms, 31
private sector, 3, 141, 188, 238
privation, 43, 50, 57
privatization, 26, 104, 114
probability, 84, 158
production, x, xii, 27, 37, 43, 44, 50, 55, 56, 57, 58, 61, 62, 63, 64, 67, 74, 151, 154, 205, 206, 208, 209, 211, 212, 217, 218, 237
productivity, 2, 58
professionalism, 184
profit, 3, 126, 172, 180, 191, 193, 211, 216
profit margin, 3
profits, 55, 58
program, viii, 6, 22, 27, 31, 35, 36, 38, 39, 41, 43, 45, 46, 50, 75, 88, 108, 118, 136, 140, 141, 153, 154, 159, 162, 163, 165, 193, 195, 219, 245, 246
proliferation, x, 39, 41, 45, 46, 47, 75, 79, 151, 153, 156, 157, 159, 160, 162, 165, 166, 172, 187, 215, 216, 246
propaganda, 42, 48, 85, 189
propagation, 200
property rights, 170, 173, 196
prosperity, 38, 46
protectionism, 8
Protestants, 171, 180
PTSD, 136
public health, 172, 183
public interest, 172, 184
public opinion, 21, 30, 113, 178, 189
public sector, 105
public service, 183
punishment, 74, 156, 211
purchasing power, 15, 33, 40, 52, 97, 210, 225
purchasing power parity, 15, 33, 40, 52, 97, 225
purity, viii, 35, 36, 37, 39, 40

Q

quality of life, 113, 186
questioning, 13, 28, 161

R

race, 41, 147, 155
radar, 20, 109, 227
range, 12, 19, 28, 37, 39, 50, 52, 73, 80, 102, 107, 143, 154, 172, 181, 182, 183, 185, 186, 187, 192, 211, 244, 248, 249
rape, 22, 31, 142
rate of return, 8
ratings, viii, 11, 28
raw materials, 9, 38, 44, 56, 67, 83
real estate, 3, 4, 7, 138
reason, 52, 157, 178, 207, 210, 233, 240, 242
recession, 12, 24, 186
recognition, 31, 45, 48, 58, 124, 131, 227
reconciliation, 16, 19, 39, 95, 96, 102, 103, 105, 108
reconstruction, 5, 16, 103, 104, 108, 112, 114, 143
recovery, 2, 52, 56, 62, 88, 108, 247
reforms, x, 9, 31, 38, 51, 53, 57, 58, 83, 89, 105, 108, 117, 129, 137, 151, 157, 169, 170, 172, 174, 175, 183, 184, 191, 228, 248
refugees, viii, 36, 41, 42, 43, 50, 52, 73, 79, 81, 84, 120, 121, 136
region, 32, 42, 79, 83, 85, 106, 110, 117, 120, 121, 157, 164, 181, 182, 213, 216, 224, 225, 227, 233, 234, 237, 243, 245, 248, 249
regulation, 115, 189
regulations, 26, 59, 161, 172, 173, 176, 177, 178, 179, 181, 187, 196
relationship, viii, xii, 12, 13, 15, 23, 24, 41, 79, 82, 83, 84, 85, 106, 107, 169, 191, 222, 226, 227, 232, 241, 243, 246, 248

relevance, 125, 183
reliability, 64, 156, 158, 161
relief, 102, 103, 104, 105, 106, 107, 118, 228, 247
religion, 111, 179, 188, 192, 200, 223, 238
remittances, 17, 38, 53, 67, 72, 73, 83, 208
remote sensing, 237
repression, 51, 112, 171, 228
reprocessing, 154, 164
reserve currency, 8, 9
reserves, vii, 1, 3, 7, 8, 9, 63, 67, 104, 208, 237
resettlement, 102
resistance, xi, 16, 94, 167, 174, 230, 232
resolution, xi, 15, 17, 20, 37, 45, 46, 47, 50, 79, 80, 81, 83, 103, 104, 125, 126, 129, 136, 141, 168, 192, 195, 203, 215
resources, viii, xii, 20, 35, 43, 55, 57, 78, 193, 211, 221, 225, 241, 242, 245
retaliation, 26, 27, 101, 155
revenue, 29, 138, 178, 183, 232, 236
rewards, 53
rhetoric, 19, 48, 96, 242
rice, 55, 58, 65, 104
risk, 43, 74, 81, 88, 117, 152, 157, 163, 171, 173, 217
rubber, 96, 104
rule of law, xi, xii, 142, 168, 169, 184, 188, 190, 193, 195, 221, 224, 245, 248
rural areas, 6, 29, 173, 180, 186, 199
rural development, 172
Russia, viii, 35, 36, 38, 41, 44, 45, 46, 48, 50, 57, 65, 69, 70, 82, 83, 84, 85, 86, 88, 90, 91, 92, 165, 188, 207, 214, 216

S

Saddam Hussein, 46
safety, 8, 19, 195
sales, 6, 44, 45, 53, 67, 73, 125, 127, 128, 129, 131, 138, 154, 163, 178, 208
sanctions, viii, ix, xi, 8, 12, 17, 26, 27, 35, 36, 37, 38, 39, 42, 44, 45, 47, 48, 50, 64, 67, 72, 74, 75, 80, 81, 84, 86, 87, 94, 153, 160, 163, 168, 169, 178, 179, 195, 206, 207, 210, 213, 214, 216, 217, 218, 220
SARS, 179
Saudi Arabia, 15, 235
savings, 3, 105
scaling, 117
scandal, 13, 25, 28, 29, 178
scarcity, 42, 50, 53, 55
school, 40, 170, 176, 179, 193, 235
scores, 19, 171, 246
Secretary of Defense, 87
Secretary of the Treasury, 87, 212, 217
securities, vii, 1, 3, 7, 8, 9, 68
seizure, 37, 116, 173, 208
selecting, 147
self-image, 101
semiconductor, 61
semiconductors, 78
Senate, xi, 31, 32, 33, 48, 119, 125, 130, 132, 152, 154, 159, 160, 162, 165, 166, 168, 192, 194, 209, 218, 220, 253
Senate Foreign Relations Committee, 130, 132, 160, 163, 165, 220
sensitivity, 152, 230
separation, 164, 169, 188
September 11, viii, x, 9, 11, 16, 134, 146, 151, 153, 157, 158, 200, 201
service provider, 26, 178
shares, 8, 9, 18, 83, 104
Sharia, 235, 251
sharing, 20, 78, 99, 158, 215, 242
shellfish, 67
shortage, 63, 89
signs, 4, 16, 230, 237
Singapore, 12, 19, 21, 50, 58, 65, 213, 225, 236, 244, 250, 252
smuggling, 72, 74, 102, 113, 219
Smuggling, 121
social change, xi, 167, 183
social class, 185
social development, 179, 181, 194
social group, 186, 187
social justice, 252
social order, 174
social participation, 171
Social Security, 8, 9, 31
social support, 104
social welfare, 105
Solomon I, 238
South Asia, 104, 105, 119, 121, 152, 154, 155, 157, 163, 164
Southeast Asia, xii, 67, 221, 227, 234, 237, 242, 245, 246, 247, 248, 252, 253
sovereignty, 39, 128, 131, 152, 158, 242
Soviet Union, 51, 80, 83, 124
SPA, 243
space, viii, 35, 39, 42, 44, 47, 208, 230, 239
Spain, 73, 215
species, 237, 238
speech, 26, 78, 131, 152, 165, 171, 240, 243, 244
Spring, 88, 198, 240
Sri Lanka, v, vii, ix, 93, 94, 95, 96, 97, 98, 99, 100, 101, 102, 103, 104, 105, 106, 107, 108, 109, 110, 111, 112, 113, 114, 115, 116, 117, 118, 119, 120, 121, 122

stability, vii, 1, 7, 19, 20, 32, 41, 46, 81, 152, 162, 172, 174, 185, 187, 188, 194, 223, 226, 228, 245
stabilization, x, 133, 137
staffing, 125, 126
standard of living, 39, 43
standards, 43, 44, 105, 111, 142, 195
starvation, 38, 41, 44, 50, 52, 53
state control, xi, 167, 177
state-owned enterprises, 3, 7, 9
statistics, 52, 63, 64, 67, 88, 90, 92, 181
steel, 6, 26, 63, 77, 81, 82, 84
stimulus, vii, 1, 6, 9, 13, 28, 79
stock, 3, 4, 56, 69, 80
stock markets, 3
stockpiling, 160
storage, 155, 157, 158
strategic assets, 155, 158
strategies, 20, 47, 155, 169
strength, 22, 54, 136, 146, 184
stress, 55, 57, 104, 158
stroke, viii, 35, 36, 39
students, 176, 186, 187, 224
Sudan, 52
sugar, 52, 104
Suharto, xii, 221, 222, 224, 228, 229, 240, 242, 250, 251
suicide, 98, 102, 115, 116, 117, 187, 241
suicide bombers, 102
summer, 19, 51, 52, 110, 115, 117, 182
supervision, 174, 211
suppliers, 65
supply, 37, 61, 67, 78, 83, 159, 166, 212
suppression, 176, 232
Supreme Court, 125, 136, 137, 142, 145, 148, 240
surplus, 76, 109
surveillance, 108, 109, 117, 156, 176, 189, 198
survivability, 155
survival, 43, 46, 238
suspects, 21, 171, 173
Sweden, 69, 70, 87
Switzerland, 40, 70, 85, 88
Syria, 41, 48, 73

T

tactics, xi, 44, 49, 99, 107, 112, 168, 178, 190, 241
Taiwan, v, vii, ix, 15, 50, 59, 80, 123, 124, 125, 126, 127, 128, 129, 130, 131, 132, 171, 186, 188
takeover, x, 151
Taliban, x, 16, 133, 134, 135, 136, 138, 140, 141, 142, 147, 148, 152, 157, 165
tanks, 101, 172
targets, 52, 58, 105, 117, 154, 217, 235, 241
tariff, 27, 107
tax base, 107
tax cuts, 6
taxation, 185
ttechnical assistance, 48
technology transfer, 91
telephone, 59, 240
television, 58, 158, 178
television stations, 178
tension, 45, 81, 232, 239
territory, 19, 20, 84, 115, 116, 206, 207, 228, 231
terrorism, 17, 21, 32, 38, 41, 47, 48, 75, 87, 88, 106, 107, 109, 112, 117, 134, 240, 244, 245, 246, 247
terrorist organization, 102, 159, 182, 240
textiles, 6, 40, 61, 67, 77, 104, 225
Thailand, 7, 50, 65, 67, 70, 81, 84, 102, 112, 113, 241
theft, 157, 174
threat, 24, 30, 42, 45, 48, 52, 64, 75, 87, 113, 117, 152, 161, 162, 163, 219, 237, 240, 241
threats, 8, 114, 117, 158, 162, 183, 191, 215, 229, 230, 238
threshold, 155, 223
timber, 225, 233, 237
time frame, 106
timing, 64, 156
Title I, 109, 203, 246
Title II, 109, 203, 246
tobacco, 137, 219
torture, xi, 141, 167, 171, 172, 173, 174, 180, 182, 240
tourism, 59, 77, 105
trade agreement, 26, 75, 85, 245
trade cycles, ix, 123
trade deficit, 12, 24, 38, 64, 67, 73, 207, 208
trade liberalization, 50
trade preference, 25
trade-off, 28, 42
trading, viii, 7, 19, 26, 27, 36, 39, 53, 54, 58, 64, 65, 67, 74, 80, 82, 84, 86, 195, 209, 213
trading partners, 26, 27, 39, 65, 82, 86
Trading with the Enemy Act, 41, 49, 75, 87, 88
traffic, 74, 176, 197
trafficking in persons, 142
training, 6, 20, 21, 31, 101, 102, 108, 117, 141, 144, 182, 193, 195, 212, 232, 246, 247, 248
trajectory, 18
transactions, 54, 58, 64, 67, 69, 71, 74, 80, 126, 188, 212, 214, 217
transcripts, 165
transformation, ix, 20, 36, 44
transformations, ix, 123, 129
transition, 43, 47, 86, 134, 222, 224, 228
transition period, 228

transitions, 156
transmission, 61, 63, 241
transparency, 159, 170, 172, 178
transport, 6, 16, 227
transportation, 59, 247
treaties, 125, 126
trial, 37, 39, 142, 171, 234, 240, 244
Turkey, 138, 141

U

U.N. Security Council, 16, 47, 50, 80, 84, 131
U.S. Department of the Treasury, 91, 219
U.S. economy, vii, 1, 7, 8, 207, 211
U.S. Treasury, vii, 1, 7, 9, 74, 88, 207, 213, 214
UK, 70, 119, 122
Ukraine, 169
UN, 80, 88, 92, 119, 120, 121, 166, 203, 216
uncertainty, viii, xi, 11, 114, 167, 226
unemployment, 12, 24, 185, 186, 236
unemployment rate, 12, 24, 186
unhappiness, 113
UNHCR, 120
unions, 72, 83, 173
United Kingdom, 24, 69, 196, 215
United Nations, 12, 16, 17, 22, 30, 37, 38, 44, 47, 50, 51, 59, 64, 68, 81, 83, 85, 90, 92, 95, 110, 119, 120, 124, 128, 131, 134, 175, 182, 188, 195, 196, 203, 213, 216, 231, 232, 233, 237, 247, 248
United Nations High Commissioner for Refugees, 92
Universal Declaration of Human Rights, 175, 188
universities, 193, 235, 245
university education, 114
university students, 187, 189
updating, 145
uranium, 48, 153, 154, 159, 163, 165
urban centers, 2
USA Patriot Act, 219
USSR, 83
Uzbekistan, 52

V

vehicles, x, 74, 81, 82, 84, 102, 139, 151, 154, 157, 166
vessels, 16, 37, 102, 108, 243
victims, 32, 33, 138, 176, 227
Vietnam, 85, 89, 92
village, 6, 197, 234
violence, xi, 94, 97, 99, 101, 107, 113, 115, 116, 147, 167, 181, 224, 231, 234, 235, 238, 239, 241, 250
Volunteers, 200
voters, xii, 29, 31, 98, 99, 143, 144, 145, 146, 147, 221, 222, 223, 232, 233
voting, 144, 196, 231
vulnerability, 145

W

wages, 58, 62, 69, 71, 173, 244
war, ix, 14, 18, 19, 21, 30, 32, 37, 46, 55, 93, 94, 96, 101, 103, 104, 105, 112, 115, 116, 120, 121, 124, 136, 149, 152, 153, 155, 157, 158, 178, 188, 215, 226, 227, 231, 232, 241, 246, 248
watches, 58, 61
water supplies, 115
Waziristan, 149
weakness, 138, 188
wealth, 3, 9, 85
weapons, ix, x, 16, 39, 42, 43, 44, 45, 48, 50, 74, 75, 83, 102, 107, 113, 123, 127, 129, 131, 141, 151, 152, 153, 154, 156, 157, 158, 159, 161, 162, 165, 166, 215, 216
weapons of mass destruction, 16, 48, 50, 74, 75, 166, 215, 216
Western Europe, 102
White House, 7, 10, 15, 25, 49, 92, 105, 119, 120, 125, 127, 220, 252
withdrawal, 94, 100, 131, 230
women, 15, 20, 30, 32, 58, 75, 136, 141, 142, 143, 145, 235, 243
worker rights, 195
workers, vii, 1, 2, 4, 31, 38, 44, 47, 56, 58, 61, 62, 67, 71, 78, 90, 91, 95, 96, 105, 111, 137, 173, 182, 185, 188, 244
working conditions, 62
World Bank, 75, 86, 88, 105, 114, 121, 236, 251
World Trade Organization, 26
World War I, vii, 11, 12, 13, 14, 16, 18, 20, 24, 31, 32, 55, 72, 75, 123, 228
worry, 152, 157
writing, xi, 130, 168, 198
wrongdoing, 18
WTO, 24, 26, 27
WWW, 220

Y

Yemen, 73, 80
yuan, 6, 8, 9, 62, 63

Z

Zimbabwe, 52